KOREAN MADE SIMPLE 3

GO! BILLY KOREAN WRITTEN BY BILLY GO

Continuing your journey of learning the Korean language

GO! Billy Korean

Korean Made Simple 3: Continuing your journey of learning the Korean language
Volume 3, Edition 1

Written by: Billy Go
Edited by: Sohyun Sohn and Patricia Brooks
Published by: GO! Billy Korean

Audio files for this book are available for free download from gobillykorean.com.

Cover and inside illustrations by: HeeJin Park (heejinbakes.tumblr.com)

Copyright © 2016 GO! Billy Korean
http://www.gobillykorean.com
All rights reserved

Printed by CreateSpace
Available from Amazon.com and other retail outlets
ISBN: 1533025223
ISBN-13: 978-1533025227

TABLE OF CONTENTS

	Preface	v
Chapter 1	Plain Form	13
Chapter 2	Making Quotes	37
Chapter 3	Expressing Thoughts	55
Chapter 4	More Questions and Commands	71
Chapter 5	Expressing Emotions	87
Chapter 6	How To	105
Chapter 7	Whether and If	121
Chapter 8	Through	141
Chapter 9	Titles	155
Chapter 10	Causatives	173
Chapter 11	Hoping and Wanting	189
Chapter 12	Making Decisions	201
Chapter 13	Looks and Sounds Like	215
Chapter 14	Since Doing	231
Chapter 15	Passive Voice	243
Chapter 16	Describing States	269
Chapter 17	More Past Tense	287
Chapter 18	Explanations	301
Chapter 19	More Explanations	319
Chapter 20	More Thought	337
	Answer Keys	357
	Appendix A. Introduction to Onomatopoeia	373
	Appendix B. Introduction to Dialects	381
	Special Thanks	399
	Glossary	400

Preface

Welcome back once more! You've come a long way. I can see that you're itching to learn more Korean (figuratively, of course... hopefully). After completing the first two books, you should now have a strong beginning foundation in the Korean language. But we're not going to stop there. There's still much more that we need to cover.

About this Book

While all three books in this series follow the same general format of presenting dialogues with grammar explanations and additional notes, each book offers something unique. The first book, "Korean Made Simple," focuses on building the basic foundations to begin studying Korean. Its lessons revolve around common themes and day-to-day situations such as introducing yourself, shopping, and telling the time. The second book, "Korean Made Simple 2," is geared toward increasing communication skills and focuses more on grammatical concepts.

This third book will concentrate mostly on introducing new grammar and concepts that you will need in real world situations. It is designed to help you reinforce and build upon the foundation started in the previous two books so that you will be able to continue learning the Korean language in your *own* way. This book will also explain increasingly difficult Korean concepts as simply as possible. Many of the concepts in this book are considered to be intermediate level, and some are even considered advanced, but are all common and necessary to know.

Preface

A major difference between this book and the previous books is how the grammar forms and concepts will be taught. In the previous two books, major grammar was taught at the beginning of the chapter before explaining the sample dialogue. That was because each chapter only introduced a small amount of new grammar. This book will introduce a much larger amount of grammar in each chapter, so new grammar will be divided and taught while examining the dialogue. I would recommend reading the dialogues again after having finished each chapter, before moving on to the next one.

Since this book will continue directly where "Korean Made Simple 2" left off, please review the previous two books before moving further. This includes completing the practice sections for each chapter and reading all of the "Advanced Notes" and appendix sections. Concepts already taught in the previous two books will not be covered again in this book. If you find a grammar form or vocabulary word in this book that you do not recognize, or find something used in an unfamiliar way, know that it was covered in one of the previous two books.

What to Expect

In the very beginning we could happily spend an entire chapter learning basic greetings, vocabulary, and simple grammar forms to use the Korean language right away. This, along with practice, would be more than sufficient to see some improvement. In the very first day you may have gone from knowing absolutely nothing about the language to being able to read and write your first few words and phrases completely in 한글. But in order to prepare for a higher level of Korean communication than "Hello" and "I like kimchi" (though I do like kimchi), there are still many additional concepts that we'll need to cover.

Just as with the previous two books, do not expect to be able to speak fluent Korean by the end of this book. Through this book we will cover *most* common grammar forms that you will need to know in order to hold actual conversations and to fully express yourself using the language. Nevertheless, know that there is much more to learn to become fluent than could fit into a single book or even a book series. However, I can promise that after competing these three books, you will have a solid foundation that will aid you in continuing to learn Korean on *your own*.

My ultimate goal is to help you to hit your own goals for learning. This third book is specifically designed to give you the foundation that you will need to continue studying on your own after you have finished this book.

Preface

About the Vocabulary

Each vocabulary word presented to you in this book has been hand selected one by one. It is all commonly used and will be useful to know. Over the course of this series, you will have learned well over 3,000 vocabulary words and phrases.

The average native Korean speaker knows between ten and thirty thousand words depending on their education. This number includes everything from foreign words in the Korean language to technical terms, medical terms, and slang. Fortunately, the daily vocabulary of most Koreans will only amount to a few thousand words at most.

Holding an actual conversation in Korean on your own – although probably rather slowly at first – is an attainable goal by the end of this book, if you only regularly practice what you learn and continue to study. Your vocabulary will be sufficient for most basic conversation if used creatively. This vocabulary should serve as a foundation to continue learning and to practice what you are learning with native Korean speakers.

Not all vocabulary listed in each chapter will be used within this book. Practice this additional vocabulary by making your own example sentences. More difficult vocabulary, more commonly used vocabulary, and vocabulary that can seem vague from only reading its definition have been given priority when creating the example sentences for each chapter.

How to Use This Book

This book builds upon itself with each new chapter. I recommend that you take your time to carefully read and understand the material as you complete each lesson, and then spend additional time to practice the concepts that you have learned. It is always better to know fewer grammatical concepts and vocabulary well than to know more of them poorly.

Chapters in this book will be slightly larger than in the previous two books, and each will be denser and contain more grammatical explanations and examples. Also, many of these concepts will be more difficult than what we have learned before and will require more time to understand and become familiar with. I recommend moving through each chapter slowly, and taking plenty of time to practice. And just like before, I will help guide you along through each chapter.

Preface

Refer to the vocabulary list at the end of each chapter whenever you notice a new word you are unfamiliar with. If you are unable to locate a word, try searching in the Glossary. Since this is the third book in the "Korean Made Simple" series, if the word is absent from this Glossary, it was covered in a previous book. Because of this, I would recommend keeping the previous two books handy. This will be useful for quickly reviewing concepts, such as grammar or vocabulary, and will help you to move through this book more smoothly. Alternatively, you can also use a dictionary to look up unfamiliar words.

Take notes as you go. Practice by writing (and speaking, if possible) your own example sentences using the concepts in each chapter. You know better than anyone else which concepts are the most difficult to you. Organize your study schedule to give yourself enough time to review those concepts.

If you're in a rush – "I have a date tomorrow with my favorite Korean idol and they don't speak any English!" – then complete all of the lessons but skip the Practice sections, and focus on the main grammar concepts instead of the vocabulary.

About the Advanced Notes

In the previous two books, I recommended skipping the "Advanced Notes" during your first time reading each chapter. This book works a bit differently, as some of the information taught in the "Advanced Notes" in each chapter will be used in the following chapters. This is to allow more concepts to be taught in a single book.

For your first time reading through each chapter, read each "Culture Notes" section but skip the "Advanced Notes" until you have a good understanding of the concepts being taught. The "Advanced Notes" in this book contain information that you will need to know for later chapters, but can be confusing before you have understood the basic concept. Read the "Advanced Notes" once you feel comfortable with the topic, and after you have had a chance to read through the chapter.

If you are using this book only as a review and have already learned the major concepts in each chapter, then read the "Advanced Notes" together with the chapter as you move through the book.

About the Answer Keys

The more grammar and vocabulary that you know, the more "right answers" you will find. Use the Answer Keys section in this book as a general guide, but do not take them as the only possible solutions. Compare your own answers with the Answer Keys, but know that they might not always match – and this is fine.

Preface

Because there can be multiple correct answers to each Practice question, I suggest focusing more on the grammar forms used in the Answer Keys than on the exact sentences.

반말 and Honorific Korean

Most of "Korean Made Simple 1" used example sentences and conversations that were written using the 니다 form, until the 요 form and polite speech (존댓말) were introduced in Chapter 19. In "Korean Made Simple 2" we learned about casual Korean (반말) and the basics of when and how to use it. We also covered honorific speech (높임말), including honorific verbs and words, as well as humble verbs and particles.

In this book, all of these forms will be utilized together in their appropriate situations. Keep an eye out for each type of speech as you see it, and try to review for yourself when it is appropriate to use each kind. Knowing when and where to use each type of speech can be one of the most challenging aspects of learning the Korean language. However, the more you practice, the more comfortable you will become with using them. Having a strong understanding of when to use each type of Korean speech will not only help you avoid sounding rude, but also will allow you to speak and write Korean more naturally.

I also want to add a few more notes on this subject. First, 반말 should be avoided when meeting someone for the first time, even if they're a bit younger than you (with the exception of little children). If you want to use 반말 with someone who is younger than you, or with someone who you are not yet friends with, it is best to ask them for permission before doing so. You can do this with the following sentence (among other ways of asking):

우리 말(을) 놓을까요?
"Should we speak casually?"

The above sentence literally means, "Should we put down our speech?"

In *most* situations when speaking with Koreans, the 요 form will work fine. However, use honorifics whenever you are talking about or asking a question to someone who is older than you and when speaking to strangers. It is best to be safe, as the more Korean you know the more you will be expected by native Korean speakers to use the appropriate levels of speech.

Preface

After Completing This Book

This book, as well as the previous two books, were designed only as stepping stones for you to use toward reaching your own language goals. In order to become fluent in Korean, or at least able to carry on a full conversation by yourself, it will take extra work outside of this book series. As much as I would love to, I cannot be your only start-to-finish resource for learning the Korean language.

If your goal is to become conversational, then you will need to practice Korean as much as possible outside of these books. Frequently practicing what you are learning is essential to being able to use the language in real world situations.

You can practice by making sentences using each grammar form and concept as you learn them, through chatting online or in person, and by exposing yourself to the language as much as possible. Listening to Korean natives speaking in their language on television, in movies, on the radio, and in real life will help to train your ears to recognize sounds and words. But ultimately, *speaking* the language yourself will provide the greatest assistance in improving your Korean ability.

I would highly recommend finding a Korean friend or pen pal as soon as possible and practicing the language with them daily through writing or speaking. Even if you do not yet feel that your Korean is "good enough" to hold a conversation, you will still be able to practice what you are learning. Having a pen pal or friend will also expose you to more of the language that you will need to know in order to hold natural conversations. There are many places to find language friends and pen pals if you search online, so I will not mention any specific ones here.

Good Luck

While good quality books and teachers can help make the process of learning Korean easier, it is likely that there will still be times when the language will frustrate you. Maybe there is a grammar form that just does not make sense in your mind, or a concept that confuses you. We have all been there. I have been there too (more times than I can count), and I want you to know that it does get better.

I have said it before, but the secret to becoming fluent in Korean (or in any language) is to simply keep going until you have reached your goal. Just like running a marathon, learning Korean is a long process, and if you want to reach your goals then you need to keep going until you are there. Sometimes it will be easy, and other times difficult. I understand exactly how difficult it can be. Know that many other people who have learned Korean have been in your shoes, and have continued past their hurdles with the language, and know that you can too.

Preface

I also hope that whatever your goals are, whether they be fluency or basic conversation, you will keep going until you are satisfied with where you want to be. I truly believe that anyone can learn Korean as long as they put forth the effort.

Again, congratulations on making it this far. I hope that through these books and your own studying and practice that you will be able to reach your own personal language goals. And as usual, I will be here if you need me.

Preface

Plain Form

Chapter 1

Conversation

소라:	난 내일 엄마랑 바다에 간다!
수현:	오, 좋겠다!
소라:	같이 갈래?
수현:	당연히 가고 싶지. 하지만 나는 일하잖아. 아직 휴가철도 안 됐는데….
소라:	아, 맞다. 미안.
수현:	괜찮아. 재미있게 놀고 와.
소라:	그래!
수현:	근데 요즘 좀 춥지 않아?
소라:	그럼 코트를 입고 나가야 되겠다.

The Plain Form is one of the most important forms in Korean that we have not covered yet, and it will be used throughout the rest of this book. We need to learn how to make the Plain Form in order to use several other essential grammar forms, such as quotations, which will be covered in the next chapter. This chapter will cover how to conjugate the Plain Form and what it is, as well as when and where to use it.

First let's look at the conversation and learn about the Plain Form along the way.

> 소라: 난 내일 엄마랑 바다에 간다!
> "Tomorrow I'm going to the beach with my mom!"

Chapter 1: Plain Form

The Plain Form

The Plain Form is used in the following situations:

When speaking...
    Announcement-style speaking (반말)
    Talking to yourself

When writing...
    News articles
    Essays
    Example sentences in textbooks
    Journals

Let's cover each of these uses one at a time. First we will focus on using the Plain Form when *speaking*. In the conversation, 소라 ends the sentence with 간다. This comes from the verb 가다 ("to go").

So what is the difference between saying **간다** (Plain Form), or just saying **가요** (요 form)? Using the Plain Form when speaking can make your sentence seem like you are making an *announcement* – as if you are holding a megaphone. Because of this, speaking using the Plain Form might sound like you are announcing something that you want the listener, or everyone to hear. Here is an example of this:

내가 이걸 다 먹는다!
"I'm eating all of this (and I want to let you know)!"

However, using the Plain Form in this way to speak as if you are making an announcement is only appropriate for situations when you would use 반말, such as when talking with close friends. It should not be used in any polite situation.

Using 가(요) instead of 간다 in this sentence would have the same *grammatical* meaning, and would also be fine to use, but the overall sentence would have a different *feeling*.

내일 바다에 가요!
"Tomorrow I'm going to the beach!"

In summary, using the Plain Form when speaking to a friend can make a sentence sound like an announcement, but does not change the actual meaning of the sentence.

Plain Form

Making the Plain Form

Let's take a look at the rules for conjugating the Plain Form. I will cover how to use the Plain Form with each of the three main tenses – past tense, present tense, and future tense. Many of these conjugations might appear familiar to you, and that is because you have already learned most of them.

Note that all forms of the Plain Form will end in 다. However, this is different from the form of a verb that you will find in a dictionary. I will explain why in a moment.

Past Tense Plain Form:
Verb Stem + 아/어/etc. + ㅆ + 다

To make the Plain Form in past tense, simply conjugate the past tense in the same way as usual without adding anything extra to the end (such as 어요). Add the 다 at the end as it would be, and you are finished. Here are a few examples.

공부하다 → 공부해
공부해 + ㅆ → 공부했
공부했 + 다 → 공부했다

놀다 → 놀아
놀아 + ㅆ → 놀았
놀았 + 다 → 놀았다

먹다 → 먹어
먹어 + ㅆ → 먹었
먹었 + 다 → 먹었다

있다 → 있어
있어 + ㅆ → 있었
있었 + 다 → 있었다

While not listed above, the verb 이다 ("to be") will become 이었다 after a *consonant*, or 였다 after a *vowel*. 아니다 ("to not be") will become 아니었다.

Let's take a look at a few example sentences with the past tense and the Plain Form.

내가 실수를 했다.
"I made a mistake."

Plain Form

엘비스는 건물을 나갔다.
"Elvis left the building."

어제는 아주 추웠다.
"Yesterday was very cold."

Culture Notes

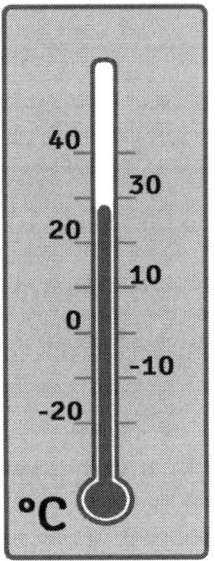

Korea uses Celsius (섭씨), and not Fahrenheit (화씨) when telling the temperature. If you want to specify one or the other, you can say it at the beginning of a sentence.

어제는 화씨 100 도였어요.
"Yesterday was 100 degrees Fahrenheit."

Present Tense Plain Form:

Action Verb Stem + (는/ㄴ) + 다

Descriptive Verb Stem + 다

To make the Plain Form in present tense, first take a look at the type of verb it is. For *action verbs*, take the verb stem and attach 는 if it ends in a *consonant*, or attach ㄴ if it ends in a *vowel*. Then attach 다, and you are finished.

Here are a few quick examples of action verbs:

가다 − 다 → 가
가 + ㄴ → 간
간 + 다 → 간다

Plain Form

먹다 → 먹
먹 + 는 → 먹는
먹는 + 다 → 먹는다

놀다 – 다 → 놀
놀 – ㄹ → 노
노 + ㄴ → 논
논 + 다 → 논다

When an action verb stem ends in ㄹ, the ㄹ will be dropped.

알다 – 다 → 알
알 – ㄹ → 아
아 + ㄴ → 안
안 + 다 → 안다

For descriptive verbs in the present tense, things get even easier. *Descriptive verbs* in the Plain Form will be the exact same as their regular verb forms. Here are a few examples.

재미없다 → 재미없다

심심하다 → 심심하다

춥다 → 춥다

있다 → 있다

> **Advanced**
>
> **Action and Descriptive 있다**
>
> The verb 있다 can actually be used as an *action verb* or a *descriptive verb*. When it is being used to mean that something or someone "exists" (its most common usage) it is a *descriptive verb*. However, when it is being used to say that *someone* (and not something) "exists and stays" somewhere, then it is an *action verb*. You can think of 있다 meaning both "to exist" and "to stay put." Here are a few examples.
>
> 철수는 친구 집에 있는다.
> "Chul-soo is (staying) at a friend's house."
>
> 철수는 친구 집에 있다.
> "Chul-soo is at a friend's house."
>
> 철수는 집이 있다.
> "Chul-soo has a house."
>
> Note that although the verb 있다 can be used as both an action verb and a descriptive verb, it is most commonly only conjugated as a descriptive verb (here, as 있다 in the Plain Form) even when it is being used as an action verb.
>
> 없다, however, is only used as a *descriptive verb*.

Chapter 1
Plain Form

The verb 이다 ("to be") will become either 이다 after a *consonant,* or simply 다 after a *vowel.*

Let's take a look at a few example sentences with the present tense and Plain Form.

나는 과자를 좋아한다.
"I like snacks."

철수는 학교에서 밥을 먹는다.
"Chul-soo eats at school."

나는 그걸 모른다.
"I don't know that."

오늘은 굉장히 덥다.
"Today is awfully hot."

한국어는 기초부터 배워야 한다.
"You must learn Korean from the basics."

그 사람은 나보다 키가 훨씬 더 크다.
"That person is much taller than me."

훨씬 is an *adverb* that's used with *descriptive verbs* to mean "much (more)." It adds *emphasis* to the descriptive verb that it is used before. It can be used *optionally* together with the adverb 더 ("more"). You will also commonly see it used with 좋다 ("to be good") to mean "much better."

Future Tense Plain Form:

Verb Stem + 겠다

Verb Stem + (을/ㄹ) 것이다

In Chapter 3 of the previous book we learned how to conjugate the future tense in these two ways. Once you have conjugated either of these two future tense forms, 겠다 or 것이다, you are finished.

하다 → 하겠다 or 할 것이다

먹다 → 먹겠다 or 먹을 것이다

있다 → 있겠다 or 있을 것이다

덥다 → 덥겠다 or 더울 것이다

Plain Form

Chapter 1

When using the 겠다 form, the verb 이다 ("to be") will become either 이겠다 after a *consonant*, or simply 겠다 after a *vowel*. When using the 것이다 form, 이다 will become 일 것이다.

We previously learned that 거다 is more commonly used than 것이다, and the same applies here.

Let's take a look at a few example sentences with the future tense and Plain Form.

지금 안 먹으면 이따가 배가 고프겠다.
"You'll be hungry later if you don't eat now."

내일 친구와 같이 공부할 거다.
"Tomorrow I'll study together with a friend."

기말시험이 어려울 거다.
"The final test will be difficult."

Culture Notes

The 수능

Another word for 기말시험 is 기말고사 ("final exam," "final test"). However, there is an even larger test given once during the last year of high school to all students in Korea – 대학수학능력시험 ("College Scholastic Ability Test"). This is more commonly abbreviated as 수능. It is a test made for showing a student's ability to perform in college, and only students who score highly on the test are able to enter Korea's most prestigious universities. Students who enter Korea's top universities currently have a much larger chance of being employed in higher paid positions. Because of this, students will stress and study daily, sacrificing their free time and sometimes much more, in order to score well on this single test.

Let's go back to the conversation, and we'll learn more about the Plain Form along the way.

Chapter 1

Plain Form

수현: 오, 좋겠다!

"Oh, that'd be great!"

"Would" & "Must": 겠다

The 겠다 ending has one more common usage – to mean "would" or "must." This form can be used for expressing your *opinion* that something would be, or must be, or must have been a certain way, or that something would happen. This form can be used when you are making a *statement*, but not when you are asking a question. It can be used with either present tense or past tense. Let's take a look at a few examples.

맛있겠다!
"That would be delicious!"

맛있었겠다!
"That must have been delicious!"

심심하겠다.
"You must be bored."

정말 춥겠다.
"That would be really cold."

재미있었겠다.
"That must have been fun."

이미 나갔겠네요.
"He already would've left."

힘들었겠네.
"That must've been difficult."

Note that this form is different from the 까(요) form we learned in the previous book, as that form is only used when making *suggestions* (in questions).

Plain Form

Chapter 1

Advanced

모르다 and 모르겠다

Both 모르다 and 모르겠다 can be used to say that you "do not know" something or someone. Using 모르겠다 shows that you might not know (would not know), and using 모르다 shows that you simply do not know. Here are examples of each.

몰라요.
"I don't know."

모르겠어요.
"I don't/wouldn't know."

소라: 같이 갈래?
"You wanna go together?"

수현: 당연히 가고 싶지. 하지만 나는 일하잖아. 아직 휴가철도 안 됐는데....
"Of course I want to go. But I work. It's not even vacation season yet."

휴가철 is a combination of 휴가 ("a break," "a leave") with 철, which means "season." While 철 cannot be used on its own (the normal word for "season" when used on its own is 계절), it can be attached to some words to mean "a season for" or "a time for." In this case, 휴가철 literally means "a season for breaks," or "vacation season."

소라: 아, 맞다. 미안.
"Ah, that's right. Oops."

Talking to Yourself with Plain Form

Using the 요 and 니다 forms or honorific speech when speaking to yourself would be awkward, since those forms are made to show a higher level of respect to other people. Instead, you can use the Plain Form when talking to yourself.

바쁘다. 싫다.
"I'm busy. I don't like it."

오! 재미있다!
"Oh! It's fun!"

너무 지루하다.
"It's so boring."

While 너무 is normally used to mean "too much" or "overly," it has one more use when speaking *casually* or with friends – "so (much)." Here is an example.

Chapter 1

Plain Form

너무 좋아!
"It's so good!"
"I like it so much!"

In the conversation, 소라 is speaking to herself at the beginning (아, 맞다.), and then is speaking to 수현 at the end (미안.).

> **Adv** — Note that 맞다 is actually an *action verb*. However, it is most often conjugated simply as 맞다 in the Plain Form.

However, the Plain Form is only used for making *statements*. It is not used for questions no matter how it is being used – both in speaking and in writing. If you want to ask a question to yourself, you do not use the Plain Form. Instead, you can use the 지 ending which we learned in the previous book.

뭐 먹지?
"What do I eat?"

내 지갑이 어디 갔지?
"Where did my wallet go?"

저 사람이 누구지?
"Who's that person?"

These two forms, the Plain Form (for statements) and the 지 ending (for questions), are two common ways of speaking to yourself. Note that using the 지 ending in this way still has the same meaning it normally does when talking to other people – it is used when asking someone (here, yourself) to *confirm* what you are saying, like saying the stereotypical "eh?" that's used by some Canadians.

> **Advanced** — While the Plain Form is not used when speaking to other people, except for when using *casual speech* (반말) to make an announcement, it can be used when speaking to *yourself* in any situation. It is fine to use Plain Form to speak to yourself, or the 지 ending to ask yourself a question, even if you are in front of someone else who you are speaking politely to. You can do this as long as it is clear that you are speaking to yourself, and as long as you avoid slang or inappropriate language. The following sentence is an example of this, with the parts in parenthesis being the parts that the speaker is saying to themselves.
>
> (이름이 뭐였지? 아, 맞다.) 어제 제가 박 선생님을 잠깐 만났는데요....
> "(What was his name? Ah, that's right) Yesterday I met Mr. Park for a moment...."
>
> However, this kind of usage should still be avoided in most formal situations, as speaking to yourself out loud can come across as being *informal*. It is best to be cautious with the way that you speak in any formal situation.

Let's continue with the conversation.

Plain Form

수현: 괜찮아. 재미있게 놀고 와.

"It's okay. Have fun."

Action Verb Stem + 고 오다

In English, we might tell someone to go do something by saying just that – "go do something." In Korean you will use the verb 오다 ("to come"). So instead of telling someone in English to "go have fun," in Korean you are actually telling them to "have fun and then *come back*."

To use this form, take an *action verb stem* and attach 고 ("and," "and then"), followed by the verb 오다. Conjugate the verb 오다 any way that you would like. Literally, this translates as "to do (something) and come (back)." Here are a few example conjugations.

공부(를) 하다 → 공부(를) 하고 오다

놀다 → 놀고 오다

먹다 → 먹고 오다

보다 → 보고 오다

However, this form cannot be used after verbs that show *movement*, such as 가다, 나가다, and others. Making the verb 나가다 into 나가고 오다 would be *incorrect*. We will learn a few phrases that we can use instead, as well as more about the 고 form later in this book.

소라: 그래!

"Okay!"

수현: 근데 요즘 좀 춥지 않아?

"But isn't it a bit cold lately?"

Negative Plain Form

The Plain Form can also be used in *negative* sentences. You can use 안 or 지 않다 to make a negative sentence, just as we learned in the first book.

To review, here are examples of each tense used with a *negative* verb.

Chapter 1: Plain Form

Negative Past Tense:

안 + Verb Stem + 아/어/etc. + ㅆ다

Verb Stem + 지 않았다

To make the negative past tense with the Plain Form you can either use 안 (depending on the verb) or the 지 않았다 ending. Here are a few examples.

하다 → 안 했다 or 하지 않았다

움직이다 → 안 움직였다 or 움직이지 않았다

있다 → 없었다 or 있지 않았다

내가 안 했다.
"I didn't do it."

어제 그렇게 피곤하지 않았다.
"I wasn't that tired yesterday."

한국어를 조금밖에 못 했다.
"I could only speak a little Korean."

국물이 별로 고소하지 않았다.
"The (soup's) broth wasn't really good."

고소하다 ("to be savory," "to be nutty") is specifically used for describing something that has a savory, or deep nutty taste of *sesame oil*. Although this descriptive verb is specifically for referring to the flavor of sesame oil, it's a commonly used verb for describing food dishes containing that flavor – in a similar way to 맛(이) 있다. It can also be used for other flavorful nuts as well, such as peanuts and almonds.

Negative Present Tense:

안 + Action Verb Stem + (는/ㄴ) 다

Action Verb Stem + 지 않는다

안 + Descriptive Verb Stem + 다

Descriptive Verb Stem + 지 않다

To make the negative Plain Form in present tense, first take a look at the type of verb that it is.

Plain Form

For *action verbs*, you can attach 안 and then use the regular present tense of the Plain Form, if it is a verb that can use 안 to become negative. Or, you can take the verb stem and attach 지 않는다. For a review of which action verbs can and cannot use 안 to become negative, re-read Chapter 14 of the first book. Here are two examples.

놀다 → 안 논다 or 놀지 않는다

나가다 → 나가지 않는다

For *descriptive verbs*, you can attach 안 before the verb. Or you can take the verb stem and attach 지 않다. Here are two examples.

덥다 → 안 덥다 or 덥지 않다

있다 → 없다 or 있지 않다

Here are a few example sentences.

난 술을 안 마신다.
"I don't drink alcohol."

오늘 날씨가 안 좋다.
"The weather today is not good."

원숭이를 좋아하지만 강아지를 좋아하지 않는다.
"I like monkeys, but I don't like puppies."

Negative Future Tense:
안 + Verb Stem + 겠다
안 + Verb Stem + (을/ㄹ) 것이다
Verb Stem + 지 않겠다
Verb Stem + 지 않을 것이다

To make the negative future tense in Plain Form, you can use 안 to make the verb negative, and then attach 겠다 or (을/ㄹ) 것이다 if it is a verb that can use 안 to become negative. Or, you can attach either 지 않겠다, or 지 않을 것이다 (shortened to 지 않을 거다) to the end of the verb stem. Here are a few examples.

내일 덥지 않겠다.
"Tomorrow will not be hot."

> **Chapter 1**

Plain Form

아무도 안 먹겠다.
"Nobody will eat that."

그 사람은 도와주지 않을 거다.
"That person will not help."

> 소라: 그럼 코트를 입고 나가야 되겠다
> "Well then, I need to wear a coat and leave."

While it might seem like there are many rules for changing a verb to Plain Form (okay, there are), the majority of these rules are ones that we have already learned. I have simply listed all of them again to use as a reference.

Journal: 나의 어제 일기

> 어제는 발렌타인 데이였다.
> 내가 좋아하는 여자한테서 초콜릿하고 카드를 받았다.
> 정말 재미있는 하루였다.
> 지금은 집에서 초콜릿을 먹으면서 쉬고 있다.
> 밤이 되면 친구의 집에 놀러 간다.
> 내일은 운동을 해야 되겠다.

We have covered the two ways that the Plain Form can be used when speaking, so now let's talk about when the Plain Form is used in writing. The Plain Form is used for writing *journals*, *news articles*, and *essays*. The Plain Form is also used for *example sentences* in many textbooks.

Plain Form

When you write something, you often do not know who the reader will be. Will your grandmother read it? Will the President look at it? Will a cat read it (hypothetically, of course)? Because of this, there would be no way of knowing which type of speech to use – casual, polite, or honorific.

This is the reason that the Plain Form is used for journals, news articles, essays, and example sentences. The Plain Form is used when what you are writing is *not directed* at anyone specifically. As long as you are not directing your writing toward a specific person, it is safe and preferred to write using the Plain Form. Let's read through the example journal.

나의 어제 일기
"My journal (from yesterday)."

Plain Form and 나

We know that using the Plain Form will replace the 니다 and 요 forms, but there is one more step that we need to take. 나, as well as its many forms (나는, 내가, etc.) are used with the Plain Form, and not 저 or any of its forms (저는, 제가, etc.). Let's take a look at an example.

나는 학교에서 공부했다.
"I studied at school."

Here is an example of an *incorrect* sentence using the Plain Form: 저는 학교에서 공부했다.

어제는 발렌타인 데이였다.
"Yesterday was Valentine's Day."

Remember that the verb 이다 ("to be") in Plain Form in the past tense will become either 이었다 after a *consonant*, or 였다 after a *vowel*.

내가 좋아하는 여자한테서 초콜릿하고 카드를 받았다.
"I received chocolate and a card from the girl I like."

Remember that on Valentine's Day in Korea, girls give chocolates and cards to boys, and not the other way around. For a review of this holiday as well as others, re-read Appendix B in the second book.

정말 재미있는 하루였다.
"It was a really fun day."

Plain Form

지금은 집에서 초콜릿을 먹으면서 쉬고 있다.
"Now I'm relaxing while eating chocolate at home."

밤이 되면 친구의 집에 놀러 간다.
"In the evening I'll go to a friend's house to play."

밤(이) 되다 literally means "to become the evening" but can translate more naturally in this sentence to "in the evening." Another translation for 밤이 되면 could be "when it is the evening."

내일은 운동을 해야 되겠다.
"I better exercise tomorrow."

Let's learn one more common use for the Plain Form.

Strong "If": Plain Form + 면

In addition to being used for making quotes (which we'll cover next chapter), the Plain Form is also used for another form – a stronger version of the (으)면 form ("if," "when").

In the previous book we learned that the (으)면 form can be used to mean "if" or "when" depending on the context of the sentence. When used with the Plain Form, its meaning changes to *only* be "if." Using this form is a *stronger* version of the normal (으)면 form. Let's take a look at two examples.

시간이 있으면....
"If/when you have time...."

시간이 있다면....
"**If** you have time...."

The second example, in addition to only meaning "if," also has a much *stronger* feeling. This form can be used to *emphasize* "if" in a sentence. Here is one more example of this difference.

내가 한국에 가면 한국말을 빨리 배울 수 있을 거야.
"If (or when) I go to Korea I'll be able to learn Korean quickly."

내가 한국에 간다면 한국말을 빨리 배울 수 있을 거야.
"**If** I go to Korea I'll be able to learn Korean quickly (but only "if" I go to Korea)."

Plain Form

Let's take a look at a few more example sentences with this form.

수학 시험이 어려웠다면 개인 과외는 어떨까요?
"If the math test was hard then how about a personal tutor?"

티파니를 만났다면 증거를 보여주세요.
"If you met Tiffany, show me proof."

내가 여기서 유일하게 한국말을 할 수 있는 사람이라면 좋겠다.
"It would be good if I'm the only person here who can speak Korean."

The verb 이다 ("to be") when used with this form becomes 이라면 after a *consonant*, or 라면 after a *vowel*.

Remember that the form (으)면 좋겠다 can be used to mean "hope" or "wish," so the same sentence could also be translated as "I hope that I'm the only person here who can speak Korean."

유일하다 is a descriptive verb that means "to be the only one," and can be used as either an *adverb* (유일하게) or as an *adjective* (유일한). It is fine to use either form, so the same sentence could have also been written like this: 내가 여기서 한국말을 할 수 있는 **유일한** 사람이라면 좋겠다.

오늘 춥다면 밖에 나가지 않는 게 낫겠어.
"If it's cold today, it would be better to not go outside."

Using an action verb (or a negative action verb) with 는 것이 낫다 is another common way to say "should" or "should not," as we learned in Chapter 14 of the second book. Another natural translation for this form is "better" or "better not."

만약에 내일 지구가 멸망한다면 뭐할 거야?
"What will you do if the world ends tomorrow?"

As we learned in the previous book, adding 만약(에) to a sentence with the (으)면 form adds more *emphasis* to the meaning of "if." Combining that together with this form (Plain Form + 면) increases the emphasis more. Because both 만약(에) and this form have a similar effect on the sentence, it is common for both of them to appear together when one or the other is being used.

등이 아프시다면 의자에 앉아 보세요.
"If your back hurts, try sitting in a chair."

Chapter 1 — Plain Form

Note how 아프다 is used in this example as 아프시다, which is *honorific speech*. Remember that honorific speech is used to show respect when talking *about* someone else. This can include talking about a person's body or body parts (such as someone's back).

"Know that": Plain Form + 는 것(을) 알다/모르다

Advanced

Another common use of the Plain Form is for saying that you know (or do not know) a *fact* or piece of *information*.

To use it, take the plain form and attach 는 것(을) 알다 if you know the fact, or 는 것(을) 모르다 if you do not know the fact. Here are a few examples.

나도 갈 수 있다는 것을 알아요.
"I know that I can go too."

You can also translate this form as "to know (or not know) the *fact* that." So this example sentence could translate as "I know the fact that I can go too."

철수가 했다는 걸 몰랐어요.
"I didn't know that Chul-soo did it."

춥다는 걸 알고 있어요.
"I know that it is cold."

조지가 한국 사람이 아니라는 걸 알고 있어.
"I know that George is not a Korean."

When used with the verb 이다 ("to be"), this becomes 이라는 after a *consonant* or 라는 after a *vowel*. The verb 아니다 ("to not be") becomes 아니라는.

한국은 겨울에 춥다는 것을 이미 잘 알고 있어요.
"I already know well that Korea is cold in the winter."

Note that this form is not used to say that you know a *noun*. To say that you know or do not know a noun (for example, "I don't know the password"), simply use 알다 or 모르다 as usual (비밀 번호를 몰라요.). This form is only used to say that you know or do not know about a *fact* or a piece of *information*.

Pronouncing 의

Advanced

Previously we learned that 의 is pronounced as 에 when used as the *Possessive Marker*. But 의 also can be pronounced differently depending on where it is used in a word.

At the beginning of a word, 의 is pronounced normally as 의.

Anywhere else in a word (in the middle or at the end), 의 *can* be pronounced as 이. This is *optional*.

So while 의자 is only pronounced correctly as 의자, here are a few *optional* examples of ways to pronounce other common words.

편의점 → 펴니점 (or 펴늬점)
주의 → 주이 (or 주의)
의의 → 의이 (or 의의)

Plain Form

Practice

Conjugate the following verbs to the present tense using the Plain Form:

1. 가르치다

   _____.

2. 믿다

   _____.

3. 살다

   _____.

4. 좋아하다

   _____.

5. 맛있다

   _____.

6. 이다

   _____.

7. 더럽다

   _____.

Conjugate the following verbs to the past tense using the Plain Form:

8. 앉다

   _____.

9. 공부(를) 하다

   _____.

Chapter 1 — **Plain Form**

10. 멀다

_____.

11. 없다

_____.

12. 크다

_____.

13. 울다

_____.

14. 스트레스(를) 받다

_____.

Translate to Korean using the Plain Form:

15. "I like kimchi."

_____.

16. "Yung-hee goes to school every day."

_____.

17. "I am an American."

_____.

18. "I ate two pieces of pizza."

_____.

19. "It wasn't a puppy. It was a cat."

_____.

Plain Form

20. "I only have 5,000 Won in my wallet."

_____.

21. "Today was a fun day, but it was extremely hot."

_____.

Translate to English:

22. 나는 다양한 취미를 가지고 있다.

_____.

23. 내일은 오늘보다 훨씬 더 좋은 하루가 될 거다.

_____.

24. 편의점에서 산 계란이랑 도시락이 별로 신선하지 않았다.

_____.

25. 아빠의 오래된 카메라를 실수로 떨어뜨렸다.

_____.

26. 오늘은 왠지 동생이 너무 귀찮다.

_____.

27. 내일은 오늘만큼 심심하지 않을 거다.

_____.

28. 초보자라면 이런 날씨에는 운전하면 안 된다.

_____.

New Phrases

미안.	"Sorry.," "Oops." (casual)

Chapter 1: Plain Form

New Vocabulary

실수(를) 하다	"to make a mistake"
계절	"season"
초콜릿	"chocolate"
카드	"card"
증거	"proof," "evidence"
증명(을) 하다	"to prove"
멸망(을) 하다	"to collapse," "to be destroyed," "to end (the world, etc.)"
망하다	"to be destroyed," "to be messed up," "to completely fail," "to go bankrupt" (casual)
터지다	"to burst," "to pop"
폭발	"explosion"
폭발(을) 하다	"to explode"
개인	"personal" (adjective)
과외	"tutoring"
과외 선생님	"tutor"
교재	"teaching materials," "textbook(s)"
유일하다	"to be the only one"
유일하게	"only" (adverb)
유일한	"only" (adjective)
왠지	"for some reason," "somehow"
스트레스(를) 받다	"to get stress"
굉장히	"extremely," "awfully"
훨씬	"much (more)" (adverb)
초보자	"beginner"
전문가	"expert"
귀찮다	"to be tiresome," "to be troublesome"
내게	나에게 (casual)
네게	너에게 (casual)
제게	저에게
다양하다	"to be various"
신선하다	"to be fresh"

Plain Form

상큼하다	"to be refreshing"
오래되다	"to be old (an object)"
계란	"(chicken) egg" (slightly casual)
도시락	"a box lunch," "a packed lunch"
기초	"(the) basics," "base," "foundation"
섭씨	"Celsius"
화씨	"Fahrenheit"
인증(을) 하다	"to authorize," "to confirm"
기말시험	"final exam," "final test"
기말고사	"final exam," "final test"
수능(시험)	"college entrance exam"
국물	"(soup) broth"
국자	"ladle"
씨(앗)	"seed(s)"
깨	"sesame seeds"
고소하다	"to be savory," "to be nutty"

Chapter 1

Plain Form

Making Quotes

Chapter 2

Conversation

유나:	아, 빨리 가야겠다.
조지:	네? 지금 나가자고요? 아직은….
유나:	모임이 5 시부터 시작할 거라고 그랬는데….
조지:	누가 5 시부터 시작한다고 했어요?
유나:	철수가 5 시까지 오라고 했어요.
조지:	철수한테 6 시 아니냐고 물어봐 주세요.
유나:	5 시가 아니라고요?
조지:	5 시가 아니고, 6 시예요.
유나:	그럼 철수에게 6 시라고 전해 줄게요.

Now that we have learned what Plain Form is and how to conjugate it, let's learn one more essential grammar form that uses it. This chapter will cover how to make *quotations* (something that someone says). There are four types of quotations that we can make in Korean, and one of them will use the Plain Form. First, here are a few examples in English of what we'll be learning:

"I *said* let's go to the store 3 minutes ago. Why aren't you ready yet?"
"I *said* that I'm going to the store today. Is there anything you need?"
"I *said* to do the dishes before mom comes back."
"I *asked* if you want to eat this. If not, then I will."

Making Quotes

These four examples show the four main types of quoting that we will cover – *suggestions* ("Let's...."), *statements* ("It is...."), *commands* ("Do it! Just do it!"), and *questions* ("Is it...?"). We will cover each of these one at a time. Let's start with the conversation.

유나: 아, 빨리 가야겠다.
"Ah, I better go right away."

조지: 네? 지금 나가자고요? 아직은....
"What? (Are you saying let's) leave now? I'm still...."

Suggestions: Action Verb Stem + 자고 (말)하다

This form is used for quoting what someone – yourself or another person – *suggests* ("Let's..."). First let's take another look at one of our earlier example sentences.

"I *said* let's go to the store 3 minutes ago. Why aren't you ready yet?"

To use this form, take the "let's" form (covered in Chapter 12 of the second book). Attach 고, and then (말)하다. Adding 말 is *optional*, as 하다 can mean "to say" on its own when used with this form. Here are a few examples.

하다 → 하자고 (말)하다
놀다 → 놀자고 (말)하다
먹다 → 먹자고 (말)하다

Here are a few example sentences.

가자고 말했어요.
"I said let's go."

피자를 먹자고 했어요.
"I said let's eat pizza."

밖에서 놀자고 했어요?
"Did you say let's play outside?"

같이 공부하자고 말했지만 아무도 대답을 안 했어요.
"I said let's study together but nobody answered."

오늘 학교에 가지 말자고 했어요.
"I said let's not go to school today."

Making Quotes

Chapter 2

However, if you look at the conversation you might notice something different from this form – 지금 나가자고요? Notice how the verb 하다 is missing. This is completely acceptable, and the verb (말)하다 is actually *optional*. Here, 말(하다) can be replaced with a 요, or with nothing (if speaking casually).

The only difference between using (말)하다 and removing it is that using it will add a stronger meaning of *saying* something. The overall meaning of the sentence will stay the same. Here are a couple of examples.

밖에서 놀자고 했어요? 전 너무 피곤해요."
"Did you say let's play outside? I'm too tired."

밖에서 놀자고요? 전 너무 피곤해요.
"Play outside? I'm too tired."

In fact, this same rule of removing (말)하다 applies to all four of the main forms that we'll learn in this chapter.

When someone is speaking *honorifically* (covered in Chapter 8 of the previous book) you can also replace (말)하다 with 말씀(을) 하시다.

선생님은 오늘 다 같이 밥을 먹자고 말씀하셨어요.
"The teacher said let's eat lunch all together today."

유나: 모임이 5 시부터 시작할 거라고 그랬는데....
"They said the meeting will start from 5 o'clock."

Statements: Plain Form + 고 (말)하다

This form is used for quoting when someone (yourself or another person) makes a *statement*. A statement can be anything from saying "it is" or "it isn't" to "I do," or any verb. It is when you or someone is *stating* something – not for questions, suggestions, or commands. Often statements will start with "(someone) says," but they can also start with "(someone) yells" or "(someone) talks" or with any verb that describes how someone speaks. Let's take another look at one of our earlier example sentences.

"I *said* that I'm going to the store today. Is there anything you need?"

To use this form, take the Plain Form (which is only used in statements) and attach 고. Then add (말)하다 like before. Again, you can *optionally* replace (말)하다 with a 요, or with nothing (if speaking casually). Here are a few examples of this form in the *present tense*.

Chapter 2 — Making Quotes

하다 → 한다고 (말)하다
놀다 → 논다고 (말)하다
먹다 → 먹는다고 (말)하다
춥다 → 춥다고 (말)하다

Here are a few example sentences.

만나고 싶다고 했어요.
"I said that I want to meet."

같이 공부하고 싶다고 했어요?
"Did you say that you want to study?"

한국의 날씨가 아주 추웠다고 했어요.
"I said that the weather was very cold in Korea."

에어컨을 틀고 싶다고 했어요.
"I said that I want to turn on the air conditioner."

In addition to meaning "to turn on (sound)," 틀다 can also be used when turning on a machine, such as the air conditioner, heater, or a TV. It can also be used for *turning* on objects by turning them, such as turning on the water (물).

미국 사람이 아니라고 했어요.
"I said that I'm not an American."

When used in the present tense with this form, the verb 이다 ("to be") becomes 이라 when used after a *consonant*, or 라 when used after a *vowel*. The verb 아니다 ("to not be") becomes 아니라.

이미 나갔다고요.
"I said that he already left."

널 사랑한다고.
"I said that I love you."

뭐라고요?
"What did you say?"

Asking 뭐라고(요) is a common, quick way to ask someone to repeat themselves. It is fine to use in casual situations and with friends, but should be avoided in any formal situation.

선생님은 제가 공부를 더 열심히 해야 된다고 하셨어요.
"The teacher said that I have to study harder."

Making Quotes

길거리에서 주웠다고 했어요.
"I said I picked it up on the street."

The verb 줍다 ("to pick up") is irregular, and conjugates in the past tense as 주웠다 (not 줍었다). This verb is also only used for picking something up from the *floor*. If you're picking something up from another location (such as a table), then use the verb 집다 ("to pick up") which can be used for picking something up from *any* location (including the floor). As another note, 집다 conjugates normally in the past tense as 집었다.

그 비싼 자동차도 사면 남는 돈이 없을 거라고 했잖아요.
"See, I told you that if you also buy that expensive car you won't have any money left over."

In the first book, we learned how to use (이)라고(요) to confirm whether or not someone said a *noun*. Now we can see where this form comes from.

> **Advanced**
>
> We also learned that we can use 저는 ____(이)라고 합니다 to say our name when introducing ourselves. When used in this way, (이)라고 하다 can translate as "I call myself ____." If you want someone else to call you a specific name, you can use the verb 부르다 instead. We learned that 부르다 means "to sing," but it can also mean "to call (a name)."
>
> (저를) 빌리라고 불러 주세요.
> "Please call me Billy."

Quoting: Plain Form + 고 그러다

You can also use the verb 그러다 ("to say so") instead of (말)하다 when quoting people. The meaning is the same, but this form is mostly used when speaking *informally* – it should be avoided when speaking formally. Note that 그러다 conjugates as 그래(요) in the 요 form.

치킨이 더 없다고 그랬어.
"He said that there's no more chicken."

> **Adv**
>
> 그러다 is originally a shortened version of the less commonly used verb 그리하다.

조지: 누가 5 시부터 시작한다고 했어요?
"Who said that it starts from 5 o'clock?"

Making Quotes

Instead of (말)하다, you can also use the quoting form with the verb 듣다 ("to listen"). When used in this way, 듣다 can be used to mean "to hear." 듣다 will be used when you want to say that you "heard" something, instead of "said" something.

내일 태풍이 올 거라고 들었어요.
"I heard that a Typhoon will come tomorrow."

생강이 감기에 좋다고 들었어요.
"I heard that ginger is good for colds."

유나: 철수가 5 시까지 오라고 했어요.
"Chul-soo said to come by 5 o'clock."

Commands: Action Verb Stem + (으)라고 + (말)하다

This form is used for quoting a *command*. Let's take another look at one of our earlier example sentences.

"I *said* to do the dishes before mom comes back."

A command is telling someone else to do something. Again, you can *optionally* replace (말)하다 with a 요, or with nothing (if speaking casually).

To use this form, take an *action verb stem* and attach 으라고 if it ends in a *consonant*, or attach 라고 if it ends in a *vowel*. *Optionally*, you can attach (말)하다, or replace it with a 요, or replace it with nothing (if speaking casually). Here are a few examples.

하다 → 하라고 (말)하다
놀다 → 놀라고 (말)하다*
먹다 → 먹으라고 (말)하다

*Verb stems ending in ㄹ will simply add 라고 (말)하다 to the end.

Here are a few example sentences.

제 친구는 하라고 했어요.
"My friend said to do it."

선생님은 오늘 학교에서 공부하라고 말씀하셨어요.
"The teacher said to study at school today."

앉으라고요.
"I said sit."

Making Quotes

Chapter 2

잘 들으라고요. 한 번만 말할게요.
"I said listen well. I'll only say it once."

Note that the verb 듣다 ("to listen") becomes 들으라고 when used with this form.

그걸 먹지 말라고 하지 않았어요?
"Didn't I say to not eat that?"

Since "don't" commands use the 지 말다 form, this will become 지 말라고 when used with quoting.

추우니까 목도리를 매라고 했어요.
"I said to wear the scarf because it's cold."

1 시간 전에 나가라고 했는데 왜 아직 여기 있지?
"I said to leave an hour ago, but why are you still here?"

먹을 거 만들어 달라고 했어요.
"I told you to (please) make me something to eat."

What is 달라고?

It might look like a completely new grammar form or verb, but 달라고 is actually a different version of the verb 주다 ("to give"). Before we go too far, I also want to add that 주라고 exists too, but we will talk about where that is used next. First, let's talk about 달라고.

When making quotations, if the person who is doing the *verb* is also the person who will be receiving the item or favor, you will use 달라고 instead of 주라고. Let's first take a look at two basic examples with 주다.

주세요.
"Please give it to me."

해 주세요.
"Please do it (for me)."

Now let's change these into quotes. Here are the two examples.

달라고 했어요.
"I said please give it to me."

해 달라고 했어요.
"I said please do it (for me)."

Chapter 2

Making Quotes

In the sentence 달라고 했어요, the person doing the verb – here, it is the speaker who is *asking* for something – is also the person who will be receiving the item or favor. Although this might sound a bit complicated the first time seeing it, 달라고 will be used most of the time instead of 주라고. Here are a few more examples of this form.

돈을 달라고 할 수 없어요.
"I can't ask him for money."

여기에 적어 달라고 했어요.
"I asked you to write it down here for me."

A more *literal* translation of this example would be "I said, 'write it down here (for me).'"

Culture Notes

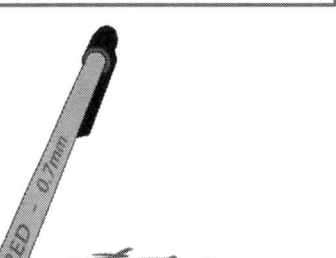

Names in Red

Avoid using the color red when writing a person's name, as it signifies blood and death. Traditionally, a person's name is only written in red after passing away (such as on a tombstone), but never while a person is alive.

철수가 5 만 원을 달라고 했어요.
"Chul-soo asked for 50,000 Won."

A more *literal* translation of this example would be "Chul-soo said, 'give me 50,000 Won.'" Since 철수 is both the person doing the verb (here, 했어요) and the person receiving the item or favor (here, the 5 만 원), the 달라고 form is used instead of the 주다 form.

도와 달라고요.
"I asked you to help me."

Notice how the verb 도와주다 becomes 도와 달라고 (note the spacing) when used in this form.

Making Quotes

Chapter 2

Just as before, it is fine to replace the verb (말)하다 with simply a 요, or with nothing (when speaking *casually*).

보여 달라고 했어.
"I asked you to show it to me."

Again, notice how 보여주다 becomes 보여 달라고 (note the spacing) when used in this form.

빨리 달라고요.
"I asked you to give it to me right away."

However, 주라고 is still used if the person doing the verb is not the same person who receives the item or favor. For example, if I told someone else to do something for someone else, or to give something to someone else, then I would use 주라고 instead of 달라고. Here are two examples.

철수에게 돈을 주라고 했어.
"I told (someone else) to give money to Chul-soo."

철수가 남은 거 너한테 주라고 했어.
"Chul-soo said to give the leftovers to you."

In both of these examples, the person doing the verb is different from the person who is receiving the item or favor. As 달라고 will be used much more often than 주라고, focus first on learning how to use 달라고.

Asking Favors with 부탁

Another common verb used with asking someone to do something is 부탁(을) 하다 ("to request"). It is commonly used with the (으)라고 (말)하다 form for quoting commands.

You can replace (말)하다 with 부탁(을) 하다 when asking a favor. While the overall meaning of the sentence will not change, using 부탁(을) 하다 adds the meaning that you or someone is making a *request* for something. Here are two of our previous examples, but using 부탁(을) 하다 instead of (말)하다.

철수가 5 만 원을 달라고 부탁했어요.
"Chul-soo requested 50,000 Won."

철수에게 돈을 주라고 부탁했어요.
"I requested (someone else) to give money to Chul-soo."

Chapter 2 — # Making Quotes

Since the verbs "to request" and "to ask" have similar meanings in English when used in this way, you can also freely translate 부탁(을) 하다 as "to ask" when used with this (으)라고 (말)하다 form.

I would recommend re-reading this section on 달라고 and 주라고 after completing this chapter, but before continuing to the next chapter, as these two forms can be tricky to become familiar with.

> **Advanced**
>
> **잘 부탁합니다.**
>
> 잘 부탁합니다 is a phrase that literally means "I request (this) well." It can be used when giving someone an assignment, in which case it could translate as "Take care of this, please" or "I trust you'll take care of it." Or it can be used when introducing someone else, in which case it could translate as "Please treat them nicely." It can also be used when introducing yourself, in which case it could translate as "Nice to meet you" or "I look forward to working together." A few other common versions of this phrase are 잘 부탁해(요), 잘 부탁드려요, and 잘 부탁드립니다.

> 조지: 철수한테 6 시 아니냐고 물어봐 주세요.
> "Please ask Chul-soo if it's not 6 o'clock."

When saying something *to* someone, remember to use the particles 에게 or 한테 (or 께 when speaking *honorifically*), and not the Object Marker. The same applies to any verb that shows *communication*.

Questions: Verb Stem + 냐고 물어보다

This form is used for quoting *questions*. Because this form is only used for asking something, the verb 물어보다 ("to ask") will be commonly added. Let's take another look at one of our earlier example sentences.

> "I *asked* if you want to eat this. If not, then I will."

To use this form, take a verb stem and attach 냐고, followed by the verb 물어보다. *Optionally*, you can replace 물어보다 with 요, or with nothing when speaking *casually*. Here are a few examples of this form.

하다 → 하냐고 물어보다
먹다 → 먹냐고 물어보다
춥다 → 추우냐고 물어보다*
그렇다 → 그러냐고 물어보다
놀다 → 노냐고 물어보다

*Remember that certain verbs have their own rules for conjugation, such as descriptive verb stems that end in ㅂ, ㅎ, and ㄹ.

Making Quotes

Chapter 2

Adv

Although 추우냐고 is the correct form, 춥냐고 (which is *incorrect*) will also be commonly used. The same applies for all descriptive verb stems ending in ㅂ. For example, you'll find 맵냐고 (from 맵다) as often as 매우냐고.

This rule also applies to using the (으)니까 form that we learned in the previous book. 춥다 with this form would become 추우니까 (not 춥으니까).

Here are a few example sentences.

엄마가 어디 가셨냐고 물어봤어.
"I asked where mom went."

철수가 나한테 제시카가 누구냐고 물어봤어.
"Chul-soo asked me who Jessica is."

내가 언제 일을 그만둘 거냐고?
"Did you ask me when I'll quit my job?"

돈이 있냐고 물어보지 마세요.
"Don't ask me if I have any money."

제가 한국에서 사냐고요?
"Did you ask if I live in Korea?"

그 사람하고 사진을 같이 찍을 수 있냐고 물어보고 싶은데 자신이 없어요.
"I want to ask if I can take a photo together with that person but I don't have confidence."

유나: 5 시가 아니라고요?

"You're saying it's not 5 o'clock?"

조지: 5 시가 아니고, 6 시예요.

"It's not 5 o'clock, it's 6 o'clock."

유나: 그럼 철수에게 6 시라고 전해 줄게요.

"Then I'll tell Chul-soo that it's 6 o'clock."

Tell Someone: 전하다 and 알려주다

While (말)하다 by itself can already mean "to tell" when used with 에게 or 한테 (or 께 when speaking *honorifically*), there are also two more verbs that are commonly used with the (으)라고 (말)하다 form – 전하다 and 알려주다.

Chapter 2: Making Quotes

The verb 전하다 means "to tell," or "to let (someone) know." Using 전하다 adds the meaning of *passing along* or *delivering* information to someone. The verb 알려주다 can be used in a similar way. 알려주다 also means "to tell" and "to let (someone) know" but does not have the added meaning of delivering information. Instead, 알려주다 has a stronger meaning of simply *informing* someone of something. Here are a few examples:

선생님에게 숙제를 못 할 거라고 전했어요.
"I let the teacher know that I won't be able to do the homework."

내일 콘서트에 간다고 전해 주세요.
"Please tell them that I'm going to a concert tomorrow."

민우에게 안부를 전해 주세요.
"Tell Min-woo hello for me."
"Please tell Min-woo I said hello."

안부(를) 전하다 means "to send (one's) regards," but it is used in Korean much more commonly than "to send (one's) regards" is used in English. A more natural translation for 안부(를) 전하다 could be "to tell (someone) hello/hi" or "to say hello/hi (to someone)."

> **Advanced**
>
> Another way to tell something to someone is with the verb 이야기(를) 하다 ("to chat," "to gossip"). This is most commonly shortened to 얘기(를) 하다 in *informal* situations. Using 이야기(를) 하다 has the meaning of "talking with someone about something" since the word 이야기 means "a conversation" or "a story."
>
> 동생에게 조용히 하라고 얘기했어요.
> "I told my younger sibling to be quiet."
>
> 민우에게 점심을 집에서 먹으라고 얘기했어요.
> "I told Min-woo to eat lunch at home."
>
> The verb 대화(를) 하다 ("to converse," "to hold a conversation") can also be used in the same way, and has a stronger meaning of *both people* in a conversation talking to each other.

Making Quotes

Chapter 2

Advanced

There are also common shortened versions of the four forms that we covered in this chapter.

Action Verb Stem + 자고 (말)하다 → 재(요)
Plain Form + 고 (말)하다 → 대(요) or (이)래(요)*
Action Verb Stem + (으)라고 (말)하다 → 래(요)
Verb Stem + 냐고 물어보다 → 내(요)

There is a good reason that these shortened versions exist. Each of these shortened versions sounds similar (somewhat) to their regular form when said quickly, and can save you time when speaking. Here is an example of each one with the verb 가다 ("to go").

가자고 해요. → 가재요.
간다고 해요. → 간대요.
가라고 해요. → 가래요.
가냐고 해요. → 가내요.

*Remember that the verb 이다 ("to be") will become (이)라고 when used with 고 in the present tense, so its shortened form will be (이)래(요).

The same thing applies for *past tense* as well.

가자고 했어요. → 가쟀어요.
간다고 했어요. → 간댔어요.
가라고 했어요. → 가랬어요.
가냐고 했어요. → 가냈어요.

Of these four forms, 대(요) and 래(요) are the two most commonly used.

Practice

Conjugate the following to a complete sentence using the 자고 form:

1. 하다

_____.

2. 가다

_____.

3. 영화를 보다

_____.

4. 가르치다

_____.

Chapter 2: Making Quotes

Conjugate the following to a complete sentence using the Plain Form + 고 form:

5. 김치를 먹다

6. 있었다

7. 시험을 통과했다

8. 잠(이) 안 오다

Conjugate the following to a complete sentence using the 라고 form:

9. 한국어를 공부하다

10. 밥을 먹다

11. 안전 벨트를 매다

12. (저에게) 설명서를 읽어 주다

Conjugate the following to a complete sentence using the 냐고 form:

13. 돈을 다 썼다

Making Quotes

14. 왜 철수에게 핑계를 대다

_____.

15. 목도리를 사 주다 (future tense)

_____.

16. 빚을 갚을 수 있다

_____.

Translate to Korean:

17. "I said let's go to see a movie."

_____.

18. "Chul-soo said that he doesn't like Yung-hee."

_____.

19. "Yesterday I said to do the homework."

_____.

20. "Did you ask if I can speak Korean?"

_____.

21. "I said that thing is an apple."

_____.

Translate to English:

22. 철수가 나한테 같이 점심을 먹자고 했어.

_____.

23. 난 이미 남자 친구가 있다고 했어.

_____.

Making Quotes

24. 철수가 나한테 그 남자하고 만나지 말라고 했어.

_____.

25. 난 왜 만나지 말아야 되냐고 물어봤어.

_____.

New Phrases

잘 자(요).	"Good night." (casual)
수고하세요!	"Keep up the good work!," "Goodbye (to a worker)"
수고하셨어요!	"You did good work!"
고생하셨어요.	"You've suffered to help me," "Thank you for your hard work (to a worker)"

New Vocabulary

모임	"meeting"
그러다	"to say so"
적다	"to write down," "to note," "to jot down"
부탁	"request," "favor"
부탁(을) 하다	"to request"
부탁(을) 드리다	"to request" (hon.)
신청	"application," "petition"
신청(을) 하다	"to apply for," "to petition for"
전하다	"to tell," "to let (someone) know"
안부(를) 전하다	"to give (one's) regards"
대화	"conversation," "dialogue"
대화(를) 하다	"to converse," "to hold a conversation"
회화	"conversation (in person)"
회화(를) 하다	"to converse (in person)," "to hold a conversation (in person)"
생강	"ginger"
태풍	"typhoon"

Making Quotes

천둥	"thunder"
번개	"lightning"
지진	"earthquake"
홍수	"flood"
화재	"fire (disaster)"
길거리	"street," "road"
안전벨트	"seatbelt"
매다	"to wear (seatbelt, backpack)"
집다	"to pick up"
돈(이) 많다	"to have a lot of money," "to be rich"
가난하다	"to be poor"
부자	"a wealthy person"
속삭이다	"to whisper"
외치다	"to shout," "to yell"
소리(를) 지르다	"to scream," "to cry out"
짖다	"to bark"
표현	"a (spoken) expression"
표현(을) 하다	"to express"
명령	"a command"
명령(을) 하다	"to command"
순종(을) 하다	"to obey," "to be obedient"
불평	"complaint"
불평(을) 하다	"to complain"
지도서	"guide book"
설명서	"(instruction) manual"
설명	"instruction"
설명(을) 하다	"to explain"
핑계	"an excuse"
핑계(를) 대다	"to make an excuse"
갚다	"to repay"
빚	"debt"
값	"value," "worth"
목도리	"scarf"
돈(을) 쓰다	"to use money"

Making Quotes

잠(이) 오다	"to feel tired," "to feel like (one) wants to sleep" (literally, "sleep comes")
수고(를) 하다	"to work hard," "to put effort into a job"
고생(을) 하다	"to go through a difficult working experience," "to go through a hardship"

Expressing Thoughts

Chapter 3

Conversation

지희:	내가 마이크를 좋아하는 거 같아.
리사:	그래? 난 마이크가 여자 친구가 있다고 생각했는데.
지희:	진짜?
리사:	친하게 지내는 1학년 여자 있잖아.
지희:	맞아. 걔가 좀 1학년들한테 잘해 줘.
리사:	머리 길고 키 작은 여자랑 같이 많이 다녀.
지희:	그래? 둘이 서로 잘 어울려?
리사:	그런 거 같아.

In this chapter we will cover one more use for the Plain Form – expressing your *thoughts*. For example, "I think...." There are two main grammar forms that we will need to know in order to say "I think...." One of them uses the Plain Form that we learned in Chapter 1. Let's jump right into the conversation and get started.

> 지희: 내가 마이크를 좋아하는 거 같아.
> "I think that I like Mike."

55

Chapter 3: Expressing Thoughts

"I think": Adjective + 것 같다

This is the most commonly used form to express your thoughts. Since this form uses the descriptive verb 같다 ("to be the same," "to be like"), a literal translation of this form is "it is the same as" or "it is like." A more natural and common translation of this form is "think."

To make this form, take an action verb or descriptive verb and conjugate it as an adjective. You can use any tense you would like. Then attach 것 ("thing") and conjugate the verb 같다. We covered how to conjugate action verbs to adjectives in Chapter 4 of the previous book. This new form will use those same conjugation rules. And while the standard form is 것 같다, it's more common to use 거 같다 as it's easier to say. Before we continue, here are a few examples using different tenses.

공부(를) 하다 → 공부(를) 하는 것 같다 ("I think he studies.")

운동(을) 하다 → 운동(을) 한 것 같다 ("I think he exercised.")

청소(를) 하다 → 청소(를) 할 것 같다 ("I think he'll clean.")

먹어 보다 → 먹어 본 것 같다 ("I think he tried eating it.")

춥다 → 추운 것 같다 ("I think it's cold.")

만들다 → 만드는 것 같다 ("I think he makes it.")

이다 → 인 것 같다 ("I think it is...")*

그렇다 → 그런 것 같다 ("I think it is so.")

알고 있다 → 알고 있는 것 같다 ("I think he knows.")

*Remember that 이다 ("to be") is used after a *noun*. For example, 고양이인 것 같다 means "I think it is a cat."

Expressing Thoughts

Each of these verbs could look slightly different with this form depending on the tense that we choose. Here is an example of the *action verb* 가다 ("to go") in different tenses using this form.

가다:
    Present: 가는 것 같다 ("I think he goes.")
    Past: 간 것 같다 ("I think he went.")
    Future: 갈 것 같다 ("I think he'll go.")*

*Note that the 겠다 future tense form *cannot* be used with the 것 같다 form.

And here is an example of the *descriptive verb* 멀다 ("to be far") in different tenses using this form.

멀다:
    Present: 먼 것 같다 ("I think it's far.")
    Past: 멀었던 것 같다 ("I think it was far.")*
    Future: 멀 것 같다 ("I think it will be far.")

*Notice the second form, 멀었던 것 같다. We have not yet covered this form (던) but we will learn about it in detail in Chapter 17. For now, here is how to make the 것 같다 form using *descriptive verbs* in the *past tense*. Take the past tense of the descriptive verb using the 요 form (for a review of this, see Chapter 20 of the first book) and replace the 요 with 던. Here are a few examples.

친절하다 → 친절했던 것 같다 ("I think he was nice.")

춥다 → 추웠던 것 같다 ("I think it was cold.")

힘들다 → 힘들었던 것 같다 ("I think it was hard.")

이다 → 이었던 것 같다 or 였던 것 같다 ("I think it was...")*

*Use 이었던 after a *consonant*, and 였던 after a *vowel*. For example, 고양이였던 것 같다 ("I think it was a cat.") or 기린이었던 것 같다 ("I think it was a giraffe.").

Note that when you are changing a *descriptive verb* into an *adjective* (to describe something), if you want the adjective to be in the *past tense* you can add 던 in the same way. Here are two examples to show the difference:

추운 날씨 ("cold weather")
추웠던 날씨 ("weather that was cold")

Chapter 3 — Expressing Thoughts

재미있는 영화 ("fun movie")
재미있었던 영화 ("movie that was fun")

For now, focus on using 던 only with the 것 같다 form. We will talk more about how to use it in Chapter 17. Now that we know how to conjugate this form, let's take a look at a few example sentences.

할 거 같아요.
"I think that I'll do it."

이건 저한테 너무 매운 거 같아요.
"I think that this is too spicy for me."

좋은 생각인 거 같아요.
"I think that it's a good idea."

지금 점심을 먹고 있는 거 같아.
"I think that they're eating lunch now."

(저는) 철수가 돈을 가지고 나간 거 같아.
"I think that Chul-soo took the money and left."

가지고 나가다 (literally, "to have and leave," or "to have and go out") or 가지고 나오다 (literally, "to have and come") can be used in the same way as 가지고 가다 and 가지고 오다.

Typically, when saying "I think" the person who does the thinking will be marked with the Topic Marker (은/는) and the person who does the action (the person who does what you think they did) will be marked with the Subject Marker (이/가).

어제도 많이 추웠던 거 같아요.
"I think yesterday was really cold too."

Depending on the sentence, you can also translate the *adverb* 많이 ("a lot") as "very" or "really."

그냥 그런 거 같아.
"I think it's just so-so."

The descriptive verb 그렇다 ("to be so") can also be used to mean "so-so."

내일은 더 더울 거 같은데.
"I think it'll be hotter tomorrow."

Expressing Thoughts

거미를 밟은 거 같아요.
"I think I stepped on a spider."

Note that the verb 밟다 ("to step on") is pronounced 밥따, but you might hear it commonly, though *incorrectly* pronounced as 발따.

어디인 거 같아?
"Where do you think it is?"

한국 사람이 아닌 거 같아.
"I don't think he's a Korean."

Note that in this example sentence, the English translation is "I don't think" while the Korean uses 아닌 거 같아. A more literal translation would be "I think he is not a Korean." It is more common in Korean to use the 것 같다 form as it is even with a negative sentence, and to instead make the verb that comes before it negative. This means that it is better to say "I think that I don't like kimchi" than to say "I don't think that I like kimchi." Here are examples of these two sentences.

    A.   김치를 안 좋아하는 것 같아요.
    B.   김치를 좋아하는 것 같지 않아요.

Of these two sentences, A sounds more natural. Although using 것 같지 않다 is grammatically correct, it is less common than simply using 것 같다. An exception would be if you want to *emphasize* that you "do not" think a certain way. In that case it would be better to use 것 같지 않다 instead.

There is no need to change this form to the past tense either. While 같았다 makes sense grammatically, it is not commonly used. Instead, if you want to say that you "thought" or "will think" a certain way, you can use the next form that we'll learn in this chapter – 생각(을) 하다.

리사: 그래? 난 마이크가 여자 친구가 있다고 생각했는데.
"Really? I thought that Mike has a girlfriend."

"I think": Plain Form + 고 생각(을) 하다

While both forms – 것 같다 and 생각(을) 하다 – can be used to mean "think," this one is used for expressing an actual *thought*. 생각(을) 하다 literally means "to think," so when you use this form it is a more *literal* translation of "think."

Expressing Thoughts

Chapter 3

For the time being, feel free to use either form to mean "to think." We'll learn more specifically about how to use the 것 같다 form, and how it differs from this 생각(을) 하다 form in Chapter 5. Of the two forms, 생각(을) 하다 is used less often, but is more flexible than 것 같다. While 것 같다 is typically only used in the present tense, you can use 생각(을) 하다 in any tense you would like.

To make this form, take the Plain Form (using any tense) and attach 고. Then conjugate the verb 생각(을) 하다. Here are a few example conjugations.

공부(를) 하다 → 공부(를) 한다고 생각(을) 하다 ("I think he studies.")

먹어 보다 → 먹어 봤다고 생각(을) 하다 ("I think he tried eating it.")

춥다 → 춥다고 생각(을) 하다 ("I think it's cold.")

놀다 → 논다고 생각(을) 하다 ("I think he plays.")

알고 있다 → 알고 있다고 생각(을) 하다 ("I think he knows.")

이다 → (이)라고 생각(을) 하다 ("I think it is...")*

*Note that 이다 ("to be") becomes 이라고 when used after a *consonant*, or 라고 when used after a *vowel*. 아니다 ("to not be") becomes 아니라고.

Here are a few examples of this form.

할 수 없다고 생각해?
"You don't think you can?"

Just like with the 것 같다 form, it is more common in Korean to say "I think" than "I don't think." An exception would be when you want to *emphasize* that you "do not" think a certain way, in which case it is fine to use this form as 생각(을) 하지 않다 or 생각(을) 안 하다.

할 수 있다고 생각하지도 않아.
"I *don't* even think I can do it."

도움이 될 거라고 생각하세요?
"Do you think it'll be helpful?"

도움(이) 되다 literally means "to become help," but it translates more naturally as "to be helpful."

Expressing Thoughts

선생님이 미국에 갔다고 생각하는데요.
"I think the teacher went to America."

마이크가 한국어를 알아들을 수 있다고 생각해요.
"I think that Mike can understand Korean."

알아듣다 means "to understand (by hearing)," and is used when you understand something that is *spoken*, such as a language. It comes from a combination of the verb 알다 ("to know") and 듣다 ("to listen"), and means that you *listen* to what someone says, and *know* what it means. 이해(를) 하다 ("to understand") is used to mean that you understand an idea or concept.

새 집을 살 수 있을 거라고 생각했어요.
"I thought I'll be able to buy a new house."

새 is an adjective that means "new." It is interchangeable with the adjective 새로운 in most cases, which comes from the descriptive verb 새롭다 ("to be new"). 새 can only be used as an adjective for "new" *items* (not people). For example, "new teacher" would be 새로운 선생님 (not 새 선생님), but "new computer" could be either 새 컴퓨터 or 새로운 컴퓨터. Be careful of context though. While 새 집 means "new house," 새집 (written without a space) means "bird house," which comes from 새 ("bird"). There are other short adjectives like this, a few of which we will cover later on.

저도 돈을 받는다고 생각을 했어요.
"I thought that I'm getting money too."

한국어가 그렇게 어렵지 않다고 생각해요.
"I don't think that Korean is that difficult."

바보라고 생각해.
"I think he's an idiot."

> 지희: 진짜?
> "Really?"

> 리사: 친하게 지내는 1학년 여자 있잖아.
> "There's a freshman girl he's close with."

The verb 친하게 지내다 is made from the descriptive verb 친하다, meaning "to be close (as friends)," and the action verb 지내다, meaning "to live" or "to associate with." The verb 지내다 is also where the expression 잘 지내세요 comes from, as well as others. Used together, 친하게 지내다 means "to have a close relationship (with someone)."

Chapter 3: Expressing Thoughts

Adv
Another similar phrase that you might find is 잘 있다 (literally, "to exist well"). It can be used in the same way as 잘 지내다.

Culture Notes

School Years: 학년

In Korea, middle school and high school are divided into 3 years each. School years are counted with *Sino-Korean numbers* (일, 이, 삼, etc.) and 학년 ("school year").

1 학년 ("1st year")
2 학년 ("2nd year")
3 학년 ("3rd year")

These can be combined with 생 as 학년생 to mean "a person in their # year of school." For example, 2 학년생 means "a person in their 2nd year of school."

To ask a person what school year they are in, you can use 몇 ("how many"). Here is an example.

몇 학년이세요?
"What school year are you?"

Note that due to sound change rules, 몇 학년 will be pronounced as 며탕년. This is because 몇 is pronounced as 멷, and a ㄷ sound will change to ㅌ when used before the consonant ㅎ. For a more detailed review of this, re-read the "Introduction to Sound Change Rules" section of the first book, as well as Appendix C.

10 대인데 벌써 대학교 3 학년이에요?
"You're a teenager but you're already in your 3rd year of college?"

To say "a person in their #s," use the counter 대 ("generation") with *Sino-Korean numbers*. For example, 20 대 means "a person who's in their 20s." This counter can also be used to mean "(one's) #0s." For example, 20 대 can also be used when you are talking about the years 20 through 29 of a person's life – "(his/her) 20s." In the same way, 30 대 can be used to mean "a person who's in their 30s" or "(one's) 30s."

30 대에 꼭 해야 할 일...
"Things I have to make sure to do in my 30s..."

Also, while 10 대 literally means "a person in their 10s" or "(one's) 10s," it can be more naturally translated as "a teenager" or "the teenage years."

Expressing Thoughts

Chapter 3

Advanced

년생

Another common way to say your age, besides using Pure Korean numbers and the age counter 살, is by saying the last *two digits* of the year you were born (using *Sino-Korean numbers*) and then attaching 년생 (literally, "birth year"). For example, if you were born in 1986, then you can say your age as 86 년생. By saying your age this way, you are instead telling them the year that you were born. Although this is not a common way to say someone's age in Western cultures, Koreans are used to calculating a person's age from knowing their birth year.

To ask a person's age, you can also use 몇 ("how many") together with 년생. Due to sound change rules, this will be pronounced as 면년생.

몇 년생이세요?
"What year were you born?"

지희: 맞아. 걔가 좀 1 학년들한테 잘해 줘.

"That's right. He's kinda nice to the freshmen."

Casual Korean: 얘, 걔, 쟤

Here are three common, but *casual* Korean words – 얘, 걔, and 쟤. Before we talk about what these words mean, I should note that all 3 of these words are shortened versions of other words.

이 아이 → 얘 ("this guy/girl")
그 아이 → 걔 ("that guy/girl")
저 아이 → 쟤 ("that guy/girl")

These three words come from a combination of 이, 그, and 저 with the word 애. The word 애 is a shortened form of 아이 ("child"), and can be used when speaking *casually* to mean "guy" or "girl." Literally, these words mean "this child" or "that child," but they are used to mean "this guy/girl" or "that guy/girl." Because they are casual, they should be avoided in any situation where you want to sound polite.

리사: 머리 길고 키 작은 여자랑 같이 많이 다녀.

"He goes around a lot together with a short girl who has long hair."

지희: 그래? 둘이 서로 잘 어울려?

"Really? Do the two of them suit each other?"

둘 can also mean "the two of them/us," and another common related word is 셋 ("the three of them/us").

| Chapter 3 | **Expressing Thoughts** |

Each Other: 서로

서로 is an *adverb* that means "each other." Here are a few examples.

우리는 서로 좋아해요.
"We like each other."

서로 친하게 지내.
"We're close (with each other)."

우리는 항상 서로에 대해 생각하고 있어요.
"We're always thinking about each other."

While 서로 is an *adverb*, it can also be used as a *noun* in some cases, such as with this example using 생각(을) 하다.

리사: 그런 거 같아.
"I think so."

그런 것 같아요 and 그렇게 생각해요 both mean "I think so." Now that you know the difference between these two forms – 것 같다 and 생각(을) 하다 – you can choose whichever you would like.

> **Adv**
> One more way to say "I think" is using 제 생각에(는), or 내 생각에(는). This phrase literally means "In my thought(s)," but translates more naturally as "In my opinion." It is often used together with either of the two forms covered in this chapter.
>
> 제 생각에는 내일 눈이 올 것 같아요.
> "In my opinion, I think that it'll snow tomorrow."

Practice

Conjugate the following in present tense using the 것 같다 form:

1. 먹고 있다

   _____.

2. 알다

   _____.

Expressing Thoughts

3. 물을 마시다

4. 무섭다

Conjugate the following in past tense using the 것 같다 form:

5. 이다

6. 발표를 녹음하다

7. 집으로 가고 있다

8. 마음에 들다

Conjugate the following in future tense using the 것 같다 form:

9. 가다

10. 세탁(을) 하다

11. 울다

12. 만들고 있다

Chapter 3: Expressing Thoughts

Conjugate the following in present tense using the 생각(을) 하다 form:

13. 이다

_____.

14. 쉬고 있다

_____.

15. 운이 좋다

_____.

16. 행사를 준비하다

_____.

Conjugate the following in past tense using the 생각(을) 하다 form:

17. 한국 사람이 아니다

_____.

18. 미신을 믿다

_____.

19. 점심을 같이 먹다

_____.

20. 잘하다

_____.

Conjugate the following in future tense using the 생각(을) 하다 form:

21. 집에서 놀다

_____.

Expressing Thoughts

22. 일하러 가다

_____.

23. 그렇게 하다

_____.

24. 지갑을 찾을 수 있다

_____.

Translate to Korean using the 것 같다 form:

25. "I think that the weather is very hot."

_____.

26. "I don't think that I'm hungry."

_____.

27. "I don't think that's a cat."

_____.

28. "Do you think that it will take a lot of time?"

_____.

Translate to Korean using the 생각(을) 하다 form:

29. "I think that this is too spicy."

_____.

30. "I think that I have 5,000 Won."

_____.

31. "I think that it's funny."

_____.

Chapter 3 — Expressing Thoughts

32. "I don't think that it's clean."

_____.

Translate to English:

33. 저는 철수가 가게에 갔다고 생각해요.

_____.

34. 철수가 영어를 못 알아듣는 것 같아요.

_____.

35. 수업에 집중을 잘하면 빨리 배울 것 같아요.

_____.

36. 확실하지 않지만 저는 맞는 것 같아요.

_____.

37. 새 차가 필요하다고 생각해요.

_____.

New Phrases

그런 것 같아요.	"I think so."
그렇게 생각해요.	"I think so."
솔직히 말하면...	"To be honest...," "To be frank..."
새해 복 많이 받으세요.	"Happy New Year."

New Vocabulary

친하게 지내다	"to have a close relationship (with someone)"
친하다	"to be close (as friends)"
지내다	"to live," "to associate with"
학년	"school year"

Expressing Thoughts

Chapter 3

얘	"this guy/girl"
걔	"that guy/girl"
쟤	"that guy/girl"
둘	"the two of them/us"
셋	"the three of them/us"
서로	"each other" (adverb)
알아듣다	"to understand (by hearing)"
집중(을) 하다	"to focus"
생각(이) 나다	"to come to mind," "to think (of something from the past)"
솔직하다	"to be honest," "to be frank"
솔직히	"honestly," "frankly"
새해	"new year"
새	"new" (adjective)
새 차	"new car"
새 집	"new house"
새집	"bird house"
힘(이) 들다	"to be hard," "to be difficult"
도움(이) 되다	"to be helpful"
대	generation counter, "a person who's in their #s," "(one's) #0s"
10 대	"teenager," "the teenage years"
20 대	"a person who's in their 20s," "(one's) 20s"
30 대	"a person who's in their 30s," "(one's) 30s"
무시(를) 하다	"to ignore," "to look down on (someone)"
동의(를) 하다	"to agree (with someone's idea)"
상상(을) 하다	"to imagine"
발표	"a presentation"
발표(를) 하다	"to present"
녹음(을) 하다	"to record (audio)"
세탁	"dry cleaning"
세탁(을) 하다	"to dry clean"

Chapter 3: Expressing Thoughts

세탁소	"the (dry) cleaner's"
다리미	"(clothes) iron"
다리미질(을) 하다	"to iron (clothes)"
운	"luck"
운(이) 좋다	"to be lucky"
운(이) 안 좋다	"to be unlucky"
미신	"superstition"
행사	"an event"

More Questions and Commands

Chapter 4

Conversation

김지우:	어? 태용 씨 아니세요? 이런 데에서 다 보네요.
서태용:	지우 씨, 안녕하세요! 영화 보러 오셨어요?
김지우:	네. 태용 씨 오늘 할 일이 많으시다더니 괜찮으세요?
서태용:	네... 대충 다 했어요.
김지우:	항상 태용 씨만 일이 많은 거 같아요.
서태용:	그런가요? 아니에요. 제가 그냥 느려서 그래요.
김지우:	에이.... 왜 자기 탓을 하세요? 태용 씨는 상을 줘야 할 만큼 부지런한데요.
서태용:	고맙습니다. 어? 지우 씨 차례인 거 같은데요.
김지우:	고마워요! 그럼 저 먼저 갈게요.
서태용:	네. 내일 또 봐요!

This chapter will cover a few more forms that we can use to ask *questions*, and to make *commands*. Let's jump right into the conversation.

> 김지우: 어? 태용 씨 아니세요? 이런 데에서 다 보네요.
> "Huh? Isn't that Tae-yong? It's surprising to see you here."

Both 데 and 곳 can mean "place" or "location," but 곳 is slightly more *formal* than 데. Both words are regularly used. Here are a couple of examples to show their similarity.

More Questions and Commands

철수가 먼 곳에서 왔어요.
철수가 먼 데에서 왔어요.
"Chul-soo came from somewhere far."

사람이 많은 곳에 있고 싶지 않아요.
사람이 많은 데에 있고 싶지 않아요.
"I don't want to be at a place with a lot of people."

However, 데 can only be used with *adjectives* that come from *descriptive verbs*. For example, it cannot be used with 이 ("this") or 새 ("new") since 이 and 새 are not from descriptive verbs, but it can be used with 좋은 (from 좋다) or 예쁜 (from 예쁘다), among many others.

이 곳에서 만났어요.
"We met at this place."

Saying 이 데에서 만났어요 would be *incorrect*. Instead, you could say 만난 데가 여기였어요 ("The place we met was here.").

> **Adv**
> The word 데 also has a couple of other less common uses, which will not be covered in this book, including being used to mean "an event" or "a case." If you see 데 in a situation where it does not translate to "place" or "location," and where it is not being used in the 데 form that we learned in the previous book, then you can know that it is being used in this way.

We learned in the second book that the 네(요) ending can be used to add the feeling of being *surprised* to your sentence. The sentence 이런 데에서 다 보네요 would literally translate as "I see you at all of these kind of places." However, since this sentence finishes with the 네(요) ending, it would be more natural to translate it as "I'm surprised to see you at these places," or simply "It's surprising to see you here."

> 서태용: 지우 씨, 안녕하세요! 영화 보러 오셨어요?
>
> "Hello, Ji-woo! You came to see a movie?"

> 김지우: 네. 태용 씨 오늘 할 일이 많으시다더니 괜찮으세요?
>
> "Yes. You said you have a lot of things to do today, but are you okay?"

In Chapter 2 of the previous book we learned that 일 ("work," "job") can also be used to mean "a matter" or "a concern" – although a more natural translation could simply be "thing." When combined with 할 (from the verb 하다), 할 일 can translate as "a thing to do" or "something to do."

More Questions and Commands

Contrasting Experiences: Action Verb Stem + 더니

In Chapter 11 of the previous book we learned how to use the 데 form to *contrast* two sentences. The 더니 form is also used to show contrast, but is only for things that you have *personally experienced* in the past (directly seen, heard, or did it yourself). Because of this, when you use this form it gives the feeling that you were there when it happened.

To use this form, take an *action verb stem* in past tense or present tense and attach 더니. Then complete the rest of the sentence. The sentence after 더니 should *contrast* (show something different or unexpected) with the sentence before 더니. This contrast can be either *good* or *bad*. Here is an example.

친구 집에 갔더니 아무도 없었어요.
"I went to my friend's house but nobody was there."

When using this form, *descriptive verb stems* will use the present tense – for example, 춥더니 – while *action verb stems* can use either the present tense or the past tense.

One reason that you might want to show the contrast of two parts of a sentence is because you are *surprised*. You could be surprised because the second part of the sentence was not what you expected and want to emphasize that.

열심히 공부했더니 시험이 너무 쉬웠어.
"I studied hard, but the test was so easy (and it surprised me)."

밤 늦게까지 잠을 자지 않더니 결국 늦게 일어났네.
"You didn't sleep until late at night, and in the end you woke up late (and that surprised me)."

그 동안 잘하더니 갑자기 왜 이래?
"You were doing so well, so why are you like this all of the sudden?"

Again, this form can be used for both good and bad outcomes, as long as the two parts of the sentence (before and after the 더니) have *contrast*, and as long as you are saying something that you personally *experienced*.

아침부터 빈대떡을 계속 먹고 싶더니 결국 비가 오네.
"I kept wanting to eat mung bean pancakes since morning, and in the end it's raining (and this is a nice coincidence)."

More Questions and Commands

A more natural translation for the above sentence could be, "I wanted to eat mung bean pancakes since morning, and now it's raining." While the *adverb* 결국 means "in the end," or "ultimately," these words are sometimes not the best choices for a natural English translation.

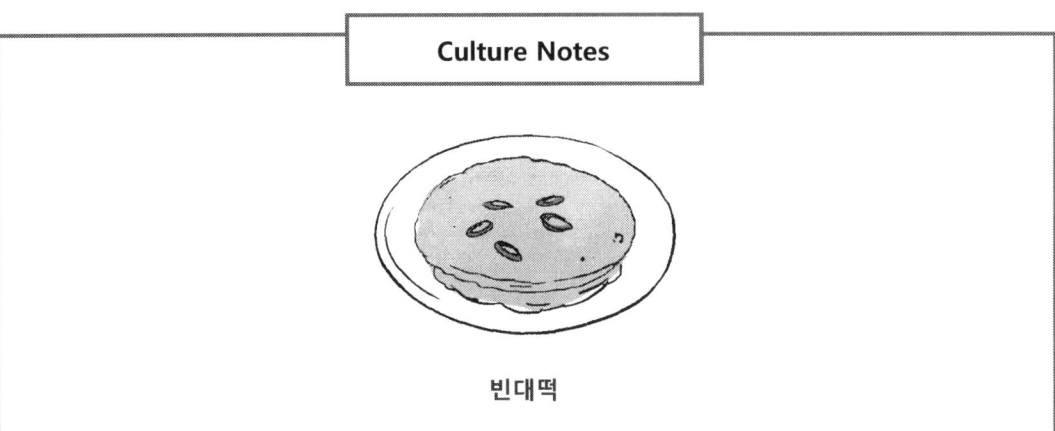

Culture Notes

빈대떡

When it rains in Korea, people often think about eating 빈대떡 ("mung bean pancakes"). Note that these types of pancakes are not eaten for breakfast with syrup – that would be disgusting – but are dipped in soy sauce and eaten piece by piece.

The 더니 form also has one more additional usage besides showing *contrast*. It can also be used to show two *events*, when the second event is a direct *result* of the first event, similar to how the 서 form is used. When using the 더니 form to show two events, these events must still have been your own *personal experiences* (or something that you directly saw or heard).

엄마를 위해서 설거지를 해 드렸더니 용돈을 주셨어요.
"I did the dishes for my mom and she gave me some allowance."

피자를 많이 먹었더니 콜라를 마시고 싶네.
"I ate a lot of pizza so I want to drink some cola."
"I ate a lot of pizza and now I want to drink some cola."

Another natural translation for the 더니 form when used to show two events is "and now."

Going back to the conversation, 다더니 – here, used in 많으시**다더니** – is a shortened version of **다고** (말)하**더니**. This 다더니 form is simply a combination of the quoting form that we learned in Chapter 2 for making statements, and the ending 더니. It's used for quoting what someone said that you also directly heard, and are *recalling* what they said. The full version of the conversation could therefore be this: "네. 태용 씨 오늘 할 일이 많으시**다고 말하더니** 괜찮으세요?"

More Questions and Commands

서태용: 네... 대충 다 했어요.

"Yes... I'm pretty much finished."

Roughly: 대충

대충 can be tricky to translate directly to English, but it is an *adverb* that means "roughly" or "approximately." It can also mean "loosely" (not "strictly"). It's best to learn how to translate 대충 through seeing it used in examples.

대충 이 정도면 충분한 거 같아.
"If it's roughly this much then I think that it's good enough."

대충 하고 빨리 가자.
"Let's just quickly get it over with and go."

그냥 대충 하지 말고 제대로 해.
"Don't just do it half-heartedly. Do it the right way."

발표를 대충 했는데 의외로 다들 좋아했어.
"I just winged the presentation, but unexpectedly everyone liked it."

Remember from Chapter 14 of the previous book that the adverb 다 ("all") can also have the meaning of "finish" when used with *action verbs*.

김지우: 항상 태용 씨만 일이 많은 거 같아요.

"I think only you have a lot of work always."

서태용: 그런가요? 아니에요. 제가 그냥 느려서 그래요.

"Yeah? No. It's just because I'm slow."

Informal Questions: Descriptive Verb Stem + (은/ㄴ) + 가(요)

We have learned many different ways to ask questions in Korean depending on the situation, but let's learn one more useful one – 가(요). This form is not as formal as using the 니까 ending (from the 니다 form), but it is a little more formal than the normal 요 ending.

Chapter 4 — More Questions and Commands

In addition, using this form is slightly less *direct* than using the normal 요 ending to ask a question. Because it makes sentences sound indirect, using this form can sound like you are not certain about what you are asking. Because of this, using the 가(요) form can also make your question sound a bit more soft – similar to using the 나(요) ending (which can be used with both action verbs and descriptive verbs).

> **Adv** Because this form is only used with descriptive verbs, instead use the 나(요) ending with action verbs.

To make this form, take a *descriptive verb stem* and attach 은 if it ends in a *consonant*, or attach ㄴ if it ends in a *vowel*. Here are a few examples.

크다 → 큰가(요)
작다 → 작은가(요)
멀다 → 먼가(요)
그렇다 → 그런가(요)
춥다 → 추운가(요)

Remember that certain descriptive verbs will conjugate differently as usual (such as ones ending in ㄹ, ㅎ, and ㅂ).

Note that this form is only used with descriptive verbs in the *present tense*, and not with descriptive verbs that are in the past tense or future tense. Here are a few example sentences.

정말 좋은가요?
"Is that really good? (I'm not certain myself.)"

Since using this form can sound like you are not certain about what you are asking, you can think of it as adding the meaning of "I'm not certain myself" to your sentence, if it helps to understand its meaning.

그런가요?
"Is that so?"
"Yeah?"

이 사과가 저 사과보다 큰가?
"Is this apple bigger than that apple?"

Using this form does not automatically make what you are saying polite or formal, but know that it is slightly less informal than using the normal 요 form. Remember to add the 요 to the end of this form in any situation where you want to be polite.

More Questions and Commands

일이 너무 힘든가요?
"Is your work too tough?"

철수가 진짜 한국 사람인가요?
"Is Chul-soo really a Korean?"

We previously learned that we can use the Plain Form and 지 ending when talking to ourselves. You can also use the 가(요) form when talking to yourself (without adding the 요).

누구지? 철수인가?
"Who's that? Is that Chul-soo?"

> **Advanced**
>
> There are also other forms that you can use when talking to yourself. Two common ones are 나 and 네. The 나 ending can be used when asking yourself a question to which you completely do not know the answer. The 네 ending can be used to show surprise at something while talking to yourself. Here is an example of each.
>
> 그랬나?
> "Was that so? (I have absolutely no idea.)"
>
> 오! 맛있네!
> "Oh! This is delicious!"
>
> These two endings are slightly different from using the 지 ending to ask yourself a question, since using 지 is literally asking yourself to confirm something that you think you know (just like when using it to someone else).
>
> 누구였지?
> "Who was that? (I'm sure I know who it was... but I can't think of their name.)"

Remember that this 가(요) form is only used for *descriptive verbs*, and not for action verbs. Since 있다 can be both an action verb and a descriptive verb, 있은가 would be *incorrect*. 재미있다 ("to be fun," "to be entertaining") is one example of a verb that will not be used with this form. Another example is the verb 맞다 ("to be correct") which is also not used with this form. 맞은가 would be *incorrect*. Instead, you can use the 나(요) ending with these verbs, and with any action verb as we previously learned.

> **Adv**
>
> It is also possible to use the 가(요) form with *action verbs*, but this is an old-fashioned usage. However, you might see this form used in older texts (if that's what you're into), so it is good to at least know about it. To make it, take an *action verb stem* and attach 는, followed by 가(요).
>
> 어디 가시는가요?
> "Where are you going?"

Chapter 4: More Questions and Commands

Informal Commands: Action Verb Stem + (으)시오

You can use this form to make a *command* when you do not know who you are speaking to – similar to how the Plain Form is used for speaking and writing when you do not know who is listening or who will read it. However, this form is usually only used on *signs*.

To make this form, take an *action verb stem* and attach 으시오 if it ends in a *consonant*, or attach 시오 if it ends in a *vowel*. Here are a few examples.

하다 → 하시오
듣다 → 들으시오*
넣다 → 넣으시오
밀다 → 미시오

Remember that action verb stems ending with ㄹ will lose the ㄹ when conjugating as usual.

*Note that the verb 듣다 often becomes 들 when conjugated, such as in this form and in the 요 form (as 들어요).

Here are a few examples of this form used on signs.

당기시오.
"Pull."

미시오.
"Push."

멈추시오.
"Stop."

This form can also be used with negative commands – "do not." Simply attach the 지 말다 ending as usual, and conjugate it to this form as 지 마시오.

멈추지 마시오.
"Do not stop."

> **Adv**
> The (으)시오 form has an additional use. It can be used as an old-fashioned version of the (으)세요 command form. It can also be used *jokingly* in this same way between friends.
>
> 자, 생일 선물을 받으시오.
> "Here, receiveth your birthday present."

More Questions and Commands

Chapter 4

Strong Commands: Action Verb Stem + (으)라

You can use this form to make a *strong* command – a stronger way to say "do it." Using this form can be very harsh, so it should be avoided in any polite or formal situation. It should also be avoided when speaking to friends (because it is not a friendly sounding form). You should be aware of this form, but I would not recommend using it for giving someone a command. Instead, use the (으)세요 form, or the regular 요 form, or 반말, depending on who you are speaking to.

We already (kind of) learned how to make this form in Chapter 1 when we learned Plain Form. This form is made in the same way. To make this form, take an *action verb stem* and attach 으라 if it ends in a *consonant*, or attach 라 if it ends in a *vowel*.

하다 → 하라
받다 → 받으라

나가라.
"Leave."

This form can also be used with *negative commands* – "do not." Simply attach the 지 말다 ending as usual, and conjugate it to this form as 지 말라. Because these two forms, (으)라 and 지 말라, are not often used in regular conversations, they can have an old-fashioned, almost Biblical feel when used.

하지 말라.
"Don't do it."
"Thou shalt not do it."

> **Advanced**
>
> ### Friendly Strong Commands: Action Verb Stem + 아/어/etc. 라
>
> You can use this form to make a strong, but friendly-sounding command. This form is also not polite or formal, but can be *jokingly* used when speaking in 반말. I would recommend avoiding this form until you are on close terms with a friend (who is the same age as you or younger). This form can be misinterpreted as being rude if it is not said in a joking way, or if it is said to the wrong person.
>
> To make this form, take an *action verb* and conjugate it to the 요 form. Then remove the 요, and attach 라.
>
> 혼자서 잘해라.
> "Do it (well) on your own."
> "Good luck doing it on your own."
>
> For *negative commands*, you can use the ending 지 마라.
>
> 하지 마라!
> "Don't do it!"

More Questions and Commands

김지우: 에이…. 왜 자기 탓을 하세요? 태용 씨는 상을 줘야 할 만큼 부지런한데요.

"Come on…. Why are you blaming yourself? You're so hard-working that they need to give you a prize."

에이 is an *exclamation* (something that you shout out) that you can use when you are *disappointed* or feel hurt. It can also be used *sarcastically* in this same way when speaking to friends.

자기 means "yourself" or "oneself," as well as also "himself" or "herself."

저 사람은 여기에 자기만 있다고 생각하나?
"Does that person think they're the only one here?"
"Does that person think only himself is here?"

> Adv: 자기 is also used between couples who are dating when referring to each other. When used this way, it can translate as "baby," "honey," or "darling," among others.

To Blame: 탓(을) 하다

The *noun* 탓 means "fault," and it can be used by itself. For example:

내 탓이 아니야!
"It's not my fault!"

탓 can also be combined with 하다 to mean "to blame." Here are two examples.

왜 내 탓을 해?
"Why are you blaming me?"

남 탓하지 마.
"Don't blame others."

"So much that…": (을/ㄹ) 만큼

We learned about 만큼 ("amount," "as much as") in Chapter 7 of the previous book, but we only used it with the *present tense* (Action Verb Stem + 는). It is also commonly used with the *future tense* (Action Verb Stem + 을/ㄹ).

먹을 만큼만 가져 가세요.
"(Please) only take the amount that you will drink."
"(Please) only take as much as you will drink."

More Questions and Commands

Chapter 4

To make a more natural translation, if necessary 만큼 can also be translated as "so much that."

그 친구 생일 파티에 갈 만큼 친하지는 않아.
"I'm not close with that friend so much that I'll go to their birthday party."

선생님이 될 수 있을 만큼 한국어를 잘하지는 못해요.
"I can't speak Korean (well) so much that that I can become a teacher."

You could also translate this sentence more literally as, "I can't speak Korean (well) *to the amount that* I could become a teacher."

서태용: 고맙습니다. 어? 지우 씨 차례인 거 같은데요.
"Thank you. Huh? I think it's your turn."

차례 means "a turn," such in a *line*, in a *game*, or in an *order*.

하하, 이제 내 차례다!
"Haha, now it's my turn!"

김지우: 고마워요! 그럼 저 먼저 갈게요.
"Thanks! Well then, I'll go first."

서태용: 네. 내일 또 봐요!
"Okay. See you again tomorrow!"

"Again": 또

또, like 다시, is an *adverb* that means "again." But while 다시 can be used in any situation to mean "again," 또 is only used to mean "again" when you want to add *emphasis*.

여기에 다시 왔네요!
"You came here again!"

여기에 또 왔네요!
"You came here *again*!"

다시 만날래?
"You want to meet again?"

# More Questions and Commands

또 만날래?
"You want to meet *again*?"

You might want to add emphasis to "again" if you are *complaining* about something or feel *embarrassed*, for example. Or, it can be used in a *friendly* way to emphasize "again."

또 약속에 늦었어.
"He was late to the appointment *again*."

그럼 다음에 또 봐!
"Well then, see you *again* next time!"

> **Advanced**
>
> **Soft Command: Action Verb Stem + (으)렴**
>
> This *command form* is much softer, but is also less common. It is typically used by mothers to children – you can think of this as a *loving command form* – but can also be used jokingly in other situations with friends. It should not be used in any polite or formal situation.
>
> 애들아, 안전벨트를 매렴!
> "Kids, put on your seatbelts (if you would be so kind)!"
>
> This form is a shortened version of (으)려무나.

Practice

Conjugate the following descriptive verbs using the 가(요) form:

1. 심심하다

   _____.

2. 배고프다

   _____.

3. 아니다

   _____.

4. 행복하시다

   _____.

More Questions and Commands

5. 너무 많다

6. 집이 넓다

Conjugate the following commands using the (으)시오 form:

7. 보다

8. 고르다

9. 받다

10. 누르다

11. 뽑다

Translate to Korean using the 더니 form:

12. "It rained yesterday, but today it's snowing."

13. "I slept late yesterday, and today I'm tired."

14. "I didn't do the homework, and I failed the test."

Chapter 4: More Questions and Commands

15. "It was cold last week, but this week it's not cold at all."

_____.

Translate to Korean:

16. "Whose turn is it?"

_____.

17. "Whose fault is it?"

_____.

18. "Don't blame yourself."

_____.

19. "I want to go someplace warmer."

_____.

Translate to English:

20. 오래된 우유를 마셨더니 화장실에 계속 가고 싶어요.

_____.

21. 평범한 차를 사 달라고 했더니 스포츠카를 사 주셨어요.

_____.

22. 갑자기 운동을 많이 했더니 제대로 걸을 수가 없어요.

_____.

23. 아침을 안 먹고 나왔더니 배가 너무 고프다.

_____.

24. 3 일 동안 샤워를 안 했더니 아무도 내 옆에 오려고 하지 않아요.

_____.

More Questions and Commands

Chapter 4

25. 도시에만 있다가 시골로 갔더니 문화 충격을 받았어요.

New Phrases

어?	"Huh?," "Oh?"
자....	"Well... (shall we?)," "Here/there (you go)...."
에이....	"Come on...."

New Vocabulary

데	"place," "location"
밤 늦게	"late at night"
아침 일찍	"early in the morning"
대충	"roughly," "approximately" (adverb)
제대로	"properly," "correctly," "right" (adverb)
의외로	"unexpectedly" (adverb)
탓	"(one's) fault"
탓(을) 하다	"to blame"
자기	"yourself," "oneself"
차례	"a turn"
상	"prize," "reward"
부지런하다	"to be diligent," "to be hard working"
게으르다	"to be lazy"
게으름쟁이	"lazy person"
욕심	"greed"
욕심(이) 많다	"to be greedy"
욕심쟁이	"greedy person"
개구쟁이	"troublemaker"
또	"again" (adverb)
빈대떡	"mung bean pancake"
용돈	"allowance," "pocket change"
스포츠카	"sports car"

Chapter 4: More Questions and Commands

네모나다	"to be square (shaped)"
나긋나긋하다	"to be gentle and soft"
버튼	"(mechanical) button"
단추	"(clothes) button"
누르다	"to push (a button)," "to press"
만지다	"to touch"
충격	"a shock," "an impact"
문화 충격	"culture shock"
충격(을) 받다	"to experience shock"
문화 충격(을) 받다	"to experience culture shock"
문화 차이	"culture difference"
평범하다	"to be plain," "to be ordinary"
뽑다	"to pick out (something)," "to choose (someone)"
거품	"bubble"
마을	"village," "town"

Expressing Emotions

Chapter 5

Conversation

사장:	민우 씨, 오늘 무슨 일 있어요?
직원 (민우):	아니요. 왜요?
사장:	그냥 좀 민우 씨가 피곤한 거 같아서요.
직원 (민우):	네. 사실은 어제 핸드폰을 잃어 버려서 잠을 못 자고 왔어요.
사장:	잠을 안 잤다고요? 그럼 피곤할 만하네요.
직원 (민우):	네. 혹시 오늘 조금 일찍 갈 수 있을까요?
사장:	그래요. 지은 씨도 오늘 일찍 가고 싶어 하니까 그렇게 해요.
직원 (민우):	지은 씨가요?
사장:	네. 고양이가 많이 아파서 슬퍼하는 거 같아요.
직원 (민우):	지은 씨네 고양이가요? 슬퍼하고 있을 만하네요.
사장:	그렇죠. 어? 근데 저거 민우 씨 핸드폰 아닌가요?
직원 (민우):	맞아요. 여기 있었네요. 오늘은 잠을 편하게 잘 수 있을 거 같아요.
사장:	잘됐네요. 그럼 1시간 뒤에 퇴근합시다.

This chapter will cover several topics, the main one being changing *descriptive verbs* into *action verbs*. I recommend moving through this chapter extra slowly. Although the topics we will cover are not particularly difficult compared to other topics we have learned, it can take several reviews to adjust to these concepts if you are not already familiar with the concept of "the third person" in English. Let's start with the conversation and learn along the way.

Chapter 5

Expressing Emotions

사장: 민우 씨, 오늘 무슨 일 있어요?
"Min-woo, is something the matter?"

In the first book we learned the word 사장님 for "boss." Whenever you are *referring* to a boss, you'll use 사장님 (and not 사장). The 님 at the end adds *politeness* when using a person's *title*. We will learn about this in detail in Chapter 9, but for now simply know that 사장님 means "boss" when you are speaking to or about a boss (such as *your* boss), and 사장 is simply the word for "*a* boss."

> Adv: 무슨 can be shortened to 뭔 when speaking *casually*. 뭔 is less common.

직원 (민우): 아니요. 왜요?
"No. Why?"

사장: 그냥 좀 민우 씨가 피곤한 거 같아서요.
"Because I think you're just kinda tired."

"To Seem"

Although we learned that we can use the 것 같다 form to mean "think," a more natural translation for the conversation sentence could be "Because you just *seem* kinda tired." This is because the 것 같다 form is used to show your own *thoughts*. In this way, it is like the boss is saying "it seems this way *to me*." It is common to translate the 것 같다 form as "to seem" when using it with *descriptive verbs*. Here are some examples.

어려운 것 같아요.
"I think it's difficult."
"It seems difficult."

지루한 것 같아요.
"I think it's boring."
"It seems boring."

웃긴 것 같아요.
"I think it's funny."
"It seems funny."

쟤 정신없는 거 같아.
"I think that guy's out of it."
"That guy seems out of it."

Expressing Emotions

Chapter 5

We will learn more about how to say "to seem" in detail in Chapter 13.

직원 (민우): 네. 사실은 어제 핸드폰을 잃어 버려서 잠을 못 자고 왔어요.
"Yes. Actually I lost my cellphone yesterday so I came here without sleeping."

Extra Emotion: Action Verb Stem + 아/어/etc. 버리다

While the verb 버리다 literally means "to throw away," it has an additional use as a grammar form to add extra *emotion* to a sentence. This emotion can be *good* or *bad*. Using this form does not change the actual meaning of a sentence.

To make this form, take an *action verb stem* and conjugate it as if you were conjugating the 요 form (but without adding the 요). Then attach the verb 버리다 and conjugate it. Most often the verb 버리다 will be conjugated in the *past tense*. Here are a few common examples of verbs that use this ending.

잊다 → 잊어 버리다 "to forget"
잃다 → 잃어 버리다 "to lose (something)"
먹다 → 먹어 버리다 "to eat"

Let's take a look at an example sentence.

숙제를 다 끝냈어요.
숙제를 다 끝내 버렸어요.
"I finished all of my homework."

Both sentences have the same meaning and translation, but the second sentence (using the 버리다 form) has more emotion attached to it. The second sentence sounds like the speaker is getting slightly *emotional* about it. In this case, the emotion is most likely *good*. Here is another example.

아! 잊었어요!
아! 잊어 버렸어요!
"Ah! I forgot!"

The second sentence shows a stronger *emotional* response to forgetting. In this case, the emotion is likely *bad*. Remember that besides this extra emotion, the meanings of the two sentences are the same. Here are a few more examples.

너무 빨리 일어났어요.
너무 빨리 일어나 버렸어요.
"I woke up too early."

Chapter 5

Expressing Emotions

10 초 안에 안 오면 그냥 나간다!
10 초 안에 안 오면 그냥 나가 버린다!
"If you don't come in 10 seconds I'm just leaving!"

안 means "inside," but when used with *time* it can translate as "within" or "in." Remember that 안, as well as all *postpositions* (위, 앞, 밖, etc.), are used *after* the noun. For a review of postpositions, see Chapter 20 of the first book.

이제 피자는 질렸어.
이제 피자는 질려 버렸어.
"Now I'm sick of pizza."

철수가 케이크를 다 먹었어요.
철수가 케이크를 다 먹어 버렸어요.
"Chul-soo ate all of the cake."

계속 같은 일만 하니까 미칠 거 같아.
계속 같은 일만 하니까 미쳐 버릴 거 같아.
"I think I'll go crazy because I keep doing only the same thing."

While the 버리다 form can be used to show both good (positive) or bad (negative) emotion, it is most commonly used to show *negative* emotions such as sadness or disappointment.

"Without": Negative Action Verb Stem + 고

When 고 ("and") is used with an *action verb*, it has the meaning of "and then." In the conversation, the sentence 잠을 못 자고 왔어요 literally means "(I) could not sleep and then (I) came (here)." Using 고 shows that one action took place after the next – just like "and then" in English.

When used with a *negative* action verb, a more natural translation for 고 can be "without."

밥을 안 먹고 왔어요.
"I didn't eat and then came (here)."
"I came (here) without eating."

공부를 안 하고 시험을 봤어요.
"I didn't study and then took the test."
"I took the test without studying."

생각하지 않고 말했어요.
"I didn't think and then spoke."
"I spoke without thinking."

Expressing Emotions

지갑을 안 가지고 나왔어요.
"I came out without bringing my wallet."
"I forgot (to bring) my wallet."

Note that just saying 지갑을 잊었어요 would be *incorrect* in this way, since that would mean that you forgot *about* your wallet, or that you forgot to *consider* your wallet. Instead, use 안 가지고 나가다 (if you forgot to take it *somewhere else*) or 안 가지고 나오다 (if you forgot to bring it *here*). Alternatively, you could also use 놓고 가다 ("to put it down and go *somewhere else*") or 놓고 오다 ("to put it down and come *here*") with the particle 에 to mean "to leave (something somewhere)." For example, 집에 놓고 왔어요 ("I left it at home.").

사장: 잠을 안 잤다고요? 그럼 피곤할 만하네요.
"You say you didn't sleep? Then it's natural that you're tired."

"Worth it": Action Verb Stem + (을/ㄹ) 만하다

You can use this form to say that something is "worth" doing. For example, "It's *worth* going to Seoul. It's really fun." In English, saying that something is "worth" doing means that it is *acceptable* to do, or *good* to do – in Korean, this form can have the same usage.

To make this form, take an *action verb stem* and attach 을 if it ends in a *consonant*, or attach ㄹ if it ends in a *vowel*. Then add the verb 만하다 and conjugate it.

서울은 갈 만해요. 정말 재미있어요.
"It's worth going to Seoul. It's really fun."

Notice how this sentence uses the Topic Marker (은/는) to mark what is *worth* doing. This is because 만하다 is a *descriptive verb*. Alternatively, you could also use the Subject Marker (이/가), or 도 ("also," "even," "too"), among other particles.

저 김밥이 먹을 만해요?
"Is that kimbap worth eating?"

Remember that saying something is "worth" doing is also saying that it is acceptable to do something, so another translation for this sentence could be "Is that kimbap *acceptable* (to eat)?" Or more naturally, "Is that kimbap *good* (to eat)?"

| Chapter 5 | **Expressing Emotions** |

Culture Notes

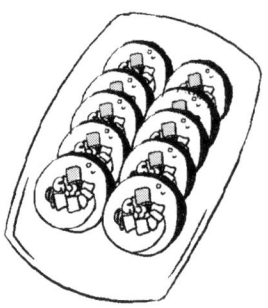

Seaweed & 김밥

There are many words for "seaweed" in Korean depending on the type. Flat, dry seaweed is called 김. Waving seaweed that you'd imagine at the bottom of the ocean is called 해초. Another variant that appears similar but is edible is 미역 (eaten in soups). 다시마 is another common type of seaweed that is thick, and is used to make flavorful soup broth.

You will find 김 commonly used to make 김밥 (literally, "seaweed and rice"). 김밥 was originally inspired by Japanese sushi, but uses no similar ingredients besides 김. Instead of using vinegar (like sushi rice), the rice in 김밥 is made with sesame oil (참기름). 김밥 is filled with vegetables, as well as sometimes meat or seafood. And since it does not use any raw ingredients it can survive fresh for a while outside of the refrigerator, so it can be easily taken on picnics.

어제 본 영화가 진짜 볼 만했어.
"The movie I saw yesterday was really worth seeing."

한국어는 공부할 만해요.
"Korean is worth studying."

이 책은 읽을 만한 거 같아요.
"I think this book is worth reading."
"This book seems worth reading."

저런 데는 별로 가 볼 만하지 않아요.
"Those kind of places aren't really worth going to."

저런 comes from 저렇다 ("to be so"), which is used for things that are far (physically, or mentally) from both the speaker and the listener. 저렇다 can be used in a similar way to 그렇다.

Expressing Emotions

"Understandably": Descriptive Verb Stem + (을/ㄹ) 만하다

This form can also be used with *descriptive verbs*. While the meaning of 만하다 is not changing in Korean, we need to change our English translation. When using this form with a descriptive verb, it translates as "to be understandably" something, or "it is natural to be" something.

배고플 만해요.
"You're understandably hungry."
"It's natural to be hungry."

둘다 비슷해서 헷갈릴 만해요.
"Both of them are similar so you're understandably confused."
"Both of them are similar so it's natural to be confused."

저 집이 우리 집보다 더 비쌀 만해요.
"That house is understandably more expensive than our house."
"It's natural for that house to be more expensive than our house."

그렇게 큰 거미를 봤으면 놀랄 만했네.
"It was understandable for you to be surprised if you saw such a large spider."
"It was natural for you to be surprised if you saw such a large spider."

철수 씨는 의사라서 돈이 많이 있을 만해요.
"Chul-soo understandably has a lot of money because he's a doctor."
"It's natural for Chul-soo to have a lot of money because he's a doctor."

직원 (민우): 네. 혹시 오늘 조금 일찍 갈 수 있을까요?
"Yes. By chance could I leave a little early today?"

사장: 그래요. 지은 씨도 오늘 일찍 가고 싶어 하니까 그렇게 해요.
"Okay. Ji-eun also wants to go early today so (you) do that."

The Third Person

Before we learn about the main topic of this chapter – changing descriptive verbs into action verbs – we first need to talk about what "the third person" means. In English, there are three ways to speak about something – using the *first person*, the *second person*, and the *third person*. If you have never learned these terms before – or if you slept through that lesson in your English class – they might seem new and confusing, but these three words are actually quite simple.

Chapter 5: Expressing Emotions

If someone is speaking using the *first person*, it means they are talking about *themselves*. For example, if I say that I am happy ("*I* am happy."), then I am speaking in the first person. If my friend tells me that he is happy, then he is also speaking in the first person, since he is talking about himself. Pretty simple, right?

If someone is speaking using the *second person*, it means that they are talking about the person to whom they are speaking. For example, if I am speaking with 철수, and I tell him I am happy, then this is the first person like before. But if I tell 철수 that he is happy while speaking to him ("*You* are happy."), then this is called the second person. If 철수 tells me that I am happy, while he is speaking to me ("No, Billy. You are happy."), then this is also the second person.

So whenever you are speaking and talking about yourself (using the word "I") you are speaking in *first person*, and whenever you're talking about the person you're speaking to (using the word "you") you're speaking in *second person*.

If someone is speaking using the *third person*, it means that they are talking about someone else – not themselves, and not the person who they are speaking to. For example, if I am speaking with 철수, and I tell him that 민우 is happy ("*He* is happy."), then this is called the third person because I am not talking about myself or about 철수. Whenever you are using the word "he" or "she" in this way you are speaking using the third person. Let's review:

1st person: "I am happy."
2nd person: "You are happy."
3rd person: "He/she is happy."

"Why is this important?" In English, it is okay to use the same adjective (here, "happy") in all three of these cases – first, second, and third person. But in Korean, it is not correct. In Korean, you can use the same descriptive verb when speaking in the first person (저는 기뻐요.) and in the second person ([당신은] 기뻐요.), but not in the third person. If you are not directly speaking with 철수, then it would be *incorrect* to tell someone else 철수는 기뻐요 ("Chul-soo is happy.") because this is speaking using the *third person*.

"Why would it be incorrect?" Because certain descriptive verbs (such as "to be happy") or the 싶다 form ("want to") are related to a person's own *desires*, *feelings*, *thoughts*, or *emotions*. Koreans do not believe that they can know for certain what another person is thinking, so it would be *incorrect* to assume that someone else is "happy" or "sad" unless we knew 100% that they were. Any descriptive verb that shows a person's *desires*, *feelings*, *thoughts*, and *emotions* cannot be used in the third person as it is – we have to change it to an *action verb* in order to use it in the third person.

Expressing Emotions

For example, currently we can say "I want to eat kimchi" (저는 김치를 먹고 싶어요.) and "You want to eat kimchi" ([당신은] 김치를 먹고 싶어요.) but not yet "He wants to eat kimchi." Saying 그 사람은 김치를 먹고 싶어요 would make sense to a Korean, but would be *incorrect* because we are assuming that we know that person's *desires*, *feelings*, *thoughts*, or *emotions*. Instead, we need to change our descriptive verb a little to make it work. Fortunately, there is a simple way to do this.

> **Adv**
> When using action verbs that end in 고 싶다, we learned that the Object Marker (을/를) is used to show what it is that you want to do. For example, 김치를 먹고 싶어요 ("I want to eat kimchi."). Actually, the Subject Marker (이/가) can also be used, and commonly is. This is because 싶다 is a *descriptive verb*. So when 고 싶다 is added to an action verb, in a way it has the function of both the action verb and the descriptive verb 싶다. For example, you can also say 김치가 먹고 싶어요 ("I want to eat kimchi."). The meaning will be the same, and both are commonly used.

Changing Descriptive Verbs to Action Verbs:
Descriptive Verb Stem + 아/어/etc. + 하다

In order to use a descriptive verb related to someone's desires, feelings, thoughts, or emotions in the *third person*, we need to change it to an action verb.

To make this form, conjugate a descriptive verb the same way as you would conjugate the 요 form, but do not add the 요. Then directly attach the verb 하다 to the end and conjugate it. The difficult part of using this form is simply remembering *to* use it when speaking in the third person. Here are some examples.

기쁘다 → 기뻐하다
슬프다 → 슬퍼하다
가고 싶다 → 가고 싶어 하다*

*Note that the 고 싶다 ending will add a space when used in this form (고 싶어 하다).

> 저는 슬퍼요.
> "*I* am sad."

> (당신은) 슬퍼요.
> "*You* are sad."

Note that I have only used 당신 as an example for the above sentence, and that 당신 would not normally be used in a real conversation. For a review of this, see Chapter 18 of the first book.

> (그 사람은) 슬퍼해요.
> "*He/she* is sad."

Chapter 5 — **Expressing Emotions**

Here are three more examples.

저는 한국 음식이 그리워요.
"I miss Korean food."

Note that 그립다 ("to miss," "to long for") is more commonly used to say that you miss or long for a *thing*, but can also be used when you miss or long for *someone*.

한국 음식이 그리워요?
"Do you miss Korean food?"

그 사람도 한국 음식을 그리워해요.
"That person also misses Korean food."

In certain cases, not using this form when speaking in the third person could also lead to misunderstandings. If you were to tell someone that your friend (using the third person) wanted to eat too, you would use 저의 친구도 먹고 싶어 해요 ("My friend wants to eat too."). It would be *incorrect* (although humorous) to say 저의 친구도 먹고 싶어요 ("I want to eat my friend too."). Unless you are a cannibal (please get help), remember to use this form whenever you are speaking in the third person.

> **Advanced**
>
> This form is used whenever you are not 100% sure about the person's desires, feelings, thoughts, or emotions. But if you are 100% sure, then you do not need to use it. For example, let's say that you are speaking together with 철수, and talking about 민우. But before meeting 철수, you met 민우 and asked him if he is happy (기뻐요?). 민우 replied that he is happy. When you later meet with 철수, you can say something like this: 민우는 기뻐요 ("Min-woo is happy."). Even though this uses the third person since you are not talking about yourself or 철수, this is okay because you are 100% sure about 민우's feelings – you spoke with him directly and confirmed it.
>
> Also, if you are an author writing a book then you do not need to use this form. This is because you can be 100% sure about your character's desires, feelings, thoughts, and emotions – after all, you are the author.
>
> In all other cases, it is necessary to use this form for descriptive verbs when speaking in the third person.

직원 (민우): 지은 씨가요?

"Ji-eun?"

사장: 네. 고양이가 많이 아파서 슬퍼하는 거 같아요.

"Yes. Her cat's really sick so I think she's feeling sad."

Expressing Emotions

Chapter 5

More on Action Verbs

If this is your first time reading through this chapter and you are still getting used to the concept of "the third person," I recommend skipping this section.

Changing a descriptive verb into an action verb can also sometimes change the meaning of the verb a bit. For example, while 슬프다 means "to be sad" and 슬퍼하다 means "to be sad" in the third person, 슬퍼하다 can also mean "to *feel* sad." While 괴롭다 means "to be distressed" or "to be in pain," 괴로워하다 can also mean "to suffer" or "to *feel* distressed." And while 힘들다 means "to be hard" or "to be difficult," 힘들어하다 can also mean "to have a hard time" or "to have trouble." Fortunately, you do not need to focus on memorizing a large list of these words as their meanings are similar to their original descriptive verb forms. Even if you forget how the meaning of a descriptive verb changes as an action verb, you should be able to figure out the general meaning of the verb from the context of the sentence. If you forget these alternate meanings, most of the time you can simply translate them as their original descriptive verb forms.

One way to remember how the meaning changes is to think of the new action verb as meaning "to *feel* (descriptive verb)" or "to *do* (descriptive verb)." So 기쁘다 ("to be happy") when changed to 기뻐하다 can also translate as "to feel happy" or "to *do* happy." By "to *do* happy" I mean that you are *doing* something that shows you are feeling happy.

Most importantly, since these new verbs are action verbs, you can use them as you would use any action verb (using the Object Marker, for example). A common usage of this form is for saying "do be" (commands) and "don't be" (negative commands) with descriptive verbs. For example, we currently can only say "don't" with action verbs. It would be *incorrect* to say "Don't be sad" as 슬프지 마세요. Instead, change 슬프다 ("to be sad") into 슬퍼하다. Now that it is an action verb, we can change it into a negative command easily – 슬퍼하지 마세요. Remember that these new verbs are action verbs, so they will conjugate as action verbs and can be used in any grammar form as if they have always been action verbs.

Since the third person form is used when speaking about other people, the phrases 건강하세요! ("Be healthy!") and 행복하세요! ("Be happy!") are grammatically *incorrect*. This is because normal descriptive verbs cannot be used as commands to mean "do be (descriptive verb)." Only action verbs can be used as commands, as we learned previously. However, these two phrases are commonly used and will be accepted as correct grammar in all polite situations, even in writing.

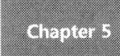

Expressing Emotions

Let's go a bit further. We learned how to change an action verb into an adjective in Chapter 4 of the second book. For example, we can take the verb 먹다 ("to eat") and attach it to 김치 in the present tense – (제가) 먹는 김치 ("The kimchi that I eat."). We can also do the same thing with our new action verbs. We can change the action verb 기뻐하다 into an adjective (기뻐하는) and use it to describe a noun in the *third person*. This might seem a bit complicated to change a descriptive verb into an action verb and then back into an adjective again, but take a look at this example.

기뻐하는 사람들이 많아요.
"There are many people who are happy."

Since this sentence is not talking directly about the speaker ("I") or the listener ("you"), but is instead talking in the third person, it is necessary to use this form for this sentence. Saying 기쁜 사람들이 많아요 would be understood, but would be *incorrect* because you are not 100% sure about their desires, feelings, thoughts, or emotions.

> **Advanced**
>
> Although this form is *necessary* when speaking in the third person (when you are not 100% sure about the person's desires, feelings, thoughts, or emotions), it *can* also be used when speaking in the *first person* or *second person*, since adding this form is not actually changing the meaning of the verb. This usage is much less common, but be aware of it in case you come across it.
>
>
>
> 저도 힘들어요.
> 저도 힘들어하고 있어요.
> "I'm also having a hard time."
>
>

> **Advanced**
>
>
>
> The verbs 좋아하다, 싫어하다, and 미워하다 were also originally made in this same way, from 좋다, 싫다, and 밉다. These three verbs are commonly used, which is why you were taught about them long before learning about this grammar form.

직원 (민우): 지은 씨네 고양이가요? 슬퍼하고 있을 만하네요.

"Ji-eun's cat? It's understandable that she is feeling sad."

Expressing Emotions

Chapter 5

Group Possessive Marker – 네

We previously learned about the Possessive Marker (의), but here is a slightly different type of Possessive Marker which is used for things that are owned by a *group* or an *organization* (not owned by just one person).

When you use 의, you are saying that one person is the sole owner of something. For example, 진희의 연필 means "Jin-hee's pencil." Jin-hee is the only owner of the pencil in this case. But if you wanted to talk about something that Jin-hee was part of (a group or organization) and did not own by herself, you would use 네 instead of 의. For example, both 진희의 집 and 진희네 집 can mean "Jin-hee's house." If Jin-hee was the sole owner of the house then you could use 진희의 집, but since she is likely just one member of the household 네 is more appropriate. Because of this, you will most commonly find 네 used with words such as 집, 학교, and pets, among others.

Note that 네 will not be attached to 저 or 나 to mean "my." Instead, 우리, 저의 (or 제), or 나의 (or 내) will be used. For a review of 우리, see Chapter 18 of the first book.

사장: 그렇죠. 어? 근데 저거 민우 씨 핸드폰 아닌가요?
"Yeah. Huh? But isn't that your cell phone?"

직원 (민우): 맞아요. 여기 있었네요. 오늘은 잠을 편하게 잘 수 있을 거 같아요.
"You're right. It was here. I think I'll be able to sleep comfortably today."

사장: 잘됐네요. 그럼 1 시간 뒤에 퇴근합시다.
"That worked out well. Then let's go home after 1 hour."

In the *past tense*, a more natural translation for 잘되다 ("to go well") is "to work out well." Or more casually, you can translate it as "to be great" when you want to express your *opinion* on something that worked out well.

잘됐어요.
"It worked out well."
"That's great."

In the *future tense*, "to be fine" or "to work out fine" is a more natural translation.

잘될 거야.
"It'll be fine."

Chapter 5
Expressing Emotions

Adv

There are also a few verbs that work differently than they might seem at first. For example, the verb 예뻐하다 comes from 예쁘다 ("to be pretty") but means "to favor and like." You can think of this verb as literally meaning "to think that someone is beautiful, and to treat them that way." In the same way, the verb 귀여워하다 comes from 귀엽다 ("to be cute") and means "to adore."

Practice

Conjugate the following action verbs using the 버리다 form:

1. 실수하다

   _____.

2. 사다

   _____.

3. 죽다

   _____.

4. 떨어지다

   _____.

5. 말하다

   _____.

Conjugate the following descriptive verbs to the third person:

6. 무섭다

   _____.

7. 속상하다

   _____.

8. 부럽다

   _____.

Expressing Emotions

9. 가지고 싶다

10. 외롭다

Translate to Korean:

11. "It seems cold today."

12. "It's worth going to Korea."

13. "You're understandably tired because you worked 10 hours today."

14. "Don't be afraid."

15. "That person is not sad."

16. "It seems that person isn't happy."

17. "There are 3 people who want to eat pizza."

Translate to English:

18. 바빠서 잊어 버렸어요.

Chapter 5 — Expressing Emotions

19. 먼저 생각을 안 하고 그 사람을 그냥 믿어 버렸어요.

_____.

20. 안 씻고 밖으로 나왔어요.

_____.

21. 저 자동차는 살 만하나요?

_____.

22. 친구가 많이 있을 만해요.

_____.

23. 철수네 집에 가고 싶어 하는 사람이 없어요?

_____.

24. 친구들이 다 저를 부러워해요.

_____.

25. 어린 아이에게 상처를 줘서 마음이 아프네요.

_____.

New Phrases

건강하세요!	"Be healthy!"
행복하세요!	"Be happy!"
동감입니다.	"I feel the same way (about it)."
기분이 어떻습니까?	"How do you feel?"

New Vocabulary

잃다	"to lose (something)"
퇴근	"leaving from work"
퇴근(을) 하다	"to leave from work"

Expressing Emotions

출근	"leaving to work"
출근(을) 하다	"to leave to work"
사장	"a boss"
안	"within/in (time)"
힘들어하다	"to have a hard time," "to have trouble"
괴롭다	"to be distressed," "to be in pain"
괴로워하다	"to suffer"
부러워하다	"to feel jealous"
부끄러워하다	"to feel embarrassed"
무서워하다	"to feel scared"
즐겁다	"to be cheerful," "to be merry"
즐거워하다	"to feel cheerful," "to feel merry"
예뻐하다	"to favor and like"
귀여워하다	"to adore"
쑥스럽다	"to be bashful"
동감(을) 하다	"to agree (with someone's feelings)"
진심	"sincerity"
편리하다	"to be convenient"
예민하다	"to be sensitive (physically/emotionally)"
민감하다	"to be touchy," "to be sensitive (emotionally)"
기분	"(one's) mood"
상처	"wound," "injury"
상처(를) 주다	"to hurt someone's feelings"
기분(이) 좋다	"to feel good"
기분(이) 안 좋다	"to not feel good"
마음	"(one's) mind," "(one's) heart," "(one's) feelings"
마음(이) 아프다	"to be hurting (emotionally)," "to feel sad"
마음(이) 편하다	"to feel at ease (emotionally)"
느끼다	"to feel," "to sense"
느낌	"a feeling," "a sensation"
딱딱하다	"to be hard," "to be firm"

Chapter 5: Expressing Emotions

부드럽다	"to be soft," "to be smooth"
외롭다	"to be lonely"
외로워하다	"to feel lonely"
미치다	"to be crazy/insane," "to go crazy/insane"
정신(이) 없다	"to be out of it," "to be extremely busy"
그립다	"to miss," "to long for"
질리다	"to get sick (of something)," "to be tired (of something)"
헷갈리다	"to be confused (about something)"
속상하다	"to be upset"
당황하다	"to be confused and flustered"
밉다	"to be detestable," "to be hated"
저렇다	"to be so"
단체	"group," "organization"
납작하다	"to be flat"
김	"flat, dry seaweed"
해초	"seaweed"
미역	"(edible) seaweed"

How To

Conversation

타일러:	실례합니다. 서울 백화점에 어떻게 가는지 아세요?
은혜:	서울 백화점이요?
타일러:	네, 이 동네에 있는 서울 백화점이요.
은혜:	서울 백화점은 여기서 좀 멀어요.
타일러:	저는 서울 백화점이 이 근처에 있는 줄 알았는데요.
은혜:	여기에 있는 건 서울 시장이에요. 지하철 탈 줄 아세요?
타일러:	네, 알고 있어요.
은혜:	그러면 가는 방법을 적어 드릴게요.
타일러:	대단히 감사합니다!

While we have already learned the adverb 어떻게 ("how"), we have not yet covered how to say "how to." For example, we can use 어떻게 in a sentence such as 어떻게 하세요? ("How do you do it?"), but we cannot yet make the sentence "I don't know *how to* do it." In English, "how to" is most often used with the verb "to know." For example, "I know how to use chopsticks." In Korean it is the same. There are two main ways to say "how to" that we will cover in this chapter. Let's get started with the conversation.

> 타일러: 실례합니다. 서울 백화점에 어떻게 가는지 아세요?
> "Excuse me. Do you know how to get to Seoul Department Store?"

How To

"How to": 어떻게 Action Verb Stem + 는지(를) 알다/모르다

To say "how to," first add the adverb 어떻게 ("how") before an *action verb stem*. Then attach 는지(를) – the Object Marker is *optional*. Then conjugate the verb 알다 ("to know") or 모르다 ("to not know") in any way that you like. For example:

가다 → 어떻게 가는지(를) 알다/모르다
받다 → 어떻게 받는지(를) 알다/모르다
팔다 → 어떻게 파는지(를) 알다/모르다

As usual, verb stems ending in ㄹ will remove the ㄹ when using this form. Let's look at a few example sentences.

어떻게 가는지 알아요.
"I know how to get there."

While 가다 literally means "to go," when there is no *destination* in the sentence a more natural English translation can be "to get (there/to somewhere)." The meaning in Korean stays the same.

어떻게 해야 하는지 몰라요.
"I don't know how I need to do it."

어떻게 받을 수 있는지를 몰랐어요.
"I didn't know how I could get it."

한국어로 길을 어떻게 물어보는지 아세요?
"Do you know how to ask for directions in Korean?"

길(을) 물어보다 comes from 길 ("a street," "a road," "a *way*") and 물어보다 ("to ask"). Together they mean "to ask the *way*," or more naturally, "to ask (for) directions."

도대체 어떻게 하는지 몰라.
"I don't know how in the world to do it."

(도)대체 is an adverb that is only used with *question words* – such as 왜, 언제, 어디, 무엇, 누구/누가, 어떻게, and others. It can translate as "in the world" or "on earth" and is used to express *shock*. It is only for *informal* or *casual* usage, and should be avoided when speaking formally.

이걸 어떻게 할 수 있는지 완전히 모르겠어요.
"I completely don't know how I can do this."

How To

완전히 ("completely") is an *adverb* and comes from the descriptive verb 완전하다 ("to be complete," "to be perfect"). A more natural translation for this example would be "I have completely no idea how I can do this."

젓가락을 어떻게 쓰는지 알아요.
"I know how to use chopsticks."

"Fish"를 한국어로 어떻게 말하는지 아세요?
"Do you know how to say 'fish' in Korean?"

Note that the English word "fish" said with Korean pronunciation would be 피쉬. While the above example is an acceptable way to ask someone *how to* say something in Korean, a more common (and simpler) way is this: (이것은) 한국어로 뭐예요?

어떻게 설명하는지 모른다는 뜻이에요?
"You mean that you don't know how to explain it?"

다는 is a common shortened version of **다고 말하는** – a quoting form. In this example, 모른다는 뜻 can literally translate as "meaning that (you're saying) you do not know." For a review of quoting forms, see Chapter 2. This type of form, which uses *quoting forms* and 는 뜻이다, is often used for asking and explaining the meaning of things. Here are a few more examples.

한국어를 잘한다는 뜻이에요.
"It means you can do (speak) Korean well."

더 없다는 뜻이에요?
"Does that mean that there's no more?"

제가 내일 나간다는 뜻이에요.
"It means that I'm leaving tomorrow."

공부를 잘하면 시험을 통과할 수 있다는 뜻이에요.
"It means that if you study well you'll be able to pass the test."

제가 그 물건을 원하지 않는다는 뜻이에요.
"It means that I don't want that item."

기숙사에 들어오지 말라는 뜻이에요.
"It means 'don't enter' the dormitory."

빨리 하라는 뜻이에요.
"It means 'do it quickly.'"

Chapter 6

How To

제가 미국 사람이라는 뜻이에요.
"It means that I'm American."

Remember that the verb 이다 ("to be") changes to (이)라고 (말)하다 when used in quoting. (이)라고 하는 shortens to just (이)라는.

줄에 사람이 많다는 뜻이에요.
"It means that there are a lot of people in line."

매운 걸 못 먹으면 김치를 안 좋아할 거라는 뜻이에요.
"If you can't eat spicy food, it means that you won't like kimchi."

In the second book we learned this phrase to ask the meaning of something:

무슨 뜻이에요?
"What does it mean?"

We can use the 뜻이다 form to reply.

사과라는 뜻이에요.
"It means 'apple.'"

한국이라는 뜻이에요.
"It means 'Korea.'"

> **Advanced**
>
> These forms, 다는 and (이)라는, are commonly shortened to 단 and (이)란.
>
> 더 없단 뜻이에요.
> "It means there's no more."
>
> 한국이란 뜻이에요.
> "It means 'Korea.'"

은혜: 서울 백화점이요?

"Seoul Department Store?"

타일러: 네, 이 동네에 있는 서울 백화점이요.

"Yes, the Seoul Department Store in this neighborhood."

How To

Chapter 6

Neighborhood: 근처, 주변, and 동네

We previously learned 근처 ("neighborhood," "vicinity"), and 주변 ("surroundings," "vicinity"), but now we will learn about 동네 ("neighborhood"). While all three of these words can translate as "neighborhood," they each have slightly different uses. 근처 is used when you mean a "neighborhood" that is close by. 주변 is used when you mean a "neighborhood" that is in the surrounding area. 동네 is used when you mean a "neighborhood" that is where someone lives.

이 근처에 있어요.
이 주변에 있어요.
이 동네에 있어요.
"It's in this neighborhood."

When used on their own, each can have an additional meaning.

근처에 있어요.
"It's close by"

주변에 있어요.
"It's in this surrounding area."

동네에 있어요.
"It's in (someone's) neighborhood."

While you can use 근처 and 주변 to say that something is in the area that you are in, using 동네 is only for when you are talking about an actual neighborhood where someone *lives* – not for saying that something is close by.

은혜: 서울 백화점은 여기서 좀 멀어요.

"Seoul Department Store is a bit far from here."

타일러: 저는 서울 백화점이 이 근처에 있는 줄 알았는데요.

"I thought that Seoul Department Store was in this neighborhood."

How To

"Think" & "Know": Verb Stem + (은/ㄴ/을/ㄹ/는) 줄(을) 알다/모르다

We previously covered two forms we can use to say "think" – 것 같다 and 생각(을) 하다. We also learned how to say that we "know" a fact or piece of information – 것(을) 알다. This new form can be used to mean both "think" and "know," but it has a slightly different usage. It is used for saying you had an *expectation* about something – whether you *knew* or *thought* that it would be as someone (perhaps yourself) expected.

To use it, take a *verb stem* and conjugate it as an *adjective* to whatever tense you would like – past, present, or future. I have included each possible conjugation in the rule itself as a reminder. For a review of these rules in detail, re-read Chapter 4 in the second book. Then attach 알다 if you know, or 모르다 if you do not know. These two verbs will typically only be conjugated in the *past tense*. Let's take a look at some example verbs before we talk more about how to use this form.

가다:
    간 줄(을) 알다/모르다 (Past Tense)
    가는 줄(을) 알다/모르다 (Present Tense)
    갈 줄(을) 알다/모르다 (Future Tense)

먹다:
    먹은 줄(을) 알다/모르다 (Past Tense)
    먹는 줄(을) 알다/모르다 (Present Tense)
    먹을 줄(을) 알다/모르다 (Future Tense)

살다:
    산 줄(을) 알다/모르다 (Past Tense)
    사는 줄(을) 알다/모르다 (Present Tense)
    살 줄(을) 알다/모르다 (Future Tense)

있다:
    있었던 줄(을) 알다/모르다 (Past Tense)
    있는 줄(을) 알다/모르다 (Present Tense)
    있을 줄(을) 알다/모르다 (Future Tense)

이다:
    이었던 줄(을) 알다/모르다 or 였던 줄(을) 알다/모르다 (Past Tense)
    인 줄(을) 알다/모르다 (Present Tense)
    일 줄(을) 알다/모르다 (Future Tense)

Note that verbs in this form will often not use their past tense conjugations. Instead, the *present tense* or *future tense* will be used. This is because the verb 알다 (or 모르다) will be in the past tense, so it's unnecessary to conjugate the verb in the past tense as well.

How To

Chapter 6

Whether this form means "think" or "know" depends entirely on the *context* – it will be simple to know whether it means "think" or "know" if you are able to keep up with the rest of the conversation. Here are a few examples. I have added some additional context in *parentheses* as suggestions for translation.

한국 사람인 줄 알았어요!
"I thought you were a Korean (but you're not)!"
"I knew you were a Korean (and you are)!"

If it helps you to understand this form, you can also translate it in your head as "expect" in both cases.

선아도 가는 줄을 알았어요.
"I thought Sun-ah is going too (but she's not)."
"I knew Sun-ah is going too (and she is)."

어제 눈이 올 줄을 알았어요.
"I thought it would snow yesterday (but it didn't)."
"I knew it would snow yesterday (and it did)."

맛있을 줄 알았어.
"I thought it'd taste good (but it doesn't)."
"I knew it'd taste good (and it does)."

좋아할 줄 알았어요.
"I thought you'd like it (but you don't)."
"I knew you'd like it (and you do)."

Notice how all of the examples use 알다 and 모르다 in the *past tense* – this is the most common way to use this form. Here are some more examples.

10 번 버스인 줄 알았는데.
"I thought/knew it was bus #10."

You can say a bus's number (or anything that can be given a number) by using *Sino-Korean numbers* with the counter 번.

그렇게 더운 줄 몰랐어요.
"I didn't think/know it was that hot."

네가 여기 있을 줄 알았어.
"I thought/knew you'd be here."

111

How To

> 그렇게 할 줄 몰랐어요.
> "I didn't think/know he'll do that."

> 나도 갈 줄을 알았어?
> "Did you think/know I will go too?"

> 귀여울 줄 알았는데....
> "I thought/knew he would be cute...."

> 고기 10 근을 사 달라고 한 줄 알았어요.
> "I thought/knew that I asked you to buy me 10 geun of meat."

근 is a traditional, but still commonly used weight counter. It is used with *Sino-Korean numbers*. A single 근 equals 600 grams (about 1.32 lbs).

> **Adv**: Another traditional, but still commonly used counter is 평, which is also used with Sino-Korean numbers. A single 평 equals 3.3058 square meters (about 10.9 square feet) and is used to measure the size of apartments and homes.

Remember that the 것(을) 알다 form we learned in Chapter 1 is used for saying that you know or do not know a *fact* or some *information*.

> 현우가 멋있다는 것을 알고 있어요.
> "I know (the fact that) that Hyun-woo is cool."

The 줄(을) 알다 form is used for saying that you know or do not know something that someone – perhaps yourself – *expected*. It is also only used in the *past tense*.

> 현우가 멋있는 줄 알았어요.
> "I thought that Hyun-woo is cool (but he isn't)."
> "I knew that Hyun-woo is cool (and he is)."

Because this form is used for something you or someone else expected, here is another way to translate this example: "I *expected* (maybe correctly or incorrectly) that Hyun-woo is cool."

> 은혜: 여기에 있는 건 서울 시장이에요. 지하철 탈 줄 아세요?
> "The one here is Seoul market. Do you know how to ride the subway?"

"How to": Action Verb Stem + (을/ㄹ) 줄(을) 알다/모르다

Here is one more common way to say "how to." We can use the same form that we just learned for "think" and "know" in a much simpler way, and with *action verbs*.

How To

Chapter 6

To use it, take an *action verb stem* and attach 을 if it ends in a *consonant*, or attach ㄹ if it ends in a *vowel*. Then add 줄(을) – the Object Marker is *optional*. Finally, conjugate the verb 알다 ("to know") or 모르다 ("to not know") in any way that you would like. Here are three example conjugations.

하다 → 할 줄(을) 알다/모르다
먹다 → 먹을 줄(을) 알다/모르다
만들다 → 만들 줄(을) 알다/모르다

Although this form looks the same as the one we just learned for "think" and "know," there is no need to choose the tense of the action verb like before. Here are a few examples of this form.

수영할 줄 알아요.
"I know how to swim."

자전거를 탈 줄 몰라요.
"I don't know how to ride a bicycle."

한국어를 할 줄 아세요?
"Do you know how to speak Korean?"

Both this form, and the previous form that we learned for saying "how to" have the same meaning when used in this way.

갈 줄 알아요.
어떻게 가는지 알아요.
"I know how to get there."

젓가락을 쓸 줄을 알아요.
젓가락을 어떻게 쓰는지 알아요.
"I know how to use chopsticks."

This form is slightly more *informal* than using the previous form, but both have the same meaning.

타일러: 네, 알고 있어요.
"Yes, I do."

은혜: 그러면 가는 방법을 적어 드릴게요.
"Then I'll write down (for you) how to go there."

How To

"How to": Action Verb Stem + 는 (방)법

"Another way to say 'how to?'" This form is not used as often as the other two that we have learned. 방법 is a *noun* that means "method" or "way," so using this form is literally asking someone if they know the method or way of doing something. Because of this it can also translate as "how to." This form is a bit more *formal* than the previous two forms that we have learned.

To use this form, take an *action verb stem* and attach 는. Then add 방법 (or just 법). Unlike our previous two forms, this one is not limited to being used with only 알다 ("to know") or 모르다 ("to not know") because its meaning is more general. First let's look at a few basic conjugations.

하다 → 하는 (방)법
먹다 → 먹는 (방)법
만들다 → 만드는 (방)법

Remember that certain verbs, such as ones ending in ㄹ, will have their own extra conjugation rules.

This form can be used with the verbs 알다 ("to know") and 모르다 ("to not know") just like before.

컴퓨터를 고치는 방법을 아세요?
"Do you know the way to repair a computer?"
"Do you know how to repair a computer?"

아직 하는 방법을 잘 몰라요.
"I don't know the way to do it well yet."
"I don't know how to do it well yet."

저는 비싼 상품을 제일 싸게 살 수 있는 방법을 알고 있어요.
"I know the way to buy expensive goods as cheap as possible."
"I know how to buy expensive goods as cheap as possible."

제일 싸게 comes from 제일, meaning "most," "(the) best," and 싸다, meaning "to be cheap." Literally, 제일 싸게 means "the most cheaply," but it can more naturally translate to "as cheap as possible."

This form can also be used with other verbs, since its meaning is more general than the previous two forms.

How To

Chapter 6

젓가락을 쓰는 법을 이미 배웠어요.
"I already learned the way to use chopsticks."
"I already learned how to use chopsticks."

쉽고 재미있는 방법을 찾고 있어요.
"I'm looking for an easy and fun method."

지하철을 타는 방법이 쉬워요.
"The way to ride the subway is easy."

제일 맛있게 먹는 방법을 가르쳐 줄까요?
"Should I teach you the most delicious way to eat it?"

타일러: 대단히 감사합니다!
"Thank you very much!"

Practice

Translate to Korean using the 어떻게 form for "how to":

1. "I know how to make cheese."

_____.

2. "I don't know how to drive."

_____.

3. "Do you know how to write a book?"

_____.

4. "I don't know how I need to start."

_____.

Translate to Korean using the 줄(을) 알다/모르다 form for "how to":

5. "I don't know how to use it well yet."

_____.

Chapter 6 — How To

6. "Do you know how to drive?"

   _____.

7. "I don't know how to eat it."

   _____.

8. "I know how to write Hangul."

   _____.

Translate to Korean using the 줄(을) 알다/모르다 form for "thought/knew":

9. "I thought/knew that it was a cat."

   _____.

10. "I didn't think/know that it was this hot."

    _____.

11. "I thought/knew that you'll visit me."

    _____.

12. "Did you think/know that I was a Korean?"

    _____.

Translate to Korean using the (방)법 form:

13. "I don't know how to find it."

    _____.

14. "Please teach me how to use this watch."

    _____.

15. "Is there a way to speak Korean well?"

    _____.

How To

16. "Is there another way?"

_____.

Translate to English:

17. 컴퓨터를 어떻게 쓰는지 아세요?

_____.

18. 학교에 어떻게 가는지 몰라요.

_____.

19. 초보자에게 한국어를 어떻게 가르칠 수 있는지 알아요?

_____.

20. 저는 이거에 대해 어떻게 생각해야 하는지 몰라요.

_____.

21. 할 수 있겠다는 뜻이에요?

_____.

22. 같이 갈 거라는 뜻이에요?

_____.

23. 한국을 정말 좋아한다는 뜻이에요.

_____.

24. 어느 동네에 있어요?

_____.

25. 더 없을 줄 알았어.

_____.

Chapter 6	**How To**

26. 경치가 아주 예쁠 줄 알았는데 별로 안 그래요.

_____.

27. 정류장을 놓칠 줄 알았어!

_____.

28. 그 장면이 무서울 줄 알았어요.

_____.

29. 여기에 줄을 설 줄 모르는 사람이 많아요.

_____.

30. 선도 못 그리는데 당연히 그림 그릴 줄 모르지.

_____.

New Phrases

대단히 감사합니다.	"Thank you very much." (formal)

New Vocabulary

백화점	"department store"
대단히	"greatly," "incredibly"
동네	"neighborhood"
번	item number counter
정류장	"(bus) stop," "(bus) station"
정거장	"(train/bus) stop," "(train/bus) station"
(도)대체	"in the world" (adverb)
기숙사	"dormitory," "dorms"
숙소	"residence," "lodging"
줄	"a line (for waiting)"
줄(을) 서다	"to make a (standing) line," "to stand in line"

How To

선	"a line (in geometry)," "a wire"
완전히	"completely"
완전하다	"to be complete," "to be perfect"
근	"geun" (600 grams)
상품	"a product," "merchandise"
물건	"an item," "stuff"
경치	"view," "scenery"
장면	"(movie) scene"
길(을) 물어보다	"to ask the way," "to ask (for) directions"

Chapter 6

How To

Whether and If

Chapter 7

Conversation

딸:	엄마, 떡이 어디 있는지 아세요?
엄마:	어제 새로 샀는데 어디 있는지 기억이 안 나네.
딸:	동생이 어제 밤에 먹었을지도 모르겠네요.
엄마:	네 동생이 어제 야식을 먹긴 했는데 떡은 아니었던 거 같아.
딸:	떡을 좋아하는 애가 떡을 먹지를 않았다고요?
엄마:	응. 식탁 위에 치킨 뼈가 있었어.
딸:	치킨을 혼자 먹었으면 떡까지 먹지는 못했겠네요.
엄마:	아, 그렇지. 냉장고 맨 밑에 떡이 있는지 확인해 봐.
딸:	찾았어요! 여기 있네요.

This chapter will introduce a new use for a form that we have already learned – the 는지(를) 알다 form. Let's jump into the conversation and learn it along the way.

> 딸: 엄마, 떡이 어디 있는지 아세요?
>
> "Mom, do you know where the rice cake is?"

To Know "Whether" and "If": Action Verb Stem + 는지(를) 알다/모르다

You can use this form to say that you know or do not know *if* (whether) something or someone does something else (such as a *verb*). For example, "I don't know *if* the teacher likes apples," or "I don't know *whether* the teacher likes apples."

Chapter 7 — Whether and If

This form is used for talking about things that are *unknown*. In the previous example, whether or not the teacher likes apples is something that is not known to the speaker. If the speaker already knew *that* the teacher liked apples, then they could say it like this: 선생님이 사과를 좋아한다는 것을 알고 있어요 ("I know that the teacher likes apples."). We will talk about this more in detail throughout this chapter.

To make this form, take an *action verb stem* and attach 는지(를) – the 를 is *optional*. Then conjugate the verb 알다 ("to know") if you know, or 모르다 ("to not know") if you do not know.

선생님이 사과를 좋아하는지 몰라요.
"I don't know whether the teacher likes apples."
"I don't know if the teacher likes apples."

아기가 자고 있는지 알아요?
"Do you know whether the baby is sleeping?"
"Do you know if the baby is sleeping?"

이쑤시개가 남았는지 아세요?
"Do you know whether there are any toothpicks left?"
"Do you know if there are any toothpicks left?"

You will see 남다 ("to be remaining," "to be left over") conjugated to the *past tense* even when it is being used to mean that something is left over in the present. It can only be used in the future tense if you want to say that something *"will* be left over." For example, you could say 100 원이 남을 거예요 to mean, "There *will be* 100 Won left over," but if you wanted to say "There *is* 100 Won left over" then you would use 100 원이 남았어요.

잠자리가 벌레를 먹는지 알아요?
"Do you know whether dragonflies eat bugs?"
"Do you know if dragonflies eat bugs?"

여기서 셀카를 찍어도 되는지 아세요?
"Do you know whether it's okay to take a selfie here?"
"Do you know if it's okay to take a selfie here?"

셀카 is a *slang* word meaning "selfie" and comes from the words 셀프 (from the English word "self") and 카메라 ("camera").

철수가 어제 일을 했는지 몰라요.
"I don't know whether Chul-soo worked yesterday."
"I don't know if Chul-soo worked yesterday."

Whether and If

Chapter 7

Note that you can use an *action verb stem* in any tense that you would like, such as past tense, present tense, or future tense (using only the 겠다 form).

공부하겠는지 아세요?
"Do you know whether he'll study?"
"Do you know if he'll study?"

However, to use *descriptive verbs*, or to use the 것이다 future tense, we will need to learn a longer and more flexible version of this same form.

To Know "Whether" and "If": Verb Stem + (은/ㄴ/을/ㄹ/는) + 지 알다/모르다

This form is an expanded version of the same form we just covered. While there are certainly many options to choose from (은/ㄴ/을/ㄹ/는), they are all the same conjugations that we have already previously learned for other forms. You can use this form for both action verbs and descriptive verbs, and in any tense.

To use it, take a *verb stem* and conjugate it as an *adjective* to whatever tense you would like – past, present, or future. For a review of how to change an action verb into an adjective, see Chapter 4 of the second book. Here are a few examples.

하다:
    했는지 (Past Tense)
    하는지 (Present Tense)
    할지 (Future Tense)*

먹다:
    먹었는지 (Past Tense)
    먹는지 (Present Tense)
    먹을지 (Future Tense)

만들다:
    만들었는지 (Past Tense)
    만드는지 (Present Tense)
    만들지 (Future Tense)

춥다:
    추웠는지 (Past Tense)
    추운지 (Present Tense)
    추울지 (Future Tense)

Chapter 7: Whether and If

있다:
    있었는지 (Past Tense)
    있는지 (Present Tense)
    있을지 (Future Tense)

이다:
    이었는지 or 였는지 (Past Tense)
    인지 (Present Tense)
    일지 (Future Tense)

*Note that 할지, 하겠는지, and 할 건지 (from 할 것인지) are all possible ways to use this form in the *future tense*.

Let's take a look at a few example sentences.

내일도 오늘처럼 더울지 아나요?
"Do you know whether/if tomorrow will also be hot like today?"

모두가 좋아할지 모르잖아요.
"We don't know whether/if everyone will like it."

모두 is a *noun* and means "everyone." We also previously learned two other words meaning "everyone," 여러분 and 다들, which are used slightly differently. 여러분 is used when *addressing* "everyone," such as when speaking in front of a group of people *formally* – 여러분, 안녕하세요! ("Hello, everyone!"). 다들 is used when speaking *about* "everyone" and is an *informal* or *casual* word – 다들, 안녕하세요. ("How's everyone doing?"). 다들 can also translate as "you all" when used in casual speech. However, 다들 is not used as a regular noun, with particles and markers (에게, 이/가, 을/를, etc.). On the other hand, 모두 is a regular noun, and can be used with particles and markers. For example, while you could say 모두에게 선물을 주었어요 ("I gave a present to everyone."), it would be *incorrect* to say 다들에게 선물을 주었어요. Finally, note that 모두 cannot be used when addressing a group of people, so it cannot take the place of 여러분. 모두 is also not specifically a formal or casual word, so it can be used when speaking Korean both casually and formally.

소현이가 바쁜지 알아?
"Do you know whether So-hyun is busy?"
"Do you know if So-hyun is busy?"

시험이 어려웠는지 알고 싶어요.
"I want to know whether the test was difficult."
"I want to know if the test was difficult."

Whether and If

할머니가 오늘 집에 계실지 몰라요.
"I don't know whether my grandmother will be at home today."
"I don't know if my grandmother will be at home today."

Remember that this form is used for things that are *unknown* – this is why it can translate as "whether" or "if." However, up until now we have only focused on using this form with the verbs 알다 and 모르다. It can also be used with many other verbs, as long as what you are talking about is something that is *unknown*. Here is a quick example.

할머니가 오늘 집에 계실지 궁금해요.
"I'm curious whether/if my grandmother will be at home today."

We are free to use whatever verb we would like with this form (besides 알다 and 모르다), as long as what we are talking about is something *unknown* to us. Here, what is unknown is whether grandmother will be at home today. Let's look at a few more examples.

철수가 바쁜지 알려주세요.
"Please tell me whether/if Chul-soo is busy."

한국어를 할 수 있는지 말해 주세요.
"Please tell me whether/if you can speak Korean."

영화가 재미있었는지 신경을 안 썼어요.
"I didn't care whether/if the movie was entertaining."

이미 했는지 물어봤어요.
"I asked whether/if he already did it."

Question Words

This same form has one additional usage with *question words* (such as 뭐, 어떻게, 언제, etc.). Here is a quick example.

그 사람의 성이 뭔지 몰라요.
"I don't know *what* that person's last name is."

Note that 이름 ("name") is most commonly used when referring to a person's *first name*.

Remember that 뭔지 is short for 무엇인지 (무엇 + 이다). Here, the form is still being used with something that is *unknown* – in this case, the person's last name. It is common to see this form used with question words. Here are some more examples.

Chapter 7

Whether and If

어디 있는지 알고 있어요.
"I know *where* it is."

Literally, this sentence translates as "I know whether/if he is *where*."

뭐라고 했는지 들었어요?
"Did you hear *what* he said?"

휴대폰을 어디서 충전할 수 있는지 몰라요.
"I don't know *where* I can charge my mobile phone."

걔가 여기에 왜 왔는지 몰라.
"I don't know *why* he came here."

몇 개를 샀는지 알아요?
"Do you know *how many* she bought?"

In addition to the normal question words, it is fine to use any word that shows that something is *unknown* (such as 몇 개, meaning "how many").

제 몸무게의 두 배면 얼마인지 아세요?
"If it's double my bodyweight, do you know how much that is?"

배 is the *counter* for "fold," such as two fold ("double"), three fold ("triple"), ten fold, and further. It is used with *Pure Korean numbers*.

언제 만났는지 말해 봐.
"Tell me *when* you met."

뭘 먹었는지 몰라요?
"You don't know *what* you ate?"

어떻게 할 수 있을지 몰라요.
"I don't know *how* I can do it."

While it might seem completely new to use the form this way with question words, it is actually similar to the "how to" form that we learned last chapter. When we learned that form as "how to" we only used it with the adverb 어떻게 ("how") and action verbs in the present tense. This chapter's focus has been on using that same form, but with a larger variety of verbs, adverbs, and tenses. Here are three quick examples that show the same grammar form used in different ways.

Whether and If

어떻게 만드는지 아세요?
"Do you know *how* to make it?"

어떻게 만드는지 가르쳐 주세요.
"Please teach me *how* to make it."

어떻게 만들어야 할지 알려주세요.
"Please let me know *how* I'll have to make it."

Before we continue the conversation, here are some more example sentences using this form with question words.

서울이 이렇게 추울지 알고 있었어요?
"Did you know whether/if Seoul would be this cold?"

어떻게 했는지 배우고 싶어요.
"I want to learn *how* he did it."

뭐가 더 쉬운지 알고 싶어요.
"I want to know *what* is easier."

누가 가장 똑똑한지 맞혀 보세요.
"Try to guess *who* is the smartest."

맞히다 is the causative form of 맞다 and is commonly used with the 보다 form to mean "to guess." You might hear this used when someone asks you to guess their age – [제 나이를] 맞혀 보세요 ("Try to guess [my age].").

어디서 시작해야 할지 고민이에요.
"I'm worried *where* I have to start from."

While we learned that 고민(을) 하다 means "to be concerned" or "to (slightly) worry," it is also commonly used with 이다 ("to be") as 고민이다 (literally, "to be a concern" or "to be a worry").

세일 기간이 언제까지인지 아세요?
"Do you know *when* the sale period is until?"

왜 했는지 이해할 수 없어요.
"I can't understand *why* he did it."

한국어를 어디서 배웠는지 얘기해 주세요.
"Please tell me *where* you learned Korean."

Chapter 7

Whether and If

도대체 누가 내 치즈를 먹었는지 몰라요.
"I don't know *who* on earth ate my cheese."

풍선을 좋아하는지 몰라요.
"I don't know whether/if he likes balloons."

Remember that this form is used for talking about things that are *unknown* – in fact, "whether" and "if" are also used in English for talking about things that are unknown. Let's get back to the conversation.

엄마: 어제 새로 샀는데 어디 있는지 기억이 안 나네.
"I bought a new one yesterday, but I don't remember where it is."

We learned about the *adjective* 새 ("new") in Chapter 3, but now let's talk about the *adverb* 새로 meaning "new(ly)," or "anew." Both 새 and 새로 can translate as "new," but they are used differently. As we learned previously, 새 is used as an *adjective*.

어제 새 전자레인지를 샀어요.
"I bought a new microwave yesterday."

새로 is used as an *adverb* when you do something *newly* – for the first time, or for the first time in a long time.

어제 프라이팬를 새로 샀어요.
"I bought a (new) pan yesterday (and it was my first time in a long time)."

새로 이사왔어요.
"I (newly) moved here (for my first time)."

새로 가입했어요.
"I'm a new member."

가입(을) 하다 means "to become a member" or "to join (a group)," so this sentence could more literally be translated as "I newly became a member" or "I newly joined."

Remember: 기억(이) 나다

In the first book we learned the verb 기억(을) 하다 ("to remember"). Let's learn another way to say "remember" using 기억(이) 나다. The noun 기억 means "memory," and the verb 나다 here means "to occur" or "to come to mind," so 기억(이) 나다 literally means "a memory comes to mind." It is used in the general sense to mean "I remember something (because it came to my mind)."

Whether and If

Chapter 7

Alternatively, you can still also use 기억(을) 하다 to mean "I remember something (because I remembered it myself)." Both have the same translation in English as "to remember."

기억해요?
기억나요?
"Do you remember?"

누가 했는지 기억하지 않아요.
누가 했는지 기억이 안 나요.
"I don't remember who did it."

Only 기억(을) 하다 can be used in *commands*. Telling someone to remember something by saying 기억(이) 나세요 would be *incorrect*.

In addition, if you want to say that you are *unable* to remember something ("can not remember...") then you must use 기억(을) 하다. Saying 기억을 하지 못해요 ("I can't remember.") would be correct, but 기억이 나지 못해요 would be *incorrect*. The reason for this is because 하다 ("to do") and 나다 ("to occur," "to come to mind") are two different types of action verbs – but do not worry about this right now. We will discuss these types of verbs in Chapter 15.

Also, while 기억(을) 하다 can be used with the Object Marker to say *what* it is that you remember, 기억(이) 나다 is used with the Subject Marker (이/가). For example:

그 사람을 기억해요.
그 사람이 기억나요.
"I remember that person."

딸: 동생이 어제 밤에 먹었을지도 모르겠네요.
"My younger sibling might've eaten it yesterday night."

"Might" and "May": Verb Stem + (을/ㄹ) + 지도 모르다

One way to say that something "might" or "may" do something, or "might" or "may" be a certain way, is by using a similar form to one that we have already learned in this chapter. For example, you could use this form to say "You might/may like fish if you try it."

To use this form, take any verb stem (action verb or descriptive verb) in the past tense or future tense (with the 것이다 form) and attach 을 if it ends in a *consonant*, or attach ㄹ if it ends in a *vowel*. Then attach 지, followed by 도 ("also," "even," "too"). Finally conjugate 모르다 (or 모르겠다) in the *present tense*.

Chapter 7

Whether and If

생선을 먹어 보면 좋아할지도 몰라요.
"You might like fish if you try it."

티비를 샀을지도 몰라요.
"He might've bought a TV."

> **Advanced**
>
> **Past Tense**
>
> Throughout this book you'll find examples of grammar forms that can use verb stems in the past tense. The past tense verb stem is commonly used in grammar forms (such as the "might" and "may" form) and it is important to be familiar with it. For example, you can even attach the future tense forms (겠다 or 것이다) to a past tense verb stem to add the meaning "would have (been/done)." This kind of usage is less common, but you will see it from time to time. Here are four examples.
>
> 추울 거예요.
> "It will be cold."
>
> 춥겠어요.
> "It will/must be cold."
>
> 추웠을 거예요.
> "It would have been cold."
>
> 추웠겠어요.
> "It would/must have been cold."
>
> We will also learn more about the past tense in Chapter 17.

엄마가 집에 계실지도 몰라요.
"Mom might be at home."

오늘 조금 일찍 잘지도 몰라요.
"I might sleep a little early today."

그럴지도 몰라요.
"It might be (so)."

옷장에 안 들어갈지도 모르겠네.
"It might not go into the closet."

While 들어가다 means "to go in," a more natural translation for this example could be "It might not fit in the closet."

Whether and If

Chapter 7

Advanced

Whether or Not

We have learned how to say "whether" and "if," but there is one more similar form that we can learn – "whether or not." While this form has the same meaning as the one we learned already, it is a bit more specific because it shows that there is an option of *not* doing something, or *not* being a certain way.

To use this form, make a regular sentence using the "whether" or "if" form as we learned. Then, add in the *negative* version of the same verb, conjugated with the same ending as the first. For example, if you use the verb 있다, then its opposite verb is 없다. If you use 가다, then its opposite verb is 가지 않다 or 안 가다. Here are a few examples.

집에 있을지 없을지 몰라요.
"I don't know if he will be at home or not."

김치를 좋아하는지 안 좋아하는지 알고 싶네요.
김치를 좋아하는지 싫어하는지 알고 싶네요.
"I want to know if he likes kimchi or not."

In the above example, the opposite verb of 좋아하다 can be either 안 좋아하다 ("to not like") or 싫어하다 ("to dislike").

비가 올지 안 올지 궁금해요.
"I'm curious if it'll rain or not."

한국 사람인지 아닌지 아세요?
"Do you know if he's a Korean or not?"

Note that if you are using a *descriptive verb*, you can use the verb 아니다 ("to not be") instead of the second negative verb. If you do this, remember to conjugate 아니다 with the same ending as the first verb.

지금 철수가 바쁜지 아닌지 알려주세요.
"Please tell me whether Chul-soo is busy now or not."

시험이 어려웠는지 아니었는지 알고 싶어요.
"I want to know if the test was difficult or not."

엄마: 네 동생이 어제 야식을 먹긴 했는데 떡은 아니었던 거 같아.

"Your younger sibling did eat a late-night snack yesterday, but I don't think it was rice cake."

Emphasizing Verbs: Action Verb Stem + 기 + (는/도/를) 하다

You can add emphasis to an action verb by using the 기 ending and the verb 하다. This does not change the meaning of the verb.

To use it, take an *action verb stem* in the *present tense* and attach 기. Then attach the particle 는, 도, or 를. The type of emphasis that is added to the verb will depend on which particle you choose, and these particles function in the same way as they normally would. Finally, conjugate the verb 하다. Here are a few examples.

Chapter 7: Whether and If

수영해요.
"I swim."

수영하기를 해요.
"I *swim*."

수영하기는 해요.
"As for swimming, I do."
"I *do* swim."

수영하기도 해요.
"I *swim* too (in addition to doing other things)."

Commonly, 기는 will be shortened to 긴, and 기를 will be shortened to 길.

> **Adv**: You can add *further* emphasis by using the same verb after 기(는/도/를) as you used before. For example, you can say 가기는 갔어요 to mean "I *did* go." You can also use this with descriptive verbs. For example, you can say 맛있기는 맛있었지만... ("It *was* good, but...").

> 딸: 떡을 좋아하는 애가 떡을 먹지를 않았다고요?
> "You're saying that a kid who likes rice cake didn't eat rice cake?"

지(를) 않다 and 지(가) 않다

We learned that we can use the 지 않다 form for both action verbs and descriptive verbs to change it into a negative verb. In addition, in the second book we learned that we can use 지는 않다 or 지도 않다 to add emphasis to the verb. This emphasis is similar to the emphasis added with the 기(는/도/를) 하다 form that we just covered, but for negative verbs. First, here are some examples using each of those.

내일 학교에 가지는 않을 거예요.
"As for going to school tomorrow, I won't."

내일 학교에 가지도 않을 거예요.
"I won't even go to school tomorrow."

The particles 를 and 가 can also be used, but only in specific cases. 지(를) 않다 can only be used after *action verbs*, and 지(가) 않다 can only be used after *descriptive verbs*.

수영하지를 않아요.
"I don't *swim*."

Whether and If

쉽지가 않아요.
"It's not *easy*."

엄마: 응. 식탁 위에 치킨 뼈가 있었어.
"Yeah. There was a chicken bone on the table."

딸: 치킨을 혼자 먹었으면 떡까지 먹지는 못했겠네요.
"If they ate chicken all by themselves, they wouldn't have been able to eat rice cakes too."

Even: 까지

In the first book we learned that 까지 can be used directly after a noun (such as a location or a time) to mean "until" or "(up) to." 까지 can also be used to mean "even."

"But doesn't the particle 도 mean 'even' too?" You can use 까지 when you want to *emphasize* the meaning of "even." Here are a few examples (emphasis has been added with italics).

저도 해야 됐어요.
"I had to do it too/also."
"Even I had to do it."

저까지 해야 됐어요.
"*Even I* had to do it."

면허증도 잃어 버렸어요.
"I lost my driver's license too/also."

면허증까지 잃어 버렸어요.
"I *even* lost my *driver's license*."

어제 비도 왔어.
"It also rained yesterday."

어제 비까지 왔어.
"It *even rained* yesterday."

나도 가도 괜찮아?
"Is it okay if I go too/also?"

Whether and If

나까지 가도 괜찮아?
"Is it okay if *even I* go?"

어제 다리가 부러졌는데 오늘은 손도 다쳤어요.
"Yesterday I broke my leg, and today I hurt my hand too."

어제 다리가 부러졌는데 오늘은 손까지 다쳤어요.
"Yesterday I broke my leg, and today I *even* hurt my *hand*."

Reviewing 지 않다 vs. 지 못하다

In the first book we learned that the 지 않다 form can be used with both action verbs and descriptive verbs to make them negative, and the 지 못하다 form can be used with action verbs to say that you "can not" do the verb.

Note that using the 지 않다 form can mean that you are *willingly* not doing the verb, while the 지 못하다 form means that you are simply *unable* to do it. This is important, because the sentence 한국어를 하지 않아요 can mean "I do not (intentionally) speak Korean," while 한국어를 하지 못해요 means "I cannot speak Korean." Using the first sentence could come across as rude to a Korean ("You speak Korean, but you're not going to use it to me?").

Let's go back to the conversation.

> 엄마: 아, 그렇지. 냉장고 맨 밑에 떡이 있는지 확인해 봐.
> "Ah, that's right. Check if there's rice cake in the very bottom of the refrigerator."

"The very": 맨

You can use 맨 before a *postposition* or an adverb related to *time* to mean "the most." A more natural translation for this is "the very."

서랍 맨 뒤에 있어요.
"It's in the very back of the drawer."

Since 뒤 means "behind" or "after," a more literal translation for this example would be "It's in the most behind of the drawer."

맨 위에 놓아 주세요.
"Please put it on the very top."

맨 먼저 손을 씻으세요.
"Wash your hands first (and before anything/anyone else)."

Whether and If

Chapter 7

A more literal translation of this example would be "Wash your hands the very first."

버스에서 맨 마지막에 내렸어요.
"I got off the bus last."

A more literal translation of this example would be "I got off the bus at the very end."

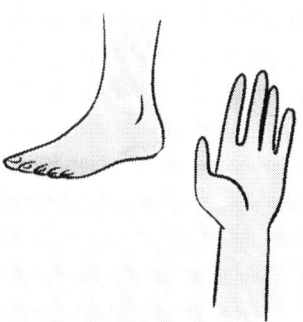

"Bare": 맨

맨 can also mean "bare," such as in 맨발 ("barefoot") and 맨손 ("bare hands"). Note that this 맨 is a different word, and is not related to 맨 ("the most," "the very").

뜨거운 냄비를 맨손으로 잡지 마세요.
"Don't grab a hot pot with bare hands."

딸: 찾았어요! 여기 있네요.
"I found it! It's here."

Practice

Translate to Korean using the "whether" and "if" form with 알다/모르다:

1. "I don't know whether/if the baby is still hungry."

   _____.

2. "I want to know whether/if it is a snake."

   _____.

3. "Do you know whether/if it is safe?"

   _____.

Whether and If

Chapter 7

4. "Do you know whether/if there is an apple on top of the kitchen table?"

_____.

Translate to Korean using the "might" and "may" form with 지도 모르다:

5. "I might go to the supermarket."

_____.

6. "It might be fun."

_____.

7. "There might be an extra room."

_____.

8. "Tomorrow it might be hotter than today."

_____.

9. "I might have to buy a new TV."

_____.

Translate to Korean:

10. "I don't know who did it."

_____.

11. "I know where the elevator is."

_____.

12. "I want to know what that is."

_____.

13. "I am curious why you met Chul-soo."

_____.

Whether and If

14. "I don't remember that person."

_____.

15. "Please check when the meeting will start."

_____.

Translate to English:

16. 병원에 자판기가 있는지 아세요?

_____.

17. 손잡이를 잡아야 하는지 아닌지 몰라요.

_____.

18. 망치를 어디서 살 수 있는지 아세요?

_____.

19. 김치가 어떻게 이렇게 맛있는지 몰라요.

_____.

20. 사람 몇 명이 올 건지 알아봤어요?

_____.

21. 제 지갑에 돈이 조금 있을지도 몰라요.

_____.

22. 맨 끝에 있을지도 몰라요.

_____.

23. 철수가 내 음식까지 먹어 버렸어!

_____.

Chapter 7: Whether and If

New Vocabulary

맞히다	"to guess (correctly)"
맞혀 보다	"to try to guess"
세일	"sale"
기간	"a period (of time)," "a term (of time)"
새로	"new(ly)," "anew" (adverb)
가입(을) 하다	"to become a member," "to join (a group)"
기억(이) 나다	"to remember," "to come to mind"
야식	"late-night snack"
식탁	"(kitchen) table"
다리(가) 부러지다	"to break a leg" (literally, "a leg breaks")
다치다	"to get (physically) hurt"
서랍	"drawer"
냄비	"a pot"
전자레인지	"microwave"
전자레인지에 데우다	"to microwave (something)"
데우다	"to heat/warm up (something)"
리모컨	"remote control"
전기	"electricity"
옷장	"closet"
옷걸이	"(clothes) hanger"
프라이팬	"(frying) pan"
풍선	"balloon"
충전(을) 하다	"to charge (electronics)"
잠자리	"dragonfly"
코끼리	"elephant"
앵무새	"parrot"
나비	"butterfly"
거북이	"turtle"
셀카	"selfie" (slang)
자판기	"vending machine"
엘리베이터	"elevator"

Whether and If

Chapter 7

에스컬레이터	"escalator"
손잡이	"handle"
이쑤시개	"toothpick"
치실	"floss"
치실질(을) 하다	"to floss"
망치	"hammer"
배	fold counter
모두	"everyone"
여부(의)	"extra," "surplus" (adjective)
성	"last name"
휴대폰	"mobile phone"
맨	"the most," "the very"
맨발	"barefoot"
맨손	"bare hands"

Chapter 7

Whether and If

Through

Conversation

은경:	아진아. 혹시 단 거 좋아해?
아진:	응, 나 단 거 진짜 좋아해. 왜?
은경:	내가 남자 친구 주려고 마카롱을 만들었는데 한 번 먹어 볼래?
아진:	그래.... 와, 이거 진짜 맛있다! 학원에서 배운 거야?
은경:	아니. 그냥 혼자 인터넷을 통해서 배웠어.
아진:	정말? 혼자 배운 거치고는 정말 잘했는데.
은경:	고마워. 처음엔 다 태웠는데 하루에 한 번씩 만들었더니 실력이 조금 늘었어.
아진:	역시, 여러 번 연습함으로써 늘지 않는 건 없지. 남자 친구가 좋아하겠다.
은경:	그렇지? 다행이다. 다음에 다른 거 만들면 또 가져올게.

은경: 아진아. 혹시 단 거 좋아해?

"A-jin. (By chance) do you like sweet things?"

아진: 응, 나 단 거 진짜 좋아해. 왜?

"Yeah, I love sweet things. Why?"

Chapter 8

Through

While we learned that the verb 사랑(을) 하다 means "to love," this verb is only used for loving *someone* and not *something* (such as food). It is more natural to use an adverb such as 많이 ("a lot"), 아주 ("very"), 정말 ("really"), or 진짜 ("really") with the verb 좋아하다 when you want to say that you love *something*.

> 은경: 내가 남자 친구 주려고 마카롱을 만들었는데 한 번 먹어 볼래?
> "I made macarons to give them to my boyfriend, so do you want to try it (once)?"

Remember that the (으)려고 form is used to show *intention*, so another translation for the conversation sentence could be "I made macarons intending to give them to my boyfriend [...]." For a review of this, see Chapter 17 of the second book.

> 아진: 그래.... 와, 이거 진짜 맛있다! 학원에서 배운 거야?
> "Sure.... Wow, these are really good! Did you learn this at an academy?"

Past Tense: Action Verb Stem + (은/ㄴ) 것이다

We have learned two main future tense forms – 겠다 and (을/ㄹ) 것이다. There are two main past tense forms as well – ㅆ다 (ㅆ어요, ㅆ습니다, etc.) as we previously learned, and (은/ㄴ) 것이다.

To make this form, take an *action verb stem* and attach 은 if it ends in a *consonant*, or attach ㄴ if it ends in a *vowel*. Then add 것, and conjugate the verb 이다 ("to be"). Let's look at a few examples.

> 누가 했어요?
> 누가 한 거예요?
> "Who did it?"
>
> 같이 갔어요.
> 같이 간 거예요.
> "We went together."
>
> 어디서 만났어요?
> 어디서 만난 거예요?
> "Where did you meet?"
>
> 벌써 다 먹어 버렸어요.
> 벌써 다 먹어 버린 거예요.
> "He already ate it all."

Through

The difference between using the normal past tense form and (은/ㄴ) 것이다 is similar to the difference between using the future tense forms 겠다 and (을/ㄹ) 것이다, which we covered in Chapter 3 of the second book. Using the normal past tense form puts more emphasis on the *verb* in a sentence, while using (은/ㄴ) 것이다 puts more emphasis on the *subject* of that verb. Here's an example.

제가 했어요.
"I **did** it."

제가 한 거예요.
"**I** did it."

While this emphasis is small, I have exaggerated it here to help explain the difference. Of these two forms, the normal past tense form will be used more commonly, but it's important to know both ways.

은경: 아니. 그냥 혼자 인터넷을 통해서 배웠어.
"No. I just learned it alone through the internet."

Through: Noun + (을/를) 통해(서)

Saying "through" in Korean works in a similar way in English. It can be used for both *physically* going through something ("I entered through the window.") and for doing something "through" or "by way of" something ("I learned art through books.").

To use it, take a *noun* and attach 을 if it ends in a *consonant*, or attach 를 if it ends in a *vowel*. Then add 통해(서) and finish the rest of the sentence – the 서 is *optional*.

창문을 통해서 들어갔어요.
"I entered through the window."

책을 통해서 미술을 배웠어요.
"I learned art through books."

친구를 통해서 만났어요.
"We met through a friend."

코를 통해서 숨쉬고 있어요.
"I'm breathing through my nose."

거울을 통해서 얼굴을 봤어요.
"I saw his face through the mirror."

Through

뉴스를 통해서 친구의 소식을 들었어요.
"I heard (the news) about my friend through the news."

While 뉴스 means "the news" when referring to the *media*, 소식 means "news" as in 소식을 들었어요? ("Have you heard the news?") or 좋은 소식이 있어요 ("I have good news.").

운동을 통해서 살을 많이 뺐어요.
"I lost a lot of weight through exercise."

Note that using 통해(서) is different than using (으)로 which is used to mean "using" or "by," among other translations. For a review of the (으)로 form see Chapter 3 of the second book.

아진: 정말? 혼자 배운 거치고는 정말 잘했는데.
"Really? For something you learned alone you did a really good job."

"For": Noun + 치고(는)

You can use this form to say that something is out of the ordinary *for* being a noun. For example, "You speak Korean well *for* a foreigner."

To use it, take a *noun* and attach 치고(는) – the Topic Marker (here, 는) is *optional*. It can also be used with verbs that have been changed into nouns using 것 ("thing").

외국 사람치고는 한국어를 잘하시네요.
"You speak Korean well for a foreigner."

초등학생치고는 키가 커요.
"He's tall for an elementary student."

새로운 자동차치고는 싸요.
"It's cheap for a new car."

큰 도시치고는 깨끗하네요.
"It's clean for a big city."

겨울치고는 별로 안 추운데요.
"It's not really cold for winter."

Through

Culture Notes

온돌

Most apartments in Korea lack centralized heating, because electricity can be rather expensive. Instead, to avoid being cold during the winters (in addition to using blankets) most Koreans utilize a heated floor system, called 온돌. A long time ago Koreans would keep actual fires underneath their homes in winter to keep the floors warm directly. Modern heated floors are a series of tubes underneath the floors that provide slow, consistent warmth when turned on.

어린 아이치고는 힘이 세네요.
"He's strong for a young kid."

백화점 물건치고는 많이 안 비싸네요.
"It's not very expensive for a department store item."

내가 만든 거치고는 아주 훌륭해.
"It's very wonderful for something that I made."

3 일 동안 잠을 자지 않은 거치고는 멀쩡하네.
"I feel fine for not having slept for 3 days."

While it is not required, this form will often appear together with the 네(요) ending.

Adv A common shortening of 치고는 is 치곤.

은경: 고마워. 처음엔 다 태웠는데 하루에 한 번씩 만들었더니 실력이 조금 늘었어.
"Thanks. At first I burned them all, but I made them once each day and I got a bit better."

Through

Chapter 8

태우다 can be used to say that someone burns something, and 타다 can be used to say that something burns (itself). For example, you can say that you burned a pizza (피자를 태웠어요), or you can say that the pizza burned in the oven (피자가 오븐에서 탔어요) without admitting guilt. We will talk about verbs such as these more in detail later in this book (in Chapter 10 and Chapter 15).

"Each," "A," and "Per": 에 & 씩

You can use the particle 에 ("to," "at", "in") to also mean "each," "a," or "per." For example, "I drink 3 glasses of water each/a/per day." Here are some examples.

하루에 물을 3 잔 마셔요.
"I drink 3 glasses of water each/a/per day."

1,000 원에 10 개를 살 수 있어요.
"You can buy 10 per 1,000 Won."

1 킬로에 만 원이에요.
"It's 10,000 Won per kilo."

1 년에 2 번 꽃이 펴요.
"Twice a year the flowers blossom."

에 is commonly used in this way together with the ending 씩. You can add 씩 directly after a word (usually a *counter*) and it emphasizes the meaning of "each" for that word. Adding 씩 is *optional*.

하루에 물을 3 잔씩 마셔요.
"I drink 3 glasses of water each day."

이틀에 한 번씩 하려고 해요.
"I try to do it once each two days."

아진: 역시, 여러 번 연습함으로써 늘지 않는 건 없지. 남자 친구가 좋아하겠다.

> "As expected, there's nothing you won't improve at through practicing a number of times. Your boyfriend will like them."

Through: Action Verb Stem + (음/ㅁ) + 으로써

You can also say "through" (or "by way of") with *action verbs* and not only nouns. For example, "I learned art through *reading* books." In this case, this "through" cannot be used for *physically* going through something.

Through

> **Adv** — Note that by using this form, you are technically transforming the action verb into a noun using the (음/ㅁ) form and then attaching 으로써. You can review this (음/ㅁ) form in Chapter 19 of the second book.

To use it, take an *action verb stem* and attach 음 if it ends in a *consonant*, or attach ㅁ if it ends in a *vowel*. Then attach 으로써 and finish the rest of the sentence. Here are a few conjugation examples.

하다 → 함으로써
먹다 → 먹음으로써
만들다 → 만듦으로써

Note that verb stems ending in ㄹ will *not* remove the ㄹ when conjugating with this form. Here are a few example sentences.

책을 읽음으로써 미술을 배웠어요.
"I learned art through reading books."

봉사를 함으로써 얻는 행복이 커요.
"The happiness that you get through doing service is large."

민속촌을 구경함으로써 역사를 공부할 수 있어요.
"You can study history by sightseeing at a folk village."

Culture Notes

민속촌 ("folk village")

A common attraction for tourists (as well as Koreans) is a 민속촌, which is a traditional style Korean village. These villages are set up as an interactive museum. You can watch performances of dance, art, music, and martial arts, taste traditional food and snacks, play games, and observe common workers recreating older techniques for their crafts. Since 민속촌 are designed to appear like a real traditional village, Korean production companies often use these as filming sites for TV dramas. If you stop by on the right day, you might even catch a glimpse of your favorite Korean celebrity.

Through

매일 도서관에서 열심히 공부함으로써 한국 역사에 대해 배웠어요.
"I learned about Korean history through studying hard in the library everyday."

친구가 알려준 방법을 씀으로써 돈을 벌었어요.
"I earned money through using a method that my friend told me about."

다른 사람에 대해 안 좋은 얘기를 함으로써 얻는 것은 아무것도 없어요.
"There's nothing that you get from saying bad things about other people."

> **Advanced**
>
> **About: 관해(서) & 관한**
>
> You can use 관해(서) in the same way as 대해(서) to mean "about" or "on." You can also use 관한 in the same way as 대한 when it is used before a noun. Using 관해(서) is a bit more *formal*, and is therefore used less. Here are two examples.
>
> 주로 한국 문화에 관해서 공부하고 싶어요.
> "I mainly want to study about the Korean culture."
>
> 한국 문화에 관한 책을 찾고 있어요.
> "I'm looking for a book on Korean culture."

매일 아침 달리기를 함으로써 건강 관리를 하고 있어요.
"I'm maintaining my health through running every morning."

"Many": 여러

여러 is an *adjective* that means "a number of" or "many." While its meaning seems similar to the adjective 많은 (from 많다), it is only used with certain nouns. Here are a few common examples of 여러.

여러 사람 ("a number of people," "many people")

오늘 여러 사람을 만났어요.
"Today I met a number of people."

여러 가지 ("a number of types," "many types," "various types")

여러 가지 음식을 먹어 보고 싶어요.
"I want to try eating various types of food."

Note that 가지 is also commonly used with *Pure Korean numbers* to mean "type(s)" or "kind(s)."

Through

여러 번 ("a number of times," "many times," "repeatedly")

여러 번 말을 안 해도 돼요.
"You don't have to repeatedly say it."

Adv | 여러분 ("everyone") originally comes from 여러 and 분, the *honorific noun* for "person."

은경: 그렇지? 다행이다. 다음에 다른 거 만들면 또 가져올게.

"Yeah? That's good. Next time if I make something different I'll bring it again."

Practice

Conjugate the following using the 으로써 form:

1. 김치를 먹다

    _____.

2. 공부(를) 하다

    _____.

3. 노래(를) 부르다

    _____.

4. 한국에서 살다

    _____.

Translate to Korean:

5. "The wind came in through the hole."

    _____.

6. "I became a singer through an audition."

    _____.

Through

7. "I learned it through the newspaper."

_____.

8. "You can prevent a cold through taking vitamins."

_____.

9. "I learn more things through meeting new people."

_____.

10. "Your hands are pretty for a man."

_____.

11. "You have a lot of money for a student."

_____.

12. "I study 5 hours each week."

_____.

Translate to English:

13. 편지를 통해서 소식을 전했어요.

_____.

14. 철수가 인터넷에 올린 여러 동영상을 통해서 한국어를 배웠어요.

_____.

15. 그 모임에 참석함으로써 많은 사람들을 만날 수 있었어요.

_____.

16. 차를 마심으로써 스트레스를 풀어요.

_____.

Through

17. 그 책의 내용 읽음으로써 새로운 사실을 깨달았어요.

_____.

18. 세금을 냄으로써 시민이 될 수 있어요.

_____.

19. 아버지께 용돈을 드림으로써 사랑을 표현해요.

_____.

20. 대부분의 사람들은 하루에 7 시간씩 잠을 자요.

_____.

21. 첫 시험치고는 정말 어려웠네요.

_____.

22. 공부를 안 한 거치고는 성적이 좋았어요.

_____.

23. 종이로 만든 것치고는 튼튼해요.

_____.

24. 이미 여러 번 봤어요.

_____.

New Phrases

다행이에요.	"That's fortunate.," "I'm glad."

New Vocabulary

마카롱	"macaron"
타다	"(something) burns"
태우다	"to burn (something)"

Chapter 8 — Through

실력	"skill," "ability"
늘다	"to be increased," "to be improved"
실력(이) 늘다	"to get better (at something)," "a skill/ability improves"
여러	"a number of," "many" (adjective)
여러 사람	"a number of people," "many people"
여러 가지	"a number of types," "many types," "various types"
여러 번	"a number of times," "many times," "repeatedly"
가지	"a type," "a kind"
오븐	"oven"
다행이다	"to be fortunate," "to be a good thing"
다행히	"fortunately" (adverb)
불행하게도	"unfortunately" (adverb)
숨	"a breath"
숨(을) 쉬다	"to breathe"
소식	"news"
살(을) 빼다	"to lose weight"
외국 사람	"foreigner"
멀쩡하다	"to have no problems," "to be/feel fine"
피다	"to blossom (flowers)"
봉사	"service (to others)"
봉사(를) 하다	"to do service (to others)"
관리	"maintenance," "administration"
관리자	"supervisor," "administrator"
관리(를) 하다	"to maintain," "to administer"
달리기	"running"
달리기(를) 하다	"to do running," "to run"
구멍	"a hole"
시민	"citizen"
세금	"tax"
요금	"a fee," "a charge"
거스름돈	"change (from a transaction)"

Through

할인	"a discount"
예약	"reservation"
예약(을) 하다	"to reserve," "to make a reservation"
구경	"sightseeing," "looking around"
구경(을) 하다	"to sightsee," "to look around"
민속촌	"folk village"
내용	"content(s)"
깨닫다	"to realize"
인식(을) 하다	"to realize," "to recognize"
오디션	"audition"
비타민	"vitamin"
비타민(을) 먹다	"to take vitamins"
예방	"prevention"
예방(을) 하다	"to prevent"
인터넷	"internet"
올리다	"to put up," "to upload"
다운(을) 받다	"to download"
파일	"(computer) file"
참석(을) 하다	"to attend"
온돌	"heated floor"
초등학생	"elementary student"
중학생	"middle school student"
고등학생	"high school student"
대학생	"college student," "university student"

Chapter 8

Through

Titles

Chapter 9

Conversation

제레미:	안녕하세요. 고급 한국어 수업 교수님이시죠?
박재석 교수:	네, 제가 고급 한국어 수업을 가르치는 박재석 교수입니다.
제레미:	질문이 있어서 찾아왔는데 지금 괜찮으세요?
박재석 교수:	미안하지만 지금은 통화 중인데 잠깐만 기다려 줄래요?
제레미:	네, 그럼 밖에서 기다리겠습니다.

10 분 뒤...

박재석 교수:	오래 걸려서 미안해요. 들어오세요.
제레미:	감사합니다.
박재석 교수:	무슨 일이라고 했죠?
제레미:	다음 학기에 제가 고급 한국어 수업을 들을 수 있는지 궁금해서요.
박재석 교수:	한국어를 어느 정도 할 수 있는지에 따라 다르지만 학생은 한국어를 잘해서 가능할 것 같네요.
제레미:	감사합니다. 한국어 공부를 열심히 하는 편이지만 제가 실수하면 고쳐 주세요.
박재석 교수:	그래요. 그럼 벌써 필요할 리는 없겠지만 지난 학기에 내 수업을 들은 선배 학생을 소개시켜 줄게요.
제레미:	네. 그게 좋을 것 같네요. 그럼 수업 시간에 뵙겠습니다.

Chapter 9

Titles

This chapter will introduce some additional *titles* (ways of referring to other people). Up until now we have been limited to using a person's name, relationship title (such as 형, etc.), or 선생님 (among a few other options) when talking to others. Along the way we will also cover how to use a new important grammar form with the verbs 가다 ("to go") and 오다 ("to come"). Let's get started.

> 제레미: 안녕하세요. 고급 한국어 수업 교수님이시죠?
> "Hello. Are you the advanced Korean class professor?"

Note that while 안녕하세요 can only be used to mean "hello," 안녕 (when speaking *casually*) can mean both "hello" ("hi") and "goodbye" ("bye").

More about Titles

In the previous two books we learned how to refer to other people using *titles* such as 선생님, 오빠, 형, 누나, 언니, 아저씨, 아줌마, and more depending on the situation. We also learned a few words for directly saying "you," as well as when and not it is and is not appropriate to use them. However, we have not finished talking about titles, so here are a few more tips.

If you want to specify who you are talking *about* (if it's not already clear) you can also add a title after a person's name – full name or last name. Here are a few examples with the name 김철수.

선생님: 김철수 선생님 or 김 선생님
대통령: 김철수 대통령 or 김 대통령
회장: 김철수 회장 or 김 회장
사장: 김철수 사장 or 김 사장

Note that if it is already clear which teacher (or other title) that you are talking about, it is *optional* to add the person's full name or last name before their title. It's perfectly fine to use a title on its own.

> **Adv** Another way to say "you" is with 그대 ("you"). This word is a much older-sounding word and is not used anymore in regular speech, but is still used commonly in *songs* and *poems*.

Using 님

In the conversation, note how 제레미 is using 교수님 when talking directly *to* the teacher.

Titles

Chapter 9

In Chapter 5 we learned about the words 사장 and 사장님. Whenever you are talking to or about a boss, you use 사장님 to be polite to him or her – the 님 at the end adds *politeness* to the title. However, when you are not directly talking about a boss, but simply speaking about a boss (or bosses) *in general*, you use 사장 (without 님). But 사장 is not the only title that can have 님 added to it, and we have already learned a few other titles that use 님.

회장 means "a president (of a company)," and you should use 회장님 when speaking directly to or about that president. It would be impolite to refer to your company's president using 회장, but it would be fine to use 회장 to talk about a president or presidents *in general*, or to talk about yourself if you are a president. This is because adding 님 to a title adds politeness (just as it does with 사장님), and it is not necessary to add *politeness* when speaking about yourself – just like you would not add honorifics to verbs when talking about yourself.

The same applies for 부모님 ("parents"). You could use 부모님 to refer to your own parents (since you should be polite to your parents) or to another person's parents, but you would not use it to refer to yourself if you are a parent – you would instead use 부모.

However, there are a few words which are always used with 님 at the end – 스님 ("monk") and 장님 ("a blind person") are two examples. Also, 선생님 is used with 님 even when referring to yourself. You can think of these words as exceptions.

Advanced

If you spend any time online in Korean chat rooms, you might notice 님 being used at the end of people's usernames. This is a common way to politely refer to a person you do not know online. As usual, remember to only add 님 after others' usernames and not after your own.

박재석 교수: 네, 제가 고급 한국어 수업을 가르치는 박재석 교수입니다.
"Yes, I'm professor Park Jae-Seok and I teach the advanced Korean class."

Notice how the professor refers to himself using his full name and the title 교수 (without 님).

Titles

제레미: 질문이 있어서 찾아왔는데 지금 괜찮으세요?

"I came here to find you because I had a question, but are you okay now (for time)?"

Note about 서

In Chapter 5 of the second book we learned that we can use the 서 ending to mean "because" to show a *cause and effect*. Then in Chapter 16 we learned how we can use the 서 ending to also show a *strong relation* in a sentence. I recommend reviewing these two concepts if this conversation sentence does not make sense (질문이 있어서 [...]), as 서 will commonly be used in both of these ways.

Also note that the 서 form is not used to make *commands*. Instead, you can use the (으)니까 ("because") ending. For example, the sentence "Buy more milk because I drank it all" would be 제가 우유를 다 마셨으니까 더 사세요 (not 마셨어서 or 마셔서).

Action Verb Stem + 아/어/etc. + 가다/오다

In the first book we learned the verbs 걷다 for "to walk," 걸어가다 for "to walk (somewhere)," and 걸어오다 for "to walk (here)." We also learned other verbs that are similar to these such as 들어오다 ("to come in") and 들어가다 ("to go in"), but we have not talked about these verbs in detail.

"Why are these verbs especially important?" Because while the English translations of these verbs might seem similar, each verb is used in different situations. If an action verb has 가다 at the end, it show that the movement of that verb is *going away* from the speaker – just like the verb 가다. And if the action verb has 오다 at the end, it shows that the movement of that verb is *coming* to the speaker – just like the verb 오다. Here are examples of each type.

걷는 것이 좋아요.
"I like walking."

This example uses the verb 걷다 without 가다 or 오다. Because of this, it does not explain *where* the speaker is going. The speaker could be walking to Seoul, or walking *here* (to where they already are), or just walking around in circles for hours and hours in their basement.

걸어가는 것이 좋아요.
"I like walking (going there)."

Titles

Chapter 9

This example uses 걷다 with 가다 – we will see how 걷다 becomes 걸어가다 in a moment – to show that the speaker is walking *to* somewhere. The speaker could be walking *to* Seoul, but they could not be walking *here* (to where they already are). They also probably would not be walking around in circles in their basement, since adding 가다 means that they are *going* somewhere.

걸어오는 것이 좋아요.
"I like walking (coming here)."

This example uses 걷다 with 오다 to show that the speaker is walking *here*. This works the same as the verb 오다 normally works. You could use this sentence if you wanted to say that you like walking *here*, perhaps after already arriving at a certain destination – "I like walking (coming here), so there's no need to drive me here to school."

Another two examples of this form that we have already learned are 가져가다 for "to take (something somewhere else)" and 가져오다 for "to bring (something here)." Both of these come from the verb 가지다 for "to hold" or "to have (on your person)," combined with the verbs 가다 and 오다.

To make this form, take an *action verb stem* and conjugate it as if you were conjugating the 요 form, but without adding the 요. Then attach the verb 가다 ("to go") or 오다 ("to come") to the end. Remember that certain types of verbs conjugate to the 요 form differently, such as the verb 걷다 (which becomes 걸어가다 or 걸어오다), among many others. Here are a few example verbs.

사다 → 사가다 ("to buy and go somewhere") and 사오다 ("to buy and bring here")
찾다 → 찾아가다 ("to look for and go somewhere") and 찾아오다 ("to look for and come here")

Note that a more natural translation for 사오다 is "to go buy (and come back)," and a more natural translation for 찾아가다 and 찾아오다 is "to go visit" and "to come visit."

씻다 → 씻어가다 ("to wash and go/take somewhere") and 씻어오다 ("to wash and come/bring here")
집다 → 집어가다 ("to pick up and go/take somewhere") and 집어오다 ("to pick up and come/bring here")
끌다 → 끌어가다 ("to drag and go somewhere") and 끌어오다 ("to drag and come/bring here")
내리다 → 내려가다 ("to go down," "to descend to somewhere"), and 내려오다 ("to come down," "to descend to here")
건너다 → 건너가다 ("to cross to somewhere"), and 건너오다 ("to descend to here").

Titles

Many of these verbs are common enough that simply memorizing them one at a time as you see them could be the easiest way to learn them. Also, this form is most commonly used with the same verbs over and over again (such as the verbs listed in this chapter) so you do not have to worry about memorizing long lists of action verbs that use 가다 or 오다. It should be enough for the time being to simply memorize the example verbs taught in this book series, and to pay attention when you hear new ones used in your own studies.

Also 가다 and 오다 are not the only verbs that can be used in this form. You might also see other action verbs used which show *movement*, such as 다니다 which means "to attend (school)" or "to commute (to work)." Here are two examples.

다녀오세요!
"Attend (school) and come (back)!"
"Commute (to work) and come (back)!"

다녀올게!
"I'll attend (school) and come (back)!"
"I'll commute (to work) and come (back)!"

다녀오다 is a commonly used verb for announcing when you are leaving the house (and expect yourself to return), or for saying to someone else when they are leaving the house (and expect them to return). A natural translation for 다녀오세요 could be "Take care!" A natural translation for 다녀올게(요) could be "I'll be back!"

> **Advanced**
>
> This form (with 가다 and 오다) has another usage. It can also be used to show *continuing* actions. When using these two forms, add a space between the verb and 가다 (or 오다).
>
> **Action Verb Stem + 아/어/etc. 가다**
>
> Using this form with the verb 가다 has the meaning of an action that *continues* from now and goes into the future. Here are a few examples.
>
> 한국어를 오래 공부해 갈 거예요.
> "I will study Korean (because I've started now, and I will continue to study in the future)."
>
> 잘돼 가요?
> "Is it going well (and will it keep going well)?"
>
> 열심히 일해 갈 거예요.
> "I'll work hard (because I work hard now, and I will continue to work hard in the future)."
>
> **Action Verb Stem + 아/어/etc. 오다**
>
> Using this form with the verb 오다 has the meaning of an action that *began* in the past and continues until now. Here are a few examples.
>
> 한국어를 오래 공부해 왔어요.
> "I have studied Korean a long time (because I started in the past, and I still do now)."
>
> 미국에서 살아 왔어요.
> "I have lived in America (because I've been here in the past, and I'm still here now)."

Titles

Chapter 9

열심히 일해 왔어요.
"I have worked hard (because I worked hard in the past, and I'm still working hard)."

While these two forms might translate the same in English as other forms (such as the regular past tense), know that their meanings are different in Korean. And while this form is a bit advanced, fortunately you do not have to memorize it with a long list of verbs as it is most commonly used with a few verbs (such as 하다, 살다, and 되다).

박재석 교수: 미안하지만 지금은 통화 중인데 잠깐만 기다려 줄래요?

"I'm sorry but right now I'm in the middle of a phone call, so do you want to wait for just a moment?

잠깐만(요) can also be used to mean "Excuse me" when *passing by* someone who is in the way, or when passing through a crowd. More *politely*, you can use 잠시만(요). Using 실례합니다 ("Excuse me.") would be *incorrect* in this situation, as 실례합니다 is used for apologizing to someone for *interrupting* them, or for *bumping into* them (as we learned in the first book).

제레미: 네, 그럼 밖에서 기다리겠습니다.
"Yes, then I will wait outside."

10 분 뒤...
After 10 minutes...

박재석 교수: 오래 걸려서 미안해요. 들어오세요.
"I'm sorry it took a long time. Come in."

"I'm sorry."

You can use 미안하다 or 죄송하다 with the 서 ending to say that you're sorry "for" doing something. Here is an example.

늦게 도착해서 죄송합니다.
"I'm sorry for arriving late."

Note that in Korean, saying that you're sorry is admitting that something is your *fault*. It is good to apologize for things that you have caused, such as making someone wait, or hurting someone, etc., but it would be *incorrect* to say you are "sorry" (using the verbs 죄송하다 or 미안하다) to someone after hearing that they lost a relative (unless of course you caused them to die) or after hearing that something bad happened to them. Instead, you can express that you are sorry to *hear* about something by using the verb 유감이다. Here are two examples.

Chapter 9

Titles

유감입니다.
"I'm sorry (to hear that)."

죄송합니다.
미안합니다.
"I'm sorry (because I did it)."

제레미: 감사합니다.

"Thank you."

박재석 교수: 무슨 일이라고 했죠?

"What did you say is the matter?"

제레미: 다음 학기에 제가 고급 한국어 수업을 들을 수 있는지 궁금해서요.

"(It's because) next semester I'm wondering if I can take the advanced Korean class."

박재석 교수: 한국어를 어느 정도 할 수 있는지에 따라 다르지만 학생은 한국어를 잘해서 가능할 것 같네요.

"It depends on how much Korean you can speak, but you speak Korean well so I think it'll be possible."

"It depends on...": Noun + 에 따라(서) 다르다

To say "it depends on" something, take a noun and attach 에 따라(서) – the 서 is *optional*. Then conjugate the verb 다르다 ("to be different"). Literally this form means "It is different depending on (noun)."

사람에 따라 달라요.
"It depends on the person."

시간에 따라 달라요.
"It depends on the time."

날씨에 따라 달라요.
"It depends on the weather."

상황에 따라 달라요.
"It depends on the situation."

Titles

Chapter 9

"It's different for each...": Noun + 마다 다르다

Here is another similar form. 마다 can be attached after a *noun* and means "each."

사람마다 달라요.
"It's different for each person."

상황마다 달라요.
"It's different for each situation."

날마다 달라요.
"It's different for each day."

"It depends on...": Action Verb Stem + 는지 에 따라(서) 다르다

You can also use this form with verbs, using the same 는지 form that we previously learned.

어디서 사는지에 따라 달라요.
"It depends on where you live."

Note that since the verbs 사다 ("to buy") and 살다 ("to live") would both conjugate as 사는지 in this form, depending on the context the sentence could also mean "It depends on where you buy it."

돈이 얼마나 있는지에 따라 달라요.
"It depends on how much money you have."

누가 하는지에 따라 달라요.
"It depends on who does it."

무슨 일을 겪었는지에 따라 달라요.
"It depends on what you went through."

You can also use this form with other tenses as well (besides 는지).

어떤 여자를 사귈지에 따라 달라요.
"It depends on what kind of girl you'll date."

어떤 ("what kind of") can also be used to mean "a certain." For example, 어떤 여자 can mean both "what kind of girl" and "a certain girl" depending on the context of the sentence.

Chapter 9 — Titles

Advanced

"It depends on...": Action Verb Stem + 느냐 에 따라(서) 다르다

Another similar form uses 느냐 instead of 는지. Both forms have the same meaning, so feel free to use whichever you would like. To use it, take an *action verb stem* and attach 느냐. As usual, verb stems ending in ㄹ will drop the ㄹ.

내일 뭘 하느냐에 따라 달라요.
"It depends on what we do tomorrow."

한국어를 얼마나 공부하느냐에 따라 달라요.
"It depends on how much you study Korean."

네 월급은 샴푸를 몇 병 팔 수 있느냐에 따라 달라.
"Your monthly wage depends on how many bottles of shampoo you can sell."

"How much?" – 어느 정도

In the second book we learned that 어느 정도 is an *adverb* that means "somewhat" or "to a certain degree." 어느 정도 can also be used to mean "how much," similarly to 얼마나 and 얼마만큼 (or 얼마큼). Literally, 어느 정도 means "to what extent" and is slightly more *formal*.

한국어를 얼마나 할 수 있어요?
한국어를 얼마(만)큼 할 수 있어요?
한국어를 어느 정도 할 수 있어요?
"How much Korean can you speak?"

Going back to the conversation, notice how the professor uses *title* of 학생 to refer to 제레미, who is a student.

제레미: 감사합니다. 한국어 공부를 열심히 하는 편이지만 제가 실수하면 고쳐 주세요.
"Thank you. I tend to study hard, but if I make a mistake please correct me."

"Tend to...": Verb Stem + (은/ㄴ/는) 편이다

편 ("a side") is normally used in words such as 맞은편 ("the opposite side") and 길 건너편 ("the other side of the street"). It can also be used with action verbs and descriptive verbs to mean "to be on the side of (verb)." For example, "I'm on the slim side."

To use this form, take an *action verb stem* and attach 는. Or, take a *descriptive verb* and conjugate it to an adjective – attach 은 if it ends in a *consonant*, or attach ㄴ if it ends in a *vowel*. Then add 편 and conjugate 이다 (typically in the *present tense*).

Titles

Chapter 9

While this form can translate as "to be on the side of (verb)," more natural translations can also be "rather" or "to have a tendency to (verb)" depending on the context. Here are some examples.

저는 날씬한 편이에요.
"I'm on the slim side."
"I'm rather slim."
"I tend to be slim."

싼 편이에요.
"It's rather cheap."

논쟁을 많이 하는 편이에요.
"I tend to argue a lot."

자주 먹는 편이에요.
"I tend to eat often."

제 남자 친구는 좀 잘생긴 편이에요.
"My boyfriend is kind of on the handsome side."
"My boyfriend is rather handsome."

박재석 교수: 그래요. 그럼 벌써 필요할 리는 없겠지만 지난 학기에 내 수업을 들은 선배 학생을 소개시켜 줄게요.

"Okay. Then there's no way that you'll need it already, but I'll introduce you to a student who took my class last semester."

Culture Notes

선배 and 후배

Parts of Korea's culture revolve around a person's age and social status. You saw some of this when we covered honorific speech, but you will also find it in other parts of Korean life. Younger Koreans are required by social norms to respect and listen to their older coworkers and classmates. Older Koreans in turn act as mentors to their younger coworkers and classmates.

In Korea, a person's *senior* – someone who is older or in a more superior position than them at work or in school, or someone who has been in that position longer – is referred to as 선배. A person's *junior* – someone who is younger or in a lower position than them at work or in school, or someone who has been in that position for less time – is referred to as 후배. These two words are important, since the word 친구 ("friend") is specifically used in Korea for a person who is the *same age* as you, and who was born in the *same year* as you were. Alternatively, you can use 동갑 ("same age") when someone is the same age as you, but when that person may or may not have been born in the same year as you were.

Chapter 9: Titles

We previously learned 소개(를) 하다 as "to introduce." 소개(를) 시키다 also means "to introduce," but is used when you are introducing *someone else* to someone. Using 시키다 changes the meaning of a regular verb to mean that someone *causes* someone else to do something. We will talk about this more in detail in the next chapter, so for now only focus on how the meaning of the verb 소개(를) 하다 changes by switching the 하다 to 시키다.

"There's no way...": Verb Stem + (을/ㄹ) 리(가) (없다)

You can use this form to say that there is "no way" for something to be a certain way. For example, "There's no way that you're not a Korean." You can also translate this form as "It can't be" depending on the context.

To use this form, take a verb stem (in present tense or past tense) and attach 을 if it ends in a *consonant*, or attach ㄹ if it ends in a *vowel*. Then add 리(가) – the 가 is *optional* (or you can use 는 instead). Finally, conjugate the verb 없다 ("to not exist"). 없다 is also *optional* when speaking *casually*.

오늘 비가 올 리가 없어요.
"There's no way it'll rain today."

벌써 나갔을 리가 없는데.
"There's no way he already left."

그럴 리가!
"No way!"
"It can't be!"

안 될 리가 없어요.
"There's no way it won't work."
"It can't not work."

아직 주름이 생길 리가 없어요.
"There's no way I'll get wrinkles yet."

이런 경우에는 용서해 줄 리가 없어요.
"In this case, there's no way he'll forgive me."

남친이 있을 리가 없는 거 같아.
"I think there's no way she has a boyfriend."

남친 is a shortened version of 남자 친구 ("boyfriend") and can be used when speaking *casually*. In the same way, 여친 is short for 여자 친구 ("girlfriend").

Titles

Chapter 9

Additional Titles

A few other common titles that you might see are 학생 ("student"), 가수 ("singer"), and 배우 ("actor," "actress"). You can use a person's *profession* as their title if you do not know a better way to refer to them but still want to be polite. For example, you could use the title 학생 after a person who you're not close with, but who you know is a student.

> 제레미: 네. 그게 좋을 것 같네요. 그럼 수업 시간에 뵙겠습니다.
> "Okay. I think that'll be good. Then I will see you in class (time)."

Culture Notes

Business in Korea

When meeting someone in *business* for the first time, it is common for people to exchange business cards if they have one. When presenting your card to the other person, hold it with both hands and accept his or hers with both hands as well, with one person giving his or her card at a time. You can also read the card carefully when you receive it (... or pretend to read it) to be extra polite.

While Korean business culture is slowly changing, it is common in Korea for most major companies to hold frequent company meals once every week or so (called 회식). Company meals often involve socializing while eating food and drinking alcohol, drinking more alcohol, and then drinking even more alcohol as the final remaining employees stumble to locate a taxi to find their way back home.

Practice

Conjugate the following verbs using both the 가다 form and the 오다 form:

1. 사다

Titles

2. 찾다

   _____.

3. 가지다

   _____.

4. 달리다

   _____.

Translate to Korean:

5. "It depends on the color."

   _____.

6. "It depends on the place."

   _____.

7. "It depends on where you do it."

   _____.

8. "It depends on what you want."

   _____.

9. "I tend to eat quickly."

   _____.

10. "There's no way Jeremy was here yesterday."

    _____.

11. "I wanted to bring snacks (here)."

    _____.

Titles

12. "I met Professor Kim yesterday in the museum."

_____.

Translate to English:

13. 어떻게 했는지에 따라 달라요.

_____.

14. 철수가 대통령을 만났을 리가 없어요.

_____.

15. 여자를 쉽게 사귀고 쉽게 헤어지는 편이에요.

_____.

16. 저는 추억을 빨리 잊어 버리는 편이에요.

_____.

17. 김치를 어느 정도 좋아해요?

_____.

18. 떡을 더 사오세요.

_____.

19. 지도를 보고 찾아갔어요.

_____.

20. 거기까지 걸어가는 게 좀 힘들 거 같아.

_____.

21. 입구에서 종이를 1 장 집어오세요.

_____.

Titles

22. 아빠를 보고 달려갔어요.

New Phrases

유감입니다.	"I'm sorry (to hear that)."
제가 실수하면 고쳐 주세요.	"If I make a mistake, please correct me."

New Vocabulary

회장	"a president (of a company)"
부모	"parents"
스님	"monk"
장님	"a blind person"
끌다	"to drag (someone)"
끌어가다	"to drag (someone somewhere)"
끌어오다	"to drag (someone here)"
찾아가다	"to go visit"
찾아오다	"to come visit"
집어가다	"to pick up and take (somewhere)"
집어오다	"to pick up and bring (here)"
씻어가다	"to wash and take (somewhere)"
씻어오다	"to wash and bring (here)"
내려가다	"to go down," "to descend (to somewhere)"
건너가다	"to cross (to somewhere)"
건너오다	"to cross (to here)"
고급	"advanced (level)," "high-grade"
중급	"intermediate (level)"
초급	"beginner (level)"
상황	"a situation"
경우	"a case," "a circumstance"
학기	"(school) term," "semester/trimester/quarter"

Titles

학교에 다니다	"to go to school," "to attend school"
일(을) 다니다	"to go to work," "to commute to work"
뛰어들다	"to jump in(to)"
월급	"(monthly) salary," "(monthly) pay"
연봉	"(yearly) salary," "(yearly) pay"
편	"a side"
맞은편	"the opposite side," "the other side (of something)"
건너편	"the other side (of something)"
길 맞은편	"the other side of the street"
길 건너편	"the other side of the street"
선배	"(one's) senior"
후배	"(one's) junior"
소개(를) 시키다	"to introduce (someone else)"
회식	"a company meal"
명함	"business card"
서명	"signature"
악수	"handshake"
악수(를) 하다	"to shake hands"
박수	"applause"
박수(를) 하다	"to applaud"
면접	"interview"
남친	남자 친구 (casual)
여친	여자 친구 (casual)
전 남자 친구	"ex-boyfriend"
전 여자 친구	"ex-girlfriend"
사귀다	"to date," "to go out with," "to associate with"
헤어지다	"to break up (with someone)"
남자 친구(를) 사귀다	"to date a boyfriend"
여자 친구(를) 사귀다	"to date a girlfriend"
친구(를) 사귀다	"to make friends"
사춘기(가) 되다	"to enter puberty"
초대	"an invitation"

Titles

청첩장	"wedding invitation"
초대장	"(written) invitation"
임신(을) 하다	"to get pregnant"
아기(를) 낳다	"to have a baby"
나이(가) 들다	"to get older"
생기다	"to come up," "to arise," "to happen"
주름(이) 생기다	"to get wrinkles"
경험	"an experience"
경험(을) 하다	"to experience"
겪다	"to go through," "to experience"
의사 선생님	"doctor" (formal)
친척	"a relative," "relatives"
부인	"(another person's) wife" (hon.)
평화	"peace"
토론	"discussion"
토론(을) 하다	"to discuss"
논쟁	"argument"
논쟁(을) 하다	"to argue"
용서	"forgiveness"
용서(를) 하다	"to forgive"
추억	"a memory (of something)"
기억력(이) 좋다	"to have a good memory (ability)"
상상력(이) 좋다	"to have a good imagination (ability)"
봉지	bag (of something) counter
입구	"entrance"
출구	"exit"
출입구	"entrance and exit"
마다	"each" (particle)
매번	"every time"
고객님	"customer," "client"
동갑	"same age" (casual)

Make and Let

Chapter 10

Conversation

딸:	엄마. 오늘 아빠 깜짝 생일 파티 어떻게 하면 될까요?
엄마:	일단 집이 더러우니까 동생이 집 좀 치우게 해 봐.
딸:	집은 제가 치웠어요. 선물은 어떻게 할까요?
엄마:	온라인으로 주문한 선물이 오늘 5시에 도착하도록 했으니까 걱정 안 해도 돼.
딸:	네, 그러면 음식은 제가 준비할게요.
엄마:	그래. 아빠가 피자를 좋아하시니까 피자도 한 판 시켜 줘.
딸:	그럼 피자를 한 판 시키고 다른 요리도 조금 더 하는 동안 아빠가 집에 못 들어오게 만들어 주세요.
엄마:	알았어. 아빠가 집에 가기 전에 2시간 정도 운동시키고 같이 들어갈게.
딸:	네. 아빠는 모자를 쓰고 운동해서 머리가 항상 눌리니까 엄마가 빗겨 주시는 것 잊지 마세요.
엄마:	그래. 그럼 집에서 보자.

This chapter will cover the grammar that we need to know in order to say "make" and "let." For example, "I *made* him do the homework." Or, "I *let* him do the homework." This type of grammar has to do with *causing* someone to do something – whether you *made* them do it, or *let* them do it. Let's jump right into the conversation.

딸: 엄마. 오늘 아빠 깜짝 생일 파티 어떻게 하면 될까요?

"Mom. What should we do about dad's surprise birthday party today?"

Chapter 10: Make and Let

어떻게 하면 될까요 is a commonly used expression that literally means "How should I do it?" A more natural translation is "What should I do about (noun)?"

엄마: 일단 집이 더러우니까 동생이 집 좀 치우게 해 봐.
"First since the house is dirty, make your younger sibling clean the house a bit."

"Make" & "Let": Verb Stem + 게 하다

While you can translate this form naturally as "make" or "let," this form is used to show that someone *caused* someone else to do something, or *caused* something to be a certain way. It can be used with both descriptive verbs and action verbs, but we will first focus on using this form with action verbs.

To make it, take a verb stem and attach 게. Then conjugate the verb 하다, and you are done. For example:

달리게 했어요.
"I made him run."
"I let him run."

You will know whether "make" or "let" is a better translation through the context of the sentence.

If you want to specify *who* or *what* you are causing to do something, you can use the Subject Marker (이/가) or the Object Marker (을/를). Or, you can also use 도 ("also," "even," "too") or 만 ("only") depending on the meaning of your sentence.

철수가 서울까지 달리게 했어요.
"I made Chul-soo run to Seoul."

마이크가 숙제를 하게 했어요.
"I made Mike do the homework."

강아지가 초콜릿을 먹게 하면 안 돼요.
"You shouldn't let a dog eat chocolate."

나도 같이 가게 해 줘.
"Please let me go together too."

내가 또 말하게 하지 마.
"Don't make me say it again."

Make and Let

저를 좀 자게 해 주세요.
"Please let me sleep a bit."

현우가 집중하게 하고 싶어.
"I want to let Hyun-woo concentrate."

> **Advanced**
>
> Whether you will use the Subject Marker or the Object Marker in this grammar form can depend on whether one of the two is already present in the sentence. To avoid confusion, the Subject Marker can be used when the Object Marker is already being used in a sentence, and vice versa. Here is an example.
>
> 제가 피자를 먹게 해 주세요.
> "Please let me eat pizza."
>
> It would be better to use 제가 than 저를 to avoid confusion, since there is already another Object Marker (피자를) in the sentence.

티비를 볼 수 있게 해 주세요.
"Please let me watch TV."

Another natural translation for this form is "to have (someone do something)."

직원이 손을 닦게 했어요.
"I had the employee wash his hands."

"Make": 게 하다 and Descriptive Verbs

This form can also be used with descriptive verbs in the same way to mean "make." Here are a few examples.

따뜻하게 했어요.
"I made it warm."

음악 소리를 더 크게 하세요.
"Make the music louder."

방을 밝게 했어요.
"I made the room bright."

> **Adv**
>
> The 게 in this form is part of another grammar form which we wll cover in the "Advanced Notes" of Chapter 19. It is enough for now to know that it can translate as "so that" and can have a similar usage to 도록, which we wll learn next.

딸: 집은 제가 치웠어요. 선물은 어떻게 할까요?
"I cleaned up the house. What should we do about presents?"

Chapter 10 — Make and Let

A literal translation of 어떻게 할까요 is "How should I do it?" This is similar in meaning to 어떻게 하면 될까요 which we saw previously. Another common form you might see is 어떡할까요, using the verb 어떡하다. 어떡하다 has the same meaning as 어떻게 하다 and is often used.

> **Adv**
> 어떡하다 comes from a combination of 어떠하게, from 어떠하다 (the original form of the verb 어떻다) and 하다. While 어떡해 ("What do/should I do?") and 어떻게 ("how") have the same pronunciation due to sound change rules, their meanings are different. Be careful not to confuse them when writing.

엄마: 온라인으로 주문한 선물이 오늘 5시에 도착하도록 했으니까 걱정 안 해도 돼.
"I made it so that the present I ordered online will arrive today at 5 o'clock so you don't have to worry."

"So that": Verb Stem + 도록

The 도록 form has two main uses. First, it can be used to mean "so that."

To use this form, take a verb stem and attach 도록. Then finish the rest of the sentence. This form is commonly used together with the 수 있다 form, and with the 지 않다 form in negative sentences.

제가 이해할 수 있도록 도와주세요.
"Please help me so that I can understand."

잊지 않도록 조심하세요.
"Be careful so that you don't forget."

한국어를 배울 수 있도록 한국인 친구들을 사귀었어요.
"I made Korean friends so that I can learn Korean."

시험에 떨어지지 않도록 공부를 많이 할 거예요.
"I'll study a lot so that I don't fail the test."

우리가 들을 수 있도록 더 크게 말해 주세요.
"Please speak louder so that we hear you."

내일 일찍 일어날 수 있도록 오늘 일찍 자야 돼요.
"I have to sleep early today so that I can wake up early tomorrow."

While the meaning of the form is the same, 도록 can also translate as "to the extent that." This can sometimes translate more naturally (though not literally) as "until."

Make and Let

배가 아프도록 소리를 질렀어요.
"I screamed until my stomach hurt."

You can think of this sentence as literally meaning "I screamed, and I did it to the extent that my stomach hurt."

햄버거를 질리도록 먹었어요.
"I ate hamburgers until I got sick of them."

죽도록 널 사랑해.
"I love you so much."

You can also translate this sentence literally as "I love you to the extent that I die (from loving you)."

도록 with 하다

The 도록 form can also be used with the verb 하다 as a more *formal* way of speaking. Because of this, you might often hear it used in speeches. You can think of this form as meaning "to make it so that."

내일 하도록 해 주세요.
"Please make it so that you do it tomorrow."
"Please do it tomorrow."

지금 시작하도록 하겠습니다.
"I'll make it so that I start now."
"I'll start now."

너무 빨리 하지 않도록 하세요.
"Please make it so you don't do it too fast."
"Don't do it too fast."

사장님과 직접 만날 수 있도록 해 줄 수 있습니까?
"Can you please make it so that I can meet with the boss face to face?"

When used with 만나다 ("to meet"), the adverb 직접 ("directly") can also translate as "face to face" or "personally."

저는 한국에 있는 동안 저는 철수가 김치를 먹어 보도록 했어요.
"I made it so that Chul-soo tried kimchi while we were in Korea."
"I made Chul-soo try kimchi while we were in Korea."

Make and Let

You can see how in some situations the 도록 하다 form can also have the same meaning as the 게 하다 form.

모든 학생들이 안전벨트를 매도록 했어요.
"I made it so that all of the students wore a seatbelt."
"I made all of the students wear a seatbelt."

딸: 네, 그러면 음식은 제가 준비할게요.
"Okay, then I'll prepare the food."

엄마: 그래. 아빠가 피자를 좋아하시니까 피자도 한 판 시켜 줘.
"Okay. Because dad likes pizza, order a pizza too."

Both 시키다 and 주문(을) 하다 mean "to order," but 시키다 is used specifically to mean "to order (food)." 주문(을) 하다 is also slightly more formal than 시키다, so 시키다 is used more often among friends.

뭐 시킬까?
"What should we order?"

족발 시키자.
"Let's order pigs' feet."

Culture Notes

족발 ("pigs' feet") is commonly eaten in Korea as a meal along with spicy noodles, or other side dishes.

딸: 그럼 피자를 한 판 시키고 다른 요리도 조금 더 하는 동안 아빠가 집에 못 들어오게 만들어 주세요.

"Then while I order a pizza and do a little more cooking, please don't let dad come into the house."

Make and Let

Chapter 10

"Make": Verb Stem + 게 만들다

This is an alternative to the 게 하다 form that we learned previously. You can use 만들다 ("to make") instead of 하다. However, this form can only be used to mean "make."

To make it, take a verb stem and attach 게. Then conjugate the verb 만들다, and you are done. Here are some example sentences.

친구들이 싸우게 만들었어요.
친구들이 싸우게 했어요.
"I made my friends fight."

광희를 화나게 만들었어요.
광희를 화나게 했어요.
"I made Gwang-hee angry."

설거지를 하게 만들었어요.
설거지를 하게 했어요.
"I made him do the dishes."

> 엄마: 알았어. 아빠가 집에 가기 전에 2 시간 정도 운동시키고 같이 들어갈게.
> "Got it. Before dad goes home I'll make him exercise for about 2 hours, and we'll go in (the house) together."

"Make" & "Let": 시키다

There is one more way to say "make" and "let," and it involves using the verb 시키다. While we learned that 시키다 can be used to mean "to order (food)," here it has a different meaning. The verb 시키다 can take the place of the 게 하다 form, but only for action verbs that end with 하다.

To use it, take an *action verb* that normally ends in 하다, and replace 하다 with 시키다. Here are two examples, using both forms.

일(을) 하다 "to work" → 일(을) 시키다 "to make (someone) work"

자꾸 같은 일만 시켜요.
자꾸 같은 일만 하게 해요.
"He repeatedly makes me do only the same work."

Chapter 10

Make and Let

공부(를) 하다 "to study" → 공부(를) 시키다 "to make (someone) study"

놀기 전에 먼저 공부를 시켰어요.
놀기 전에 먼저 공부를 하게 했어요.
"I made her study before playing."

청소(를) 하다 "to clean (the house)," "to vacuum" → 청소(를) 시키다 "to make (someone) clean (the house)," "to make (someone) vacuum"

화장실 청소를 시켰어요.
화장실 청소를 하게 했어요.
"I made him clean the bathroom."

준하가 억지로 시켰어요.
준하가 억지로 하게 했어요.
"Joon-ha made him do it by force."
"Joon-ha forced him to do it."

억지로 ("by force," "forcefully") is an *adverb* that can more naturally translate as "to force (someone)" when used with causative grammar forms.

시키다 is more often used than the 게 하다 form when the action verb ends in 하다, but both forms are grammatically correct. In addition, 시키다 is more often used to mean "make" than "let."

딸: 네. 아빠는 모자를 쓰고 운동해서 머리가 항상 눌리니까 엄마가 빗겨 주시는 것 잊지 마세요.

"Okay. Because dad wears a hat and exercises so his hair is always pressed down, (mom) don't forget to make him brush his hair."

Causative Verbs

We were just introduced to 시키다, which is a verb that can be used to show that someone *causes* someone else to do something. 시키다 is unique, because it adds this meaning by itself and does not need a special grammar form to work. But 시키다 is not the only verb that can have this extra meaning, and this type of verb has a special name – "causative verbs" (because they *cause* people to do things). 시키다 is one of the most commonly used causative verbs, but there are others that you should also be familiar with.

Make and Let

Chapter 10

The causative verbs that we will learn here are all versions of *Pure Korean verbs*. For *Sino-Korean verbs* (action verbs ending in 하다), continue to use the 게 하다 form or 시키다. If you feel more comfortable with saying "make" and "let" using the 게 하다 form, you can feel free to keep using that form on your own in every situation for the time being. Also know that native Koreans will not only use the 게 하다 form (or the 게 만들다 form), but will more commonly use 시키다 and other causative verbs in their conversations. At least, it is important to be able to recognize these new causative verbs for now, and to focus on slowly learning them later as needed.

> **Adv** Note that you cannot use 시키다 with descriptive verbs that have been changed to action verbs (using the 하다 form we learned in Chapter 5). This is because those are not Sino-Korean verbs, and the 하다 cannot be *separated* like it can be from Sino-Korean verbs, such as 공부(를) 하다.

These causative verbs, just like 시키다, have the same general meaning and use as the 게 하다 form. However, you will notice that many of these verbs are preferable to their 게 하다 forms because of their more natural sounding definitions (in bold). Here are a few common causative verbs.

먹다 "to eat" → 먹이다 "to make (someone) eat," "**to feed**"
앉다 "to sit" → 앉히다 "to make (someone) sit," "**to seat**"
자다 "to sleep" → 재우다 "to make (someone) sleep," "**to put to sleep**"
깨다 "to awake" → 깨우다 "to make (someone) wake up," "**to awaken**"
죽다 "to die" → 죽이다 "to make (someone) die," "**to kill**"
입다 "to wear" → 입히다 "to make (someone) wear," "**to dress**"
살다 "to live" → 살리다 "to make (someone) live," "**to save**"
웃다 "to laugh" → 웃기다 "to make (someone) laugh"
울다 "to cry" → 울리다 "to make (someone) cry"
남다 "to be remaining," "to be left over" → 남기다 "to make left over," "**to leave (over)**"
낮다 "to be low" → 낮추다 "to make low," "**to lower**"
높다 "to be high" → 높이다 "to make high," "**to raise**"
비다 "to be empty," "to be blank" → 비우다 "to make empty," "to make blank," "**to empty**"
타다 "to ride" → 태우다 "to let (someone) ride," "**to give (someone) a ride**"
알다 "to know" → 알리다 "to make known," "**to inform**"*

*Note that 알리다 is where 알려주다, which means "to tell" or "to let (someone) know," is originally from.

If it makes things easier, you can ignore that these verbs are "causative verbs" and instead simply learn them as you would learn any vocabulary word. After all, we have already learned several causative verbs already before this chapter without any issues.

> **Adv** Here is a tip for recognizing new causative verbs – 이히리기우구추. These are the 7 sounds that you will find in causative verbs. For example, 먹**이**다, 앉**히**다, 울**리**다, 웃**기**다, 태**우**다, and 낮**추**다. Of these, 구 is rarely used (and not needed for this book's level), but it is included because it is one of the possible sounds that you can find in causative verbs.

Make and Let

> **Adv**: Note that 눌리다 ("to be pressed down," "to be held down") is a *passive verb*, and comes from the verb 누르다, meaning "to push (a button)." Although it uses 리, it is not a causative verb. We will cover passive verbs in detail in Chapter 15.

"Who" and Causatives

When using one of these causative verbs, you must use a different particle to show *who* is being made to do it. Previously, we used the Subject Marker (이/가) and the Object Marker (을/를), among others, with the 게 하다 form. For causative verbs (including 시키다) you use the particle 에게 instead. Here are a few examples.

명수**에게** 공부시켰어요.
명수**가** 공부하게 했어요.
"I made Myung-soo study."

홍철 씨**가** 피자를 먹게 했어요.
"I made Hong-chul eat pizza."

홍철 씨**에게** 피자를 먹였어요.
"I made Hong-chul eat pizza."
"I fed pizza to Hong-chul"

> **Adv**: In addition, you can also use the particle 에게 with the 게 하다 form (or 게 만들다 form), although this is less common.

친구**가** 식탁 앞에 앉게 했어요.
"I made/let my friend sit at the front of the kitchen table."

친구**를** 식탁 앞에 앉혔어요.
"I seated my friend at the front of the kitchen table."

However, remember that many causative verbs have their own unique meanings, such as 앉히다 ("to seat") and 죽이다 meaning "to kill." In these cases, you can use them as you would normally – with the Object Marker (을/를). You only need to use 에게 when someone *makes* or *lets* someone do something, and when you want to specify *who*.

> **Adv**: If what makes or lets someone do something is not a person (such as a thing), use the particle 에 (instead of 에게).

엄마: 그래. 그럼 집에서 보자.
"Okay. Then see you at home."

Make and Let

Adv 없애다 ("to make not exist," "to get rid of") is a causative verb that does not apply to the 이히리기우구추 rule. It comes from 없다 ("to not exist").

Practice

Change the following verbs into causative verbs:

1. 사과(를) 하다

2. 입다

3. 살다

4. 타다

Translate to Korean:

5. "I let my friend sit next to me."

6. "I made Mark read the book."

7. "I slept early so that I won't be tired tomorrow."

8. "Please empty the trashcan."

Chapter 10: Make and Let

9. "I gave her a ride to school."

10. "Please let me use the computer for 1 hour."

11. "I can't put the baby to sleep now."

Translate to English:

12. 둘을 결혼시켰어요.

13. 친구를 내 옆에 앉혔어요.

14. 버스를 놓치지 않도록 뛰었어요.

15. 열심히 공부하도록 하세요.

16. 저도 사용하도록 해 주세요.

17. 아기에게 옷을 입혔어요.

18. 울려서 미안해.

Make and Let

19. 제가 소리를 질러서 사람들이 옆으로 비키게 했어요.

_____.

20. 구급차가 먼저 지나가게 했어요.

_____.

21. 아이들이 낙엽을 줍게 했어요.

_____.

22. 찜질방에서 달걀을 먹어 보게 했어요.

_____.

23. 집에 돌아올 때 두부를 사오게 할 거예요.

_____.

New Vocabulary

깜짝 생일 파티	"surprise birthday party"
깜짝	"surprise," "with a startle" (adverb)
치우다	"to clean up," "to tidy up," "to clear (away)"
준비	"preparations"
눌리다	"to be pressed down," "to be held down"
빗다	"to brush," "to comb"
빗기다	"to make (someone) brush," "to make (someone) comb"
어떡하다	"to do what/how"
시키다	"to order (food)"
화(가) 나다	"to be angry (due to someone/something)"
자꾸	"repeatedly" (adverb)
먹이다	"to make (someone) eat," "to feed"
앉히다	"to make (someone) sit," "to seat"

Chapter 10: Make and Let

재우다	"to make (someone) sleep," "to put to sleep"
깨다	"to awake"
깨우다	"to make (someone) wake up," "to awaken"
죽이다	"to make (someone) die," "to kill"
입히다	"to make (someone) wear," "to put (clothes) on (someone)," "to dress"
껍질	"peel," "wrapper"
껍질(을) 벗기다	"to (take off the) peel," "to take off the wrapper"
젖다	"to be wet"
젖히다	"to make wet," "to wet"
웃기다	"to make (someone) laugh"
울리다	"to make (someone) cry"
낮추다	"to make low," "to lower"
높이다	"to make high," "to raise"
비우다	"to make empty," "to make blank," "to empty"
알리다	"to make known," "to inform"
없애다	"to make not exist," "to get rid of"
남기다	"to make left over," "to leave (over)"
숨다	"to be hidden"
숨기다	"to make (something) hidden," "to hide (something)"
쓰레기통	"trashcan"
두부	"tofu"
잎	"leaf (on a tree)"
낙엽	"leaf (on the ground)"
구급차	"ambulance"
경찰차	"police car"
응급실	"emergency room"
찜질방	"sauna"
목욕탕	"bath house"

Make and Let

욕조	"bathtub"
달걀	"(chicken) egg"
비키다	"to move out of the way"
조심하다	"to be careful" (descriptive verb)
조심히	"carefully"
생신	"birthday" (hon.)
늘리다	"to make increase/improve," "to increase/improve (something)"
줄이다	"to make decrease/get worse," "to decreasen/worsen (something)"
억지로	"by force," "forcefully" (adverb)
이용하다	"to use (someone)," "to exploit"
기능	"function (of something)"
놀리다	"to make fun of," "to mock," "to tease"

Chapter 10

Make and Let

Hope and Want

Chapter 11

Conversation

민주:	승아야, 정말 오랜만이다.
승아:	그래, 민주야. 그런데 지아는 오늘도 없네.
민주:	응. 오늘 아침에 아무리 연락을 해도 지아가 안 받았어.
승아:	잘 시간도 없이 바쁘다니 어쩔 수 없지. 너는 요즘 어때?
민주:	부모님이 빨리 결혼하길 원하셔. 자꾸 남자 친구를 집에 데려오거나 아니면 조건이 더 좋은 다른 사람을 만나래.
승아:	정말? 아직 3개월밖에 안 만났잖아.
민주:	응. 우린 아직 결혼할 준비가 안 됐는데 괜히 남자 친구가 있다고 집에 말해 뒀어.
승아:	너도 고민이 많겠다. 근데 내가 결혼해 보니까 일찍 결혼하는 것도 나쁘지 않아.
민주:	나도 오빠랑 결혼하고 싶은데 아직 오빠가 취업 준비 중이라서 결혼 얘기를 못 하겠어.
승아:	그래. 난 둘이 잘됐으면 좋겠는데 잘 생각해 보고 어떻게 할지 결정하길 바라.
민주:	잘 생각해 봐야지. 얘기 들어 줘서 고마워.

In the first book we learned how to express our own desires, such as "I want" using the 고 싶다 form and "I hope" using the (으)면 좋겠다 form. Then in Chapter 5 of this book we learned how to express the desires and emotions of other people using the 하다 form with descriptive verbs. In this chapter we will cover how to say that you want *someone else* to do something. We will also talk about a few other important grammar forms. Let's get started.

Chapter 11

Hope and Want

민주: 승아야, 정말 오랜만이다.

"Seung-ah, it's been so long."

승아: 그래, 민주야. 그런데 지아는 오늘도 없네.

"Yeah (it has), Min-ju. But Ji-ah isn't here today again."

민주: 응. 오늘 아침에 아무리 연락을 해도 지아가 안 받았어.

"Yeah. No matter how much I contacted her this morning Ji-ah didn't answer."

"No matter how": 아무리 Verb Stem + 아/어/etc. + 도

You can use 아무리, along with a verb and the particle 도 ("also," "even," "too") to mean "no matter how" or "no matter how much." For example, "No matter how tired you are, you shouldn't sleep yet."

To make this form, first use the *adverb* 아무리. Then take a verb and conjugate it as if you were conjugating the 요 form, but attach 도 instead of 요, just like the "even" form that we learned in the previous book. Then finish the rest of the sentence. Here are a few examples.

아무리 피곤해도 아직은 자면 안 돼요.
"No matter how tired you are, you shouldn't sleep yet."

아무리 바빠도 꼭 해야 돼요.
"No matter how busy you are, you have to make sure to do it."

아무리 갖고 싶어해도 살 수 없어요.
"No matter how much you want (to have) it, you can't buy it."

아무리 어른이라도 아이스크림은 맛있다.
"Ice cream is delicious no matter how much of an adult you are."

When combined with the particle 도 in this way, 이다 will become 이라도 after a *consonant*, or 라도 after a *vowel*.

승아: 잘 시간도 없이 바쁘다니 어쩔 수 없지. 너는 요즘 어때?

"She's busy without even having time to sleep, so it can't be helped. How are you these days?"

Hope and Want

Chapter 11

(을/ㄹ) Noun

In Chapter 4 of the previous book we covered using (을/ㄹ) with the noun 것 to mean "something to." For example, 집에 먹을 것이 없어요 ("There is nothing to eat at home."). This form can also be used with other nouns, and not only 것. Here are a few examples.

집에 갈 시간이에요.
"It's time to go home."

쉴 시간 좀 주세요.
"Please give me some time to rest."

요리할 준비를 다 했어요?
"Did you finish preparing to cook?"

아직 밖에 나갈 준비가 안 됐어.
"I'm not ready to go outside yet."

오늘 여기로 올 필요가 없어요.
"There's no need to come here today."

정말 그렇게 할 필요가 있을까요?
"Could there really be a need to do that?"

Emotional Reaction: The 다니 Form

Plain Form + 니

This form is used to quote something that you *heard* someone else say, and to show an *emotional reaction* to hearing it. Because of this, it is often used together with sentences that show an *emotion* or a *feeling* or *thought*.

Adv: This form is originally a shortening of the quoting form that we learned in Chapter 2. The full version would be 다고 하니(까) ("because someone said...").

To make this form, conjugate a verb using the *statement* quoting form that we learned in Chapter 2. Then attach 니. Here are a few examples.

케이크를 다 먹었다니 슬퍼요.
"I'm sad that (I heard) there's no more cake."

항상 밤에 안 잔다니 이상하네.
"It's strange that (I heard) he always doesn't sleep at night."

Chapter 11

Hope and Want

그게 사실이라니 믿을 수 없어.
"I heard that it's true and I can't believe it."

With this form the verb 이다 will become 이라니 after a *consonant*, or 라니 after a *vowel*.

그 드라마에 관심이 없다니 답답해요.
"I heard that you're not interested in that drama and I'm frustrated."

영희도 남자 친구가 생겼다니 정말 부럽다.
"I heard that Yung-hee also got a boyfriend and I'm so jealous."

> **Advanced**
>
> This form is not to be confused with the ending 다니까(요), although both forms are made in the same way. 다니까(요) is also a shortened version of 다고 하니까(요) ("because I said…"), but is used for emphasis when you are *repeating* yourself to someone ("I already said…"). It is only used when speaking *informally*. Here are a few examples.
>
> 바나나가 더 없다니까!
> "I (already) told you there are no more bananas!"
>
> 내가 안 했다니까.
> "I (already) said I didn't do it."
>
> 아니라니까요.
> "I (already) said it's not."
>
> This form will become 이라니까(요) when used after a *consonant*, or 라니까(요) when used after a *vowel*.

민주: 부모님이 빨리 결혼하길 원하셔. 자꾸 남자 친구를 집에 데려오거나 아니면 조건이 더 좋은 다른 사람을 만나래.

> "My parents want me to hurry up and get married. They keep saying to bring my boyfriend home, or to meet a person with better qualifications."

Note that 조건 is pronounced differently from how it is written, as 조껀. This is an exception to the normal sound change rules.

"Want someone to...": Verb Stem + 기(를) 원하다

In the first book we learned that the form 가지고 싶다 is used more often than the verb 원하다 ("to want") to say "I want (something)." But 원하다 is still useful, and you can use it when you want *someone else* to do something, or when you want something to be a certain way.

To use this form, take a verb stem and attach 기. *Optionally*, although most commonly, attach the Object Marker (here, 를). Then conjugate the verb 원하다. You can mark *who* you want to do the verb using the Subject Marker (이/가). Here are a few examples.

Hope and Want

Chapter 11

제가 지금 공부하기를 원하세요?
"Do you want me to study now?"

네가 나를 사랑하기를 원해.
"I want you to love me."

아이들이 가만히 있기를 원해요.
"I want the kids to stay still."

영수가 숙제에 집중하길 원해요.
"I want Yung-soo to focus on his homework."

Commonly, the 기를 verb ending is shortened to 길.

You can also use the (으)면 좋겠다 form ("I/you hope that...") that we learned in Chapter 14 of the second book to say that you want someone else to do something, although using this form is less direct than 원하다.

철수가 숙제에 집중하면 좋겠어요.
"I hope that Chul-soo focuses on his homework."
"I want Chul-soo to focus on his homework."

승아: 정말? 아직 3 개월밖에 안 만났잖아.
"Really? You only dated him for 3 months still."

만나다 ("to meet") is often used to mean "to date" when talking about couples.

민주: 응. 우린 아직 결혼할 준비가 안 됐는데 괜히 남자 친구가 있다고 집에 말해 뒀어.
"Yeah. We're not ready to get married yet, so I told my family that I had a boyfriend for nothing."

Here, 집 ("home," "house") can also be used to mean "family," since telling your "home" means that you are telling the people who live in it. This is a similar concept to how we say "to phone home" (meaning "to phone the *family*") in English.

"Doing for later": Action Verb Stem + 아/어/etc. 놓다/두다

This form can be used to do something *for later* or *in preparation* for something. Literally, the verbs 놓다 and 두다 mean "to put down," but have a different meaning when used in this form.

Chapter 11

Hope and Want

To use this form, take an *action verb stem* and conjugate it as if you were conjugating the 요 form, but without adding the 요. Then conjugate the verb 놓다 or 두다 – either verb is fine. Here are two examples to show how it's used.

오늘 집을 청소할 거예요.
"Today I'll clean the house."

오늘 집을 청소해 놓을 거예요.
"Today I'll clean the house (for later)."

While both sentences can translate the same in English, the second sentence means that the speaker is doing something in preparation for something else, or just for later. Perhaps the speaker in the second example is cleaning the house today because they are going to have guests tomorrow, or because they will be too busy later. Here are a few more examples.

샌드위치를 만들어 놓을게요.
"I'll make some sandwiches (for later)."

오늘 밤까지 설거지를 해 둬.
"Do the dishes by tonight (in preparation for later)."

신발을 여기에 벗어 놓을게요.
"I'll take off my shoes here (so I don't have to later)."

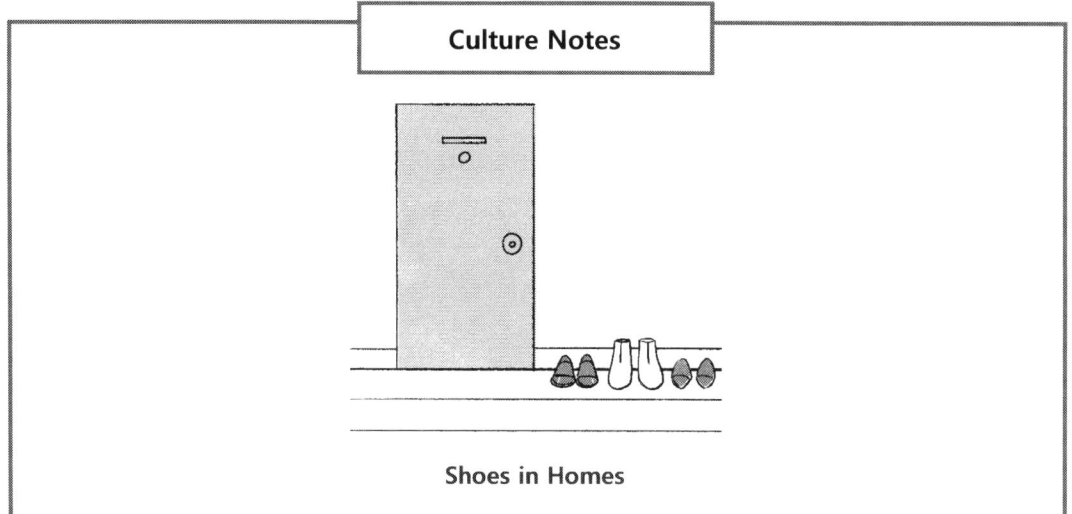

Culture Notes

Shoes in Homes

When entering a Korean home, first remove your shoes and place them together in the entryway. This not only is polite, but also is a cultural requirement. Koreans will not wear shoes inside of their home to avoid bringing in dirt from outside.

Hope and Want

문을 열어 놓았어요.
"I opened the door (and left it open for later)."

내일까지 여행을 갈 준비를 해 놓으세요.
"Please get ready to go on the trip by tomorrow (in preparation for traveling)."

기억해 둘게요.
"I'll remember that (for later when I'll need it)."

불을 켜 놓아.
"Turn on the light (and leave it on for later)."

While you can use either 놓다 or 두다, know that 놓다 is used more often.

> *Informally*, 놓다 will commonly be conjugated as 놔(요), or as 놨어(요) in the past tense.

승아: 너도 고민이 많겠다. 근데 내가 결혼해 보니까 일찍 결혼하는 것도 나쁘지 않아.
"You must have a lot of concerns too. But having gotten married myself, getting married early isn't bad too."

"Having done...": Action Verb Stem + 아/어/etc. 보니(까)

You can use this form to say what you *felt* or *experienced* after having done (here, "tried") something. For example, "Having written a book, it's not that easy."

To use this form, conjugate an *action verb* using the 보다 form ("Try and See") that we learned in the previous book. Conjugate 보다 as 보니(까) – the 까 is *optional*. This form literally means "because I tried (verb)...." Here are two example conjugations.

하다 → 해 보니(까)
먹다 → 먹어 보니(까)

Let's look at a few example sentences.

책을 써 보니까 그렇게 쉽지 않네요.
"Having written a book, it's not that easy."

먹어 보니까 괜찮네.
"Having tried (eating) it, it's alright."

대학생이 돼 보니까 정말 좋네요.
"Having become a college student, it's really nice."

Chapter 11

Hope and Want

한국어를 공부해 보니까 영어에 대해서도 많이 배웠어요.
"Having studied Korean, I learned a lot about English too."

2 달 동안 한국에서 살아 보니까 한국 음식이 얼마나 맛있는지 깨달았어요.
"Having lived in Korea for 2 months, I realized how delicious Korean food is."

생각해 보니까 안 하는 게 나을 거 같아요.
"Having thought about it, I think it'll be better to not do it."

> **Advanced**
>
> This form is different from a similar looking one – Action Verb + 보니(까). For example, 하다 보니(까). This form is also used to show what you *felt* or *experienced*, except *while* the action is still happening. This form is a combination of the 다(가) form for "while" that we learned in Chapter 20 of the previous book, and the 보니까 form. Here are a couple of examples.
>
> 티비를 보다 보니까 엄마가 생각이 났어요.
> "While watching TV, I thought of my mom."
>
> 늦잠을 자다 보니까 3 시가 됐어요.
> "While sleeping (I experienced that) it became 3 o'clock."

민주: 나도 오빠랑 결혼하고 싶은데 아직 오빠가 취업 준비 중이라서 결혼 얘기를 못 하겠어.

> "I want to marry him too, but because he's still in the middle of preparing to find a job I can't talk about marriage (with him)."

Note that you can use a *noun* with 얘기 (or 이야기) and 하다 ("to do") to mean "to talk about (noun)." Or, you can use (noun)에 대해(서) 얘기(를) 하다 as usual – "to talk about (noun)."

승아: 그래. 난 둘이 잘됐으면 좋겠는데 잘 생각해 보고 어떻게 할지 결정하길 바라.

> "Okay. I hope (things between) the two of you work out well, so I hope you think about it (well) and decide what you'll do."

Note that 잘되다 ("to go well") can also mean "to work out well."

잘 생각(을) 하다 (literally, "to think well") can translate more naturally as "to think hard about (something)."

"Hope that...": Verb Stem + 기(를) 바라다

This form works in a similar way to the 원하다 form. You can use the verb 바라다 ("to hope") to say that you *hope* that someone does something (or that something is a certain way).

Hope and Want

To use this form, take a verb stem and attach 기. *Optionally*, although more commonly, attach the Object Marker (here, 를). Then conjugate the verb 바라다. Here are a few examples.

시험 잘 보길 바랄게요.
"I hope you'll do well on the test."

항상 행복하시길 바랍니다.
"I hope that you're always happy."

빨리 낫길 바라요.
"I hope that you'll get better soon."

낫다 ("to be preferable," "to be better") is also commonly used to mean "to recover" or "to get better (from an illness)."

누나도 오길 바라요.
"I hope that you'll come too."

어떻게 되길 바라요?
"How do you hope that it'll go?"

> **Advanced**
>
> **The Vowel ㅏ**
>
> For a small amount of words, the ㅏ sound can sometimes be pronounced *incorrectly* as ㅐ or ㅔ. For example, 바라(요) can be pronounced as 바래(요), 같아(요) can be pronounced as 같애(요), and 아기 can be pronounced as 애기. This only happens with a few specific words in spoken Korean, so I would only recommend learning more words as you hear them. Also note that while these words may be fairly common in spoken Korean, they are *incorrect*.

건강하길.
"Hope that you're healthy."

When speaking *casually* the 기(를) verb ending (or 길) can also be used on its own without 바라다 to have the same meaning. This form will most often appear in writing, such as in a letter to a friend.

민주: 잘 생각해 봐야지. 얘기 들어 줘서 고마워.
"I need to think about it (well). Thanks for listening (to me)."

Remember that it's common in casual speech (or writing) to remove the verb 하다 or 되다 when saying "have to," as both 하다 and 되다 have a similar meaning. In the conversation sentence, 봐야지 comes from the verb 보다 and 야 하지 (or 야 되지).

| Chapter 11 | **Hope and Want** |

> **Adv**
> The 원하다 form can also be used to say that *you* want to do something (similar to the 고 싶다 form). However, this usage sounds a bit more formal and is not commonly used.
>
> 집으로 가고 싶어요.
> 집으로 가기를 원해요.
> "I want to go home."

Practice

Translate to Korean:

1. "Is it time to eat?"

   _____.

2. "No matter how much I want it, I can't get it."

   _____.

3. "I'm happy that (I heard) you did well on the test."

   _____.

4. "I want Jeremy to do the dishes today."

   _____.

5. "I want you to shave your beard."

   _____.

6. "I'll study the science textbook (for later)."

   _____.

7. "I bought a ticket (for later)."

   _____.

8. "Having tried (eating) liver, it's not bad."

   _____.

Hope and Want

9. "Having worked in a factory, I don't want to recommend it."

10. "I hope that you will succeed."

Translate to English:

11. 식사할 준비를 했어요.

12. 아무리 울어도 도와주는 사람이 없었어요.

13. 지갑을 잃어 버렸다니 안됐네요.

14. 취직했다니 잘됐네요.

15. 네가 좀 더 잘 생각해 보길 원해.

16. 우유를 냉장고에 넣어 놓았어요.

17. 신문을 책상 위에 펴 놓았어요.

18. 한 번 사 보니까 또 사고 싶어요.

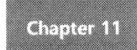

Hope and Want

19. 아이를 키워 보니까 부모님의 마음을 이해할 수 있어요.

_____.

20. 다 잘되길 바라.

_____.

New Phrases

어쩔 수 없어요.	"It can't be helped."

New Vocabulary

준비(가) 되다	"to be prepared"
남자 친구(가) 생기다	"to get a boyfriend"
여자 친구(가) 생기다	"to get a girlfriend"
어쩔 수(가) 없다	"to be inevitable," "to be nothing one can do about something"
가만히 있다	"to stay still," "to keep still"
조건	"qualification," "a condition (for something)"
두다	"to put down"
취업	"getting/finding a job"
취직(을) 하다	"to get a job"
바라다	"to hope"
필요	"a necessity," "a need"
소원	"a desire," "a wish"
수염	"beard," "mustache"
염소	"goat"
염소 수염	"goatee" (literally, "goat beard")
깎다	"to trim," "to mow"
펴다	"to open up (something)," "to unfold"
공장	"factory"
간	"liver"
늦잠(을) 자다	"to sleep late"

Making Decisions

Chapter 12

Conversation

마크:	만기야, 나 드디어 새로운 텐트를 사기로 결정했어.
만기:	와. 축하해. 그런데 텐트 말고 뭐 살 거 있다고 하지 않았어?
마크:	응. 원래 침낭을 새로 살 계획이었는데 그거 대신에 텐트를 먼저 사려고.
만기:	그렇구나. 그럼 이제 캠핑을 자주 가기 시작하겠네.
마크:	응. 사실 다음 주 주말에 여자 친구와 캠핑을 갈 생각인데 너도 같이 갈래?
만기:	나도 가고 싶은데 다음 주 주말까지 마무리해야 되는 일이 있어서 아직 잘 모르겠어.
마크:	나는 개인적으로 네가 같이 갈 수 있으면 좋겠어. 갈 수 있으면 꼭 얘기해 줘.
만기:	그래. 그렇게 할게.

This chapter will focus on a few grammar forms that relate to making decisions, such as how to *decide* to do something, how to *plan* to do something, how to *think* of doing something, and more. Let's go right into the conversation.

마크: 만기야, 나 드디어 새로운 텐트를 사기로 결정했어.
> Hey Man-gi, I finally decided to buy a new tent."

Chapter 12: Making Decisions

"Decide to": Action Verb Stem + 기로 하다

You can use this form to "decide to" do something. For example, "I decided to go to the store."

To use it, take an *action verb stem* and attach 기, followed by 로. Then conjugate the verb 하다 ("to do") anyway that you like. Here are a few examples.

가게에 가기로 했어요.
"I decided to go to the store."

Notice how in this form the main action verb – here, 가다 ("to go") – remains in the *present tense*, and only the verb 하다 at the end is conjugated to the *past tense*.

오늘은 설거지를 하기로 했어요.
"Today I decided to do the dishes."

새로운 지갑을 사기로 했어요.
"I decided to buy a new wallet."

친구의 이사를 도와주기로 했어요.
"I decided to help my friend move."

공부하지 않기로 했어요.
공부를 안 하기로 했어요.
"I decided not to study."

원래 가기로 했는데, 감기에 걸려서 못 갔어요.
"Originally I had decided to go, but I caught a cold so I couldn't (go)."

The *adverb* 원래 ("original," "originally") is also commonly used together with this form.

술을 끊기로 했어요.
"I decided to quit alcohol."

Another verb that can be used with this form is 결정(을) 하다 ("to decide," "to make a decision"). The meaning is the same.

술을 끊기로 결정했어요.
"I decided to quit alcohol."

소방관이 되기로 결정했어요.
"I decided to become a firefighter."

Making Decisions

Chapter 12

2 시에 공원에서 만나기로 결정했어요.
"We decided to meet at the park at 2 o'clock."

Advanced

This form can also be used with other verbs that can be related to making a *decision*, such as 약속(을) 하다 ("to promise") and 결심(을) 하다 ("to be determined to do," "to resolve to do").

오늘 요리해 주기로 약속했어요.
"I promised to cook for him today."

대학원에 가기로 결심했어요.
"I was determined to go to graduate school."

> 만기: 와. 축하해. 그런데 텐트 말고 뭐 살 거 있다고 하지 않았어?
>
> "Nice. Congrats. But didn't you say there was something (else) that you'll buy, (and) not a tent?"

We learned that 와아 is an *exclamation* that can be used to mean "Wow!" 와 has the same meaning, but is slightly less enthusiastic. A natural translation for 와 could be "Nice."

Remember that due to sound change rules, 거 in this sentence (살 거) would be pronounced as 꺼 since it comes after ㄹ.

> 마크: 응. 원래 침낭을 새로 살 계획이었는데 그거 대신에 텐트를 먼저 사려고.
>
> "Yeah. Originally I was planning to buy a new sleeping bag, but instead of that I'm going to buy a tent first."

"Plan to": Action Verb Stem + (을/ㄹ) 계획이다

You can "plan to" do something by using the noun 계획 ("plan").

To use this form, take an *action verb stem* and attach 을 if it ends in a *consonant*, or attach ㄹ if it ends in a *vowel*. Then add 계획 and conjugate 이다 ("to be") any way that you would like. Here are a few examples.

내일 서울로 갈 계획이에요.
"I'm planning to go to Seoul tomorrow."

그 날은 숙제할 계획이에요.
"I'm planning to do my homework that day."

오늘 밤에 머리를 감을 계획이라서 만나지 못할 거 같아요.
"Tonight I'm planning to wash my hair so I don't think we can meet."

Chapter 12

Making Decisions

원래 갈 계획이었는데, 감기에 걸려서 못 갔어요.
"Originally I was planning to go, but I caught a cold so I couldn't (go)."

The *adverb* 원래 is also commonly used with this form.

일찍 퇴직할 계획이세요?
"Are you planning to retire early?"

여자 친구하고 같이 저녁을 먹을 계획이었는데....
"I was planning to eat dinner together with my girlfriend...."

> **Advanced**
>
> This form can also be used with the noun 예정 ("schedule") in the same way. It has the same meaning, but is slightly more *formal* than using 계획. Here are a few examples.
>
> 주말에 뭐할 예정이에요?
> "What are you planning to do this weekend?"
>
> 3시 전에 집에 돌아갈 예정이라고 했어요.
> "He said that he's planning to return home before 3 o'clock."
>
> 오늘 회장님과 같이 저녁을 먹을 예정입니다.
> "I'm planning to eat dinner together with the president tonight."

"Instead of": Noun 대신에

You can say something "instead of" something else by using this form. For example, "I ate an apple instead of an orange."

To use this form, take a *noun* and put 대신에 after it (with a space). Then finish the rest of the sentence. For example:

오렌지 대신에 사과를 먹었어요.
"I ate an apple instead of an orange."

Note that 대신에 is used *after* what it is "instead of," and not before like in English.

그거 대신에 이거 하세요.
"Do this instead of that."

노트북 대신에 컴퓨터를 사는 건 어때요?
"How about buying a computer instead of a laptop?"

치마 대신에 바지를 입었어요.
"I wore pants instead of a skirt."

Making Decisions

Chapter 12

저 대신에 해 주세요.
"Please do it instead of me."

철수 대신에 민우한테 물어보려고요.
"I'll ask Min-woo instead of Chul-soo."

Adv | Note that the 에 in 대신에 is *optional*, but is most commonly added.

"Instead of": Action Verb Stem + 는 대신에

You can also use this form with *action verbs*, simply by adding 는 (just as you would when changing an action verb into an adjective). For example, "I read a book instead of *watching* a movie."

영화를 보는 대신에 책을 읽었어요.
"I read a book instead of watching a movie."

파티에 가는 대신에 시험 공부를 했어요.
"I studied for my test instead of going to the party."

도서관에서 공부하는 대신에 공원에 놀러 갔어요.
"I went to the park to play instead of studying at the library."

뭘 먹는 대신에 물을 마실래요.
"I want to drink water instead of eating something."

잠을 자는 대신에 밤 늦게까지 남자 친구랑 전화 통화했어요.
"I talked on the phone with my boyfriend until late at night instead of sleeping."

Chapter 12 — Advanced

Making Decisions

This same form is also commonly used to mean "in exchange for" or "in return for." Here are two examples.

내가 이걸 하는 대신에 그걸 해 줘.
"Please do that for me in return for me doing this."

제가 숙제를 도와주는 대신에 저녁을 만들어 주세요.
"Please make me dinner in exchange for helping your homework."

만기: 그렇구나. 그럼 이제 캠핑을 자주 가기 시작하겠네.
"I see. Then you'll start going camping often from now."

The ending 구나 is similar to the 군(요) ending that we learned in the previous book. It can be used in a sentence when you want to add the feeling of *realizing* something. However, while 군(요) can be used in formal speech, 구나 is only used in *casual* speech. Here are a couple of examples.

맛있군(요)!
맛있구나!
"Oh, it's really good!"

김치를 진짜 좋아하는군(요).
김치를 진짜 좋아하는구나.
"Wow, he really likes kimchi."

Just as 군(요) becomes 는군(요) when used with *action verbs*, 구나 will become 는구나.

To Start: Action Verb Stem + 기(를) 시작(을) 하다

You can use this form to "start" or "begin" doing something.

To use this form, take an *action verb stem* and attach 기(를) – the 를 is *optional*. Then conjugate the verb 시작(을) 하다 ("to begin," "to start") any way that you would like.

언제부터 운동하기 시작했어요?
"From when did you start exercising?"

벌써 밥 먹기 시작했어요.
"He already started eating."

지금 새로운 컴퓨터를 만들기 시작하고 있어요.
"Now I'm starting to make a new computer."

Making Decisions

내일부터 열심히 공부하기 시작할 거예요.
"From tomorrow I'll start studying hard."

To Stop: 그만 Action Verb

To say to "stop" doing something, you can use the *adverb* 그만 before an *action verb*. Here are a few examples.

그만하세요.
"Stop (doing it)."

Note that the verb 그만하다, which we previously learned, comes directly from this adverb.

그만 봐.
"Stop looking."

그만 만나요.
"Stop meeting her."

그만 먹었어요.
"He stopped eating."

> **Adv** 그만 literally means "only (up to) that amount." The sentence 그만 먹었어요 literally means "He ate only up to that amount."

마크: 응. 사실 다음 주 주말에 여자 친구와 캠핑을 갈 생각인데 너도 같이 갈래?
"Yeah. I'm actually thinking of going camping with my girlfriend next weekend, but do you want to go together too?"

"Thinking of": Action Verb Stem + (을/ㄹ) 생각이다

You can say that you are *thinking* of doing something using the noun 생각 ("an idea," "a thought") with the verb 이다 ("to be") – just as we learned how to use 계획.

Sentences using this form will translate slightly differently from the 생각(을) 하다 form that we learned in Chapter 3. Here are examples of both forms.

내일 갈 거라고 생각해요.
"I think that I'll go tomorrow."

Chapter 12

Making Decisions

내일 갈 생각이에요.
"I'm thinking of going tomorrow."

Here are a few more examples of this form.

버스를 탈 생각이에요.
"I'm thinking of taking a bus."

어떻게 할 생각이세요?
"What are you thinking of doing (about it)?"

Note that depending on the context you could also translate the above sentence as "How are you thinking of doing it?" Literally 어떻게 means "how," but when used with 하다 it can translate more naturally as "what." For example, 그건 어떻게 했어요? can translate naturally as "What did you do (about it)?" or literally as "How did you do that?" This works in a similar way to using the phrase 취미가 어떻게 돼요? when asking someone to tell you *about* their hobbies.

우선 부모님께 선물을 사 드릴 생각이에요.
"First of all I'm thinking of buying a present for my parents."

오늘은 잠을 자지 않을 생각이에요.
"I'm thinking of not sleeping today."

To say that you are *not* thinking of doing something, you can use a negative verb before 생각이다, such as in the above example, or you can use the verb 없다 ("to not exist") instead of 이다 – as 생각(이) 없다.

지금은 먹을 생각이 없어요.
"I'm not thinking of eating now."

난 거기 갈 생각이 없어.
"I'm not thinking of going there."

만기: 나도 가고 싶은데 다음 주 주말까지 마무리해야 되는 일이 있어서 아직 잘 모르겠어.

> "I want to go too, but there's something I have to finish up by next weekend so I don't know yet."

마크: 나는 개인적으로 네가 같이 갈 수 있으면 좋겠어. 갈 수 있으면 꼭 얘기해 줘.

> "Personally I hope you can go together (with us). Make sure to tell me if you can go."

Making Decisions

Chapter 12

The Suffix 적

적 is a common *suffix* (a word ending). It can be attached to certain *Sino-Korean words* – words that originally comes from the Chinese language – to change their meaning. However, it is best to simply learn the words that can use 적 one at a time, and to be able to recognize new ones as you see them than to worry about guessing if a word is Sino-Korean or not, as there is no easy way to guess.

적 can be used to change a Sino-Korean noun into an *adverb*, a *descriptive verb*, and an *adjective*. Let's first look at one example.

Noun: 기본 ("the basics," "fundamentals")
Adverb: 기본적으로 ("basically," "fundamentally")
Descriptive Verb: 기본적이다 ("to be basic," "to be fundamental")
Adjective: 기본적인 ("basic," "fundamental")

There are many Sino-Korean nouns that can use 적. Fortunately, it is only necessary to focus on learning the most common ones at first. Later on, as you see and hear new ones used you will be able to recognize them and understand their meaning without having to look them up in a dictionary. Once you are familiar with how 적 works, as long as you know the meaning of the original Sino-Korean noun you will be able to understand its meaning when used with 적.

To use it, take a Sino-Korean noun and attach 적. Then, to turn it into an *adverb* add 으로. Or, to turn it into a *descriptive verb* add the verb 이다 ("to be"). You can then change that descriptive verb into an *adjective* by conjugating 이다 to 인 (or 이었던, depending on the sentence). Let's take a look at another example.

Noun: 문화 ("culture")
Adverb: 문화적으로 ("culturally")
Descriptive Verb: 문화적이다 ("to be cultural")
Adjective: 문화적인 ("cultural")

You might think that adding 적 is simply like adding "al" to the end of a word in English. In most cases, this is correct. In other cases, know that 적 is used to show that something has the *properties* of something else. For example, 문화적 means that something has the properties of 문화. Here is one more example.

Noun: 과학 ("science")
Adverb: 과학적으로 ("scientifically")
Descriptive Verb: 과학적이다 ("to be scientific")
Adjective: 과학적인 ("scientific")

| Chapter 12 | # Making Decisions |

Review this chapter's vocabulary list for more words.

> **Adv**: You can also use the suffix 적 as an *adjective* without adding the verb 이다. This is more common in *print* (such as in a newspaper). For example, 문화적(인) 문제 would mean "cultural problem."

만기: 그래. 그렇게 할게.
"Okay. I will (do that)."

Practice

Translate to Korean:

1. "I decided to teach Korean to a friend."

   _____.

2. "I decided to watch a movie with my parents tonight."

   _____.

3. "I decided to (go on a) diet."

   _____.

4. "I'm planning to study for 4 hours tomorrow."

   _____.

5. "I'm planning to wake up at 8 o'clock."

   _____.

6. "I'm planning to buy a truck next year."

   _____.

7. "I want to relax instead of going to work."

   _____.

Making Decisions

8. "I wrote a letter instead of buying a present."

_____.

9. "I'll buy you lunch instead of dinner."

_____.

10. "Many people started giving up."

_____.

11. "I started saving up money to buy a house."

_____.

12. "I'm thinking of helping."

_____.

13. "I was thinking of doing that."

_____.

14. "I'm not thinking of exercising in the morning."

_____.

Translate to English:

15. 책을 빌려 주기로 했어요.

_____.

16. 동생에게 좋은 오빠가 되기로 했어요.

_____.

17. 방학 동안 규칙적인 생활을 할 계획이에요.

_____.

Chapter 12 Making Decisions

18. 내년에는 피아노를 배울 계획이에요.

    _____.

19. 엄마 대신에 아빠한테 허락 받았어요.

    _____.

20. 주말에 일을 하는 대신에 보너스를 받았어요.

    _____.

21. 아기가 걸어 다니기 시작했어요.

    _____.

22. 언제부터 요리를 배우기 시작할 건지 궁금했어요.

    _____.

23. 계속 직진할 생각이세요?

    _____.

24. 쭉 가서 다음 신호등에서 우회전할 생각이에요.

    _____.

New Phrases

와.	"Wow.", "Nice."
우선	"First of all..."

New Vocabulary

텐트	"tent"
침낭	"sleeping bag"
개인적	"personal"
그만	"stop" (adverb)

Making Decisions

마무리(를) 하다	"to finish (up)," "to complete (something)"
소방관	"firefighter"
소방서	"fire station"
결심(을) 하다	"to be determined to do," "to resolve to do"
대학원	"graduate school"
이사	"a move (to another residence)"
예정	"schedule"
머리(를) 감다	"to wash (one's) hair"
(옷[을]) 빨다	"to wash (clothes)"
과학적	"scientific"
문화적	"cultural"
역사적	"historic"
경제적	"economical"
지리적	"geographical"
사회적	"social"
전통	"tradition"
전통적	"traditional"
기계적	"mechanical"
충격적이다	"to be shocking"
자발적	"voluntary"
자동적	"automatic"
효과	"effect"
효과적	"effective"
규칙적	"regular," "orderly"
구체적	"concrete," "specific"
조언	"advice," "counsel"
허락	"permission"
허락(을) 받다	"to get permission"
보너스	"bonus"
걸어 다니다	"to walk around," "to move about"
포기(를) 하다	"to give up"
신호등	"traffic light"

Chapter 12: Making Decisions

쭉 가다	"to go straight"
직진(을) 하다	"to drive straight (forward)"
후진(을) 하다	"to reverse (when driving)"
우회전(을) 하다	"to turn to the right (when driving)"
좌회전(을) 하다	"to turn to the left (while driving)"
멈춰 서다	"to come to a halt"
퇴직(을) 하다	"to resign (from a job)," "to retire (from work, from a task)"
은퇴(를) 하다	"to retire (from working)"
출장	"company trip"
야근	"(overtime) night work"
트럭	"truck"
오토바이	"motorcycle"

Looks and Sounds Like

Chapter 13

Conversation

민아:	어머, 새로운 잡지가 나왔나 보네. 크리스야, 이 연예인 너랑 정말 많이 닮았다.
크리스:	그래? 그 연예인은 조금 토끼처럼 생겼는데?
민아:	아니야. 이 사진이 각도가 이상해서 그렇게 보이나 보네. 원래 잘생겼어.
크리스:	그 연예인보다는 옆에 있는 연예인이 나랑 비슷해 보이지 않아? 분위기가 닮았다는 얘기를 종종 들어.
민아:	내가 보기에는 별로 안 닮았는데.
크리스:	최근에 머리를 잘라서 그런가 봐.
민아:	그럴 수도 있겠다.

This chapter will focus on learning how to say that something "looks like" something else. There are several forms that we will cover, and each is a bit different. We will learn one form that we can use with *descriptive verbs*, and one form that we can use with *action verbs*. There are also a few more forms for specific situations that we will also cover, and I will explain each one along the way. Let's get started.

민아: 어머, 새로운 잡지가 나왔나 보네. 크리스야, 이 연예인 너랑 정말 많이 닮았다.

"Oh my, it seems the new magazine came out. Chris, this celebrity really looks like you a lot."

어머 ("Oh dear.") can also translate as "Oh my," depending on the context.

Chapter 13 — Looks and Sounds Like

"I guess (that)..." & "It seems (like)...": Action Verb Stem + 나 보다

You can use this form to say "I guess (that)" or "It seems (like)." Because this form is used with action verbs, you can use it to *assume* that someone *does* (or *did*) something. For example, you could use this form to say "I guess that he doesn't *eat* cheese," or "It seems like he doesn't *eat* cheese."

To use it, take an *action verb stem* (in any tense) and attach 나. Then conjugate the verb 보다 to the *present tense*. Here are some examples.

치즈를 안 먹나 봐요.
"I guess that he doesn't eat cheese."
"It seems like he doesn't eat cheese."

선생님이 아직 안 오셨나 보네.
"I guess the teacher hasn't come yet."
"It seems the teacher hasn't come yet."

어린이가 공원에서 노나 봐요.
"I guess the child is playing in the park."
"It seems the child is playing in the park."

Note that verb stems ending in ㄹ will conjugate without the ㄹ, which is usual when adding grammar forms that use the consonant ㄴ.

옆 집에서 파티를 하나 봐요.
"I guess that they're having a party next door."
"It seems like they're having a party next door."

벌써 나갔나 봐요.
"I guess she already left."
"It seems she already left."

못 하겠나 봐.
"I guess he won't be able to do it."
"It seems he won't be able to do it."

많이 좋아하나 보죠?
"I guess he likes it a lot, right?"
"It seems he likes it a lot, right?"

Looks and Sounds Like

Chapter 13

올해 장마가 일찍 왔나 봐.
"I guess the rainy season came early this year."
"It seems the rainy season came early this year."

Culture Notes

장마 comes once a year in Korea in the summertime. During 장마, it rains for several days continually (with random breaks). Unfortunately, this is not cool and refreshing rain, but warm rain that increases the humidity even more (like taking a shower with your clothes on). If you are in Korea during 장마, be sure to carry around an umbrella at all times.

정말 재미있나 봐요.
"I guess it's really entertaining."
"It seems really entertaining."

Note that 있다 ("to exist") and 없다 ("to not exist") can conjugate with this form as 있나 and 없나.

> **Adv** Another possible natural English translation for this form is "It looks like." Focus on first learning it as "I guess (that)" or "It seems (like)" in order to understand how it's different from the other forms in this chapter.

Resembling Someone: 닮다

You can use the *action verb* 닮다 ("to resemble," "to look like") to say that someone resembles someone else, or looks like someone else. Note that this verb is not used for saying that someone seems like someone else – you can use the other forms in this chapter for that – but is only used for talking about *physical* similarities. 닮다 is used in the *past tense*. You can use either the Object Marker (을/를) or "with" – (이)랑, 과/와, and 하고 – to mark *who* someone resembles. Here are a few examples.

Chapter 13

Looks and Sounds Like

내가 누구(를) 닮았어?
내가 누구(랑) 닮았어?
"Who do I resemble?"
"Who do I look like?"

걔랑 조금 닮았어.
"It resembles him a little."
"It looks like him a little."

아기가 아빠를 닮았어요.
"The baby resembles the father."
"The baby looks like the father."

정말 대통령을 닮은 거 같아?
"Do you really think I resemble the President?"
"Do you really think I look like the President?"

크리스: 그래? 그 연예인은 조금 토끼처럼 생겼는데?
"Really? That celebrity looks a little like a rabbit."

"To look like...": Noun + 처럼 생겼다

You can use this form to say that someone or something looks like someone or something else. It is used for describing someone or something *physically*. For example, this form is *not* used to say that something looks like a good idea since that is not a physical description. Instead, it could be used to say that something physically looks like, for example, a wristwatch. This form uses 처럼 ("like," "as") along with 생기다 ("to come up," "to arise," "to happen") in the past tense. Just as 잘생겼다 (literally, "came up well" or "arose well") can be used to mean "handsome," 처럼 생겼다 can be used to mean "appears like" a noun.

To use it, take a *noun* and attach 처럼. Then conjugate 생겼다, which is already in the past tense, any way that you would like. Here are a few examples.

손목시계처럼 생겼어요.
"It looks like a wristwatch."

무서운 사람처럼 생겼어요.
"He looks like a scary person."

원숭이처럼 생긴 고양이를 샀어요.
"I bought a cat that looks like a monkey."

Looks and Sounds Like

바보처럼 생겼어.
"He looks like an idiot."

Adv

As we learned in the previous book, you can also use 같이 in place of 처럼 in the same way. Remember that 처럼 is more commonly used than 같이.

Advanced

"To look like...": Noun + 처럼 보이다

You can also use the verb 보이다 ("to be seen," "to appear") in place of 생겼다. 보이다 can then be conjugated to any tense you would like. Compare this form with 생겼다, which is only conjugated to the *past tense* but is used to mean the *present tense* ("He looks..."). We will cover how to use 보이다 more in this chapter. Here is a quick example.

바보처럼 보여요.
"He looks like an idiot."

바보처럼 보였어요.
"He looked like an idiot."

바보 처럼 보일 거예요.
"He will look like an idiot."

Although the verb 보이다 can be used in different tenses, it is less common than 생겼다 in this form.

민아: 아니야. 이 사진이 각도가 이상해서 그렇게 보이나 보네. 원래 잘생겼어.
"No. I guess he looks like that because the photo angle is strange. Normally he's handsome."

"Looks...": Descriptive Verb Stem + 아/어/etc. 보이다

Now that we have learned how to say that something "looks like" a noun using the 처럼 생겼다 form, let's learn how to say that someone or something physically "looks" a certain way using a *descriptive verb*. For example, "You look tired."

To use this form, take a *descriptive verb* and conjugate it to the 요 form, but without adding the 요. Then conjugate the verb 보이다 ("to be seen," "to appear") any way that you would like. Note that 보이다 conjugates as 보여(요) in the 요 form. Here are a few examples.

피곤해 보여요.
"You look tired."

힘들어 보인다.
"It looks difficult."

Chapter 13

Looks and Sounds Like

재미있어 보인다.
"It looks fun."

Note that 있다 ("to exist") and 없다 ("to not exist") can conjugate with this form as 있어 and 없어.

그래 보여요.
"You look like that."

When using 그렇다 ("to be so") with this form, you can use either 그래 보이다 or 그렇게 보이다. Both have the same meaning.

> **Advanced**
>
> **Descriptive Verb Stem + 게 보이다**
>
> Although much less common, this form can also be used with *adverbs* made from descriptive verbs using 게. This form has the same meaning as the 아/어/etc. 보이다 form.
>
> To use it, take a *descriptive verb stem* and attach 게 (as we learned in Chapter 6 of the second book). Then conjugate the verb 보이다. For example:
>
> 맛있어 보였어요.
> 맛있게 보였어요.
> "It looked delicious."

조금 슬퍼 보이지 않았어?
"Didn't he look a little sad?"

오늘은 너무 바빠 보여요.
"She looks busy today."

그 기사를 읽으면서 행복해 보였겠다.
"He must've looked happy while reading that article."

> **Adv**
>
> 보이다 ("to be seen," "to appear") is a *passive verb*, and originally comes from the verb 보다 ("to see"). We will learn about passive verbs in detail in Chapter 15.

Going back to the conversation, 원래 ("original," "originally") can also be translated as "normally."

크리스: 그 연예인보다는 옆에 있는 연예인이 나랑 비슷해 보이지 않아? 분위기가 닮았다는 얘기를 종종 들어.

"More than that celebrity, doesn't the celebrity next to him look similar to me? Sometimes I hear that my image resembles him."

Looks and Sounds Like

Chapter 13

You can use the descriptive verb 비슷하다 ("to be similar") and the 보이다 form that we just learned to say that someone (or something) looks *similar* to someone else (or something else). It can be used with the particle "with" – (이)랑, 과/와, 하고. In Korean, "to be similar to" is literally said as "to be similar *with*." For example, "He looks similar to me" could be 저와 비슷해 보여요. The same applies to other verbs, such as 다르다 ("to be different") which literally becomes "to be different with" in Korean when you want to *compare* two people or things. Keep an eye out for other examples of the "with" particles as you see them in the future.

분위기 ("atmosphere," "an image") is most commonly used to mean the atmosphere of a *situation* or *location* ("The restaurant has a nice atmosphere"), but it can also be used to mean an image (or "air") of a *person*.

식당의 분위기가 좋아요.
"The restaurant has a nice atmosphere."

철수의 분위기가 나랑 많이 달라.
"Chul-soo's image is a lot different from me."

Plain Form + 는 Noun

분위기가 닮았다는 얘기 from the example conversation literally means "talk (saying) that I resemble his image." This grammar is similar to the 뜻이다 form that we learned in Chapter 6, but this grammar can be used with more nouns than only 뜻. It is also similar to the 것(을) 알다 form that we learned in Chapter 1, but this grammar can be used with more verbs than only 알다 and 모르다.

This form is a shortened version of **다고 말하는**, which is a quoting form that we learned in Chapter 2. It means "that (someone says) (Plain Form)." For example, "I know that (someone says) Chul-soo speaks Korean well." We previously used this same grammar with the verbs 알다 and 모르다 to say that we "know" or "do not know" a *fact* or piece of *information*. Here is an example with the 것(을) 알다 form.

제레미가 한국어를 잘한다는 것을 알고 있어요.
"I know (the fact) that (someone says) Jeremy speaks Korean well."

First, let's change just the final verb to something different to show more about how this form can work.

제레미가 한국어를 잘한다는 것을 믿지 못했어요.
"I couldn't believe (the fact) that (someone says) Jeremy speaks Korean well."

Chapter 13

Looks and Sounds Like

In addition to changing the final verb, we can also change the noun 것 ("thing") – which here is being used to mean "the fact" – to other nouns. For example, we can use the noun 이야기 (or 얘기) to mean "*talk* that (someone says) (Plain Form)." By "talk," I mean "the story," "the gossip," or "the conversation." This will commonly be used with the verb 듣다 ("to listen").

영희가 했다는 얘기를 들었어요.
"I heard (the gossip) that (someone said) Yung-hee did it."

이번 시험이 어려울 거라는 얘기를 들었어요.
"I heard (the story) that (someone said) the test this time will be difficult."

돈이 더 없다는 얘기를 들었어요.
"I heard (the conversation) that (someone said) there's no more money."

This 이야기(를) 듣다 form might appear to be similar to the normal quotation form that we learned with the Plain Form and 듣다 (for example, 했다고 들었어요), and they are not that different. This form simply adds a bit of extra meaning to the sentence through the noun being used. For example, you could also say 돈이 더 없다고 들었어요 ("I heard that there's no more money.") to mean the same general thing, but it would be missing the meaning of "the talk that" (or "the gossip that," etc.) which gives the meaning that people are also *talking* about it, and not just that you heard it. The same applies to the conversation example. 분위기가 닮았다는 얘기를 종종 들어 could also be written as 분위기가 닮았다고 들어 to have the same general meaning.

Now we can go back to the 뜻이다 form again that we learned in Chapter 6 and look at it in a new way. We can think of it as meaning literally "meaning that (someone says) (Plain Form)."

제레미가 한국어를 잘한다는 뜻이에요.
"It means that (someone says) Jeremy speaks Korean well."

We can also go back to the 것(을) 알다 form that we learned in Chapter 1 and look at it again as meaning "the fact/thing that (someone says) (Plain Form)."

영희가 했다는 것을 알고 있어요.
"I know (the fact) that (someone says) Yung-hee did it."

Looks and Sounds Like

Chapter 13

You will also see this same form used with other nouns and verbs, but we will not go into them in detail in this book. Understanding the general form first will help you to later become comfortable with using it in any way. For example, if you understand that the 것(을) 알다 form means "to know the fact (that)," then if you saw 거짓말 ("lie") used with the verb 듣다 ("to listen") in the same way (with the Plain Form) then you would be able to know that it meant "to hear the lie (that)." For example, 민우가 했다는 거짓말을 들었어요 ("I heard the lie that Min-woo did it.").

If learning the overall meaning of this form is difficult at first, it might be easier to first memorize these forms one at a time separately. Here is a simpler way to remember these three forms. The 것(을) 알다 form means "to know (the fact) *that*." The 뜻이다 form means "it means (that)." And the 이야기(를) 듣다 form means "to hear *that*."

> 민아: 내가 보기에는 별로 안 닮았는데.
> "As I see it he doesn't really look like you."

내가 보기에(는), or 제가 보기에(는) literally means "In me seeing it." More naturally, you can translate this phrase as "The way I see it," "As I see it," or even "In my opinion."

> **Advanced**
>
> **"Because": Verb Stem + 기에**
>
> The 기 ending can also be used after verb stems with the particle 에 in the same way as 기 때문에. This form is much less common, and is occasionally used in writing. More *casually*, the 기에 form can also be said as 길래. Here's an example.
>
> 엄마가 나가셨**기 때문에** 친구를 초대했어요.
> 엄마가 나가셨**기에** 친구를 초대했어요.
> 엄마가 나가셨**길래** 친구를 초대했어요.
> "I invited a friend because my mother left."

> 크리스: 최근에 머리를 잘라서 그런가 봐.
> "I guess it's (so) because I cut my hair recently."

"I guess (that)..." & "It seems (like)...": Descriptive Verb Stem + (은/ㄴ) + 가 보다

You can use this form to say "I guess (that)" or "It seems (like)" with *descriptive verbs*. For example, you could use this form to say "I guess that the water is cold," or "It seems like the water is cold."

To use it, take a *descriptive verb stem* and conjugate it in the same way that we learned how to conjugate *informal questions* in the *present tense* (covered in Chapter 4). Then conjugate the verb 보다 to the *present tense*. Here are some examples.

Chapter 13

Looks and Sounds Like

물이 차가운가 봐요.
"I guess that the water is cold."
"It seems like the water is cold."

날씨가 더운가 봐.
"I guess the weather's hot."
"It seems the weather's hot."

한국 사람인가 봐요.
"I guess she's a Korean."
"It seems she's a Korean."

심심한가 보네요.
"I guess that you're bored."
"It seems like you're bored."

아주 좋은가 봐요.
"I guess it's very good."
"It seems very good."

배고프지 않은가 봐요?
"I guess you're not hungry?"
"It seems you're not hungry?"

안 할 건가 봐요.
"I guess that he won't do it."
"It seems like he won't do it."

수영장이 깊은가 보네요.
"I guess that the swimming pool is deep."
"It seems that the swimming pool is deep."

Note that 깊다 ("to be deep") can be used for describing the *depth* of something (such as a body of water), or for describing *thoughts*. Its opposite, 얕다 ("to be shallow") can also be used to describe both depth and thoughts. However, 짧다 which means "to be short (in length)" is more commonly used to describe a shallow *thought*.

Remember that the *informal questions* form that we learned is used with descriptive verbs in the *present tense*. So to use this form in the *past tense*, you will need to switch back to the 나 보다 form. Here are a few of the previous examples re-written in the past tense.

Looks and Sounds Like

Chapter 13

물이 차가웠나 봐요.
"I guess that the water was cold."
"It seems like the water was cold."

한국 사람이었나 봐요.
"I guess she was a Korean."
"It seems she was a Korean."

안 했나 봐요.
"I guess that he didn't do it."
"It seems like he didn't do it."

> **Advanced**
>
> **More on 나 보다 and 가 보다**
>
> We learned that the 나 보다 form is used with *action verbs*, and the 가 보다 form is used with *descriptive verbs*. However, there is an exception. The 나 보다 form can also be used with descriptive verbs in certain cases. This is common only when the descriptive verb stem ends in a *consonant*. Here are a few examples.
>
> 작다 → 작은가 보다 or 작나 보다
> 덥다 → 더운가 보다 or 덥나 보다
> 많다 → 많은가 보다 or 많나 보다
> 바쁘다 → 바쁜가 보다 (not 바쁘나 보다)
>
> However, the 가 보다 form cannot be used with *action verbs*.
>
> In addition, the verb 보다 in the forms 나 보다 and 가 보다 can also be conjugated simply as 보다 in the Plain Form. This is an exception for 보다 when used with this form.
>
> 다 먹었나 보다.
> "I guess he ate it all."
> "It seems he ate it all."
>
> 그런가 보다.
> "I guess it is (so)."
> "It seems it is (so)."

In Chapter 5 we learned how to use the 것 같다 form to say that something "seems" like something, or to say that you "think" something. The 나보다 and 가 보다 forms are different from the 것 같다 form because they are used for making an *assumption* about something that you are not certain about. The 것 같다 form is used for simply stating your *opinion* ("It seems...") or *thoughts* ("I think...") on something.

민아: 그럴 수도 있겠다.

"That's possible too."

> **Adv**
>
> Koreans typically prefer using the forms 것 같다, 나 보다 or 가 보다, and 보이다 over directly saying that something is or is not a certain way. Rather than saying "it *is*," it can be less direct and therefore more *polite* in Korean to say "I think" or "it seems," among other forms.

Chapter 13 — Looks and Sounds Like

Practice

Conjugate the following verbs using the 나 보다 or 가 보다 form, as appropriate:

1. 싫어하다

    _____.

2. 맵다

    _____.

3. 매웠다

    _____.

4. 멀다

    _____.

5. 있다

    _____.

6. 심심하다

    _____.

7. 할 수 없다

    _____.

8. 아니다

    _____.

9. 아니었다

    _____.

10. 살다

    _____.

Looks and Sounds Like

Translate to Korean:

11. "I guess that she went home."

12. "I guess that the movie finished."

13. "Yung-hee looks like a model."

14. "It looks like oil."

15. "The puppy looks cute."

16. "The house looks very small."

17. "The movie looked fun."

18. "I guess it's just a scam."

19. "I guess it's a good idea."

20. "I guess I made a mistake."

Looks and Sounds Like

21. "I guess there are a lot of people."

_____.

22. "I guess there were a lot of people."

_____.

Translate to English:

23. 한국어를 정말 잘하나 봐요.

_____.

24. 휴지를 다 썼나 봐요.

_____.

25. 새로운 방법을 발견했나 보네요.

_____.

26. 벌써 문을 닫았나 보네요.

_____.

27. 내가 했다는 걸 아나 봐.

_____.

28. 민우가 했다는 얘기를 들었어요.

_____.

29. 우리는 전혀 안 닮았어요.

_____.

30. 그 부부는 서로 많이 닮았어요.

_____.

Looks and Sounds Like

Chapter 13

31. 사탕처럼 생긴 장식을 샀어요.

_____.

32. 그거랑 비슷해 보여요.

_____.

33. 상자가 가벼워 보여요.

_____.

34. 동생이 아직 너무 어린가 보네요.

_____.

35. 다른 차들보다 속도가 더 빠른가 봐요.

_____.

36. 우리 나라보다 기온이 높은가 봐요.

_____.

New Vocabulary

잡지	"magazine"
닮다	"to resemble," "to look like"
각도	"angle"
분위기	"atmosphere," "an image"
평소(에)	"normally," "usual(ly)"
장마	"rainy season"
보이다	"to be seen," "to appear"
깊다	"to be deep"
얕다	"to be shallow"
부부	"married couple," "husband and wife"
장식	"decoration," "ornament"
속도	"speed"
사기	"scam"

Chapter 13 — Looks and Sounds Like

사기꾼	"a scammer"
수상하다	"to be suspicious" (descriptive verb)
기온	"temperature (of weather)"
온도	"temperature (of a thing)"
발견	"discovery"
발견(을) 하다	"to discover"
잘못	"an error," "a mistake"
잘못(을) 하다	"to do something wrong," "to make a misake"
잘못	"incorrectly," "wrong(ly)" (adverb)
기사	"news article"
손목	"wrist"
손톱	"fingernail"
발톱	"toenail"

Since Doing

Conversation

혜정:	자기야, 여기 옷 예쁘다. 우리 사귄 지 100 일 됐으니까 커플티 살까?
벤:	그래. 나는 사실 우리가 사귀기로 하고 나서 바로 커플티를 사고 싶었어.
혜정:	그랬어? 그럼 진작 얘기하지.
벤:	네가 사귀자마자 커플티 사는 것을 싫어할 줄 알았어.
혜정:	아니야. 나도 항상 커플티를 입어 보고 싶었어.
벤:	그랬구나. 그럼 지금 입어 보고 바로 살까?
혜정:	응. 생각이 이렇게 똑같다니 우린 역시 서로 사랑할 수밖에 없어.

This chapter will cover a few forms that you can use for showing actions happening over a period of time. For example, we will cover how to say that time has passed "since" something happened. We will also talk about a few grammar forms that relate to things happening "after" each other. Let's get started.

혜정: 자기야, 여기 옷 예쁘다. 우리 사귄 지 100 일 됐으니까 커플티 살까?

"Honey, the clothes here are pretty. It's been 100 days since we've been dating, so should we buy a couple t-shirt?"

Since Doing

Since: Action Verb Stem + (은/ㄴ) 지 Time + (이/가) 되다

You can use this form to say how long it has been since you *started* or *began* to do something, or since you *first* did something. For example, "It's been 1 year since I (first) began studying Korean."

To use it, take an *action verb stem* and attach 은 if it ends in a *consonant*, or attach ㄴ if it ends in a *vowel*. Then add a *space*, and 지. Add the amount of time that has passed – a day, a year, or 오래 ("a long time"), among other possibilities. *Optionally* you can add the Subject Marker (이/가) after the amount of time. Finally conjugate the verb 되다 ("to become") – this will most often be conjugated to the *past tense*. Here are some examples.

한국어를 공부한 지 1 년이 됐어요.
"It's been one year since I (first) began studying Korean."

한국에 온 지 얼마나 됐어요?
"How long has it been since you (first) came to Korea?"
"How long have you been in Korea?"

The question word 얼마나 ("how much," "to what extent") when used with this form translates more naturally as "how long."

강이 흐른 지 거의 100 년이 됐어요.
"It's been almost 100 years since the river flowed."

한국에서 산 지 1 주일밖에 안 됐어요.
"It's only been one week since I've lived in Korea."
"I've only been living in Korea for 1 week."

Verb stems ending in ㄹ will drop the ㄹ when using this form, just as with other forms.

그림을 그려 본 지 몇 년이 됐어요.
"It's been a few years since I (first) tried drawing (a drawing)."

You can use 몇 ("how many") to also mean "some" when it is used with *counters*. Whether it is being used to mean "how many" or "some" will be clear depending on the context of the sentence. For example, you could say 파티에 몇 명이 왔어요 ("A few people came to the party.") or ask 파티에 몇 명이 왔어요? ("How many people came to the party?").

결혼한 지 5 년 넘게 됐어요.
"It's been over 5 years since we (first) got married."
"We've been married for over 5 years."

Since Doing

10 주일이 된 거 같아요.
"I think it's been 10 weeks."

This form can also be used without saying what the action is – by only using the amount of time with the verb 되다. This can be useful to avoid sounding repetitive. For example, if someone asks you 거기 간 지 얼마나 됐어요? ("How long has it been since you went there?") it would sound more natural to simply say the amount of time that has passed using 되다 instead of repeating the entire phrase.

만난 지 정말 오래됐어요.
"It's really been a long time since I (first) met him."

여기서 일한 지 2 달이 됐어요.
"It's been 2 months since I (first) started working here."

> **Advanced**
>
> Note that this form is only used for things which you have done and are still doing, or things that you are still under the effects of such as getting married. It is typically not used for saying something like "It's been 3 days since I've taken a shower" (if so, then please go take a shower). To say how long it has been since you have done something that you are not still doing, use 동안 together with a negative verb. Remember that 동안 means "*for* (a period of time)." Here's an example.
>
> 3 일 동안 샤워를 안 했어요.
> "I didn't shower for 3 days."
>
> Alternatively, you can use this form with actions that you are not still doing only if you are using a *negative verb*. Here are a few examples.
>
> 샤워를 안 한 지 3 일이 됐어요.
> "It's been 3 days since I took a shower (and I'm not showering right now)."
> "I haven't taken a shower in 3 days."
>
> 안 만난 지 거의 10 년이 됐어요.
> "It's been almost 10 years since we haven't met (and we still don't meet)."
> "We haven't met in 10 years."
>
> While the actual meaning of this form does not change – it is still used for actions that you are *still* doing – here the sentence uses a negative verb to show that it has *still* been a certain amount of time since first *not* doing the action. Here is another example.
>
> 제대로 운동을 안 한 지 너무 오래됐어요.
> "It has been so long since I've properly exercised (and I'm not exercising now)."
> "I haven't properly exercised in so long."
>
> This example would translate literally as "It has been so long since I *haven't* properly exercised."

> **Adv**
>
> This form can be used with 있다 as 있은 지 when it is being used as an *action verb*. Note that 있다 is not commonly used with this form, and instead other verbs are preferred (such as 가다 or 오다). 없다 can be used as 없은 지 in this same way. For example:
>
> 핸드폰이 없은 지 오래됐어요.
> "It's been a long time since not having a cell phone."
> "I haven't had a cell phone in a long time."

Chapter 14

Since Doing

Culture Notes

커플티 and Dating

Some Korean couples enjoy wearing matching clothes in public while dating. This can include buying matching t-shirts, shoes, couple rings, or entire outfits.

100 days is often considered to be a special milestone in Korean dating, and couples will celebrate having made it to their 100th day by going on a date. After that, couples will often celebrate yearly from the day that they first started dating.

벤: 그래. 나는 사실 우리가 사귀기로 하고 나서 바로 커플티를 사고 싶었어.

"Okay. I actually wanted to buy a couple t-shirt right after we decided to date."

After: Action Verb Stem + 고 나서

We previously learned that when 고 ("and") is used with an *action verb* it has the meaning of "and then." We can also attach 나서 to *emphasize* the meaning of something happening after something else. You can think of the 고 나서 form as meaning "after (doing)."

공부하고 쉬었어요.
"I studied and (then) rested."

공부하고 나서 쉬었어요.
"I rested after studying."

Advanced

You can use 먹고 가다 ("to eat and go") to mean "to eat here" when asked whether you are ordering your food "for here" or "to go." Here are two examples.

드시고 가세요?
"Will you eat it (and then go)?"
"Is it for here?"

네, 먹고 갈 거예요.
"Yes, I'll eat it (and then go)."
"Yes, it's for here."

Since Doing

Chapter 14

Here are a few more examples.

아침을 먹고 나서 운동했어요.
"I exercised after eating breakfast."

숙제를 하고 나서 3시간 동안 시험 공부를 할 거예요.
"I'll study for the test for 3 hours after doing the homework."

편지를 쓰고 나서 읽었어요.
"I read the letter after writing it."

> **Adv** This form is slightly different from using 후에 or 뒤에 to mean "after," which we learned in Chapter 16 of the previous book. While 후에 and 뒤에 can be used with both nouns and verbs, 나서 can only be used with verbs. Also, using 나서 *emphasizes* that the action is completed, so it means that you are doing something *after* or *upon* finishing something.

영화를 보고 나서 팝콘을 더 샀어요.
"I bought more popcorn after watching the movie."

아빠가 돈을 주시고 나서 사탕을 사지 말라고 하셨어요.
"Dad told me not to buy sweets after he gave me the money."

철수가 나가고 나서 영희도 나갔어요.
"After Chul-soo left, Yung-hee left too."

> **Adv** If the same person is doing both actions, and if you are using a verb that shows *movement* (나가다, 오다, etc.), then simply use the 서 form instead of 나서.
>
> 병원에 가서 약을 먹었어요.
> "I took medicine after going to the hospital."
> "I went to the hospital and took medicine."

> **Adv** This form can also be shortened to 고서. This shortened form is less common.

혜정: 그랬어? 그럼 진작 얘기하지.

"You did? Then you should have told me that before."

We learned that the 지 ending is used to ask someone to *confirm* something that you've said. Because of this, when used as a *command* it can also translate as "should" when speaking about the present or "should have" when speaking about the past.

Since Doing

Chapter 14

그럼 빨리 하지.
"Then you do it quickly, okay?"
"Then you should do it quickly."
"Then you should have done it quickly."

벤: 네가 사귀자마자 커플티 사는 것을 싫어할 줄 알았어.
"I thought you didn't want to buy a couple t-shirt as soon as we started dating."

"As soon as": Action Verb Stem + 자마자

You can say that something happens *as soon as* something else has happened by using this form. For example, "I ate kimchi and rice as soon as I woke up."

To use it, take an *action verb stem* in the present tense and attach 자마자. Then finish the rest of the sentence. Here are a few examples.

일어나자마자 김치랑 밥을 먹었어요.
"I ate kimchi and rice as soon as I woke up."

사진을 보자마자 울었어요.
"I cried as soon as I looked at the photo."

왕복 비행기표를 사자마자 가격이 내려갔어요.
"As soon as I bought the round trip plane ticket, the price went down."

병원에 도착하자마자 토했어요.
"I vomited as soon as I arrived at the hospital."

집에서 한국어를 1 시간 동안 공부하자마자 친구를 만나러 나갔어요.
"As soon as I had studied Korean for 1 hour at my house I left to meet my friend."

어제 밤 침대에 눕자마자 잠이 들었어요.
"Yesterday night I fell asleep as soon as I lied down in bed."

월급을 받자마자 다 써 버렸다고요?
"You (say that you) used your salary as soon as you got it?"

밖에 나가자마자 비가 내리기 시작했어요.
"As soon as I went outside, it started to rain."

Since Doing

Both 비(가) 내리다 and 비(가) 오다 can be used to mean "to rain." Using 내리다 ("to come down") simply adds emphasis that the rain is falling *down*. In the same way, you can also use both 눈(이) 내리다 and 눈(이) 오다 to mean "to snow."

Let's go back to the conversation. [...] 사는 것을 싫어할 줄 알았어 literally translates as "I thought you disliked buying [...]." This part of the sentence could also have been written as 사고 싶지 않을 줄 알았어 ("I thought you did not want to buy [...]"), but it would have a slightly different meaning. Using the 는 것 or 기 verb forms together with 좋아하다 ("to like") or 싫어하다 ("to dislike") means that the speaker likes or dislikes the *act* of doing something. Liking or disliking the *act* of doing something – liking or disliking doing something – is slightly different from *wanting* to do something (using the 고 싶다 and 고 싶지 않다 forms). However, in the *English language* these forms can be translated in the same way at times, as they are in the conversation here.

혜정: 아니야. 나도 항상 커플티를 입어 보고 싶었어.
"No. I also always wanted to try on a couple t-shirt."

벤: 그랬구나. 그럼 지금 입어 보고 바로 살까?
"Oh you did. Then should we try them on now and buy them right away?"

혜정: 응. 생각이 이렇게 똑같다니 우린 역시 서로 사랑할 수밖에 없어.
"Yeah. Considering our thoughts are exactly the same, of course we can't help but love each other."

역시 is an *adverb* meaning "(just) as expected" which we have previously learned and used. At times, this adverb can be difficult to translate naturally into English. For these situations, feel free to translate it as "of course" or "I knew (it)," depending on the sentence. Here are a few examples.

역시 그랬구나!
"As expected, it was so!"
"I just *knew* it (was so)!"
"Of course it was."

역시 여기 없네.
"As expected, it isn't here."
"I *knew* it. It's not here."
"Of course it's not here."

| Chapter 14 |

Since Doing

역시 여름에 과일은 수박이 최고지.
"As expected, when it comes to fruits in the summer, watermelon is the best."
"I *knew* that watermelons are the best summer fruit."
"Of course watermelons are the best summer fruit."

"Can't help but...": Verb Stem + (을/ㄹ) 수밖에 없다

In the second book we learned that 밖에 can be used with negative verbs to mean "only" or "nothing but." It can also be used together with the 수 없다 form ("can not") to mean "can only (do)." This can more naturally translate as "can't help but," or "there is nothing that (someone) can do/be but (verb)."

To use it, take the 수 없다 form and attach 밖에 after 수. Then conjugate 없다 any way that you would like. Here are a few examples.

이걸 마실 수밖에 없나 봐요.
"I guess I can't help but drink it."
"I guess there's nothing I can do but drink it."

도와줄 수밖에 없었어요.
"There was nothing I could do but help."

밖에 나가기 위해서는 화장을 할 수밖에 없어요.
"I can't help but put on makeup to go outside."

You might find the Topic Marker (here, 는) used after 위해(서) or 대해(서) or other forms ending in 서. When used in this way, the Topic Marker *emphasizes* the form, similar to adding the meaning of "as for" to the sentence. For example, 밖에 나가기 위해서 화장을 해야 돼요 ("I have to put on makeup to go outside.") could be changed to 밖에 나가기 위해서는 화장을 해야 돼요 ("In order to go outside, I have to put on makeup.").

사장님이 모두 오라고 하셨으니까 나도 갈 수밖에 없어.
"The boss told everyone to come so I can't help but go."
"The boss told everyone to come so there's nothing I can do but go."

아르바이트를 하면서 학교를 다닐 수밖에 없어요.
"I can't help but attend school while doing a part time job."
"There's nothing I can do but attend school while doing a part time job."

Since Doing

Practice

Translate to Korean:

1. "It's been 1 day since I (first) met Chul-soo."

   _____.

2. "It's already been 10 days since I (first) started my diet."

   _____.

3. "How long has it been since you started to (first) like hiking?"

   _____.

4. "It's been a few years since I (first) came to Korea."

   _____.

5. "I'll clean the house after I do the dishes."

   _____.

6. "I'll sleep after I exercise."

   _____.

7. "I ate (food) as soon as I met my friend."

   _____.

8. "Yung-hee met a new person as soon as she broke up with her boyfriend."

   _____.

9. "I can't help but think that."

   _____.

10. "I can't help but like cake."

    _____.

Since Doing

Chapter 14

11. "In order to wake up early tomorrow, I can't help but go to sleep now."

_____.

Translate to English:

12. 기자를 만나서 인터뷰를 한 지 2 시간이 됐어요.

_____.

13. 아빠와 노래 연습을 시작한 지 3 일 됐어요.

_____.

14. 수영을 배우기 시작한 지 조금밖에 안 됐어요.

_____.

15. 찜질방을 다녀오고 나서 몸무게를 쟀어요.

_____.

16. 선생님은 철수가 쓴 글을 읽고 나서 눈물을 흘리셨어요.

_____.

17. 졸업을 하고 나서 직장을 구할 거예요.

_____.

18. 밥을 먹고 나서 바로 달리기를 했어요.

_____.

19. 의자에 앉자마자 영화가 시작했어요.

_____.

20. 아빠가 안아주자마자 아기가 그만 울었어요.

_____.

Since Doing

Chapter 14

21. 그 사람은 연기를 잘해서 국제적으로 유명할 수밖에 없어요.

_____.

22. 성공하기 위해서 잠을 조금 잘 수밖에 없어요.

_____.

New Vocabulary

커플티	"couple t-shirt"
바로	"right away" (adverb)
진작	"before(hand)" (adverb)
비(가) 내리다	"to rain (down)"
눈(이) 내리다	"to snow (down)"
비(가) 그치다	"to stop raining"
눈(이) 그치다	"to stop snowing"
흐르다	"to flow (liquid)"
토(를) 하다	"to vomit," "to throw up"
왕복	"round trip"
편도	"one-way trip"
기자	"reporter"
연기	"act," "acting"
연기(를) 하다	"to act"
국내	"national," "domestic" (adjective)
국제	"international" (adjective)
국제적	"international"
국내 전화	"domestic phone call"
국제 전화	"international phone call"
무게	"weight (of something)"
몸무게	"body weight," "weight (of someone)"
재다	"to weigh"
글	"(written) words," "letters"
눈물(을) 흘리다	"to shed tears," "to cry"
직장	"(one's) place of work"
안아주다	"to hug"

Chapter 14: Since Doing

| 키스(를) 하다 | "to kiss" |
| 뽀뽀(를) 하다 | "to kiss" (children's word) |

Passive Voice

Chapter 15

Conversation

나라:	동진 씨, 미안해요. 길이 막혀서 지하철을 늦게 타게 됐어요.
동진:	괜찮아요. 서울은 길이 막혀서 조금 늦는 거에 어느 정도 익숙해졌어요.
나라:	15 분 정도 늦게 도착할 것 같아요.
동진:	그래요. 서류는 이미 준비가 다 됐으니 천천히 오세요.
나라:	서류 준비가 벌써 다 됐어요? 그럼 이제 뭐가 해결되어야 하죠?
동진:	나라 씨의 서류가 전부 한글로 쓰인 것이라서 번역을 해야 돼요.
나라:	지난 달부터 한글로 쓰인 서류를 제출해도 되는 걸로 바뀐 건 아니었나요?
동진:	한글로 쓰인 서류는 접수가 되는 데에 시간이 더 오래 걸려요.
나라:	그럼 오늘 번역을 해야겠어요. 고마워요.
동진:	제가 도움이 돼서 다행이에요. 잠시 후에 봐요.
나라:	네.

This chapter will introduce *passive voice*, as well as *passive verbs*. We have actually already learned a few passive verbs throughout this series, but we have not talked about this concept in detail. The majority of what we have learned so far has been only using active voice and active verbs.

Passive Voice

Chapter 15

"What do passive voice and active voice mean?" In English, we use the terms "passive voice" and "active voice" to describe sentences. If a sentence is in *active* voice, it means that the subject of that sentence is the one *doing* an action. For example, the sentence "I stared at Chul-soo" is active voice because the subject (here, "I") is the one doing an action (here, staring at Chul-soo). Most sentences in English and Korean use active voice. But if a sentence is in *passive* voice, it means that the subject of that sentence is the *object* of an action. For example, the sentence "I was stared at by Chul-soo" is passive voice because the subject (here, "I") is the object of an action (here, being stared at). Another example of active voice is "I ate the cat food," and another example of passive voice is "The cat food was eaten (by me)."

In English, to make a sentence passive we have to reorganize the words in the sentence and change the conjugation of the verbs. For example, in the previous examples "stared at" became "was stared at," and "ate" became "was eaten." In Korean, the order of the words and the conjugation of the verbs does not change. Instead, Korean uses different *verbs* in passive voice – *passive verbs*.

Unfortunately, there are many passive verbs (just as there are many causative verbs) and you will simply need to memorize the most common ones in order to use passive voice. Fortunately, passive voice is not commonly used in spoken Korean. More often, a sentence is simply said using active voice. Learning only the most commonly used passive verbs should be sufficient for most conversation. Let's jump into the conversation and learn more about passive voice and passive verbs.

> 나라: 동진씨, 미안해요. 길이 막혀서 지하철을 늦게 타게 됐어요.
> "Dong-jin, I'm sorry. The road was blocked so I ended up riding the subway late."

Our first passive verb in this chapter is 막히다 ("to be blocked," "to be obstructed"), which is the passive verb form of the active verb 막다 ("to block," "to obstruct"). We will learn more about how to use passive verbs in detail later in this chapter. For now, simply concentrate on this one passive verb and how it is being used.

"To end up": Action Verb Stem + 게 되다

You can say that you *ended up* doing something, or that you *eventually* did something using this form. For example, "I ended up watching a movie last night."

To use it, take an *action verb stem* and attach 게. Then conjugate the verb 되다 any way that you would like. Here are a few examples.

> 어제 밤 영화를 보게 됐어요.
> "I ended up watching a movie last night."

Passive Voice

가고 싶지 않았는데 결국 가게 됐어요.
"I didn't want to go but ultimately I ended up going."

어떻게 만나게 됐어요?
"How did you end up meeting?"

항상 같은 일을 하게 돼요.
"I keep ending up doing the same work."

나한테 필요없는 걸 사게 됐어.
"I ended up buying something I don't need."

The above example literally translates as "I ended up buying something that is unnecessary to me," since 필요(가) 없다 means "to be unnecessary."

다음에 알게 될 거예요.
"You'll find out next time."

Note that while 알게 되다 literally means "to end up knowing," it's commonly used to mean "to find (out)."

자주 만나면 좋아하게 될 거야.
"If you meet him often you'll end up liking him."

동진: 괜찮아요. 서울은 길이 막혀서 조금 늦는 거에 어느 정도 익숙해졌어요.

> "It's okay. I've gotten somewhat used to being a little late because the roads are blocked in Seoul."

We previously learned the *descriptive verb* 늦다 ("to be late") used for describing the time. There is a second version of 늦다 ("to not be on time") used for arriving late that is an *action verb*. While both verbs (늦다 and 늦다) look and sound the same, when using the action verb remember to conjugate it as an action verb – here, 늦는 것 ("being late").

Become & Get: Descriptive Verb Stem + 아/어/etc. + 지다

We can use this form with *descriptive verbs* to say that something "becomes" or "gets" a certain way. For example, "Korean will *get* easier." Here, the verb 쉽다 ("to be easy") can be changed into 쉬워지다 ("to become/get easy"). These new verbs made with the 지다 ending are *action verbs*.

Chapter 15: Passive Voice

To use this form, take a *descriptive verb* and conjugate it as if you were conjugating the 요 form. But instead of adding 요 to the end, attach 지다 and conjugate it as an *action verb*. Here are a few examples.

한국어가 더 쉬워질 거예요.
"Korean will get easier."

갑자기 피곤해졌어.
"I suddenly got so tired."

10월부터 한가해질 거예요.
"I'll be free from October."

지난 주부터 날씨가 더워졌어요.
"The weather got hot from last week."

그 연예인은 성형 수술을 통해서 예뻐졌어요.
"That celebrity became pretty through plastic surgery."

내일부터 정말 바빠질 거 같아요.
"I think I'll become really busy from tomorrow."

벌써 많이 나아졌어요.
"He already got a lot better."

나아지다 comes from the verb 낫다.

최근에 노트북이 조금 느려졌어요.
"Lately my laptop got a little slow."

펜이 없어졌어요.
"The pen disappeared."

없다 ("to not exist") can be used with this form as 없어지다 ("to disappear") to literally mean "to become non-existant." 있다 ("to exist") is not typically used with this form on its own. Instead, 있다 will commonly use this form with *descriptive verbs* like 재미(가) 있다 ("to be fun," "to be entertaining"). For example:

만기가 훨씬 멋있어졌어요.
"Man-gi became much cooler."

Passive Voice

Chapter 15

Advanced

The 게 되다 form can also be used with *descriptive verbs* to have the same meaning as the 지다 form. However, this is uncommon and usually sounds unnatural. Here's an example.

갑자기 눈이 와서 바쁘게 됐어요.
"I became busy because it suddenly snowed."

It is important to be aware of this usage as you might see it occasionally, but I recommend avoiding using it.

나라: 15 분 정도 늦게 도착할 것 같아요.
"I think I'll arrive about 15 minutes late."

동진: 그래요. 서류는 이미 준비가 다 됐으니 천천히 오세요.
"Okay. The documents are already all prepared so take your time (coming here)."

하다 and 되다

The verb 되다 ("to become," "to be okay," "to work") is also the *passive verb* form of the verb 하다 ("to do"). If an *action verb* ends with 하다, you can change it to a *passive verb* by using the verb 되다 instead.

Note that the meaning of the sentence changes when using passive voice, so remember to use the appropriate *markers* – Object Marker, Subject Marker, and Topic Marker. Here are a few example sentences.

서류를 준비했어요.
"I *prepared* the documents."

서류가 준비됐어요.
"The documents *were prepared*."

준비(가) 되다 ("to be prepared") is a passive verb that we previously learned in Chapter 11. Most passive verbs can simply be learned separately as their own verbs, just like causative verbs.

모임이 2 시에 시작했어요.
"The meeting *started* at 2 o'clock."

모임이 2 시에 시작됐어요.
"The meeting *was started* at 2 o'clock."

추가할 거예요?
"Will you *add* it?"

Chapter 15
Passive Voice

추가될 거예요?
"Will it *be added*?"

아직 결정을 한 건 아니에요.
"It's not something I *decided* yet."

아직 결정이 된 건 아니에요.
"It's not something that's *been decided* yet."

이해했어요?
"Did you *understand*?"

이해됐어요?
"Was it *understood*?"

> **Adv**
> You can also use the expression 이해(가) 가다, or 이해(가) 안 가다 to say that you understand or do not understand something. You can translate these expressions as "to (not) understand" or "to (not) follow." Here is an example.
>
> 잘 이해 안 가요.
> "I'm not following you well."

지난 달 (제가) 주문한 물건을 다 보냈어요?
"Did you send all of the items that I *ordered* last month?"

지난 달 주문된 물건이 다 왔어요?
"Did the items that *were ordered* last month all arrive?"

Note that 되다 can only be used in this way with action verbs that are a combination of a noun and the verb 하다, and that can be separated into two pieces as such. For example, 공부(를) 하다 ("to study") is a combination of a noun (공부) and the verb 하다, and can be separated into two pieces. However 좋아하다 ("to like") is an action verb that ends in 하다 that cannot be separated into two pieces and therefore cannot be used with 되다 in this way. 좋아되다 would be *incorrect*. Action verbs that can be separated into two pieces like this have been taught as separate pieces – 공부(를) 하다 – so review the vocabulary in these books if you are not sure which verbs apply.

About (으)니

In the second book we learned how to use (으)니까 to mean "because." This form (으)니 has the same meaning and usage as (으)니까, but sounds a bit less strong. Because of that it is used more often in *writing* than in speaking. In addition, (으)니 is not used at the end of a sentence. Here is an example.

Passive Voice

이제 충분하니 그만하세요.
"That's enough now so stop (doing it)."

Going back to the conversation, note that the *adverb* 천천히 ("slowly") can also be translated as "to take (one's) time" when used with an action verb.

천천히 먹었어요.
"He ate slowly."
"He took his time eating."

The verb 되다 can also still be used by itself to mean "to become," as usual.

가수가 될 거예요.
"He will become a singer."

2 살이 된 아이
"a child that has become 2 years old"
"a 2 year old child"

Remember to use 되다 to mean "to become," and not (이)겠다 ("will be") – the future tense of the verb 이다 ("to be"). Saying 가수겠어요 ("He would/must be a singer.") would not mean "He will become a singer."

나라: 서류 준비가 벌써 다 됐어요? 그럼 이제 뭐가 해결되어야 하죠?
"The documents are already all prepared? Then now what needs to be taken care of?"

동진: 나라 씨의 서류가 전부 한글로 쓰인 것이라서 번역을 해야 돼요.
"I have to translate them because your documents are all written in Hangul."

About 전부

전부, which can translate as "whole (thing)," "entire (thing)," or "all" can be used as both an *adverb* and as a *noun*.

전부 먹었어요.
"I ate the whole thing."
"I ate the entire thing."
"I ate it all."

전부 사실인가요?
"Is it all true?"

Passive Voice

Chapter 15

가지고 있었던 돈을 전부 잃어 버렸어요.
"I lost all of the money that I had."

Unique Passive Verbs

So far we have learned how to change some action verbs ending in 하다 into passive verbs using 되다. Let's talk about what to do for other action verbs.

Unfortunately, just as we needed to learn several unique causative verbs in Chapter 10, we will need to do the same for passive verbs. However, Koreans typically avoid *speaking* in passive voice. Learning just the most commonly used passive verbs will be enough for most conversations. You will more often see passive verbs used in *writing*, where you will be able to use a dictionary to look up new words. First let's learn a few common passive verbs. More are listed in this chapter's vocabulary section.

바꾸다: "to change (something)"
바뀌다: "to be changed"

> **Advanced**
>
> **Transitive and Intransitive**
>
> 바꾸다 is not only an action verb, but is also known as a *transitive verb*. 바뀌다 is also known as an *intransitive verb*. In Korean, transitive verbs are any verbs that *can* have an object, and intransitive verbs are verbs that *can not* have an object. For example, you can say 저는 메뉴를 바꿨어요 ("I changed the menu"). Because 바꾸다 can use an object, it is a transitive verb. You can also say 메뉴가 바뀌었어요 ("The menu was changed."). However, it would be *incorrect* to say 메뉴를 바뀌었어요 because 바뀌다 is an intransitive verb and can not have an object.
>
> You might find the terms *transitive* and *intransitive* used in other resources and grammar books. As long as you know the definition of a verb and how to use it, it is not required to know whether it is transitive, intransitive, passive, causative, or anything.

쓰다: "to use," "to write"
쓰이다: "to be used," "to be written"

먹다: "to eat"
먹히다: "to be eaten"

쌓다: "to stack," "to pile (up)"
쌓이다: "to be stacked," "to be piled (up)"

잠그다: "to lock"
잠기다: "to be locked"

찍다: "to chop," "to hack," "to take (a photo)"
찍히다: "to be chopped," "to be hacked up," "to be taken (a photo)"

Passive Voice

Chapter 15

Here are some example sentences using these passive verbs.

신호등이 곧 바뀔 거예요.
"The traffic light will change soon."

Note that while 바뀌다 means "to be changed," it translates better here as "changed." Using 바꾸다 (an active verb) instead in this example would be *incorrect* (unless you have telekinesis... or work for the electric company), because that would mean that you (the speaker) are the one who is changing the light.

Also note that 신호등 is followed by the Subject Marker (이/가) here, and not the Object Marker (을/를). Using the Object Marker with passive voice is *incorrect*, and would not be understood. For example, this sentence would be *incorrect*: 신호등을 곧 바뀔 거예요.

영어로 쓰여서 못 읽겠어요.
"I can't read it because it's written in English."

You can use the particle (으)로 to say that something was done *using* something, just as we learned previously.

원숭이가 (사자한테) 먹혔어요.
"The monkey was eaten (by the lion)."

Just like with *causative verbs*, if you want to specify *who* it was that did the action you can use the particle 에게 (or 한테). Most of the time it is not necessary to specify this, and it is more commonly not used. If what did the action was *not* a person, use the particle 에 instead.

> **Advanced**
>
> **"By": Noun + 에 의해(서)**
>
> Although much less common, you can also specify who or what did the action in passive voice with this form. You can translate this form as "by." This form is more often used in *writing*.
>
> To use it, attach the particle 에 to a *noun*. Then add 의해(서) – the 서 is *optional*. Here is an example.
>
> 원숭이가 사자에 의해서 먹혔어요.
> "The monkey was eaten by the lion."

밖에 눈이 쌓였어요.
"Snow was piled up outside."

문이 잠길 거예요.
"The door will be locked."

사진이 이미 찍혔어?
"Was the photo taken already?"

Chapter 15 — Passive Voice

Another useful verb to use when talking about photos is 사진(이) 잘 나오다, which literally means "a photo comes out well." You can use this to mean that a photo looks good after you have taken it.

There are two more passive verbs which are commonly used that we will talk about next – 들리다 ("to be heard") and 보이다 ("to be seen").

> **Adv**
> While *causative verbs* follow the form of using 이히리기우구추 as we learned in the Advanced Notes of Chapter 10, some *passive verbs* will follow the form of using the syllables 이히리기. This means that you might not be able to tell a passive verb from a causative verb if it is your first time seeing the verb and you do not know its meaning yet. Since causative verbs and passive verbs are used in different ways as we learned, understanding a sentence's context will help you to know whether a verb is causative or passive. Keep a dictionary on hand for whenever you encounter new words.

들리다 and 보이다

While passive voice is commonly avoided in Korean, these two verbs, 들리다 ("to be heard") and 보이다 ("to be seen"), are often used.

들리다 ("to be heard") comes from 듣다 ("to listen"), and 보이다 ("to be seen") comes from 보다 ("to see"). While these verbs are passive, they are often used to show that someone is *able* to hear something, or *able* to see something. If it helps to understand their meanings, you can also translate 들리다 as "to be audible" and 보이다 as "to be visible," depending on the context of the sentence. Here are a few examples.

제 목소리가 잘 들려요?
"Is my voice heard well?"
"Is my voice audible?"
"Can you hear my voice (well)?"

저기 보이는 거 같아.
"I think it's seen over there."
"I think it's visible over there."
"I think I can see it over there."

지금은 들리세요?
"Is it heard now?"
"Is it audible now?"
"Can you hear (it) now?"

집이 아직 안 보여요.
"The house isn't seen yet."
"The house isn't visible yet."
"I can't see the house yet."

Passive Voice

Chapter 15

As a note, remember to avoid using 안 듣다 ("to not listen") and 안 보다 ("to not see") in these situations. Using these verbs would mean that you are not listening or looking at someone or something *on purpose* (you rebel). Instead, you can use 안 들리다 ("to not be heard") and 안 보이다 ("to not be seen") to say that you do not ("can not") hear or do not ("can not") see something.

> **Adv**
>
> When speaking *honorifically*, instead of 보이다 and 들리다 you can use 보이시다 and 들리시다.
>
> 제 얼굴이 보이세요?
> "Can you see my face?"
>
> 잘 들리십니까?
> "Can you hear (me/it) well?"

The Passive Ending 나다

Some active verbs that end in 내다 can be changed to passive verbs using 나다 ("to occur," "to come to mind"). Here's an example.

끝내다: "to finish (something)," "to end (something)"
끝나다: "to be finished," "to end," "to be over"

We have seen these two verbs used often. 끝나다 has been hiding under our noses as a verb used in the passive voice this whole time. Here are a few more verbs that use 내다 and 나다.

소리(를) 내다: "to make a sound," "to make a noise"
소리(가) 나다: "a sound is made," "a noise is made"

화(를) 내다: "to get angry (at someone/something)"
화(가) 나다: "to be angry (due to someone/something)"

짜증(을) 내다: "to get annoyed (at someone/something)"
짜증(이) 나다: "to be annoyed (by someone/something)"

Here are a few more common passive verbs that use 나다.

땀(이) 나다: "to sweat." Literally, "sweat occurs."
사고(가) 나다: "to have an accident." Literally, "an accident occurs."
불(이) 나다: "to have a fire." Literally, "a fire occurs."
전쟁(이) 나다: "to have a war." Literally, "a war occurs."

Chapter 15: Passive Voice

Passive Verbs with 받다

A small number of active verbs can be changed to passive verbs using the verb 받다 ("to get," "to receive"). For example:

버리다: "to throw away"
버림(을) 받다: "to be thrown away"

You can also think of these verbs as translating as "to get (verb)," since 받다 means "to get" or "to receive." For example, you can translate 버림(을) 받다 in your head as "to *get* thrown away" if it helps you to understand the meaning. Here are three more examples.

감동(을) 시키다: "to move (emotionally)," "to touch (emotionally)"
감동(을) 받다: "to be moved (emotionally)" "to be touched (emotionally)"

존경(을) 하다: "to respect," "to look up to"
존경(을) 받다: "to be respected," "to be looked up to"

사랑(을) 하다: "to love"
사랑(을) 받다: "to be loved"

When to Use Passive Voice

Let's take a look at a couple of previous examples.

저는 철수를 쳐다봤어요.
"I stared at Chul-soo."

저는 철수에게 쳐다보였어요.
"I was stared at by Chul-soo."

저는 고양이 먹이를 먹었어요.
"I ate the cat food."

고양이 먹이가 저에게 먹혔어요.
"The cat food was eaten by me."

While these examples are grammatically accurate, they are *unnatural*. Remember that the passive voice is not commonly used in Korean. If you find yourself unable to remember a certain passive verb, feel free to say the sentence using active voice instead. More often than not, a sentence will sound more natural in active voice than in passive voice.

Passive Voice

Chapter 15

However, there are still times when passive verbs are *necessary*. This can happen when passive verbs are being used to *describe* other parts of a sentence. Here is an example.

영어로 쓰인 책을 샀어요.
"I bought a book written in English."

This sentence cannot be said in a different way using active verbs. This is because the passive verb (here, 쓰이다) is being used as an *adjective*. It is not possible to say "a book written" using an active verb unless you change it to "a book that (someone) wrote." Because of this, it is still important to learn about passive verbs. But do not stress about memorizing all of them at first. Take your time. Learn them one at a time until you feel confident with what they mean and are able to use them yourself. Let's go back to the conversation and learn more about passive verbs.

나라: 지난 달부터 한글로 쓰인 서류를 제출해도 되는 걸로 바뀐 건 아니었나요?
"Wasn't it changed from last month so that it's okay to submit documents written in Korean?"

"Change for": Noun + (으)로 바꾸다/바뀌다

You can "change (something) for" something else by using the active verb 바꾸다 ("to change") or the passive verb 바뀌다 ("to be changed").

To use it, take a noun (the thing that you will change something *for*) and attach the particle (으)로. Then conjugate the verb 바꾸다 if you are "changing" something (active voice), or the verb 바뀌다 if something is *being* "changed" for something (passive voice). Depending on the sentence, it can also translate as "exchange." Here are a few examples.

이걸 그걸로 바꿀래요.
"I want to change this for that."

Note that 것으로 can, and is commonly shortened to 걸로 when speaking *informally*.

더 새로운 제품으로 바꿔 주세요.
"Please (ex-)change it for a newer product."

색깔이 바뀔 수 있는 걸로 바꿔 달라고 했어요.
"She told me to (ex-)change it for one that the colors can change."

그렇게 하면 안 되는 걸로 바꿔 놓았어요.
"I changed it so that you can't do that."

Chapter 15

Passive Voice

1년 동안 친구에게 전화를 안 했더니 전화 번호가 바뀌었어요.
"I didn't call my friend for a year, and now her phone number has changed."

동진: 한글로 쓰인 서류는 접수가 되는 데에 시간이 더 오래 걸려요.
"It'll take a longer time for documents written in Hangul to be received."

"(In order) to": Action Verb Stem + 는 데(에)

In Chapter 19 of the previous book (in the Advanced Notes) we learned how to use the 데 form with the verb 걸리다 to say "it takes (time) to" do something. Note that there is an extra space when using the 데 form in this way. Let's talk a bit more about this form.

This 데 form is different from the other 데 form that we learned in the previous book, which was used for *contrasting* and *explaining*. Instead, this 데 form (with a space) is used only with *action verbs* and is used to mean "(in order) to." It can be used in the same way as you would use 위해(서) with verbs.

To use it, take an *action verb stem* and attach 는. Then add a space, followed by 데(에) – the 에 is *optional*.

여기서 거기까지 가기 위해(서) 1시간 넘게 걸려요.
여기서 거기까지 가는 데(에) 1시간 넘게 걸려요.
"It takes over 1 hour (in order) to go from here to there."

Note that while both forms can be used in a similar way – 위해(서) and this 데 form – using the 데 form is more common and natural. You might find the 위해(서) form used more often in *writing*.

나라: 그럼 오늘 번역을 해야겠어요. 고마워요.
"Then I'll need to translate it today. Thanks."

동진: 제가 도움이 돼서 다행이에요. 잠시 후에 봐요.
"I'm glad I was helpful. I'll see you after a short while."

More Passive Verbs: Action Verb Stem + 아/어/etc. + 지다

So far we have talked about using the verb 되다 to make verbs passive, learned several common passive verbs, covered the verbs 들리다 and 보이다, discussed the passive ending 나다, and showed a few passive verbs that use 받다. However, this does not include all types of active verbs that we might need to change into passive verbs.

Passive Voice

Chapter 15

Fortunately, if there is an active verb that does not already apply to the rules that we have covered in this chapter and that does not have its own passive verb form, there is an easy way to change it into a passive verb.

In order to change one of these active verbs into a passive verb, simply conjugate it as if you were conjugating the 요 form. Instead of adding the 요, add 지다 and conjugate it as an *action verb*. This form should not be confused with the previous 지다 form that we covered in this chapter, which is used with only descriptive verbs. Here are some examples with action verbs that do not apply to the other rules that we have covered so far.

주다: "to give"
주어지다: "to be given"

새로운 과제가 주어졌어요.
"A new assignment was given (to us)."

짓다: "to build"
지어지다: "to be built"*

집이 빨리 지어졌어요.
"The house was built quickly."

*Note that 짓다 conjugates in the 요 form as 지어(요).

정하다: "to set (something)," "to decide (something)"
정해지다: "to be set," "to be arranged," "to be decided"

정해진 날짜까지 못 만났어요.
"We couldn't meet by the arranged date."

당기다: "to pull"
당겨지다: "to be pulled"

갑자기 가방 끈이 당겨졌어요.
"Suddenly my bag's string was pulled."

Note that while 밀다 ("to push") has its own passive verb, 밀리다 ("to be pushed"), 당기다 uses this 지다 form instead.

Chapter 15: Passive Voice

펴다: "to open up (something)," "to unfold"
펴지다: "to be opened up," "to be unfolded"

> 옷의 주름이 펴졌어요.
> "The clothes' wrinkles were unfolded."

만들다: "to make"
만들어지다: "to be made"

> 그 책상은 쇠로 만들어진 거예요.
> "That desk is made of metal."

Note that 만들어지다 is used with (으)로 to mean "made from" or "made of."

깨다: "to break (something)," "to smash (something)"
깨어지다: "to be broken," "to be smashed"

> 유리가 떨어져서 깨졌어요.
> "The glass fell and broke."

Note that 깨어지다 is commonly shortened to 깨지다.

> **Advanced**
>
> Certain *causative verbs* can also be used together with this passive 지다 ending to create *passive causative verbs* (Okay, I admit I made that word up). We will not cover this in detail, but be aware of it for when you will see it. For an example, let's take a look at the verb 울다 ("to cry") and its causative verb 울리다, which means "to make (someone) cry." The passive form of this would be 울려지다 ("to be made to cry"). Here is another common example.
>
> **알다:** "to know," "to understand"
> **알리다:** "to make known," "to inform"
> **알려지다:** "to be (made) known," "to be understood"
>
> > 그 식당은 이미 많이 알려졌어요.
> > "That restaurant was already known a lot."

Again, focus now more on learning passive verbs one at a time and on understanding the general ways that they can be made, instead of memorizing every specific rule and every passive verb right away. It will be more beneficial to you to be able to use a small handful of common passive verbs correctly and regularly than it would be to memorize a long list of passive verbs and rules which might rarely be used.

Passive Voice

Chapter 15

Passive + Passive

You might see and hear Koreans attaching this 지다 form to verbs that are already passive. This is known as "double passive." This is a common grammatical mistake. However, you should be aware of it and be able to recognize it, as many passive verbs are commonly made using this "mistake" (sometimes more often than their regular forms). Here are just a few commonly used examples of this.

찢다: "to tear," "to rip (up)"
찢기다: "to be torn," "to be ripped (up)"
Or, 찢겨지다: "to be torn," "to be ripped (up)"

Another commonly used passive verb is 찢어지다, made from the verb 찢다 and the 지다 ending that we learned in this chapter. While 찢기다 is the more correct passive verb form, 찢어지다 is more commonly used.

쓰다: "to use," "to write"
쓰이다: "to be used," "to be written"
Or, 쓰여지다: "to be used," "to be written"

읽다: "to read"
읽히다: "to be read"
Or, 읽혀지다: "to be read"

연구(를) 하다: "to research"
연구(가) 되다: "to be researched"
Or, 연구(가) 되어지다: "to be researched"

나라: 네.
"Okay."

Final Notes: Causatives and Passive Verbs

As you practice using passive verbs (and causative verbs) you will be able to recognize a verb as passive simply by noticing the 지다 at the end of the active verb stem. Unfortunately, passive verbs can be a time-consuming topic, but know that it is not necessary to learn every common causative verb and every common passive verb in order to have a complete, intelligent conversation in Korean.

| Chapter 15 | **Passive Voice** |

These two types of verbs are used sparingly in conversation (especially passive verbs) and you will be able to get along fine at first knowing only a few of the most common ones and their general rules. As you become more comfortable conjugating them, remembering exceptions and rules, as well as seeing and hearing them used in real conversation, these types of verbs will lose their fear factor. And if it makes you feel any better, know that even most Koreans are unable to explain, or even understand the rules of passive verbs and passive voice – this is why there are so many exceptions to the rules. Relax, take your time studying and reviewing these concepts, and feel free to come back to review them again anytime.

Practice

Change the following active verbs to passive verbs:

1. 약속(을) 하다

   _____.

2. 배달(을) 하다

   _____.

3. 마음(을) 바꾸다

   _____.

4. 책(을) 쓰다

   _____.

5. 겁(을) 내다

   _____.

6. 케이크(를) 만들다

   _____.

7. 소리(를) 듣다

   _____.

Passive Voice

8. 사람(을) 보다

_____.

Change the following passive verbs to active verbs:

9. 주문(이) 되다

_____.

10. 찍히다

_____.

11. 놓이다

_____.

12. 팔리다

_____.

13. 살(이) 빠지다

_____.

14. 차이다

_____.

15. 허락(을) 받다

_____.

16. 화(가) 나다

_____.

Translate to Korean:

17. "I ended up eating food that I dislike."

_____.

Passive Voice

18. "I'll end up learning a lot of Korean."

_____.

19. "My clothes got small."

_____.

20. "The baby got cuter."

_____.

21. "It was started 1 hour ago."

_____.

22. "The apples were all sold yesterday."

_____.

23. "It takes a lot of time (in order) to learn Korean."

_____.

24. "I hope that it can be made quickly."

_____.

25. "Sweets were given to the children."

_____.

Translate to English:

26. 제가 모르는 사람들 앞에서 노래를 부르게 됐어요.

_____.

27. 컴퓨터를 고치면 훨씬 더 빨라질 거예요.

_____.

Passive Voice

28. 이미 완료된 줄 알았어요.

_____.

29. 그 책이 영어로도 쓰였어요.

_____.

30. 멀어서 안 들려요.

_____.

31. 어두워서 잘 안 보여요.

_____.

32. 선생님이 수업에 늦은 학생에게 화를 냈어요.

_____.

33. 멀리서 큰 소리가 났어요.

_____.

34. 누군가가 던진 공에 거울이 깨졌어요.

_____.

New Phrases

몸 조리 잘하세요.	"Take care of yourself.," "Get well soon."

New Vocabulary

없어지다	"to disappear"
막다	"to block," "to obstruct"
막히다	"to be blocked," "to be obstructed"
길(이) 막히다	"road is blocked," "road is obstructed"
알게 되다	"to find (out)"
익숙하다	"to be used to" (descriptive verb)

Chapter 15: Passive Voice

익숙해지다	"to become/get used to" (action verb)
정하다	"to set (something)"
정해지다	"to be set"
수술	"surgery," "operation"
성형 수술	"plastic surgery"
서류	"document," "paper(s)"
해결(을) 하다	"to resolve," "to settle," "to take care of (a problem)"
해결(이) 되다	"to be resolved," "to be settled," "to be taken care of (a problem)"
전부	"whole (thing)," "entire (thing)," "all"
시작(이) 되다	"to be started"
추가(가) 되다	"to be added (to something)"
결정(이) 되다	"to be decided"
이해(가) 되다	"to be understood"
주문(이) 되다	"to be ordered"
켜지다	"to be turned on"
꺼지다	"to be turned off"
열리다	"to be opened"
닫히다	"to be closed"
놓이다	"to be put down," "to be let go"
바꾸다	"to change (something)"
바뀌다	"to be changed"
마음(을) 바꾸다	"to change (one's) mind"
마음(이) 바뀌다	"(one's) mind changes"
찍히다	"to be chopped," "to be hacked up," "to be taken (a photo)"
쓰이다	"to be used," "to be written"
읽히다	"to be read"
먹히다	"to be eaten"
잡히다	"to be grabbed," "to be caught"
팔리다	"to be sold"
쌓다	"to stack," "to pile (up)"
쌓이다	"to be stacked," "to be piled (up)"

Passive Voice

Chapter 15

덩어리	"a pile," "a lump"
묶이다	"to be tied"
풀리다	"to be untied," "to be solved"
잘리다	"to be cut (off)," "to be severed"
잠그다	"to lock"
잠기다	"to be locked"
살(이) 빠지다	"weight is lost"
살(이) 찌다	"weight is gained"
들리다	"to be heard"
쳐다보이다	"to be stared at"
먹이	"(animal) food," "feed"
소리(를) 내다	"to make a sound," "to make a noise"
소리(가) 나다	"a sound is made," "a noise is made"
화(를) 내다	"to get angry (at someone/something)"
짜증(을) 내다	"to get annoyed (at someone/something)"
짜증(이) 나다	"to be annoyed (by someone/something)"
혼(을) 내다	"to scold," "to tell off"
혼(이) 나다	"to be scolded," "to be told off"
땀	"sweat"
땀(이) 나다	"to sweat"
사고(가) 나다	"to have an accident"
불(이) 나다	"to have a fire"
전쟁	"war"
전쟁(이) 나다	"to have a war"
큰 일(이) 나다	"to be a big problem"
한가하다	"to be free," "to have (spare) time," "to be at leisure"
호기심	"curiosity"
호기심(이) 많다	"to be curious"
용기	"courage"
용기(를) 내다	"to be courageous," "to show (one's) courage"

Chapter 15: Passive Voice

겁	"cowardice," "fear"
겁(을) 내다	"to show (one's) cowardice"
겁(이) 나다	"to be afraid," "to be cowardly"
겁쟁이	"a coward"
인내심	"patience"
인내심(이) 많다	"to be (very) patient"
죄책감	"(feeling of) guilt"
죄책감(을) 느끼다	"to feel guilt(y)"
제출(을) 하다	"to submit," "to turn in"
제출(이) 되다	"to be submitted," "to be turned in"
제품	"(manufactured) good," "(manufactured) product"
접수(를) 하다	"to receive (and accept)"
접수(가) 되다	"to be received (and accepted)"
완료(를) 하다	"to complete"
완료(가) 되다	"to be completed"
부담	"burden"
부담(이) 되다	"to be a burden"
주어지다	"to be given"
짓다	"to build"
지어지다	"to be built"
밀리다	"to be pushed"
당겨지다	"to be pulled"
펴지다	"to be opened up," "to be unfolded"
깨(어)지다	"to be broken," "to be smashed"
찢다	"to tear," "to rip (up)"
찢기다	"to be torn," "to be ripped (up)"
울려지다	"to be made to cry"
알려지다	"to be (made) known," "to be understood"
지우다	"to erase"
지워지다	"to be erased"
취소(를) 하다	"to cancel"
취소(가) 되다	"to be cancelled"

Passive Voice

Chapter 15

연구	"research"
연구(를) 하다	"to research"
연구(가) 되다	"to be researched"
감동(을) 시키다	"to move (emotionally)," "to touch (emotionally)"
감동(을) 받다	"to be moved (emotionally)," "to be touched (emotionally)"
존경(을) 받다	"to be respected," "to be looked up to"
사랑(을) 받다	"to be loved"
배달	"delivery"
배달(을) 하다	"to deliver"
배달(이) 되다	"to be delivered"
허락(을) 하다	"to permit," "to allow"
혜택	"benefit"
혜택(이) 되다	"to (be a) benefit"
속다	"to be tricked," "to be deceived"
속이다	"to trick (someone)," "to deceive (someone)"
차이다	"to be kicked"
치이다	"to be hit"
부딪(치)다	"to bump into/against"
부딪치이다	"to be bumped into/against"
두들기다	"to knock (door)," "to beat (drum)"
깨다	"to break (something)," "to smash (something)"
쇠	"metal"

Chapter 15

Passive Voice

Describing States

Conversation

Chapter 16

손님:	안녕하세요. 내년 초에 신혼여행을 가려고 하는데요.
직원:	네, 이쪽 자리가 비어 있으니 여기에 앉으세요. 어디를 생각 중이세요?
손님:	고맙습니다. 제가 중국어를 해서 홍콩이나 중국 본토를 생각 중이에요.
직원:	먼저 여행을 다녀온 사람으로서 말씀드리면 신혼여행으로는 홍콩이 더 좋을 것 같네요.
손님:	제가 생각하기에도 지금 상태로는 홍콩이 더 좋겠네요.
직원:	잘 생각하셨어요. 홍콩 여행은 호텔과 비행기표가 패키지로 준비돼 있는데 가격도 아주 저렴해요.
손님:	홍콩에서 만 원짜리 기념품도 많이 살 수 있을까요?
직원:	그럼요. 홍콩은 야시장이 유명하니까 기념품도 많이 살 수 있어요.
손님:	그럼 야시장에 대한 정보도 조금 찾아 주실 수 있으세요?
직원:	네, 제가 준비해 드릴게요. 아, 참! 홍콩 시장에서 물건을 사실 때는 여행객이 아닌 척하시면 더 좋아요.
손님:	아주 기대되네요. 그럼 여권이 준비되는 대로 바로 연락드리겠습니다.
직원:	네. 가시는 길에 문 앞에 있는 오픈 기념 우산을 하나 가져가세요.

Chapter 16: Describing States

We learned that the Progressive Tense can be used to show something that's *currently* happening, or "in the process of" happening:

창문을 열고 있어요.
"I am (currently) opening the window."
"I am (in the process of) opening the window."

We also learned that passive voice can be used to show that the *subject* of a sentence is the *object* of an action:

창문이 열렸어요.
"The window (was) opened."

We can combine these two – Progressive Tense and passive voice – to show that the subject of a sentence is *currently* the object of an action, or that the subject of a sentence is "in the process of" being the object of an action:

창문이 열리고 있어요.
"The window is (currently) opening."
"The window is (in the process) of opening."

While all of these sentences are correct, what we need to be able to say is "The window is *open*." We will need to learn a new tense in order to say this. Simply saying 창문이 열려요 would mean "The window opens" or "The window will open," which is not what we want to say. Saying "The window is open" is describing the *state* (the condition or status) of the window.

This chapter will discuss how to make this form, along with a few other grammar concepts. Let's first jump into the conversation.

손님: 안녕하세요. 내년 초에 신혼여행을 가려고 하는데요.
"Hello. I'm going to go on a honeymoon at the beginning of next year."

초, 중순, and 말

You can use 초 ("beginning"), 중순 ("middle") or 말 ("end") after a *noun* related to *time* to mean "the beginning of," "the middle of," or "the end of" that noun. These three words can also be used with the particle 에 to mean "at." However, 중순 can only be used to mean "the middle" of a *month*. Here are examples of each.

올해 말에 할 계획이에요.
"I'm planning to do it at the end of this year."

Describing States

작년 6월 중순에 봤어요.
"I saw it in the middle of last June."

3월 초부터 다시 만날 수 있어요.
"We can meet again from the beginning of March."

Note that these words *must* be used after a noun related to time, and will have a different meaning if used in other situations. A different word with the same sound as 초 means "candle," and two other words with the same sound as 말 are "word" and "horse." Remember that 초 can also be used with Sino-Korean numbers as the *second counter*, and is another unrelated word that has the same sound.

직원: 네, 이쪽 자리가 비어 있으니 여기에 앉으세요. 어디를 생각 중이세요?
"Okay, this seat is open so please sit here. Where are you thinking?"

"In the State Of": Action Verb Stem + 아/어/etc. 있다

You can use this form to describe the *state* (the condition or status) of someone or something. This is used for showing that an action has *finished*, and that someone or something is still in the *state* it was (or the person was) when that action finished. For example, if you are "sitting" in a chair, you have already sat down (앉았다) and are still in the state you were in when you finished sitting down.

To make this form, take an *action verb stem* and conjugate it as if you were conjugating the 요 form, but do not add the 요. Instead, add a space and then conjugate the verb 있다. Let's take a look at a few examples.

앉다: "to sit"
앉고 있다: "to be in the process of sitting (but not yet seated)"
앉아 있다: "to be sitting," "to be seated"

회장님이 저기에 앉아 계세요.
"The president is sitting over there."

You can use 계시다 instead of 있다 when using *honorific speech*.

> **Adv** When used before a noun, 계시다 can become either 계시는 or 계신. Both conjugations are correct. For example:
>
> 밖에 앉아 **계시는** 분은 누구예요?
> 밖에 앉아 **계신** 분은 누구예요?
> "Who is the person sitting outside?"

Chapter 16

Describing States

열리다: "to be opened"
열리고 있다: "to be in the process of opening"
열려 있다: "to be open"

창문이 열려 있어요.
"The window is open."

살다: "to live"
살고 있다: "to be in the process of living"
살아 있다: "to be alive"

거미가 아직 살아 있어요.
"The spider is still alive."

서다: "to stand"
서고 있다: "to be in the process of standing"
서 있다: "to be standing"

철수가 문 앞에 서 있어요.
"Chul-soo is standing in front of the door."

눕다: "to lie down"
눕고 있다: "to be in the process of lying down"
누워 있다: "to be lying down"

영희는 소파에 편하게 누워 있어요.
"Yung-hee is comfortably lying on the sofa."

Note that 눕다 becomes 누워(요) in the 요 form.

죽다: "to die"
죽고 있다: "to be in the process of dying"
죽어 있다: "to be dead"

원숭이가 죽어 있어요.
"The monkey is dead."

깨어지다: "to be broken," "to be smashed"
깨어지고 있다: "to be in the process of breaking," "to be in the process of being smashed"
깨어져 있다: "to be (in the state of having been) broken," "to be (in the state of having been) smashed"

Describing States

창문이 깨어져 있지 않아요.
"The window isn't broken."

To make this form *negative*, use 있지 않다. Do not change 있다 to 없다.

연결(이) 되다: "to be(come) connected"
연결(이) 되고 있다: "to be in the process of being connected"
연결(이) 되어 있다: "to be (in the state of having been) connected"

선이 연결되어 있어요.
"The wires are connected."

들다: "to enter," "to go in"
들고 있다: "to be in the process of entering," "to be in the process of going in"
들어 있다: "to have entered," "to be in"

이 주스에 10 가지 비타민이 들어 있어요.
"There are 10 kinds of vitamins in this juice."

> **Adv** 들어오다 ("to come in") and 들어가다 ("to go in") originally come from this verb.

손님: 고맙습니다. 제가 중국어를 해서 홍콩이나 중국 본토를 생각 중이에요.
"Thank you. I speak Chinese so I'm thinking of Hong Kong or mainland China."

직원: 먼저 여행을 다녀온 사람으로서 말씀드리면 신혼여행으로는 홍콩이 더 좋을 것 같네요.
"Speaking as someone who's traveled there before, I think Hong Kong would be better as a honeymoon."

"As": Noun + (으)로서

You can do something "as" someone by using this form. For example, you can use this form to say "*as* a parent" or "*as* a good friend."

To use this form, take a noun and attach 으로서 after a *consonant*, or attach 로서 after a *vowel*. While the 서 at the end is *optional*, it is more commonly used. Here are a few examples.

이건 부모로서 꼭 해야 할 일이에요.
"This is something I must do as a parent."

Chapter 16: Describing States

좋은 친구로서 해 줄 수 있어?
"Can you do it for me as a good friend?"

학생으로서 그런 걸 하면 안 돼요.
"He shouldn't do those things as a student."

선생님으로서 학생들에게 가르쳐 주고 싶은 게 많아요.
"As a teacher there are many things I want to teach to the students."

Let's take another look at the conversation sentence. 말씀(을) 드리다 is the *humble verb* form of 말(을) 하다 ("to speak," "to say"). Note that a more *literal* translation of 먼저 여행을 다녀온 사람으로서 말씀드리면 is "If I speak as someone who has traveled (and came back) before (you have)."

> **Advanced**
>
> **Avoiding Repetitive Korean**
>
> While the 서 at the end of (으)로서 is *optional*, it is most often used. The conversation sentence uses 신혼여행으로 instead of 신혼여행으로서 simply to avoid using 서 twice. This is a stylistic choice, as it sounds better in Korean (and in English as well) to avoid repeating words in the same sentence.
>
> This same principle is also what influences people when using markers in their sentences, especially the Object Marker. Here is an example.
>
> 한국어(를) 공부(를) 했어요.
> "I studied Korean."
>
> In order to avoid using the Object Marker twice in the same sentence so close together, typically only one or neither of these two will be used. While it is grammatically correct to use both, it is unnecessary and unnatural. In longer sentences where Object Markers are more spaced apart, it is fine and natural to use more of them.

손님: 제가 생각하기에도 지금 상태로는 홍콩이 더 좋겠네요.
"In my situation now Hong Kong would be better in my opinion too."

In Chapter 13 we learned how to use the verb 보다 ("to see") in the phrases 내가 보기에(는) and 제가 보기에(는) to mean "The way I see it," "As I see it," or "In my opinion." We can also use the verb 생각(을) 하다 ("to think") in this same way as 내가 생각하기에(는) or 제가 생각하기에(는) to mean "As I think" or "In my opinion."

직원: 잘 생각하셨어요. 홍콩 여행은 호텔과 비행기표가 패키지로 준비돼 있는데 가격도 아주 저렴해요.
"Good thinking. The Hong Kong trip is prepared in a package with a hotel and a plane ticket, and the price is very inexpensive too."

In the conversation, 잘 생각하셨어요 literally means "You thought well."

Describing States

Chapter 16

Remember that 되다 can be conjugated as either 돼 or 되어. Both are commonly used, but 되어 is more commonly found in *writing*.

> 손님: 홍콩에서 만 원짜리 기념품도 많이 살 수 있을까요?
> "Would I also be able to buy a lot of souvenirs that are worth 10,000 Won in Hong Kong?"

Counter + 짜리 Noun

짜리 can be attached to certain *counters* to mean "worth (of)" or "amount (of)," and has a few common uses. After attaching 짜리, add the noun that it will be describing. Most commonly, 짜리 is used together with an amount of 원 ("Won") to mean "something that is worth (amount)."

> 1,000 원짜리 쿠폰을 샀어요.
> "I bought a coupon that's worth 1,000 Won"

짜리 can also be used with other counters. For example, it can be used with 층 (building floor counter) when describing a building.

> 4 층짜리 건물에서 머물고 있어요.
> "I'm staying at a 4-story building."

Literally, this would mean "I live in an apartment that is *worth* 4 stories." Note that 머무르다 ("to stay," "to remain") is commonly shortened to 머물다. To help understand this usage, you can think of 짜리 as translating as "something that *has* or *contains* an amount of something." For example, we could translate the previous sentence in this way as "I live in a building that has/contains 4 stories."

Culture Notes

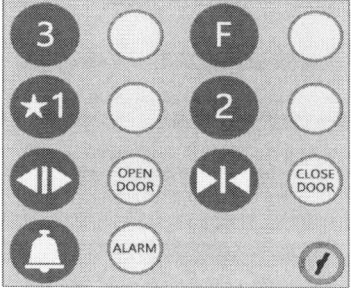

The number **4** is associated with bad luck in Korea. This is because 사 ("four") has the same sound as the Chinese character for "death," which is also pronounced 사. You might find elevators in Korea that instead label the 4th floor with an "F" (short for "four"). Knocking on doors four times is also considered bad luck.

Chapter 16: Describing States

짜리 can also be used to describe a person's age using 살 (age counter).

네 살짜리 어린이 2 명을 만났어요.
"I met 2 children that were 4 years old."

Again, using our alternate translation for 짜리, we could also translate this sentence as "I met 2 children that had 4 years (of age)."

> 직원: 그럼요. 홍콩은 야시장이 유명하니까 기념품도 많이 살 수 있어요.
> "Of course. Hong Kong is famous for its outdoor night markets so you can also buy a lot of souvenirs."

> 손님: 그럼 야시장에 대한 정보도 조금 찾아 주실 수 있으세요?
> "Then could you please find a little information about night markets too?"

> 직원: 네, 제가 준비해 드릴게요. 아, 참! 홍콩 시장에서 물건을 사실 때는 여행객이 아닌 척하시면 더 좋아요.
> "Okay, I'll prepare it for you. Ah! When you buy stuff at a Hong Kong market, it's better if you pretend you're not a tourist."

아, 참 is a *stronger* version of simply saying 아.

"To Pretend": Adjective 척(을) 하다

You can use the verb 척(을) 하다 to show that someone is *pretending* to do something, or pretending *like* something, or *acting* like something. For example, "I pretended that I was cool," or "I acted like I was cool."

To use it, first choose an *adjective* (this can be made from a descriptive verb or an action verb) and then conjugate the verb 척(을) 하다 after. First, here are a few examples using *descriptive verbs*.

멋있는 척을 했어요.
"I pretended that I was cool."
"I acted like I was cool."

안 무서운 척했어요.
"I pretended that I wasn't afraid."
"I acted like I wasn't afraid."

Describing States

Chapter 16

아픈 척을 했어요.
"I pretended to be hurt."
"I acted like I was hurt."

귀여운 척하지 마.
"Don't act cute."

There are times when using either "pretend" or "act" will sound more natural in English, such as in the previous example. Next, here are a few examples using *action verbs*.

철수는 모든 걸 아는 척해요.
"Chul-soo pretends to know everything."

대화를 하기 싫어서 자는 척했어요.
"She didn't want to talk, so she pretended to sleep."

우는 척했어요.
"He pretended to cry."

게임을 하면서 공부하는 척했어요.
"She pretended to study while playing games."

제 한국어가 서툴러서 인터뷰할 시간이 없는 척했어요.
"My Korean is poor, so I pretended I didn't have time to do an interview."

Adv
You might also see 체(를) 하다 used in the same way. 체(를) 하다 has the same meaning as 척(을) 하다, but is used much less commonly.

Advanced

"To Pretend" & Future Tense: Action Verb Stem + (을/ㄹ) 것처럼 행동(을) 하다

척(을) 하다 can not be used with adjectives in the *future tense*. In order to say that someone is pretending that they will do something in the future, or acting like they will do something in the future, you need to use a different form. This form uses the 것이다 future tense and literally means "to *behave* like someone will do something."

시험 공부를 안 할 것처럼 행동하고 있어.
"He's acting like he won't study for the test."

손님: 아주 기대되네요. 그럼 여권이 준비되는 대로 바로 연락드리겠습니다.
"I'm really looking forward to it. Then I will contact you as soon as the passport is prepared."

Chapter 16: Describing States

기대(가) 되다 is the passive form of 기대(를) 하다, but is commonly used in many of the same situations. Here is an example:

발표를 기대하고 있어요.
발표가 기대돼요.
"I'm looking forward to the presentation."

Note that while 기대(를) 하다 can be used in any tense, 기대(가) 되다 is typically only used in the *present tense*.

"As soon as": Action Verb Stem + 는 대로

You can use 대로 with action verbs to mean "as soon as." For example, "Please tell me as soon as your class finishes." Remember that the 자마자 form is also used to mean "as soon as." While both forms have the same meaning, 자마자 is more commonly used. However, it is important to be able to recognize 대로 as well.

To use it, take an *action verb stem* and attach 는, just as you would when changing an action verb to an *adjective*. Then add 대로 and finish the rest of the sentence. Here are a few examples.

수업이 끝나는 대로 말해 주세요.
"Please tell me as soon as your class finishes."

옷을 입는 대로 나갈 거예요.
"I'll leave as soon as I put on my clothes."

철수가 집을 나가는 대로 전화해 주세요.
"Please call me as soon as Chul-soo leaves the house."

학교에 도착하는 대로 전화할게요.
"I'll call you as soon as I arrive at school."

To use this form with the *past tense*, conjugate the action verb to a past tense adjective using 은/ㄴ as we previously learned.

서류를 받은 대로 연락했어요.
"I contacted him as soon as I received the documents."

Describing States

Chapter 16

"As" & "In the way": Adjective + 대로

Another common use of 대로 is to mean "as" or "in the way." For example, "Please draw it as you saw it," or "Please draw it in the way you saw it."

To use it, change an *action verb* into an *adjective* using any tense you would like. Then attach 대로 and finish the sentence. Here are a few examples.

본 대로 그려 주세요.
"Please draw it as you saw it."
"Please draw it in the way you saw it."

어제 한 대로 하세요.
"Do it as you did it yesterday."

제가 들은 대로 썼어요.
"I wrote it as I heard it."

철수가 하라고 한 대로 했어요.
"I did it the way that Chul-soo said to do it."

Noun + 대로

대로 can also be used with a small number of *nouns*. When using 대로 in this way, it attaches directly to the noun (without a space). Here are two examples.

순서대로 읽어 주세요.
"Please read it in order."

선생님의 말대로 하니까 성공했어요.
"We succeeded because we did as the teacher said."

This example literally translates as "We succeeded because we did it *in the way* of the teacher's words."

Note that this form is also where the idiom 마음대로 하다 ("to do as one wishes") comes from.

Going back to the conversation, 연락(을) 드리다 is the *humble verb* form of 연락(을) 하다 ("to contact").

직원: 네. 가시는 길에 문 앞에 있는 오픈 기념 우산을 하나 가져가세요.
"Okay. On your way take an opening commemorative umbrella in front of the door."

"On the way": Action Verb Stem + 는 길

You can use this form with verbs that show *movement* to say that something happened "on the way" to doing something, or that you're "on the way" to doing something. This form uses the word 길 ("a street," "a road," "a way").

Describing States

Chapter 16

To use it, take an *action verb stem* (one that shows *movement*) and attach 는, followed by 길. This can then be used with the particle 에 if used in the middle of a sentence, or with the verb 이다 if used at the end of a sentence. Here are a few examples.

학교로 가는 길에 친구를 만났어요.
"I met a friend while on my way (going) to school."

아빠는 지금 회사에서 오는 길이에요.
"Dad is now on his way (coming) from work."

산을 올라가는 길에 꽃을 땄어요.
"On my way (climbing) up the mountain I picked flowers."

Adv

길 and 중

This 길 form is different from the 중 form that we learned in the previous book, because the 중 form can be used with any type of action verb. The 길 form can only be used with verbs that show *motion*, such as 가다, 오다, and others. In addition, the 중 form *emphasizes* that you are *currently* doing something and therefore might not be finished for awhile. The 길 form has no such emphasis.

Going back to the conversation, while "commemoration" is not a commonly used word in English, 기념 is commonly used in Korean. 오픈 (literally "open") is referring to the "opening" of the store. 기념 ("commemoration") is referring to *celebrating* that opening.

하나 ("one") can be used in place of 한 개 to mean "one (thing)." This is an exception. Other numbers will be more commonly used together with the counter 개.

하나 주세요.
"Please give me one."

두 개 주세요.
"Please give me two."

Practice

Change the following verb states using the 있다 form:

1. 추가(가) 되다

_____.

2. 티비가 켜지다

_____.

Describing States

3. 티비가 꺼지다

   _____.

4. 사랑에 빠지다

   _____.

5. 규칙이 바뀌다

   _____.

6. 한글로 쓰이다

   _____.

7. 도둑이 잡히다

   _____.

8. 건물이 지어지다

   _____.

9. 책이 펴지다

   _____.

10. 눈이 떠지다

    _____.

11. 팔이 부러지다

    _____.

12. 정해지다

    _____.

Chapter 16 — Describing States

Translate to Korean:

13. "I can't meet until the end of June."

_____.

14. "The air conditioner is off."

_____.

15. "Is the door locked?"

_____.

16. "The garbage is already separated."

_____.

17. "That guy is the best as a singer."

_____.

18. "I bought sweets worth 100 Won."

_____.

19. "The princess lives in a 10-story tower."

_____.

20. "I pretended that I wasn't cold."

_____.

21. "I am on my way home."

_____.

22. "I met Jeremy on my way to school."

_____.

Describing States

Translate to English:

23. 정원에 꽃이 다 피어 있어요.

24. 집에 돌아왔더니 창문이 깨져 있었어요.

25. 닫혀 있는 문을 열었어요.

26. 제가 대표자로서 얘기할게요.

27. 제가 하지 않은 척했어요.

28. 돈이 모아지는 대로 여행을 갈 거예요.

29. 나가는 길에 쓰레기를 버려 주세요.

30. 그 과자에 중독이 되어 있어요.

31. 아직 시차에 적응이 안 되어 있어요.

New Phrases

아, 참!	"Ah!"

Chapter 16: Describing States

New Vocabulary

초	"beginning"
중순	"middle (of a month)"
말	"end"
신혼여행	"honeymoon"
신혼여행(을) 가다	"to go on a honeymoon"
연결	"connection"
연결(이) 되다	"to be connected"
(양)초	"candle"
눈(을) 뜨다	"to open (one's) eyes"
눈(이) 떠지다	"(one's) eyes open"
눈(을) 감다	"to close (one's) eyes"
눈(이) 감기다	"(one's) eyes close"
눈(을) 깜빡이다	"to blink (eyes)"
눈썹	"eyebrow"
속눈썹	"eyelash"
코(를) 골다	"to snore"
들다	"to enter," "to go in"
홍콩	"Hong Kong"
본토	"(the) mainland"
상태	"state," "condition," "situation"
패키지	"package"
기념	"commemoration"
기념품	"souvenir"
기념일	"anniversary"
짜리	"worth (of)," "amount (of)"
야시장	"(outdoor) night market"
여행객	"traveler," "tourist"
관광객	"sightseer," "tourist"
관광	"sightseeing," "tourism"
관광(을) 하다	"to sightsee," "to tour"
척(을) 하다	"to pretend (to/like)," "to act (like)"
기대(가) 되다	"to be expected," "to look forward"

Describing States

분리(를) 하다	"to separate"
분리(가) 되다	"to be separated"
순서	"order," "sequence"
따다	"to pick (a plant)"
오픈	"open(ing)"
(돈[이]) 모아지다	"to be saved up (money)"
쿠폰	"coupon"
중독	"addiction"
중독성(이) 있다	"to be addicting"
중독(이) 되다	"to be addicted"
탑	"tower"
시차	"time difference"
적응(을) 하다	"to adapt to," "to adjust to"
적응(이) 되다	"to be adapted to," "to be adjusted to"
서투르다	"to be unskilled," "to be poor at"
인터뷰	"interview"

Chapter 16 Describing States

More Past Tense

Chapter 17

Conversation

제니퍼:	영선아, 정말 오랜만이다.
영선:	응. 우리가 커서 만나면 어색할 거라고 생각하곤 했는데, 생각보다 어색하지 않네.
제니퍼:	그렇지? 난 지난번에 미주를 우연히 만났는데 많이 달라졌더라고.
영선:	그래? 내가 미주랑 많이 친했었는데, 이제 연락처도 모르고 정말 아쉬워.
제니퍼:	내가 미주의 연락처를 받았으니까 알려줄게.
영선:	고마워. 여기 우리가 좋아했던 음식점인데 하나도 안 변했네.
제니퍼:	맞아. 사장님이 친절하고 음식이 맛있었던 곳인데 지금도 맛있어.
영선:	오랜만에 옛날 생각나서 좋네. 우리 앞으로도 자주 만나자.
제니퍼:	그래. 다음에는 미주도 함께 만나자.

In the first book we learned how to conjugate the *past tense*, but we have not gone back to look at it since then. There is still more that we can learn about the past tense. For example, in English we can say "I *went* to the store," but we can also say "I *had gone* to the store" and "I *used to* go to the store." These three sentences are in the past tense but have slightly different meanings and uses. Korean has similar forms, but they work slightly differently from how they do in English. Let's jump right into the conversation and learn along the way.

Chapter 17

More Past Tense

> 제니퍼: 영선아, 정말 오랜만이다.
> "Yung-sun, it's been a really long time (since we've met)."

> 영선: 응. 우리가 커서 만나면 어색할 거라고 생각하곤 했는데, 생각보다 어색하지 않네.
> "Yeah. I used to think it'd be awkward when we meet after becoming adults, but it's not as awkward as I thought."

Literally 커서 means "after getting big," but it can be used to mean that someone gets *older* (becomes an adult).

커서 뭐가 되고 싶어?
"What do you want to be when you're older?"

커서 돈을 많이 벌 거예요.
"She'll grow up and earn a lot of money."

"Used to": Action Verb Stem + 곤 하다

You can use this form to say that you *used to* do something. For example, "I *used to* contact him often."

To use it, take an *action verb stem* and attach 곤. Then conjugate the verb 하다 to the *past tense*. Here are some examples.

연락을 자주 하곤 했어요.
"I used to contact her often."

지난 학기까지 도서관에서 숙제를 하곤 했어요.
"I used to do my homework at the library until last semester."

주말에 할머니 집에 가곤 했어요.
"I used to go to my grandmother's house on the weekends."

조지는 일본어를 공부하곤 했지만 지금은 한국어를 공부해요.
"George used to study Japanese, but now he studies Korean."

아기는 어렸을 때 많이 울곤 했어요.
"He used to cry a lot when he was young."

매일 건강하지 않은 음식을 먹곤 했지만 요즘은 야채만 먹고 운동해요.
"Everyday I used to eat unhealthy food, but these days I only eat vegetables and exercise."

More Past Tense

Chapter 17

> A d v
>
> 곤 is a shortened version of 고는, although 곤 is much more commonly used.

Going back to the conversation, 생각보다 literally means "more than thought." It can translate more naturally as "more than one thought" or "more than one thinks."

생각보다 좋았어요.
"It was better than I thought."

생각보다 오래 걸릴 거예요.
"It'll take longer than you think."

생각보다 많이 웃었어요.
"He laughed a lot more than I thought (he would)."

제니퍼: 그렇지? 난 지난번에 미주를 우연히 만났는데 많이 달라졌더라고.
"Right? The other day I happened to meet Mi-joo, and she's changed a lot."

Another translation for 우연히 ("by coincidence," "by chance") is "to happen to do" something.

Another translation for 지난번 ("last time") is "the other day."

Describing Personal Experiences: Verb Stem + 더라고(요)

You can use the 더라고(요) form describe something that you personally experienced, realized, saw happening, or found out. This form can translate as "I recall" or "I remember." Its English translation will depend on the context, and often it is not even necessary to translate it. This form is only used for describing experiences in the *past tense*.

To use it, take a *verb stem* and attach 더라고. When speaking *politely*, add a 요 to the end.

아주 맛있더라고요.
"It was really delicious (and I know because I tried it)."
"I recall it was really delicious."

When using this form, *descriptive verb stems* will be left in the present tense. For example, use 좋더라고(요) and not 좋았더라고(요), even when talking about something in the past. *Action verb stems* can be used in the present tense or in the past tense, depending on the meaning of the sentence. Here are two examples.

Chapter 17

More Past Tense

매일 학교로 가더라고요.
"I recall that he goes to school everyday."

매일 학교로 갔더라고요.
"I recall that he went to school everyday."

Both of these example sentences with *action verbs* are describing something that happened in the past; if not, then the speaker would not be able to use this form. The first example means that the person went to school at least once (because the speaker knows about it), and still goes to school. The second example simply expresses something that happened in the past and does not add the meaning that the person still does it. It is likely that the person in the second example no longer goes to school, as far as the speaker knows. Remember that this only applies when using this form with action verbs.

Descriptive verbs that use this form can translate as both the present tense and the past tense at the same time. Its translation will depend on the context of the sentence. For example:

맵더라고요.
"(I recall) it is spicy."
"(I recall) it was spicy."

Here are a few more examples.

좋더라고.
"It was good (and I experienced it)."
"I recall it was good."

벌써 나갔더라고요.
"He already left (and I saw him leave)."
"I recall him leaving."

시내에 사람이 많더라고.
"There were a lot of people downtown (and I was there)."
"I recall there were a lot of people downtown."

저에게 주지 않았더라고요.
"He didn't give it to me (and I was there, waiting to receive it)."
"I recall that he didn't give it to me."

한국은 여름에 너무 덥더라고.
"Korea was so hot in the summer (and I was there)."
"I recall in Korea the summer was so hot."

More Past Tense

Chapter 17

돈이 어디있는지 철수한테도 물어봤는데 모르더라고요.
"I asked Chul-soo too where the money is but he doesn't know (and I heard him say he didn't know)."

나도 그렇게 생각하게 되더라고.
"I end up thinking that too (and I realized it myself)."

학생들이 숙제를 안 하더라고요.
"The students don't do the homework (and I've realized it myself)."

> **Advanced**
>
> **Verb Stem + 더라**
>
> You can use 더라 in the same way as 더라고(요). Using 더라 shows a strong *emphasis* when describing what you personally experienced, realized, saw happening, or found out. It can be used when speaking *casually* (since there is no 요 on the end), but should not be used when speaking politely or formally.
>
> 지난 주엔 다들 너무 바쁘더라.
> "Everyone was so busy last week (and I experienced this)."

Going back to the conversation, 달라지다 literally means "to become/get different," but it's used when you want to say that a *person* has become "different," or has "changed" from how they used to be.

영선: 그래? 내가 미주랑 많이 친했었는데, 이제 연락처도 모르고 정말 아쉬워.

"Really? I had been really close with Mi-joo, but now it's too bad that I don't even know her phone number."

Past Perfect Tense: Past Tense Verb Stem + 었다

Just as we can say "I *went* to the store" in English, we can also say "I *had gone* to the store." This is known as *past perfect tense*, and it is used in Korean too. You can also think of this as a *double* past tense because of the way it is conjugated.

To use this form, take a verb and conjugate it to the past tense. Then take that new past tense verb and conjugate it to the past tense again. For example, the verb 하다 would first become 했다 in the past tense. Since all past tense verbs will end in ㅆ, we can simply add 었다 to the end of the stem (here, 했), and we are finished – 했었다.

옛날에 거기 자주 갔었어요.
"In the old days I had gone there often."

작년에는 제가 아르바이트를 했었어요.
"I had worked a part-time job last year."

Chapter 17
More Past Tense

"But I don't often use this type of *past perfect tense* in English. Why would I need it in Korean?" We have learned how to use the 곤 하다 form to say that you "used to" do something. Past perfect tense can also be used to say that you "used to" do something. While both forms, 곤 하다 and past perfect tense, can be used to mean that you "used to" do something, past perfect tense is more commonly used. Here are a few examples using previous sentences.

연락을 자주 했었어요.
"I had contacted him often."
"I used to contact him often."

주말에 할머니 집에 갔었어요.
"I had gone to my grandmother's house on the weekends."
"I used to go to my grandmother's house on the weekends."

조지는 일본어를 공부했었지만 지금은 한국어를 공부해요.
"George had studied Japanese, but now he studies Korean."
"George used to study Japanese, but now he studies Korean."

Going back to the conversation, while 연락처 literally means "contact information," it is most often used to refer to a person's phone number.

제니퍼: 내가 미주의 연락처를 받았으니까 알려줄게.
"I got Mi-joo's phone number so I'll tell it to you."

영선: 고마워. 여기 우리가 좋아했던 음식점인데 하나도 안 변했네.
"Thanks. Here's the restaurant that we used to like, and it hasn't changed a bit."

Past Tense Adjectives: Verb Stem + 던

We were introduced to 던 in Chapter 3 (with the 것 같다 form) when conjugating a descriptive verb to an adjective in the *past tense*. With *descriptive verbs*, it is necessary to use 던 in order to change it into a past tense adjective. But this 던 form can also be used with action verbs. Note that whether 던 is being used with an action verb or a descriptive verb, it is only used as an *adjective* (before a noun).

With *action verbs*, using 던 adds the meaning of "had done," similar to using the past perfect tense. In addition, it can also add the meaning of "used to," similar to using the 곤 하다 form or past perfect tense. Remember that using the 던 form with an action verb changes it into an *adjective* in the past tense.

More Past Tense

Chapter 17

To use it, take a verb stem and attach 던. *Action verb stems* can be in present tense (for example, 가던) or past tense (for example, 갔던). *Descriptive verb stems* are most commonly used in the past tense (for example, 좋았던). First let's take a look at three examples using the action verb 좋아하다 ("to like").

제가 좋아하는 영화를 봤어요.
"I saw a movie that I like."

제가 좋아한 영화를 봤어요.
"I saw a movie that I liked."

제가 좋아하던 영화를 봤어요.
제가 좋아했던 영화를 봤어요.
"I saw a movie that I had liked."
"I saw a movie that I used to like."

Here are a few more examples using *action verbs*.

여기는 제가 다니던 학교예요.
"Here is the school I used to attend."

일본어는 옛날에 제가 공부했던 언어예요.
"Japanese is a language I used to study in the past."

내가 원했던 거야.
"It's what I had wanted."

친구가 살았던 집이에요.
"It's the house where my friend used to live."

작년에 매일 읽던 책은 이거였어요.
"This was the book I used to read everyday last year."

철수가 쓰고 있었던 우산을 되게 사고 싶어.
"I very much want to buy the umbrella that Chul-soo used to use."

일요일마다 갔던 공원에 다시 가 봤어요.
"I went to the park again that I used to go to each Sunday."

작년에 거기서 샀던 모자는 더 이상 안 팔리나 봐요.
"I guess the hat I had bought there last year is not sold anymore."

| Chapter 17 | **More Past Tense** |

더 이상 is an *adverb* that can be used with *negative* sentences to mean "anymore" or "any longer."

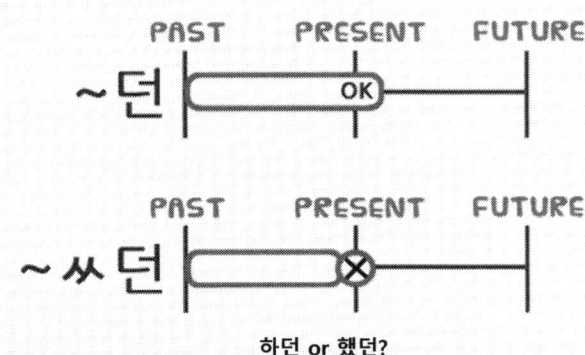

하던 or 했던?

While *action verb stems* can use this form in both the present tense (하던) or in the past tense (했던), these two forms are slightly different. Using the present tense shows that the action might still be happening now, and has happened in the past. For example, 하던 일 could mean "work that I used to do (and might still do now)." Using the past tense shows that the action happened in the past, and (to the speaker's knowledge) is not happening now. For example, 했던 일 could mean "work that I used to do (and do not do anymore)." This difference in meaning is similar to the difference between using the 더라고(요) form in the present tense and in the past tense.

Again, the present tense will not be used when (to the speaker's knowledge) the action is not happening anymore. For example, you would not use 사던 모자 to mean "the hat I had bought" because that would mean that you might still be buying the hat (unless you really like it and buy the same hat often). Instead, you would use 샀던 모자 because using the past tense shows that it does not happen anymore. However, you could use the action verb 입다 ("to wear") as either 입던 옷 or 입었던 옷 depending on the sentence. This is because "to wear" can be both an action that still happens (if you still wear it sometimes) and an action that no longer happens (if you no longer wear it).

Finally, when it is okay to use either the present tense or the past tense with an *action verb*, using the past tense can add *emphasis* that the action was in the past. Here are two examples.

제가 좋아하던 음식이에요.
"It's food that I used to like (and I still like it)."

제가 좋아했던 음식이에요.
"It's food that I *used to* like (but I don't like it anymore)."

Here are a few examples using *descriptive verbs*.

키가 컸던 친구가 기억나요?
"Do you remember our friend who used to be tall?"

항상 좋았던 건 아니에요.
"It didn't use to always be good."

어렸을 때 예뻤던 언니는 지금도 예뻐요.
"My older sister who used to be pretty when I was young is pretty now too."

More Past Tense

Chapter 17

만큼 ("as much as") is also commonly used together with the 던 form.

생각했던 만큼 좋지 않았어요.
"It wasn't as good as (much as) I'd thought."

원했던 만큼 돈을 많이 못 벌었어요.
"I couldn't make a lot of money as (much as) I'd wanted."

> **Adv**
>
> **있은 and 있던**
>
> While the 던 form can be used in place of the regular past tense form as an adjective, there is an exception with the verb 있다. 있다, as an *action verb*, can conjugate as an adjective in the past tense as 있은, although this conjugation is actually not often used. More commonly, 있던 (or 있었던) will be used. For example, instead of 집에 있은 사람 ("a person who was home"), it is much more common to use 집에 있(었)던 사람 ("a person who was home."). The same applies to 없다.

Going back to the conversation, 음식점 means "restaurant," just as 식당 means "restaurant." However, while 음식점 can only be used to refer to a store that sells food ("a restaurant"), a 식당 can also be used to refer to a cafeteria or lunchroom.

"Not one bit": 하나도

하나도 is an *adverb* that can be used with *negative verbs* to mean "not one bit" or "not at all."

하나도 안 보여요!
"It's not visible at all!"
"I can't see (it) at all!"

하나도 먹지 못했어요.
"I couldn't eat even one bit."

하나도 can also be used literally to mean "even one."

선물을 하나도 못 받았어요.
"I didn't even get one present."

"Change": 바뀌다 and 변하다

바뀌다 ("to be changed") and 변하다 ("to change," "to transform") seem similar, but are used in different situations. First, both 바뀌다 and 변하다 are used with the Subject Marker or Topic Marker – not with the Object Marker. Here is an example.

More Past Tense

A. 색깔이 변했어요.
B. 색깔이 바뀌었어요.
"The color changed."

While 바뀌다 can be used for something that's changed, 변하다 is used for something that has changed by being transformed. Example A means that the color changed due to something such as the *sunlight*, or a *chemical*, or due to *time* (etc.). Example B means that the color was changed due to being *switched* or *exchanged* with another color. Because of this difference, you could use 변하다 to say that your friend's *personality* has changed, but you would not use 바뀌다 (unless aliens switched one of your friends for an emotionless clone).

> **Adv**
>
> 더
>
> The forms 더니, 더라고(요), and 던 all originally come from the same form – 더. This 더 is used for showing something that you have personally experienced, saw happening, or heard about, just like the three forms we just learned. 던 comes from this 더 form and ㄴ, which changes it into an adjective. You will not see 더 used by itself, but it appears in several grammar forms, including the three above.

제니퍼: 맞아. 사장님이 친절하고 음식이 맛있었던 곳인데 지금도 맛있어.

> "That's right. It was a place where the boss was nice and the food was delicious, and it's delicious now too."

영선: 오랜만에 옛날 생각나서 좋네. 우리 앞으로도 자주 만나자.

> "It's nice remembering the old days after a long time. Let's meet often from now on too."

We learned how to use 앞 ("in front of") together with nouns, but it can also be used with the particle (으)로 to mean "from now on" or "in the future."

"To Come to Mind": 생각(이) 나다

Just as we learned that 기억(이) 나다 can be used to mean "to remember," you can also use 생각(이) 나다 in the same way to mean "to come to mind," "to remember," or "to think of" depending on the sentence. The noun 생각 means "an idea" or "a thought," so literally 생각(이) 나다 means "a thought comes to mind."

갑자기 이름이 생각이 안 나요.
"Suddenly his name doesn't come to mind"
"I suddenly can't remember his name."
"I suddenly can't think of his name."

More Past Tense

Chapter 17

Both 기억(이) 나다 and 생각(이) 나다 share the meanings of "to remember" and "to come to mind," but note that 기억(이) 나다 is used to emphasize a *memory*, and is not used to translate as "to think of." Here is another example of each one.

여기 올 때마다 아빠가 생각나요.
"I think of my dad each time I come here."

Just as 마다 ("each") can be attached to *nouns*, it can also be attached to the 때 form with *verbs* to mean "each time."

여기 올 때마다 아빠가 기억나요.
"I remember my dad each time I come here."

제니퍼: 그래. 다음에는 미주도 함께 만나자.
"Yeah. Next time let's meet together with Mi-joo too."

> **Advanced**
>
> **"Would have...": Verb Stem + ㅆ을 것이다**
>
> You can use this form to say "would have." This form has the same usage as the 겠다 form, though it does not translate as "must." It is used for expressing your *opinion* that something would have been, or would have happened. It is not as commonly used as the 겠다 form.
>
> To use it, take a verb stem in the *past tense* and attach 을, followed by 것이다. This form is conjugated the same way as the future tense 것이다 form, simply using a past tense verb stem instead of a present tense verb stem. Here are two examples.
>
> 나갔을 거예요.
> "She would have left."
>
> 추웠을 거예요.
> "It would have been cold."

Practice

Translate to Korean:

1. "I used to wear these pajamas."

_____.

2. "I used to dislike peanuts."

_____.

More Past Tense

Chapter 17

3. "I used to live here."

_____.

4. "I used to sleep at 10 o'clock at night."

_____.

5. "I used to meet friends each weekend."

_____.

6. "I used to like going to see movies together with my mom."

_____.

7. "It was easier than I thought."

_____.

8. "This is the book that I used to read often."

_____.

9. "That's not the movie I used to like."

_____.

10. "I sold the house that I used to live (in)."

_____.

11. "The teacher who used to be handsome became a grandfather."

_____.

Translate to English:

12. 어렸을 때 낮잠을 자곤 했어요.

_____.

More Past Tense

Chapter 17

13. 겨울이면 스키를 타곤 했어요.

_____.

14. 질이 좋아서 하나만 사도 되겠더라고요.

_____.

15. 계속 옆에 있었는데 알아채지 못했더라고.

_____.

16. 듣던 것과 많이 달랐어요.

_____.

17. 제 옆에서 울고 있던 아기가 어디 갔어요?

_____.

18. 매일 가던 웹사이트가 없어졌어요.

_____.

19. 아침마다 정원에 물을 뿌리던 기계가 어제 고장났어요.

_____.

20. 하나도 기억이 안 나요.

_____.

21. 좀 전에 들었던 노래 제목을 아세요?

_____.

22. 키가 작았던 누나를 만났더니 이제 저보다 키가 훨씬 커요.

_____.

New Vocabulary

| 우연 | "coincidence" |

Chapter 17: More Past Tense

우연히	"by coincidence," "by chance" (adverb)
시내	"downtown"
그 때에	"at that time"
동시에	"at the same time" (adverb)
매우	"very," "greatly"
몹시	"terribly," "exceedingly," "very (much)"
되게	"terribly," "exceedingly," "very (much)" (casual)
더 이상	"anymore," "any longer" (negative)
연락처	"contact information"
음식점	"restaurant"
변하다	"to change," "to transform"
변화	"change," "transformation" (noun)
하나도	"not one bit," "not at all" (negative)
앞으로	"from now on," "in the future"
생각보다...	"... than (one) thought/thinks"
스키	"ski(s)," "skiing"
스키(를) 타다	"to ski"
질(이) 좋다	"to be good quality"
질(이) 안 좋다	"to be bad quality"
알아채다	"to recognize," "to notice"
뿌리다	"to sprinkle," "to spray"
조금 전에	"a short time ago," "a little while ago"
제목	"title (of something)," "name (of something)"
달라지다	"to get/become different"
땅콩	"peanut"
콩	"bean"
오이	"cucumber"
파자마	"pajamas"
잠옷	"sleep wear," "night clothes" (literally, "sleep clothes")

Explanations

Chapter 18

Conversation

아들:	아버지, 다녀오셨어요? 오늘은 조금 늦으셨네요?
아빠:	그래. 우리 아들이 좋아하는 치킨집에 들렸다가 오느라고 조금 늦었네.
아들:	정말요? 치킨 맛이 다 비슷할 테니까 굳이 거기까지 다녀오실 필요는 없으셨을 텐데, 고맙습니다.
아빠:	그 집 치킨 맛은 다를 걸. 아빠는 우리 아들이 맛있게 먹는 모습을 보고 싶었어.
아들:	고마워요, 아빠. 같이 먹어요.
아빠:	아빤 괜찮아. 우리 아들이 맛있게 먹어 주면 아빤 그걸로 만족스러워.
아들:	혼자서 다 먹으면 당분간 치킨은 안 먹어도 될 것 같아요. 그럼 피곤하실 텐데 제가 안마해 드릴게요.
아빠:	그래. 우리 아들이 커 갈수록 아빠 생각을 많이 해 줘서 아빠가 많이 행복해.
아들:	아빠가 실망하시지 않도록 더 열심히 잘할게요. 사랑해요, 아빠.
아빠:	아빠도 우리 아들 많이 사랑해.

This chapter will introduce a few verb endings and grammar forms that we can use when giving explanations to people. Let's jump right into the conversation.

Chapter 18

Explanations

아들: 아버지, 다녀오셨어요? 오늘은 조금 늦으셨네요?
"Dad, welcome home! You're a little late today?"

In Chapter 9 we learned that we can use the verb 다녀오다 to announce that you are leaving the house and are expecting to return, or to say to someone else when they leave the house and are expected to return. It can also be used in the *past tense* when you or someone else returns home – literally meaning "someone commuted somewhere and *returned*."

While 다녀오셨어요? literally is a question that means "Have you commuted (to school/work) and returned?" it can also be used to welcome someone home, or to announce that you have arrived back from somewhere. Here is an example.

다녀왔어!
"Welcome back (home)!"
"I'm home!"

아빠: 그래. 우리 아들이 좋아하는 치킨집에 들렸다가 오느라고 조금 늦었네.
"Yeah. I'm a little late because I came (here) after stopping by the chicken restaurant that you like."

Notice how the father refers to his son as 우리 아들, meaning "my son." Using titles in this way is a more *loving* way of referring to another family member. For a review of how to use 우리 in this way, see Chapter 18 of the first book.

"Because": Action Verb Stem + 느라고

We have learned several ways to say "because," such as 때문에, (으)니까, and the 서 form. Each one is unique and can be used in different situations. You can use this 느라고 form to mean "because" or "due to" when the result is *negative*. For example, "I couldn't study Korean because I was working." This negative result might be due to *regret*, for example. Note that the negative result does not have to be a strong result – you do not have to be angry – there simply has to be some kind of negative result.

To use it, take an *action verb stem* in the present tense and attach 느라고. Then finish the rest of the sentence. Note that this form can only be used when the *subject* of the sentence stays the same. For example, it cannot be used to say "*I* couldn't study Korean because *you* were working." Here are a few examples with additional meaning added in parentheses.

일하느라고 한국어를 공부하지 못했어요.
"I (regret that I) couldn't study Korean because I was working."

Explanations

저녁을 먹느라고 문자를 못 봤어요.
"I (regret that I) couldn't see the text message because I was eating dinner."

신발을 사느라고 돈을 다 써 버렸어.
"I (regret that I) used all my money because I bought shoes."
"I (regret that I) used all my money buying shoes."

Note that this form might translate slightly differently in English depending on the sentence. Here are some more examples.

지금 공부하느라고 내일까지 바쁠 거 같아요.
"I think I'll be busy until tomorrow because I'm studying now."

뭐하느라고 늦게 왔어?
"Because of doing what did you come (here) late?"
"Why did you come (here) late?"

제가 제일 좋아하는 티비 프로그램을 보느라고 못 가서 미안해요.
"I'm sorry I couldn't go because I was watching my favorite TV program."

어제는 부모님을 도와 드리느라고 시간이 없었어요.
"Yesterday I didn't have time because I was helping my parents."

밥을 만드느라고 빨래하는 걸 잊어 버렸어요.
"I forgot to do the laundry because I was making my meal."

Note that verb stems ending in ㄹ will drop the ㄹ when used with this form.

> **Adv**
> Although less common, this form can also be shortened to 느라.

After: Verb Stem + 다(가)

In Chapter 20 of the previous book (in the Advanced Notes) we learned how to use the 다(가) ending after an action verb to mean "while." Literally, this 다(가) ending means that one action happens immediately *after* another action. Here is an example from the second book.

영화를 보다가 잠들었어요.
"I watched a movie, then fell asleep."
"I fell asleep after watching a movie."
"I fell asleep while watching a movie."

Chapter 18

Explanations

The 다(가) ending is also commonly used together with verbs that show *movement* (such as 가다, 오다, etc.) to mean that you did something *after* going somewhere. This is actually the same general concept that we have already learned for the 다(가) ending simply applied to movement verbs.

To make it, first take a verb stem that shows movement in the *past tense*, and attach 다(가). For example, 가다 would become 갔다가. The 가 is *optional* and more commonly added, but some frequently used phrases will remove it such as in this example:

갔다 와!
"Come back (here) after you go!"

Because this is a commonly used expression – 갔다 오세요 or 갔다 와(요) – a more natural translation would be "Come back soon!" or "See you later (when you come back)." You can also use 갔다 왔어(요) when you have returned from somewhere to mean "I'm back," or more literally "I went and came back," similarly to the verb 다녀오다. Here are a few more examples of the 다(가) ending.

집에 들렸다가 할게요.
"I'll do it (right) after I stop by home."

들렸다(가) comes from the verb 들르다 ("to stop by," "to drop by").

집에 갔다가 바로 갈게요.
"I'll go (there) right away after I go home."

친구가 잠깐 왔다 갔어요.
"My friend came for a short while and left (right) after."

밖에 나갔다가 친구를 만났어요.
"I met a friend (right) after I went outside."

아들: 정말요? 치킨 맛이 다 비슷할 테니까 굳이 거기까지 다녀오실 필요는 없으셨을 텐데, 고맙습니다.

"Really? The chicken flavors are all similar so there shouldn't have really been a need to go all the way there (and come back), but thank you."

정말요 is a combination of the adverb 정말(로) ("really") and the 요 ending.

Explanations

Chapter 18

Making Assumptions:
Verb Stem + (을/ㄹ) 테니까
Verb Stem + (을/ㄹ) 텐데

Both of these forms use previous forms that we have already learned – (으)니까 and the 데 form – but they can have an additional purpose when used here. You can use these two forms to make an *assumption* or *guess* about something. The 테니까 form can be used in the same way as the (으)니까 form ("because"), and the 텐데 form can be used in the same way as the 데 form (for contrasting sentences). While both of these can be used in the same way as their original forms, they are used only for making assumptions. These two forms can be used for talking about either the *future* or the *present*, depending on the context of the sentence.

To conjugate these, take a verb stem (in the present tense) and attach 을 if it ends in a *consonant*, or ㄹ if it ends in a *vowel*. Then add a space and use 테니까 to give the meaning of (으)니까, or 텐데 to give the meaning of the 데 form. Note that this form usually does not need to translate to English, but I have added translations in parentheses to help you understand how these forms are used. Here are two examples of each form.

심심할 테니까 밖에 나가서 좀 놀아.
"Because (I assume that) you're bored, go outside and play a little."

심심할 텐데 밖에 나가서 좀 놀아.
"(I assume that) you're bored, so go outside and play a little."

난 내일 공부를 해야 할 테니까 오늘 만날 수 없을까?
"Because (I assume that) I have to study tomorrow, couldn't we meet today?"

난 내일 공부를 해야 할 텐데 오늘 만날 수 없을까?
"(I assume that) I have to study tomorrow, so couldn't we meet today?"

Notice how the meaning of the sentence changes whether we're using 테니까 or 텐데, just as the meaning would change if we were using the (으)니까 ending or the 데 form. Here are some more examples.

한국 사람일 텐데요.
"(I assume that) he's a Korean."

자기 전에 핸드폰을 쓰는 것보다 책을 읽는 게 나을 텐데.
"(I assume that) reading a book before sleeping will be better than using your cell phone (so you should read a book instead)."

Explanations

Notice how an assumption can sometimes mean that you are *suggesting* something, just as it can in English. For example, telling someone "I assume he'll want to eat pizza" can imply that you are *suggesting* that they eat pizza. Another common use of these two forms is for making *suggestions*. Here are some examples of this.

피자를 먹고 싶어할 텐데요.
"(I assume) he will want to eat pizza (so we should order pizza)."

많이 추울 테니까 조심하세요.
"Be careful because (I assume that) it'll be really cold (so you should bring a jacket)."

많이 추울 텐데, 괜찮겠어요?
"(I assume) it'll be really cold (and you should bring a jacket), but will you be okay?"

이건 제가 할 테니까 그걸 해 주세요.
"Because I'll do this, (I assume that you will) please do that."

You'll often find this form used together with *commands* and *suggestions*. When the form is used in this way, it adds more *emphasis* to the command or suggestion that comes after it. For example, the previous example could also be written as 이건 제가 할 거니까 그걸 해 주세요, and would have the same meaning but with less emphasis on the command or suggestion in the sentence.

이번에 내가 밥 사 줄 테니까 다음에 네가 사 줘.
"Because I'll buy you food this time, (I'll assume that) you buy it next time."

제가 그 시간에 집에 없을 텐데요.
"(I assume that) I won't be home at that time (so you shouldn't stop by)."

제가 갈 테니까 걱정 안 해도 돼요.
"Because I'll go, (I'm assuming that) you don't have to worry."

철수가 싫어할 테니까 하지 마.
"Don't do that because (I assume that) Chul-soo won't like it."

이미 너무 늦었을 텐데 가지 마세요.
"(I assume that) it's already too late, so don't go."

This form can also be used with verb stem stems in the *past tense* to make assumptions and suggestions about the past. Here are two examples.

컴퓨터가 고장났을 테니까 쓰지 마세요.
"Because (I assume that) the computer broke, don't use it."

Explanations

정말 가고 싶었다면 같이 갔을 텐데.
"(I assume that) if you really wanted to go you would've gone together."

> **Adv**
>
> Both 테니까 and 텐데 originally come from the word 터 meaning "a will (to do something)" or "a plan (to do something)," among other definitions, and the verb 이다 ("to be"). 터 is not used as a word by itself, and only appears in certain grammar forms such as these two.

Going back to the conversation, 굳이 is an *adverb* that means "really," "absolutely," or "obstinately." You can use it in the same way that you would use 정말 ("really"), but 굳이 adds *emphasis* that someone is doing something *obstinately* (even though others may disagree with him or her). It is most commonly used in questions. Here are two examples.

굳이 가고 싶어요?
"Do you absolutely want to go?"
"Do you *really* want to go?"

이걸 왜 굳이 해야 돼요?
"Why do I absolutely have to do this?"
"Why do I *really* have to do this?"

> **Advanced**
>
> 야: "Only if..."
>
> When using the forms 야 하다 and 야 되다, the 야 ending literally translates as "only if...." For example, 이걸 해야 돼요 ("I have to do this") can literally translate as "It is okay only if I do this." This 야 ending can also be used with other verbs besides 하다 and 되다. Remember that this 야 ending is used after conjugating the verb before it to the 요 form, and then removing the 요. Here are a few examples.
>
> 지금 공원으로 가야 영희를 만날 수 있어요.
> "You can only meet Yung-hee if you go to the park now."
>
> 한국어를 잘할 수 있어야 통역사가 될 수 있어요.
> "You can become an interpreter only if you can speak Korean well."
>
> 잘 먹고 자주 운동을 해야 살이 빠져요.
> "You'll lose weight only if you eat well and exercise often."

We previously learned two main uses for 까지 – "until" (or "by" with time) and "even." There is one more usage, which is similar to "until" or "(up) to" with locations and is used in the same way. This usage literally means "all (of) the way (to)." It can be used to emphasize that someone went all of the way to a *location*. For example:

철수가 서울까지 걸어갔다고?
"You're saying that Chul-soo walked (up) to Seoul?"
"You're saying that Chul-soo walked all the way to Seoul?"

아빠: 그 집 치킨 맛은 다를 걸. 아빠는 우리 아들이 맛있게 먹는 모습을 보고 싶었어.
"That restaurant's chicken flavor is different. I wanted to watch you enjoy eating it."

Chapter 18 — Explanations

Notice how the father refers to himself as 아빠 instead of simply using 나. Using titles like this instead of using 저 or 나 to refer to yourself is also a more *loving* way of talking with another family member.

"Contrary to what you might think...": Verb Stem + (을/ㄹ) 걸(요)

You can use this form to say something that you think *contradicts* what someone else might have *said* or *thought* about someone or something. In other words, you can use this form to mean "Contrary to what you might *think*...." It is *informal* and should not be used when speaking formally.

However, this form does not mean that you are strongly disagreeing with the other person. Instead, it is a *soft* disagreement, so depending on the sentence you might want to translate it simply as "Probably (contrary to what you might think...)."

To use this form, take a verb stem in present tense or past tense and attach 을 if it ends in a *consonant*, or attach ㄹ if it ends in a *vowel*. Then add 걸(요) – the 요 can be removed when speaking *casually*. Note that although this form is written as 걸, it's pronounced 껄 due to sound change rules. Here are a few examples.

한국 사람이 아닐 걸요.
"(Contrary to what you might think...) he's (probably) not a Korean."

안 매울 걸요.
"(Contrary to what you might think...) it's not spicy."

Remember that certain types of verbs will conjugate with their own rules, such as descriptive verb stems ending in ㅂ.

해도 될 걸요.
"(Contrary to what you might think...) it's (probably) okay to do it."

돈이 많고 유명할 걸.
"(Contrary to what you might think...) he (probably) has a lot of money and is famous."

Explanations

택배가 이미 도착했을 걸요.
"The package has (probably) already arrived."

그렇게 하면 안 될 걸요.
"You (probably) shouldn't do that (contrary to what you might think)."

그 책을 읽었을 걸요.
"He read that book (even if you might think that he didn't)."

영희의 남자 친구가 아주 잘생겼을 걸.
"(Contrary to what you might think...) Yung-hee's boyfriend is (probably) very handsome."

지금 가면 늦을 걸요.
"If you go now you'll (probably) be late (even if you think that you'll make it in time)."

Note that since this form is used for contradicting what someone else might be thinking or saying about someone or something else, it is not used when speaking about *yourself*. For example, the sentence 내가 한국 사람이 아닐 걸 ("Contrary to what you might think, I'm not a Korean.") would be *incorrect*.

> **Advanced**
>
> When speaking using this form, the very *last* syllable used (걸 or 요) will have a rising intonation. This rising intonation will be the same as if you were asking a *question* – although this form is not written using a question mark. Here are two examples, with intonation and a question mark added in bold.
>
> 공부를 안 할 걸**요?**
> "(Contrary to what you might think...) he won't study."
>
> 먹을 수 있을 **걸?**
> "(Contrary to what you might think...) he can eat it."

Going back to the conversation, the noun 모습 ("figure," "image") can be used with action verbs (using 는) to mean "the figure/image of (someone doing something)." For example, 웃는 모습 is "the figure/image of someone smiling," and 공부하는 모습 is "the figure/image of someone studying." You can also think of 모습 as meaning "appearance" or "what someone or something looks like." So 웃는 모습 can also mean "what someone looks like (when they are) smiling," and 공부하는 모습 can also mean "what someone looks like (when they are) studying." Here are a couple of examples.

영희가 웃는 모습이 너무 귀엽다.
"It's so cute what Yung-hee looks like when she is smiling."
"Yung-hee looks so cute smiling."

Chapter 18

Explanations

어제 철수가 도서관에서 공부하는 모습을 봤어요.
"Yesterday I saw what Chul-soo looks like when he's studying in the library."
"Yesterday I saw Chul-soo studying in the library."

아들: 고마워요, 아빠. 같이 먹어요.
"Thanks, dad. Let's eat it together."

아빠: 아빠 괜찮아. 우리 아들이 맛있게 먹어 주면 아빠 그걸로 만족스러워.
"I'm okay. If you enjoy eating it (for me) I'm satisfied with that."

The 스럽다 Ending

스럽다 is a common ending that can attach to several *nouns*, and changes them into *descriptive verbs*. Attaching 스럽다 to a noun adds the meaning that something has the *properties* of that noun. This is similar to the 적 ending that we learned in Chapter 12. Although there are many nouns that can use 스럽다, it should be enough to learn only a few of the most common ones at first. Here are some frequently used descriptive verbs ending in 스럽다.

자연: "nature"
자연스럽다: "to be natural"

실망: "disappointment"
실망스럽다: "to be disappointing"

만족: "satisfaction"
만족스럽다: "to be satisfying"

사랑: "love"
사랑스럽다: "to be lovely"

자랑: "pride," "bragging," "boasting"
자랑스럽다: "to be proud," "to be boastful"

남성: "male"
남성스럽다: "to be masculine"

여성: "female"
여성스럽다: "to be feminine"

어른: "adult"
어른스럽다: "to be like an adult," "to be mature"

Explanations

Chapter 18

Going back to the conversation, you can use the (으)로 particle along with descriptive verbs to mean that you are "(descriptive verb) *with* (something)." Here's an example.

난 그걸로 행복해.
"I'm happy with that."

아들: 혼자서 다 먹으면 당분간 치킨은 안 먹어도 될 것 같아요. 그럼 피곤하실 텐데 제가 안마해 드릴게요.

"I think it'll be okay to not eat chicken for awhile if I eat it all alone. Then (I assume that) you're tired, so I'll give you a massage."

아빠: 그래. 우리 아들이 커 갈수록 아빠 생각을 많이 해 줘서 아빠가 많이 행복해.

"Okay. I'm really happy that the more you continue to grow up, the more you think about me a lot."

"The more you (verb), the more...":
Action Verb Stem + (을/ㄹ) + 수록

You can use this form to mean "the more you do something, the more that something happens." For example, "The more you read books, the more you learn."

To use it, take an *action verb stem* and attach 을 if it ends in a *consonant*, or attach ㄹ if it ends in a *vowel*. Then attach 수록, and complete the rest of the sentence. *Optionally*, before this form you can also attach the same verb conjugated with the (으)면 form. Here are some examples.

책을 (읽으면) 읽을수록 더 많이 배워요.
"The more you read books, the more you learn."

돈을 (벌면) 벌수록 더 벌고 싶어요.
"The more money you earn, the more you want to earn."

화장을 (하면) 할수록 예뻐지는 거 같아요.
"I think that the more I do my makeup, the prettier I get."

(빠르면) 빠를수록 더 좋아요.
"The quicker (you do it), the better."

(싸면) 쌀수록 더 많이 팔려요.
"The cheaper it is, the more that are sold."

Explanations

이 과자를 (먹으면) 먹을수록 엄마가 생각나요.
"The more I eat this candy, the more I think of my mom."

(바쁘면) 바쁠수록 건강에 신경을 더 쓰세요.
"The busier you are, the more you should care about your health."

Note that this form can also be used with *commands*, such as the (으)세요 ending and others. When used with commands, a better translation can be "should." The above example could also be more literally translated as "The busier you are, please care more about your health."

(보면) 볼수록 더 먹고 싶어져요.
"The more I look (at it), the more I want to eat it."

나이가 (많으면) 많을수록 피부에 신경을 써야 돼요.
"The older you are, the more you have to worry about your skin."

머리가 (길면) 긴 사람일수록 샴푸가 많이 필요해요.
"The longer a person's hair is, the more shampoo they need."

This form will become 일수록 when used with the verb 이다 ("to be"). The above example would also translate more literally as "The more someone is a person with long hair, the more shampoo they need."

한국어를 (공부하면) 공부할수록 한국에 더 가고 싶어져요.
"The more I study Korean, the more I want to go to Korea."

In the conversation, 커 갈수록 comes from 커 가다. For a review of this grammar form re-read the Advanced Notes of Chapter 9.

> **Adv**
>
> This form is also commonly used simply as 갈수록, which literally means "the more (someone) goes. " It's used to mean "as time goes by." Here is an example.
>
> 한국어는 갈수록 쉬워져요.
> "Korean gets easier as time goes by."

아들: 아빠가 실망하시지 않도록 더 열심히 잘할게요. 사랑해요, 아빠.

"I'll try harder so that you're not disappointed. I love you, dad."

아빠: 아빠도 우리 아들 많이 사랑해.

"I love you too, son."

Explanations

Chapter 18

Another Use of 걸

You might see 걸 used in sentences where the translation of "Contrary to what you might think..." does not seem to fit. 걸 is also used in one more separate form – "should have." This form is not the same as 걸(요), despite looking similar. It is also *informal*, and should not be used when speaking formally.

"I Should Have": Action Verb Stem + (을/ㄹ) 걸 (그랬다)

This form can be used to mean "should have" when talking about *yourself* (first person). For example, "*I* should have gone to the party too." To use this form, take an *action verb stem* and attach 을 if it ends in a *consonant*, or attach ㄹ if it ends in a *vowel*. Then add 걸, and *optionally* conjugate 그랬다 (the past tense of 그러다). Here are some examples.

나도 파티에 갈 걸 그랬어.
"I should have gone to the party too."

어제 할 걸 그랬어.
"I should've done it yesterday."

더 일찍 잠을 잘 걸.
"I should've slept earlier."

그냥 기다릴 걸.
"I should've just waited."

그걸 하지 말 걸 그랬나?
"Should I not have done that?"

Attach 지 말다 when using these two forms with *negative verbs* (instead of 안 or 지 않다).

"You Should Have": Action Verb Stem + 지 그랬다

This form can be used to mean "should have" when talking directly to *someone else* (second person). For example, "*You* should have gone to the party too." To use this form, take an *action verb stem* and attach 지. Then conjugate 그랬다 – it is *not* optional with this form.

너도 파티에 가지 그랬어.
"You should have gone to the party too."

숙제를 하지 그랬어.
"You should've done the homework."

그 남자한테 좋아한다고 말하지 그랬어.
"You should've told that boy that you like him."

저녁을 만들지 그랬어요.
"You should've made dinner."

내 말대로 우산을 가져가지 그랬어.
"You should've brought an umbrella like I said."

Finally, although the 걸 그랬다 form is normally only used when talking about yourself ("I"), it *can* also be used when talking to someone else ("you") – just like the 지 그랬다 form. For example, 너도 파티에 갈 걸 그랬어 ("You should have gone to the party too."). Note that when using the 걸 그랬다 form in this way (second person), 그랬다 is *not* optional. In addition, this form is most commonly *not* used in this way and can sound unnatural at times, but I would recommend being able to at least recognize it. However, the 지 그랬다 form *cannot* be used when talking about yourself (first person).

When talking about other people (third person), use the basic 야 되다 or 야 하다 forms instead as we have previously learned.

| Chapter 18 | **Explanations** |

Practice

Translate to Korean using the 느라고 form:

1. "I couldn't go to the park because I was studying."

    _____.

2. "I couldn't talk because I was coughing."

    _____.

Translate to Korean using the 테니까 form:

3. "I will give you money, so please do it now."

    _____.

4. "You can do it tomorrow, so go home."

    _____.

Translate to Korean using the 텐데 form:

5. "Nobody can predict it."

    _____.

6. "You should do that with a computer."

    _____.

Translate to Korean using the 걸(요) form:

7. "It's fun."

    _____.

8. "It's snowing in Seoul."

    _____.

Explanations

Translate to Korean using the 수록 form:

9. "The more you exercise, the healthier you become."

10. "The more you meet Chul-soo, the more you will end up liking him."

Translate to English:

11. 살을 빼느라고 운동을 하고 있어요.

12. 드라마를 보느라고 밤을 샜어요.

13. 세수를 하느라고 안경을 벗어 놓았어요.

14. 화장을 하느라고 오래 걸렸어요.

15. 더 자면 후회할 텐데요.

16. 두 선수의 수준이 비슷할 테니까 걱정하지 마세요.

17. 서로 도와주면서 일을 하면 장점이 될 수 있을 텐데.

18. 최대한 싸게 해 드릴 테니까 오늘 사세요.

Chapter 18 — **Explanations**

19. 조금씩 기부하면 많은 사람을 도울 수 있을 텐데.

_____.

20. 한국어 실력이 늘테니까 열심히 공부해요.

_____.

21. 빨리 끝낼 수 있을 걸요.

_____.

22. 형도 저녁을 먹었을 걸요.

_____.

23. 저를 기억할 걸요.

_____.

24. 그렇게 운전하면 사고가 날 걸요.

_____.

25. 아기가 아파하는 모습을 보니까 눈물이 났어요.

_____.

26. 정확하게 하려고 할수록 시간이 오래 걸릴 거예요.

_____.

27. 더 많이 공부할수록 쉬워져요.

_____.

28. 생각할수록 화가 나요.

_____.

29. 참을수록 더 아파질 거예요.

_____.

Explanations

30. 의사가 설명을 계속 할수록 엄마의 표정이 심각해졌어요.

_____.

New Vocabulary

치킨집	"chicken restaurant"
굳이	"really," "absolutely," "obstinately" (adverb)
모습	"figure," "image"
실망	"disappointment"
실망하다	"to be disappointed"
실망스럽다	"to be disappointing"
만족	"satisfaction"
만족하다	"to be satisfied"
만족스럽다	"to be satisfying"
조심스럽다	"to be cautious" (adjective)
조심히 하다	"to be cautious," "to be careful" (action verb)
자랑	"pride," "bragging," "boasting"
자랑스럽다	"to be proud," "to be boastful"
남성	"male"
남성스럽다	"to be masculine"
여성	"female"
여성스럽다	"to be feminine"
당분간	"for the time being," "for awhile," "for now"
안마	"massage"
안마(를) 하다	"to massage," "to give a massage"
안마(를) 받다	"to get a massage"
밤(을) 새다	"to stay up all night"
수준	"level," "standard"
장점	"an advantage," "a pro"
단점	"a weakness," "a con"

Chapter 18

Explanations

최대한	"as (much as) possible," "maximum" (adverb)
최소한	"as (little as) possible," "minimum" (adverb)
조금씩	"little by little," "gradually" (adverb)
기부	"donation"
기부(를) 하다	"to donate"
예상	"expectation," "prediction"
예상(을) 하다	"to expect," "to predict"
정확하다	"to be precise"
자세하다	"to be detailed"
표정	"(facial) expression"
심각하다	"to be serious"

More Explanations

Conversation

Chapter 19

준영:	우와, 이게 뭐야?
재호:	초콜릿. 너도 알다시피 오늘이 발렌타인 데이잖아.
준영:	아무래도 우리 학교는 남학생과 여학생의 비율이 안 맞는 것 같아.
재호:	그래?
준영:	응. 왜냐하면 나한테 초콜릿을 준 여학생이 한 명도 없거든. 여학생이 더 적은가 봐.
재호:	그러게. 왜 아무도 너한텐 안 줬을까? 근데 우리 학교는 오히려 여학생이 더 많던데.
준영:	친구야, 이럴 때는 차라리 아무 말 하지 말아 줘.
재호:	미안해. 하나 줄까?
준영:	괜찮아. 난 어차피 초콜릿 안 좋아해.
재호:	너는 뭐든지 다 좋아할 것 같은데 생각보다 안 먹는 게 많네. 근데 너 미진이랑 서로 좋아하는 거 아니었어?
준영:	아니야. 미진이랑 친하지만 그냥 친구야.
재호:	그렇구나. 난 너희가 친해서 서로 좋아하는 줄 알았어.
준영:	그냥 친구야. 아, 심지어 유치원에 다니는 내 동생도 여자 친구가 있는데 정말 슬프다.
재호:	미진이랑 그냥 친구라면 내가 다음 달에 내 친구들 소개시켜 줄게.
준영:	고마워. 너밖에 없다.

| Chapter 19 | **More Explanations** |

This chapter will follow in the previous chapter's footsteps and will continue to introduce several more verb endings and grammar forms that we can use when giving explanations to people. We will also be introduced to a few other grammar concepts. Let's jump right into the conversation.

> 준영: 우와, 이게 뭐야?
> "Wow, what's this?"

우와 is another exclamation that is similar to 와아 or 와 and can be used to mean "Wow!"

> 재호: 초콜릿. 너도 알다시피 오늘이 발렌타인 데이잖아.
> "Chocolate. As you also know, today's Valentine's Day."

"As you...": Action Verb Stem + 다시피

You can use this grammar form to say "as you (do something)." Most commonly you will see this form used with "as you *know*" or "as you *see*," but it can also be used with a few other different verbs.

To make it, take an *action verb stem* (in present tense or past tense) and attach 다시피. Here are a few commonly used examples.

알다시피: "as you know..."

> 알다시피 내일부터 방학이야.
> "As you know, it's school vacation from tomorrow."

보다시피: "as you see..."

> 어제 봤다시피 저는 차가 있어요.
> "As you saw yesterday, I have a car."

말하다시피: "as you say..."

> 철수가 말했다시피 영희는 남자 친구가 있어.
> "As Chul-soo said, Yung-hee has a boyfriend."

듣다시피: "as you hear..."

> 방송으로 들었다시피 가게가 곧 문을 닫을 거야.
> "As you heard on the broadcast, the store will close its doors soon."

More Explanations

Chapter 19

Note that you can also use this form with *honorific verbs* when speaking politely. For example, instead of 알다시피 and 보다시피, you could use 아시다시피 and 보시다시피.

> **다시피 and 하다**
>
> A
> d
> v
> a
> n
> c
> e
> d
>
> The 다시피 form can also be used together with 하다 to mean "almost." Note that this is different from the 뻔하다 form that we learned in Chapter 14 of the second book, because the 뻔하다 form is used when you almost did something *by mistake*. This 다시피 form is also commonly used together with the *adverb* 거의 ("almost") to add *emphasis*. Here are two examples.
>
> 그 책을 (거의) 매일 읽다시피 했어요.
> "I read that book almost every day."
>
> 이번 달에 생일인 친구가 많아서 선물을 사느라고 돈을 (거의) 다 쓰다시피 했어요.
> "There are a lot of friends whose birthdays are this month, so I almost used all of my money buying presents."

준영: 아무래도 우리 학교는 남학생과 여학생의 비율이 안 맞는 것 같아.

"Anyway I think that our school's male student and female student ratio doesn't match."

아무래도 is a common shortened version of 아무리 해도, and literally means "No matter (how much you do it)." A more natural translation might be "Anyway" or "Either way." It is used at the *beginning* of a sentence, and is also frequently used together with the 것 같다 form.

아무래도 철수가 안 올 거 같아.
"Anyway I don't think Chul-soo will come."

아무래도 내가 실수한 거 같아.
"Either way I think I made a mistake."

남학생 and 여학생 are shortened, but more commonly used versions of 남자 학생 and 여자 학생.

We previously learned that the verb 맞다 means "to be correct," but it also has another commonly used meaning – "to fit," or "to match." For example, you might say 안 맞아요 when the clothes you try on are too big, or if you think that two people do not match each other's personalities. Or, you can say 잘 맞아요 if you think that something or someone does fit or match.

More Explanations

Using 맞다 is different from 어울리다 ("to match well," "to suit," "to go with"). Although both 맞다 and 어울리다 can be used to say that two people "match" each other, each has a different meaning. 어울리다 is not used to say that something *fits* something else (such as clothes, or a puzzle piece). Instead, 어울리다 is used for describing how something or someone "looks." For example, you could use 어울리다 to describe a couple to mean "These two people *look* good together, so they go well together." And while 맞다 can be used for saying that someone's *personality* matches another person, 어울리다 cannot.

재호: 그래?
"Really?"

준영: 응. 왜냐하면 나한테 초콜릿을 준 여학생이 한 명도 없거든. 여학생이 더 적은가 봐.
"Yeah. Because there wasn't even one female student who gave me chocolate. I guess there are fewer female students."

왜냐(하)면 can be *optionally* added to the *beginning* of a sentence when you are about to explain something. It literally means "If you ask why...," but can be translated naturally as "Because...."

"For Your Information": Verb Stem + 거든(요)

You can use this form to say something that you believe the listener does not already know. This form can translate as "For your information..." or "Just so you know...," among other ways.

To use it, take a verb stem and attach 거든. When speaking *politely*, add a 요 to the end. Here are some examples.

저는 생선을 되게 좋아하거든요.
"(For your information...) I like fish very much."

제가 한국 사람이 아니거든요.
"(Just so you know...) I'm not Korean."

어제 다 했거든요.
"(Just so you know...) I did it all yesterday."

More Explanations

Chapter 19

다음 주에는 비가 올 거거든요.
"(Just so you know...) it will rain next week."

Note how the 것이다 future tense (here, 거다) will become 거거든(요) when used in this form.

나도 친구 많거든!
"(For your information...) I have a lot of friends too!"

저는 배고픈 걸 참을 수 없거든요.
"(Just so you know...) I can't endure being hungry."

제가 지금 티비를 보고 있거든요.
"(For your information...) I'm watching TV now."

김치가 그렇게 안 맵거든요.
"(Just so you know...) kimchi isn't that spicy."

됐거든요.
"(Just so you know...) I'm not interested."

We learned that 되다 in the *past tense* can be used to mean "No thanks" or "I'm not interested." It can also be used together with the 거든(요) form, such as when you want to avoid a conversation with a sales worker, or with someone trying to flirt with you.

그 시험은 10 개 이상 틀리면 안 되거든.
"For that test, (just so you know...) if more than 10 are incorrect, it's not good."

A more natural translation for the above sentence could be "You can't miss more than 10 on that test." Note that you can use 이상 ("more than") or 이하 ("less than"), when used after a *counter*.

저는 김치를 좋아하지 않아요. 왜냐하면 매운 음식을 잘 못 먹거든요.
"I don't like kimchi. It's because I can't eat spicy food well (for your information)."

왜냐(하)면 is also frequently used together with the 거든(요) form.

Note that you should be careful when using this form, as it can sound rude if used in the wrong situations – just as "For your information..." or "Just so you know..." can sound rude in English when used in the wrong situations.

Chapter 19

More Explanations

Intonation for 거든(요)

The 거든(요) form can be said with either a *rising* or a *falling* intonation. When said with a rising intonation, it can sound a bit condescending, like you are talking down to someone. When said with a falling intonation, it can sound informative, like you're simply passing on information. Here are examples of each, with intonation added in bold.

Rising Intonation: 이미 도착했거든**요**.
"It already arrived (and I can't believe that you didn't know this... 바보)."

Only the *last* syllable (요, or 든 when used without 요) will have a rising intonation.

Falling Intonation: 이미 도착했**거든요**.
"It already arrived (and I'm just letting you know)."

The *full* 거든(요) form will have a falling intonation.

This does *not* mean that using a rising intonation will always sound rude, or that using a falling intonation will always sound informative. When used in the wrong situation, such as informing someone of something that they clearly knew about, it can sound rude with either intonation. Because of this, it should be avoided in situations where you would speak *honorifically*, and with people who you are not close with.

재호: 그러게. 왜 아무도 너한텐 안 줬을까? 근데 우리 학교는 오히려 여학생이 더 많던데.

"Yeah. Why did nobody give it to you? But our school has more girl students."

Asking for Explanations: Action Verb Stem + 게(요)

You can use this ending when *asking* someone for more information, usually about something they previously said. While it does not have a direct translation in English, it can be loosely translated as "Are you..." or "Do you want to...," depending on the context.

To make it, take a verb stem and attach 게. When speaking *politely*, add a 요 to the end. Here are a few example questions.

뭐하시게요?
"What are you doing?"
"What do you want to do?"

When asking someone for more information, this form is most commonly used with *honorific verbs*. In addition, this form sounds a bit *friendly* and polite.

생일 케이크를 찾으시게요?
"Are you looking for a birthday cake?"
"Do you want to find a birthday cake?"

More Explanations

Chapter 19

Take a Guess: Action Verb Stem + 게(요)

Advanced

This form can also be used as a playful way of asking the listener to take a *guess*. Because this usage sounds playful, it should only be used with friends. Here are two examples.

지금 어디게?
"(Take a guess!) Where am I now?"

뭘 샀게?
"(Take a guess!) What did I buy?"

While less common, you can also use the 게(요) ending to give an *answer* to someone after they have asked you for more information about something that you previously said. The most common use of the 게(요) form in this way is the phrase 그러게(요), which comes from 그러다 ("to say so") and means "Yes, I agree (in answer to your question)."

"So that": Verb Stem + 게(끔)

Advanced

Another use of the 게 ending is one that we have previously seen many times before but have not talked about yet. The actual meaning of 게 is "so that," and can have the same usage as 도록. We used 게 in this way throughout Chapter 10 with the 게 하다 and 게 만들다 forms. Literally the 게 하다 form means "to do (something) so that (someone does something)." This is why the 게 하다 form can be used to mean that you are "causing" someone to do something.

To use this form, take a verb stem and attach 게(끔). The 끔 is *optional*. Here are a few examples.

저도 할 수 있게(끔) 가르쳐 주세요.
"Please teach me so that I can do it too."

철수가 나가게(끔) 문을 열었어요.
"I opened the door so that Chul-soo could leave."

마이크가 한국어를 빨리 배우게(끔) 한국에 데려왔어요.
"I brought Mike to Korea so that he'll learn Korean quickly."

Going back to the conversation, 너한텐 is a shortened version of 너한테는.

"On the Contrary": 오히려

오히려 is an *adverb* that means "on the contrary," and is used when something happens that was the complete opposite of what you expected. Here are a few examples.

오히려 잘됐어.
"(On the contrary...) it went well."
"It went better than I expected."

컴퓨터를 만드는 게 오히려 싸네요.
"(On the contrary...) making a computer is cheap."
"Making a computer is cheaper than I expected."

More Explanations

철수보다 영수가 오히려 잘생겼어요.
"(On the contrary...) Yung-soo is more handsome than Chul-soo."
"Yung-soo is more handsome than Chul-soo (and that's the opposite of what I expected)."

Expecting an Answer: Verb Stem + 던데(요)

While the 던데(요) form does not have a direct translation to English, it can be used at the end of a sentence when you are speaking to someone else. When you make a sentence that ends in the 던데(요) form, it adds *emphasis* that you are expecting to hear a *reply*. You can think of this form as meaning that you are asking a question through making a statement. For example:

좋아해요.
"He likes it."

좋아하던데요.
"He likes it (and what do you think of that?)."

To use it, take a verb stem (action verb or descriptive verb) in the *present tense* and attach 던데. When speaking *politely*, add a 요 to the end. When speaking, the final syllable of this form – 데 or 요, depending on whether you are speaking informally or politely – will have a *rising* intonation. Here are a few examples.

먹을 만하던데.
"It's good to eat (but what do you think?)."

한국 사람이 아니던데.
"She's not a Korean (but what do you think?)."

Note that 이다 ("to be") becomes 이던데(요) after a *consonant* or 던데(요) after a *vowel* when used with this form. 아니다 ("to not be") becomes 아니던데(요).

아직 수영하러 가긴 너무 춥던데요.
"It's still too cold to go swimming (but do you agree?)."

그렇게 말하던데요.
"He says so (but do you know differently?)."

아까 집에 가던데요.
"She went home earlier (but do you know differently?)."

More Explanations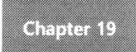

생각했던 것보다 재미있던데.
"It was more entertaining than what I had thought (but what do you think?)."

Note that past tense verb stems are not used with the 던데(요) form. The sentence 좋아하던데요 can be used to mean either "He likes it" or "He liked it."

> **Advanced**
>
> **Expecting an Answer: Plain Form + 던데(요)**
>
> In the "Advanced Notes" of Chapter 2 we learned that we can use 대(요), or (이)래(요), as a common shortened version of Plain Form + 고 (말)하다 to mean "(someone) says...":
>
> 좋아한다고 해요.
> 좋아한대요.
> "He says that he likes it."
>
> We can also use the 던데(요) form to add a similar meaning – "(someone) says" – but when we are also expecting an *answer*. To use it this way, attach 던데(요) to the *Plain Form* of a verb. Here are some examples.
>
> 좋아한다던데요.
> "He says that he likes it (but what do you think?)."
>
> 우리 그걸 하면 안된다던데.
> "They say that we shouldn't do that (but should we?)."
>
> 영수도 그 연예인을 알고 있다던데.
> "Yung-soo said that he also knows that celebrity (but is it true?)."
>
> 한국 사람이라던데.
> "They say that he's a Korean (but did you hear differently?)."
>
> Note that 이다 ("to be") becomes 이라던데(요) after a *consonant*, and 라던데(요) after a *vowel* when used with this form. 아니다 ("to not be") becomes 아니라던데(요).

준영: 친구야, 이럴 때는 차라리 아무 말 하지 말아 줘.

"(My) friend, I'd rather you don't say anything at times like these, please."

"Rather": 차라리

차라리 is an *adverb* that means "rather," and is used to say that you would *prefer* one thing over something else. Here are a few examples.

차라리 공부를 더 해.
"Rather, study more."
"I'd prefer that you study more."

이렇게 오래 걸리면 차라리 내일 다시 여기 오자.
"If it will take this long, let's come here again tomorrow."
"I'd rather come here again tomorrow if it will take this long."

Chapter 19

More Explanations

차라리 내가 만드는 게 낫겠다.
"It would be better if I made it."
"I'd rather make it."
"I'd prefer to make it."

차라리 is commonly used together with the verb 낫다 ("to be preferable," "to be better").

> **Advanced**
>
> **"Rather than...": Action Verb Stem + 느니**
>
> You can use the 느니 form to say that you would rather do something *than* do something else.
>
> To use it, take an *action verb stem* – the action that you do not prefer – and attach 느니. Then complete the rest of the sentence, using 차라리 as usual with the action that you would prefer. Here are a few examples.
>
> 비싸게 사느니 차라리 만드는 게 나아요.
> "I'd rather make it than buy it for a high price."
>
> 서울까지 걸어가느니 차라리 버스를 타지.
> "I'd rather take a bus than walk all the way to Seoul."
>
> 오늘 집에서 낮잠을 자느니 차라리 공원에 가서 운동이나 하는 게 낫겠다.
> "I'd rather go to the park and exercise or something, than take a nap at home today."

재호: 미안해. 하나 줄까?

"Sorry. Should I give you one?"

준영: 괜찮아. 난 어차피 초콜릿 안 좋아해.

"It's okay. I don't like chocolate anyway."

"Anyway": 어차피

어차피 is an *adverb* that means "in any case," or "one way or the other." Another more natural translation is "anyway." Here are a few examples.

어차피 너무 늦었어.
"Anyway it's too late."

어차피 저는 초콜릿을 안 좋아하니까 다 드셔도 돼요.
"In any case, since I don't like chocolate you can eat it all."

어차피 해야 하는 거면 그냥 오늘 해.
"If it's something that you have to do anyway, just do it today."

More Explanations

Chapter 19

재호: 너는 뭐든지 다 좋아할 것 같은데 생각보다 안 먹는 게 많네. 근데 너 미진이랑 서로 좋아하는 거 아니었어?

"I think you'll like whatever (there is), but there are a lot more things that you don't eat than I thought. But didn't you and Mi-jin like each other?"

Showing Options: Verb Stem + 든(지)

You can use this grammar form to show that there are multiple *options* to choose from. You can think of it as translating as "whether." For example, "It doesn't matter *whether* you do it now or do it later."

"But didn't we already learn how to say whether?" While both forms – the 지 form that we learned in Chapter 7 and this 든(지) form – translate as "whether" (or "if") in English, they have different uses. The 지 form in Chapter 7 was used for talking about things that are *unknown*. For example, you would use the 지 form to say "I wonder whether/if he likes me," or to say "Please tell me whether/if this dress makes me look fat." This 든(지) form is used for showing that there are multiple *options* to choose from. It is not used for showing information that is unknown to the speaker. For example, you would use this 든(지) form to say "It doesn't matter whether/if you want to eat ice cream or make kimchi," or to say "I'll study Korean whether/if I have free time or not."

To make it, take a verb stem (in the *present tense*) and attach 든지. For example, 하다 would become 하든지, 먹다 would become 먹든지, and 놀다 would become 놀든지. Repeat again with a second verb. While the 지 is *optional*, it is more commonly added. Here are some examples.

지금 하든지 나중에 하든지 상관없어요.
"It doesn't matter whether/if you do it now or do it later."

This form is also commonly used together with 상관없다 ("to not matter").

멀든지 가깝든지 꼭 가야 돼요.
"Whether/if it's far or close, I have to go."

화장을 하든지 안 하든지 항상 예뻐요.
"You're always pretty whether/if you put on make-up or not."

학교에 가든지 집에 가든지 빨리 결정하세요.
"Whether/if you go to school or go home, decide quickly."

고기든지 생선이든지 둘다 좋아요.
"Whether/if it's meat or fish, I like both."

Chapter 19 — More Explanations

When used with the verb 이다 ("to be"), this form will become 이든(지) after a *consonant* or 든(지) after a *vowel*.

> **Adv**
>
> When the 든지 form is used with *nouns* (with 이다) it has the same meaning and usage as (이)나, which we covered in Chapter 15 of the previous book. For example:
>
> 고기나 생선이나 둘다 좋아요.
> "I like both, meat or fish."

하든지 말든지 마음대로 해.
"Whether you do it or not, do as you wish."

When using this form to tell someone to do something (as a *command*), use 말다 instead of the negative verb. This will become 말든지.

Question Words and 든(지)

This form is also commonly combined with certain *question words* to mean "-ever." Here are a few common examples.

뭐든지 (or 무엇이든지): "whatever," "anything"

뭐든지 잘 먹을 수 있어요.
"I can eat whatever."
"I can eat anything."

While 뭐든지 literally translates as "whatever," it is also fine to translate it as "anything" because this might sound more natural. Each of these question words also has an alternative, more natural sounding translation.

어디든지: "wherever," "anywhere"

어디든지 여행가도 돼요.
"It's okay if I travel wherever."
"It's okay if I travel anywhere."

언제든지: "whenever," "anytime"

언제든지 전화하세요.
"Call me whenever."
"Call me anytime."

More Explanations

Chapter 19

누구든지: "whoever," "anyone"

한국어는 누구든지 배울 수 있어요.
"Whoever can learn Korean."
"Anyone can learn Korean."

Question words can also be used in sentences with the 든지 form, but on their own without a second verb. Here are a few examples.

뭘 하든지 끝까지 하세요.
"Whatever you do, do it to the end."

오늘은 어딜 가든지 사람이 많을 거야.
"Wherever you go today, there will be a lot of people."

언제 시작하든지 중요하지 않아요.
"It's not important whenever you start."

누가 오든지 상관없어요.
"It doesn't matter whoever comes."

Although 누구든지 comes from 누구 (누가든지 is *incorrect*), remember to still use the appropriate word – 누구 or 누가 – depending on how it is being used in a sentence.

준영: 아니야. 미진이랑 친하지만 그냥 친구야.

"No. I'm close with her but we're just friends."

재호: 그렇구나. 난 너희가 친해서 서로 좋아하는 줄 알았어.

"I see. I thought you liked each other because you're close."

준영: 그냥 친구야. 아, 심지어 유치원에 다니는 내 동생도 여자 친구가 있는데 정말 슬프다.

"We're just friends. Ah, even my younger brother who goes to preschool also has a girlfriend, so I'm really sad."

"Even (still)": 심지어

심지어 is an *adverb* that means "even (still)." It can be *optionally* added to a sentence which already uses a particle for "even," such as 도 or 까지, to *emphasize* the meaning of "even." Here are a few examples.

Chapter 19

More Explanations

심지어 나도 가고 싶어.
"Even I want to go too."

심지어 한국어도 공부하고 있어요.
"He's also even studying Korean."

성격이 좋은데 심지어 얼굴까지 잘생겼어.
"His personality is good, and even his face is handsome too."

> **"Even": Noun + 조차**
>
> You can use 조차 to add emphasis to a *noun*. It can be used in the same way as 도 ("also," "even," "too").
>
> 엄마조차 그 종교를 안 믿어요!
> "Even mom doesn't believe that religion!"

재호: 미진이랑 그냥 친구라면 내가 다음 달에 내 친구들 소개시켜 줄게.
"If you're just friends with her, next month I'll introduce my friends (to you)."

준영: 고마워. 너밖에 없다.
"Thanks. You're the best."

When using the 밖에 없다 form with *people*, a more natural translation instead of "I only have you" could be "You're the best."

Practice

Translate the following to Korean using the 던데(요) form:

1. "It's not that simple."

_____.

2. "It was expensive."

_____.

3. "The line is too long."

_____.

More Explanations

Chapter 19

4. "Dad also liked that singer."

_____.

5. "The teacher says he doesn't have time now."

_____.

Translate to Korean:

6. "As you know, I'm a student."

_____.

7. "(For your information...) I don't like pizza."

_____.

8. "(For your information...) I'm not at home yet."

_____.

9. "(For your information...) I can cook well."

_____.

10. "It doesn't matter whether you do it or not."

_____.

11. "The flavor will be exactly the same, whether you buy it or make it."

_____.

12. "It doesn't matter where you learn Korean."

_____.

13. "(On the contrary...) it was easier studying alone."

_____.

Chapter 19

More Explanations

14. "I'd rather watch a children's movie."

_____.

Translate to English:

15. 보시다시피 이미 다 팔렸어요.

_____.

16. 제가 여기 사장이거든요.

_____.

17. 선물을 하나도 못 받았거든요.

_____.

18. 세일이라서 싸게 팔던데요.

_____.

19. 듣던 것보다 힘들던데요.

_____.

20. 코로 숨을 쉬든지 입으로 숨을 쉬든지 그냥 숨만 쉬면 돼요.

_____.

21. 연필이든지 펜이든지 아무거나 빨리 주세요.

_____.

22. 뭐든지 다 잘 어울려요.

_____.

23. 심지어 엄마도 생일 파티에 오셨어요.

_____.

More Explanations

Chapter 19

24. 어차피 제 말을 안 들을 거잖아요.

New Phrases

우와.	"Wow."
아무래도…	"Anyway…," "Either way…"
왜냐(하)면…	"If you ask why…," "Because…"
알다시피…	"as you know…"
보다시피…	"as you see…"
말하다시피…	"as you say…"
듣다시피…	"as you hear…"
그러게(요).	"Yes (in answer to your question)."

New Vocabulary

비율	"proportion," "ratio"
평균	"average," "mean"
남학생	"male student"
여학생	"female student"
적다	"to be few (in number)"
이상	"more than"
이하	"less than"
오히려	"on the contrary" (adverb)
이럴 때	"(at) times like these"
차라리	"rather" (adverb)
어차피	"anyway," "in any case," "one way or the other" (adverb)
뭐든지	"whatever," "anything" (or 무엇이든지)
어디든지	"wherever," "anywhere"
언제든지	"whenever," "anytime"
누구든지	"whoever," "anyone"
심지어	"even (still)" (adverb)
유치원	"preschool," "kindergarten"

Chapter 19: More Explanations

종교	"religion"
천국	"heaven"
지옥	"hell"
낙원	"a paradise"
인류	"human race"

More Thought
Conversation

Chapter 20

직원:	어서 오세요. 무엇을 찾으세요?
손님:	엄마 생일 선물을 살까 생각 중인데요.
직원:	이건 어때요?
손님:	무늬가 낙서처럼 보이는데 이걸 추천하시는 이유가 있으세요?
직원:	요즘 인기가 많은 디자인이에요. 이 가방이 나이에 상관없이 쓸 수 있지 않을까 싶어서 조금 비싸더라도 추천했어요.
손님:	가격이 얼마인데요?
직원:	50만 원이에요. 감각이 있는 분이시라면 반드시 좋아할 거예요.
손님:	제 생각에 저희 엄마는 그 디자인보다는 이게 더 어울리지 않나 싶은데요.
직원:	그것도 가격에 비해 품질이 아주 좋아서 어머니들 사이에서 좋은 평가를 받고 있어요.
손님:	이 가방과 저 옷을 세트로 사면 돈을 너무 많이 쓰는 걸까요?
직원:	아니요. 부모님 선물에 돈을 아껴 써야 할 필요는 없지 싶어요.
손님:	엄마가 가격을 알게 되시면 돈 낭비라고 선물 받기를 아예 거절하실까 봐요.
직원:	걱정 마세요. 어머니께서 맘에 안 들어하시면 언제든지 환불해 드릴게요.
손님:	고맙습니다. 혹시 길이 수선도 해 주시나요?
직원:	그럼요. 수선이 필요하면 가져오세요.
손님:	그럼 이 가방과 저 옷을 함께 계산해 주세요.
직원:	네. 이쪽으로 오세요.

Chapter 20: More Thought

This chapter will cover several grammar forms that will appear to be very similar, but each form has slightly different uses. Do not worry if these forms seem complicated, too similar to each other, or difficult to understand while you are reviewing them. This is normal. Many of these grammar forms are considered advanced compared to others that we have studied so far. However, they are commonly used and will be essential to know in order to continue learning Korean to a higher level. This chapter will not cover every possible variation of these forms – as you'll see there are many – but it will cover the most common ones that you may encounter. Let's jump right into the conversation.

> 직원: 어서 오세요. 무엇을 찾으세요?
> "Come in. What are you looking for?"

> 손님: 엄마 생일 선물을 살까 생각 중인데요.
> "I'm thinking of buying my mom's birthday present."

"Thinking about..." & "Wondering if..."
Verb Stem + (을/ㄹ) + 까 (생각)하다

This form can be used with both action verbs and descriptive verbs. First, let's cover how to use it with action verbs.

You can use this form with *action verbs* to say that you are "thinking about" doing something. Using this form means that you have not yet decided. For example, "I'm thinking about meeting Sun-ah today." If you have already made a decision about what you will do, you can use another form that we have learned, such as 계획이다.

To use this form, take a verb stem and attach 을 if it ends in a *consonant*, or attach ㄹ if it ends in a *vowel*. Then conjugate the verb 생각(을) 하다. Using 생각 is *optional*. Here are a few examples with *action verbs*.

> 오늘 선아를 만날까 생각하고 있어요.
> "I'm thinking about meeting Sun-ah today."

> 드라마를 볼까 해요.
> "I'm thinking about watching a drama."

> 아직 갈까 생각 중이에요.
> "I'm still thinking about going."

You will also commonly find this form used with 중, as 생각 중이다. For a review of using 중, see Chapter 20 of the previous book.

More Thought

Chapter 20

말까

Advanced

You will also find this form used together with 말까 ("or not"), from the verb 말다. In this way, 말까 acts as a second part of the form, and can be added after the first verb. This can only be used with *action verbs*. Here is an example.

갈까 말까 하고 있어.
"I'm thinking of going or not."
"I'm thinking if I should go or not."

같이 운동할까 했어요.
"I thought about exercising together."

영화를 볼 때마다 팝콘을 먹을까 해요.
"I think about eating popcorn each time I watch a movie."

Remember that this form means that you are "thinking about" *doing* something – not that you are "thinking about" a noun – when used with *action verbs*.

When used with *descriptive verbs*, this form means that you are "wondering if" something will be a certain way. For example, "I'm wondering if it'll be too cold tomorrow." Here are a few examples with descriptive verbs.

내일 너무 추울까 해요.
"I'm wondering if it'll be too cold tomorrow."

그 날에 바쁠까 생각해요.
"I'm wondering if I'll be busy on that day."

오늘 다 하면 좋지 않을까 생각해요.
"I'm wondering if I should do it all today."

아닐까

Advanced

You will also find this form used together with 아닐까 ("or is not"), from the verb 아니다 ("to not be"). This works in the same way as 말까, but can only be used with *descriptive verbs*. Here is an example.

너무 오래됐을까 아닐까 해요.
"I'm wondering if it's too old or not."

To help you understand why the English translation of this form can change from "thinking about" to "wondering if," take a look at its parts. This form is a combination of the 까 form ("Shall we...," "would/could") and the verb 생각(을) 하다 ("to think"). Literally, 오늘 선아를 만날까 생각하고 있어요 means "I'm thinking, *shall* I meet Sun-ah tomorrow?" In the same way, 내일 너무 추울까 해요 means "I think, *would/could* it be too cold tomorrow?"

More Thought

Chapter 20

Because of this, sometimes with action verbs this form can also translate more naturally as "wondering if." This happens whenever an action verb would normally translate in a sentence as "would/could (verb)" when used with the 까 form. For example, while 저도 갈까요? translates as "*Shall* I go, too?" 민우도 갈까요? translates as "*Would/could* Min-woo go too?" We can then use this new form to change that sentence to 민우도 갈까 해요 ("I'm wondering if Min-woo will go too."). Here are a few more examples.

잘할 수 있을까 생각해요.
"I'm thinking, would/could I do it well?"
"I'm wondering if I can do it well."

정말 했을까 하네요.
"I'm thinking, would/could he have really done it?"
"I'm wondering if he really did it."

3천 원만 할인해 주실 수 있으실까 해요.
"I'm thinking, would/could you please give me a discount of only 3,000 Won?"
"I'm wondering if you could please give me a discount of only 3,000 Won."

This chapter will deal with several forms that appear to be similar to each other, and being able to separate these forms into their original parts will be helpful when learning and understanding them.

직원: 이건 어때요?

"How is this?"

손님: 무늬가 낙서처럼 보이는데 이걸 추천하시는 이유가 있으세요?

"The pattern looks like scribbles, but do you have a reason for recommending this?"

직원: 요즘 인기가 많은 디자인이에요. 이 가방이 나이에 상관없이 쓸 수 있지 않을까 싶어서 조금 비싸더라도 추천했어요.

"It's a popular design these days. I recommended it because even though it's a little expensive, I'm thinking she could use this bag regardless of her age."

"Wondering if...": Verb Stem + (을/ㄹ) + 까 싶다

You can use this form similarly to the 까 (생각)하다 form to mean that you are "wondering if" something will happen, or "wondering if" something is a certain way. For example, you could use this form to say that you are "wondering if" Min-woo will be at the party too, or that you are "wondering if" next week will be colder than this week.

More Thought

Chapter 20

To use it, take a *verb stem* and attach 을 if it ends in a *consonant*, or attach ㄹ if it ends in a *vowel*. Then conjugate the verb 싶다.

This form is a combination of the 까 form and the *descriptive verb* 싶다. So far we've only seen 싶다 used in the 고 싶다 form when saying that you "want to" do something. When used in this 까 싶다 form, 싶다 has a different meaning – "to think about" or "to worry about." This can be translated more naturally as "wondering." First, here is an example of an *action verb* using this form.

민우도 파티에 있을까 싶어요.
"I'm wondering, would/could Min-woo be at the party too?"
"I wonder if Min-woo will be at the party too."

Here is an example of a *descriptive verb* using this form.

다음 주는 이번 주보다 더 추울까 싶어요.
"I'm wondering, would/could next week be colder than this week?"
"I wonder if next week will be colder than this week."

Here are a few more examples.

사람들이 많이 올까 싶네요.
"I wonder if a lot of people will come."

이렇게 할 필요가 있을까 싶네.
"I'm wondering if there's a need to do this."

재미있을까 싶어서 가 보고 싶네.
"I want to go (and see) because I'm wondering if it'll be fun."

Note that although this form can be used similarly to the 까 (생각)하다 form, this form cannot be used to show that you (or someone else) are "thinking about" *doing* something. However, at times this form can translate naturally as "thinking about if," or "thinking that," depending on the sentence. Here is an example.

이게 좋은 생각일까 싶어요.
"I'm wondering, would/could this be a good idea?"
"I'm wondering if this is a good idea."
"I'm thinking about if this is a good idea."

Chapter 20 — More Thought

Going back to the conversation, notice how 쓸 수 있**지 않을까** 싶어서 (literally, "wondering if she *can not* use...") is used instead of 쓸 수 **있을까** 싶어요 ("wondering if she *can* use..."). While this negative meaning does not always translate directly to English, it can be used as a *suggestion*. English has a similar grammar concept to this too. Asking "Don't you agree?" ("Do you not agree?") can also be used to *suggest* that someone agrees with you in English too. For example, 좋지 않을까요? could literally translate to English as "*Wouldn't* it be good?" Or, it could translate simply as "*Would* it be good?" Here are a few more examples, with the original negative meaning in parentheses.

좋아하지 않을까 싶었어요.
"I wondered if you'd (not) like it."

너도 배고프지 않을까 싶어서 산 거야.
"I wondered if you were (not) hungry too so I bought it."

우유가 너무 차가워서 아기가 먹는 걸 거부하지 않았을까 싶어요.
"I wonder if the milk is too cold so the baby will (not) reject eating it."

Most commonly you will find the 까 싶다 form used with negative verbs in this way.

"Even if" & "Even though": Verb Stem + 더라도

You can use this form to mean "even if" or "even though." For example, "Even though I like pizza, I don't want to eat it everyday." Note that using this form adds more *emphasis* than using the regular 도 form after a verb.

To use it, take a *verb stem* in *past tense* or *present tense* and attach 더라도. Then finish the rest of the sentence. Here are some examples.

피자를 좋아하더라도 매일 먹고 싶지는 않아요.
"Even though I like pizza, I don't want to eat it everyday."

그 영화를 이미 봤더라도 줄거리를 얘기하지 마세요.
"Even if you already saw that movie, don't tell me the plot."

차가 있더라도 어디든지 갈 수 있는 건 아니에요.
"Even if you have a car, you can't go wherever (you want)."

매일 공부를 하더라도 6개월 안에 한국어를 유창하게 할 수 없을 것 같아요.
"I think that even if you study everyday you won't be able to speak Korean fluently within 6 months."

More Thought

Chapter 20

제가 조금 늦더라도 걱정하지 마세요.
"Don't worry even if I'm a little late."

혼자 하더라도 금방 다 할 수 있어요.
"Even if I do it alone, I can do it all right away."

Going back to the conversation, 상관없이 is an *adverb* that comes from 상관없다 ("to not matter") and means "regardless." When used with a noun and the 에 particle, it means "regardless of (noun)."

손님: 가격이 얼마인데요?
"How much is the price?"

직원: 50 만 원이에요. 감각이 있는 분이시라면 반드시 좋아할 거예요.
"It's 500,000 Won. If it's someone with taste, they'll surely like it."

When using honorific speech and the verb 이다 ("to be"), the Strong "If" form becomes 이시라면 after a *consonant*, and 시라면 after a *vowel*. The verb 아니다 ("to not be") becomes 아니시라면.

손님: 제 생각에 저희 엄마는 그 디자인보다는 이게 더 어울리지 않나 싶은데요.
"In my opinion, I'm wondering if this would match with my mom more than that design."

"Wondering...": Verb Stem + 나 싶다

This form's meaning is similar to the 까 싶다 form, but originally comes from the 나(요) verb ending. We previously learned that the 나(요) ending can be used to add the feeling of being especially *curious* when asking a question and can also make your sentence sound a bit *softer*. Because of this, using the 나 싶다 form shows more curiosity than the 까 싶다 form and sounds a bit softer as well. Note that using this form does not mean that you are asking a question to someone, unlike using the 나(요) form on its own. Sentences made using this form will be statements.

To use it, take a *verb stem* and attach 나. Then conjugate the verb 싶다. Here are a few examples.

왜 수영을 할 수 없나 싶어요.
"I wonder why he can't swim."

Chapter 20: More Thought

뜨겁나 싶어서 만졌어요.
"I touched it because I wondered if it was hot."

철수가 집에 있나 싶어서 전화했어요.
"I called because I wondered if Chul-soo is home."

선물을 좋아하시나 싶어요.
"I wonder if she likes the present."

이미 나갔나 싶어요.
"I wonder if he left already."

그냥 화를 낼 걸. 괜히 참았나 싶어.
"I should have just gotten angry. I wonder if I repressed it for nothing."

Just like the 까 싶다 form, this form can also translate sometimes as "thinking about if," depending on the sentence. Also, just like the 까 싶다 form you will often find it used with *negative sentences*. Here are a few example sentences, with their original negative meaning in parentheses.

이미 너무 늦지 않나 싶은데.
"I'm wondering if it's (not) already too late."
"I'm thinking about if it's (not) already too late."

안 보이는 곳에 낙서를 하는 건 괜찮지 않나 싶었어요.
"I wondered if it'd (not) be okay to scribble somewhere that's not visible."
"I was thinking about if it'd (not) be okay to scribble somewhere that's not visible."

이 정도면 두 명이 먹기에 적당하지 않나 싶어요.
"I wonder, if it's roughly this much then would it (not) be adequate for two people to eat?"
"I'm thinking about if it's roughly this much then it would (not) be adequate for two people to eat."

그 제안은 거절하는 게 좋지 않나 싶어요.
"I wonder if it's (not) good to reject that offer."
"I'm thinking about if it's (not) good to reject that offer."

More Thought

Chapter 20

> **Culture Notes**
>
>
>
> Speaking Indirectly
>
> In addition to using negative verbs with the 까 싶다 form and with other forms covered in this chapter, you will notice that in some cases the Korean language will use *indirect* grammar. Speaking directly in Korean can sometimes sound a bit strong, and speaking indirectly is one more way to make a sentence sound softer. For example, instead of telling an employee "That's too expensive," it can sound softer to speak indirectly – "I wonder if that's not too expensive."
>
> However, this does not mean that you cannot or should not speak directly in Korean. On the contrary, most conversation will be direct (and many relationships will prefer direct speech). Using indirect speech is simply one way that you can soften a sentence when you want to avoid sounding too strong.

직원: 그것도 가격에 비해 품질이 아주 좋아서 어머니들 사이에서 좋은 평가를 받고 있어요.

"The quality of that is really good compared to the price too, so it gets good reviews among mothers."

"Compared to": Noun + 에 비해(서)

You can use this form to compare something to something else.

To use it, take a *noun* and attach the particle 에. Then add 비해(서) – the 서 is *optional*. Here are a few examples.

택시를 타는 것은 버스를 타는 것에 비해 비싸요.
"Taking a taxi is expensive compared to taking a bus."

음식이 지난번에 비해서 별로네요.
"The food isn't really good compared to last time."

Chapter 20 — More Thought

The *negative adverb* 별로 ("not really") can also be used on its own, or with 이다 ("to be") as a shortened version of 별로 안 좋다 ("to not be really good") or 별로 안 그렇다 ("to not be really so").

5천 원짜리 우산이 3천 원짜리 우산에 비해서 훨씬 좋아요.
"The umbrella that's worth 5,000 Won is much better compared to the umbrella that's worth 3,000 Won."

> **Advanced**
>
> This form originally comes from the verb 비하다 ("to compare"), which is not used outside of grammar forms (such as this one). Instead, you can use the verb 비교(를) 하다 ("to compare") when outside of this form.
>
> Another use of 비하다, although less common, is in the form 비하면 ("if one compares..."). This form uses the (으)면 form and works similarly to 비해(서). For example:
>
> 옛날에 비하면 많이 나아진 거예요.
> "It got a lot better, if you compare it to the past."

"Between" & "Among": 사이

사이 literally means a "space" or a "gap" between two things. It has two main uses – "between" and "among."

When used with *things*, you can use 사이 with the particle 에 to mean "between."

병원은 학교와 은행 사이에 있어요.
"The hospital is between the school and the bank."

When used with *people*, you can use 사이 with the particle 에서 to mean "among."

요리하는 사람들 사이에서는 이게 제일 좋은 도구예요.
"This is the best tool among people who cook."

You can also use 사이 to talk about someone's "relationship," such as the relationship *between* two people. For example, 사이(가) 좋다 means "to have a good relationship" or "to be on good terms."

철수하고 영희는 사이가 별로 안 좋아.
"Chul-soo and Yung-hee's relationship isn't really good."

손님: 이 가방과 저 옷을 세트로 사면 돈을 너무 많이 쓰는 걸까요?
"Would I be spending too much money if I buy this bag and those clothes?"

More Thought

Chapter 20

직원: 아니요. 부모님 선물에 돈을 아껴 써야 할 필요는 없지 싶어요.

"No. I don't think that that there's a need to save money on a parent's presents."

You can use the verb 아끼다 – meaning "to cherish" or "to save (by not using)" – together with an action verb to mean that you do something without *wasting* it. This form is most commonly used with the verbs 쓰다 ("to use") and 먹다 ("to eat"). To use it, place 아껴(서) before the action verb – the 서 is *optional*. Here are two examples.

형에 비해서 저는 돈을 아껴 써요.
"I spend money wisely, compared to my older brother."

이번에 사온 김치는 맛있어서 아껴 먹는 게 좋지 않을까 싶어요.
"The kimchi I bought this time is delicious so I wonder if it'd (not) be good to eat it slowly."

"Thinking...": Verb Stem + 지 싶다

You can use this form to say that you're "thinking" something. While this form appears similar to the 까 싶다 form and 나 싶다 form, it is used differently. It originally comes from the 지/죠 ending, which can be used to add the meaning of "right?" or "isn't it?" or "aren't you?" to a sentence. The 지/죠 ending is used in this way as if you are asking someone to *confirm* what you are saying. Because of this, using the 지 싶다 form shows that you are hoping that the other person will *confirm* what you are saying and agree with you. In this way, expressing your thoughts using the 지 싶다 form can sound a bit *stronger* than with the 것 같다 form.

To use it, take a *verb stem* and attach 지. Then conjugate the verb 싶다. First, here is an example.

아니지 싶은데요.
"I don't think it is (don't you agree?)."

Remember that this form is a combination of the 지/죠 form with 싶다 ("to think about," "to worry about"). If it helps you to understand this form, you can also translate the above example in your head as, "It's not, right? I think so." Here are a few more examples.

이건 내가 너보다 잘하지 싶다.
"I think I can do this better than you (don't you?)."

수영이 다이어트에 도움이 많이 됐지 싶어요.
"I think swimming was really helpful to the diet (don't you?)."

Chapter 20

More Thought

그렇게 생각하는 건 너 혼자이지 싶은데.
"I think you'd be alone thinking that (don't you agree?)."

집에서 만드는 게 더 좋지 싶어요.
"I think it'd be better to make it at home (right?)."

이 옷은 저 부츠와 함께 입는 게 제일 잘 어울리지 싶어요.
"I think wearing these clothes together with those boots would match the best (don't you?)."

> **Adv**
>
> This form can also be used when speaking your thoughts to *yourself*, just like the 지 ending. For example:
>
> 차라리 잠을 자는 게 낫지 싶어.
> "I think I'd rather sleep."

손님: 엄마가 가격을 알게 되시면 돈 낭비라고 선물 받기를 아예 거절하실까 봐요.

> "If my mom found out the price, I'm worried she'll say it's a waste of money and will completely reject (getting) the present."

Note that the conversation uses a quote – here, 낭비라고 – without adding (말)하다. This usage is common too, and is similar to using the (이)라고(요) form that we learned in the first book.

아예 is an *adverb* that's used with sentences that have *negative* meanings to mean "at all," "absolutely," or "completely" (depending on which sounds more natural in English). Here are a few examples.

저는 아예 몰랐습니다.
"I absolutely didn't know."

아예 싫어할 거 같아요.
"I think he'll completely dislike it."

아예 하지 말았어야지.
"You shouldn't have done it at all."

"Worrying...": Verb Stem + (을/ㄹ) + 까 보다

You can use this form to show that you're *worried* about something happening (with action verbs), or *worried* about something being a certain way (with descriptive verbs). This form is a combination of the 까 form and verb 보다.

More Thought

Chapter 20

To use it, take a *verb stem* and attach 을 if it ends in a *consonant*, or attach ㄹ if it ends in a *vowel*. Then attach 까, and conjugate the verb 보다. Here are a few examples.

진짜로 할까 봐요.
"I'm worried he'll really do it."

돈이 부족할까 봐요.
"I'm worried I won't have enough money."

부족하다 ("to be lacking") can more naturally translate as "to not be enough," and is the opposite of 충분하다 ("to be enough").

영수가 피자를 다 먹을까 봐 두 조각을 빨리 먹어 버렸어요.
"I was worried Yung-soo would eat all of the pizza, so I quickly ate two pieces."

The 까 보다 form is most commonly used in the middle of a sentence, with 보다 conjugated as 봐.

고장날까 봐 안 썼어요.
"I didn't use it, worried it would break."

> **Adv**
> It's also okay to add the word "maybe" or "might" when translating the 까 보다 form into English.
>
> 내일 가면 없을까 봐 오늘 샀어요.
> "I bought it today, worried it might not be (there) if I go tomorrow."

This form is also commonly used with 걱정, such as 걱정(을) 하다 ("to worry"), 걱정(이) 되다 ("to be a worry," "to become worried"), or 걱정이다 ("to be a worry"). When used in this way, the verb 보다 from the 까 보다 form becomes *optional*. Here are a few examples.

이번 주말에 비가 올까 (봐) 걱정이에요.
"I'm worried it'll rain this weekend."

추울까 (봐) 걱정했어요.
"I worried it would be cold."

철수가 제 선물을 안 좋아할까 (봐) 걱정이에요.
"I'm worried Chul-soo won't like my present."

Chapter 20

More Thought

"Thinking of (maybe)...": Action Verb Stem + (을/ㄹ) + 까 보다

You can also use this same form with action verbs to show that you are *thinking* of doing something, but are not sure about it. In this way, it can be used in the same way as the 까 (생각)하다 form. Here are a few examples.

내일 갈까 봐요.
"I'm thinking of maybe going tomorrow."

새로운 핸드폰을 살까 봐요.
"I'm thinking of maybe buying a new cell phone."

친구한테 얘기할까 봐.
"I'm thinking of maybe telling my friend."

직원: 걱정 마세요. 어머니께서 맘에 안 들어하시면 언제든지 환불해 드릴게요.
"Don't worry. If your mother doesn't like it, we'll refund it for you anytime."

맘 is a common shortened version of 마음 ("mind," "heart," "feelings").

손님: 고맙습니다. 혹시 길이 수선도 해 주시나요?
"Thank you. By chance can you mend the length for me also?"

The 니 Ending in 반말

You might find 니 used in place of the 나(요) ending. Both 니 and 나 are used similarly – for asking questions – but 니 is only used when speaking in 반말. In addition, the 니 ending has a softer sound and is more often used by women than men.

좋아하**나**(요)?
좋아하**니**?
"Do you like it?"

직원: 그럼요. 수선이 필요하면 가져오세요.
"Of course. Bring it here if you need mending."

손님: 그럼 이 가방과 저 옷을 함께 계산해 주세요.
"Then please ring me up for this bag and those clothes."

In addition to meaning "to calculate" and "to take care of payment," you can also translate 계산(을) 하다 as "to ring up" when purchasing items.

직원: 네. 이쪽으로 오세요.
"Okay. Come this way."

More Thought

Chapter 20

Advanced

"Why are there so many ways to say the same thing?" The more Korean you learn, the more ways you will find to say the same things. The same applies in English, and perhaps in every language. Fortunately, as many of the forms in this chapter have the same uses, you can switch between the similar ones as you feel without worrying about being right or wrong.

Here are a few more similar grammar forms that you might find. These forms are less common than the ones already explained in this chapter, but are still important to be aware of. All of these forms have similar meanings – "wondering" or "thinking." Know that it is not necessary to be able to use these forms yourself yet, as the ones taught already in this chapter are much more commonly used – 까 (생각)하다, 까 싶다, 나 싶다, 지 싶다, 까 보다, and others (such as 나 보다 and 가 보다 from Chapter 13).

Action Verb Stem + 나 하다

This form is a combination of the 나(요) ending and the verb 하다.

어디 가시나 했어요.
"I wondered where you're going."

Plain Form + 싶다

This form is a combination of the Plain Form and 싶다.

어쩐지 너무 많이 먹는다 싶더니 결국 배가 아프잖아.
"For some reason I thought you were eating too much, and then now your stomach hurts."

어쩐지 ("for some reason," "somehow") has the same meaning as 왠지, and can be used in the same way.

Action Verb Stem + 가 싶다

This form is a combination of the *informal questions* form and 싶다.

밖에 사고가 났는가 싶어서 나가 봤어요.
"I went out to see, thinking there might be an accident outside."

Practice

Translate to Korean using the 까 (생각)하다 form:

1. "I'm thinking of going to the birthday party."

   _____.

2. "I thought of buying a new car."

   _____.

3. "I think it's (not) good if I do that."

   _____.

More Thought

Chapter 20

Translate to Korean using the 까 싶다 form:

4. "I wondered why he'll make a cake."

_____.

5. "I wonder if this house is (not) too small."

_____.

6. "I'm wondering if my friend will write one more book."

_____.

Translate to Korean using the 나 싶다 form:

7. "I wonder if he likes pizza."

_____.

8. "I wondered if there are too many."

_____.

9. "I wonder if that idea is (not) alright."

_____.

Translate to Korean using the 지 싶다 form:

10. "I think I can make it well."

_____.

11. "I think Korea's July weather is hot."

_____.

12. "I think she already has two watches."

_____.

More Thought

Chapter 20

Translate to Korean using the 까 보다 form:

13. "I'm worried Yung-hee won't like me."

_____.

14. "I ran, worried I'll be late to the test."

_____.

15. "I brought it, worried I'll be hungry."

_____.

Translate to Korean:

16. "I want to buy it, even if it's expensive."

_____.

17. "Come even if you're late."

_____.

18. "Compared to the price, the size is too small."

_____.

19. "Compared to the location, it's fairly inexpensive."

_____.

Translate to English:

20. 내일부터 시작할까 생각 중이에요.

_____.

21. 생각보다 너무 늦어서 먼저 나갈까 했어요.

_____.

More Thought

22. 꼭 비싼 선물을 사야 했었을까 싶어요.

_____.

23. 내가 오늘 밤에 요리해야 하나 싶어서 전화했어.

_____.

24. 내가 너무 일찍 도착했나 싶어.

_____.

25. 너무 멀어서 친구가 올까 싶어요.

_____.

26. 냄새가 날까 봐 옷을 갈아입었어요.

_____.

27. 이렇게 해도 되지 않나 싶어요.

_____.

28. 내년에는 시간이 없더라도 반드시 여행을 갈 거예요.

_____.

New Vocabulary

낙서	"scribbling," "scribbles," "doodling"
낙서(를) 하다	"to scribble," "to doodle"
반드시	"certainly," "surely," "no matter what" (adverb)
평가	"review"
평가(를) 하다	"to review"
평가(를) 받다	"to be reviewed," "to get a review"
아끼다	"to cherish," "to save (by not using)"
아껴 쓰다	"to spend (money) wisely," "to use wisely"

More Thought

아껴 먹다	"to eat without wasting," "to not waste (food)"
낭비	"a waste" (noun)
낭비(를) 하다	"to waste"
수선	"mending," "repair"
수선(을) 하다	"to mend," "to repair"
아예	"at all," "absolutely," "completely" (negative)
거절	"rejection (of item, request, suggestion, demand)"
거절(을) 하다	"to reject (item, request, suggestion, demand)"
거부	"rejection (of suggestion, demand)"
거부(를) 하다	"to reject (suggestion, demand)"
걱정(이) 되다	"to become a worry," "to become worried"
어쩐지	"for some reason," "somehow"
무늬	"pattern (on something)," "design (on something)"
디자인	"design"
상관없이	"regardless" (adverb)
감각	"a sense," "a sensation"
감각(이) 있다	"to have sense," "to have taste" (idiom)
냄새(를) 맡다	"to smell (something)"
품질	"quality (of an item)"
사이	"space," "gap," "relationship"
사이(가) 좋다	"to have a good relationship," "to be on good terms"
사이에	"between (things)"
사이에서	"among (people)"
세트	"a set (of things)"
환불	"refund"
환불(을) 하다	"to refund"
길이	"length"

Chapter 20: More Thought

크기	"size"
넓이	"width," "area"
높이	"height"
양	"quantity"
위치	"location"
줄거리	"plot," "story"
적당하다	"to be adequate (for something)," "to be suitable"
제안	"offer," "proposal," "suggestion"
비교	"a comparison"
비교(를) 하다	"to compare," "to make a comparison"
갈아입다	"to change (clothes)"
꽤	"quite," "comparatively," "fairly" (adverb)
부츠	"boots"

Answer Keys

Chapter 1

1. 가르친다
2. 믿는다
3. 산다
4. 좋아한다
5. 맛있다
6. (이)다
7. 더럽다
8. 앉았다
9. 공부(를) 했다
10. 멀었다
11. 없었다
12. 컸다
13. 울었다
14. 스트레스(를) 받았다
15. 나는 김치를 좋아한다.
16. 영희는 매일 학교에 간다.
17. 나는 미국 사람이다.
18. 나는 피자 두 조각을 먹었다.
19. 강아지가 아니었다. 고양이였다.
20. 내 지갑에 5,000 원밖에 없다.
21. 오늘은 재미있는 하루였지만, 굉장히 더웠다.
22. "I have various hobbies."
23. "Tomorrow will be a much better day than today."
24. "The eggs and box lunch that I bought at the convenience store weren't really fresh."
25. "I dropped dad's old camera by mistake."
26. "For some reason today my younger sibling is so troublesome."
27. "Tomorrow I won't be as bored as today."
28. "If you're a beginner you shouldn't drive in this kind of weather."

Chapter 2

1. 하자고 (말)했어요.
2. 가자고 (말)했어요.
3. 영화를 보자고 (말)했어요.
4. 가르치자고 (말)했어요.
5. 김치를 먹는다고 (말)했어요.
6. 있었다고 (말)했어요.
7. 시험(을) 통과했다고 (말)했어요.
8. 잠(이) 안 온다고 (말)했어요.

Answer Keys

9. 한국어를 공부하라고 했어요.
10. 밥을 먹으라고 했어요.
11. 안전벨트를 매라고 했어요.
12. (저에게) 설명서를 읽어 달라고 했어요.
13. 돈을 다 썼냐고 물어봤어요.
14. 왜 철수에게 핑계를 대냐고 물어봤어요?
15. 목도리를 사 줄 거냐고 물어봤어요?
16. 빚을 갚을 수 있냐고 물어봤어요.
17. 저는 영화를 보러 가자고 했어요.
18. 철수는 영희를 안 좋아한다고 했어요.
19. 어제 숙제를 하라고 했어요.
20. 제가 한국어를 할 수 있냐고 물어봤어요?
21. 저는 그것이 사과라고 했어요.
22. "Chul-soo said let's eat lunch together."
23. "I said that I already have a boyfriend."
24. "Chul-soo told me not to meet that guy."
25. "I asked why I need to not meet him."

Chapter 3

1. 먹고 있는 것 같아요.
2. 아는 것 같아요.
3. 물을 마시는 것 같아요.
4. 무서운 것 같아요.
5. 이었던 것 같다 or 였던 것 같아요.
6. 발표를 녹음한 것 같아요.
7. 집으로 가고 있었던 것 같아요.
8. 마음에 든 것 같아요.
9. 갈 것 같아요.
10. 세탁할 것 같아요.
11. 울 것 같아요.
12. 만들고 있을 것 같아요.
13. (이)라고 생각해요.
14. 쉬고 있다고 생각해요.
15. 운이 좋다고 생각해요.
16. 행사를 준비한다고 생각해요.
17. 한국 사람이 아니었다고 생각해요.
18. 미신을 믿었다고 생각해요.
19. 점심을 같이 먹었다고 생각해요.
20. 잘했다고 생각해요.
21. 집에서 놀 거라고 생각해요.
22. 일하러 갈 거라고 생각해요.
23. 그렇게 할 거라고 생각해요.

Answer Keys

24. 지갑을 찾을 수 있을 거라고 생각해요.
25. 날씨가 아주 더운 것 같아요.
26. 배고프지 않은 것 같아요.
27. 그게 고양이가 아닌 것 같아요.
28. 시간이 많이 걸릴 것 같아요?
29. 이게 너무 맵다고 생각해요.
30. 5,000 원이 있다고 생각해요.
31. 웃기다고 생각해요.
32. 깨끗하지 않다고 생각해요.
33. "I think that Chul-soo went to the store."
34. "I don't think Chul-soo can understand English."
35. "I think you'll learn quickly if you focus well on the lesson."
36. "I'm not certain, but I think that's right."
37. "I think that I need a new car."

Chapter 4

1. 심심한가요?
2. 배고픈가요?
3. 아닌가요?
4. 행복하신가요?
5. 너무 많은가요?
6. 집이 넓은가요?
7. 보시오
8. 고르시오
9. 받으시오
10. 누르시오
11. 뽑으시오
12. 어제는 비가 오더니 오늘은 눈이 오네요.
13. 어제 늦게 잤더니 오늘은 피곤해요.
14. 숙제를 안 했더니 시험에 떨어졌어요.
15. 지난 주는 춥더니 이번 주는 전혀 안 추워요.
16. 누구 차례예요?
17. 누구 탓이에요?
18. 자기 탓을 하지 마세요.
19. 더 따뜻한 데로 가고 싶어요. Or, 더 따뜻한 곳으로 가고 싶어요.
20. "I drank old milk and now I keep wanting to go to the bathroom."
21. "I asked him to buy me an ordinary car, but he bought me a sports car."
22. "I suddenly did a lot of exercise and now I can't walk properly."
23. "I left without eating breakfast and now I'm so hungry."
24. "I didn't shower for three days and now nobody's coming near me."
25. "After only staying in the city, I went to the countryside and experienced culture shock."

Answer Keys

Chapter 5

1. 실수해 버리다
2. 사 버리다
3. 죽어 버리다
4. 떨어져 버리다
5. 말해 버리다
6. 무서워하다
7. 속상해하다
8. 부러워하다
9. 가지고 싶어 하다
10. 외로워하다
11. 오늘은 추운 것 같아요.
12. 한국은 갈 만해요.
13. 오늘 10시간 일했으니까 피곤할 만해요.
14. 무서워하지 마세요.
15. 그 사람은 슬퍼하지 않아요.
16. 그 사람은 기뻐하지 않는 것 같아요.
17. 피자를 먹고 싶어 하는 사람은 3명이 있어요.
18. "I forgot because I was busy."
19. "I just believed that person without thinking first."
20. "I came outside without bathing."
21. "Is that car worth buying?"
22. "It's understandable that he has a lot of friends."
23. "Is there nobody who wants to go to Chul-soo's house?"
24. "My friends are all jealous of me."
25. "I feel sad because I hurt a young child's feelings."

Chapter 6

1. 치즈를 어떻게 만드는지 알아요.
2. 어떻게 운전하는지 몰라요.
3. 책을 어떻게 쓰는지 아세요?
4. 어떻게 시작해야 하는지 몰라요.
5. 아직 잘 쓸 줄 몰라요.
6. 운전할 줄 알아요?
7. 먹을 줄 몰라요.
8. 한글을 쓸 줄 알아요.
9. 고양이인 줄 알았어요.
10. 이렇게 더운 줄 몰랐어요.
11. 저를 방문할 줄 알았어요.
12. 제가 한국 사람인 줄 알았어요?

Answer Keys

13. 찾는 방법을 몰라요.
14. 이 시계를 쓰는 방법을 가르쳐 주세요.
15. 한국어를 잘하는 방법이 있어요?
16. 다른 방법이 있어요?
17. "Do you know how to use a computer?"
18. "I don't know how to go to school."
19. "Do you know how to teach Korean to a beginner?"
20. "I don't know how I have to think about this."
21. "Does it mean that you'll be able to do it?"
22. "Does it mean that they'll go together?"
23. "It means that you really like Korea."
24. "What neighborhood is it in?"
25. "I thought/knew there wouldn't be any more."
26. "I thought/knew that the view would be very pretty, but it's not really."
27. "I thought/knew that I'd miss the (bus) stop!"
28. "I thought/knew that that scene would be scary."
29. "There are a lot of people here who don't know how to stand in a line."
30. "I can't even draw a line, so of course I don't know how to draw (a drawing)."

Chapter 7

1. 아기가 아직 배고픈지 몰라요.
2. 뱀인지 알고 싶어요.
3. 안전한지 아세요?
4. 식탁 위에 사과가 있는지 아세요?
5. 슈퍼에 갈지도 몰라요.
6. 재미있을지도 몰라요.
7. 여분의 방이 있을지도 몰라요.
8. 내일은 오늘보다 더 더울지도 몰라요.
9. 새 티비를 사야 할지도 몰라요. Or, 티비를 새로 사야 할지도 몰라요.
10. 누가 했는지 몰라요.
11. 엘리베이터가 어디에 있는지 알아요.
12. 그게 뭔지 알고 싶어요.
13. 왜 철수를 만났는지 궁금해요.
14. 그 사람을 기억하지 않아요. Or, 그 사람이 기억나지 않아요.
15. 모임이 언제 시작할지 확인해 주세요.
16. "Do you know whether/if there's a vending machine at the hospital?"
17. "I don't know whether/if I have to hold the handle or not."
18. "Do you know where I can buy a hammer?"
19. "I don't know how kimchi is this delicious."
20. "Did you find out how many people will come?"
21. "There might be a little money in my wallet."
22. "It might be at the very end."

Answer Keys

23. "Chul-soo even ate my food!"

Chapter 8

1. 김치를 먹음으로써
2. 공부(를) 함으로써
3. 노래(를) 부름으로써
4. 한국에서 삶으로써
5. 바람이 구멍을 통해서 들어왔어요.
6. 오디션을 통해서 가수가 됐어요.
7. 신문을 통해서 배웠어요.
8. 비타민을 먹음으로써 감기를 예방할 수 있어요.
9. 새로운 사람들을 만남으로써 더 많은 것을 배워요.
10. 남자치고는 손이 예쁘네요.
11. 학생치고는 돈이 많네요.
12. 일주일에 5 시간(씩) 공부해요.
13. "I told him the news through a letter."
14. "I learned Korean through a number of videos that Chul-soo uploaded to the internet."
15. "I could meet many people through attending that meeting."
16. "I relieve stress through drinking tea."
17. "I realized a new fact through reading the contents of that book."
18. "You can become a citizen through paying taxes."
19. "I express my love for my father through giving him pocket change."
20. "Most people sleep 7 hours each day."
21. "For a first test, it was really difficult."
22. "My score was good for not studying."
23. "It's strong for something made of paper."
24. "I already saw it a number of times."

Chapter 9

1. 사가다, 사오다
2. 찾아가다, 찾아오다
3. 가져가다, 가져오다
4. 달려가다, 달려오다
5. 색깔에 따라 달라요.
6. 장소에 따라 달라요.
7. 어디서 하는지에 따라 달라요.
8. 뭘 원하는지에 따라 달라요.
9. 저는 빨리 먹는 편이에요.
10. 제레미가 어제 여기 있었을 리가 없어요.

Answer Keys

11. 과자를 가져오고 싶었어요.
12. 어제 박물관에서 김 교수님을 만났어요.
13. "It depends on how you did it."
14. "There's no way Chul-soo met the President."
15. "He tends to easily date and easily break up with girls."
16. "I tend to quickly forget memories."
17. "How much do you like kimchi?"
18. "Go buy more rice cakes (and come back)."
19. "I looked at the map and found it (and went there)."
20. "I think it'll be a little hard to walk to there."
21. "Pick up and bring a piece of paper from the entrance."
22. "I saw my dad and ran to him."

Chapter 10

1. 사과(를) 시키다
2. 입히다
3. 살리다
4. 태우다
5. 친구를 내 옆에 앉게 했어요.
6. 마크가 책을 읽게 했어요. Or, 마크에게 책을 읽혔어요.
7. 내일 피곤하지 않도록 일찍 잤어요.
8. 쓰레기통을 비워 주세요.
9. 학교까지 태워 줬어요.
10. 컴퓨터를 1시간 (동안) 쓰게 해 주세요.
11. 지금은 아기를 재울 수 없어요.
12. "I made the two of them get married."
13. "I sat my friend next to me."
14. "I ran so that I won't miss the bus."
15. "Please study hard."
16. "Please let me use it too."
17. "I put clothes on the baby."
18. "I'm sorry for making you cry."
19. "I screamed and made the people move (out of the way) to the side."
20. "I let the ambulance pass by first."
21. "I had the kids pick up leaves."
22. "I made him try (eating) an egg at the sauna."
23. "I'll make him buy tofu (and bring it here) when he comes home."

Answer Keys

Chapter 11

1. 밥 먹을 시간이에요?
2. 아무리 가지고 싶어도 받을 수 없어요. Or, 아무리 원해도 받을 수 없어요.
3. 시험을 잘 봤다니 기뻐요.
4. 오늘 제레미가 설거지하기를 원해요.
5. 수염을 깎기를 원해요.
6. 과학 교과서를 공부해 놓을 거예요.
7. 표를 사 놓았어요.
8. 간을 먹어 보니까 나쁘지 않아요.
9. 공장에서 일해 보니까 추천하고 싶지 않아요.
10. 성공하길 바라요.
11. "I prepared to have a meal."
12. "No matter how much I cried there was nobody to help (me)."
13. "It's too bad that (I heard) you lost your wallet."
14. "I heard that you got a job, and that's great."
15. "I want you to try thinking about it a little bit harder."
16. "I put the milk in the refrigerator (for later)."
17. "I opened up the newspaper on top of the table (for later)."
18. "Having bought it once, I want to buy it again."
19. "Having raised a child, I can understand a parent's mind."
20. "I hope it all goes well."

Chapter 12

1. 친구에게 한국어를 가르치기로 (결정)했어요.
2. 오늘 저녁에 부모님과 영화를 보기로 (결정)했어요.
3. 다이어트를 하기로 (결정)했어요.
4. 내일 4시간 동안 공부할 계획이에요.
5. 8시에 일어날 계획이에요.
6. 내년에 트럭을 살 계획이에요.
7. 일하러 가는 대신에 쉬고 싶어요.
8. 선물을 사는 대신에 편지를 썼어요.
9. 저녁 대신에 점심을 살게요.
10. 많은 사람들이 포기하기 시작했어요.
11. 집을 사기 위해 돈을 모으기 시작했어요.
12. 도와줄 생각이에요.
13. 그렇게 할 생각이었어요.
14. 아침에 운동할 생각이 없어요.
15. "I decided to loan him the book."
16. "I decided to be a good older brother to my younger sister."
17. "I'm planning to live a regular life during school vacation."

Answer Keys

18. "Next year I'm planning to learn the piano."
19. "I got permission from dad instead of mom."
20. "In exchange for working on the weekend I got a bonus."
21. "The baby started walking around."
22. "I was curious when he'll start learning cooking."
23. "Are you thinking of continually driving straight?"
24. "I'm thinking of going straight and then going to the right at the next light."

Chapter 13

1. 싫어하나 봐(요)
2. 매운가 봐(요)
3. 매웠나 봐(요)
4. 먼가 봐(요)
5. 있나 봐(요)
6. 심심한가 봐(요)
7. 할 수 없나 봐(요)
8. 아닌가 봐(요)
9. 아니었나 봐(요)
10. 사나 봐(요)
11. 집에 갔나 봐요.
12. 영화가 끝났나 봐요.
13. 영희가 모델처럼 생겼어요.
14. 기름처럼 생겼어요.
15. 강아지가 귀여워 보여요.
16. 집이 아주 작아 보여요.
17. 영화가 재미있어 보였어요.
18. 그냥 사기인가 봐요.
19. 좋은 생각인가 봐요.
20. 내가 잘못했나 봐요.
21. 사람들이 많은가 봐요.
22. 사람들이 많았나 봐요.
23. "It seems like he speaks Korean really well."
24. "I guess that he used all of the toilet paper."
25. "It seems like you discovered a new method."
26. "I guess that they closed the doors already."
27. "I guess he knows that I did it."
28. "I heard that Min-woo did it."
29. "We don't resemble each other at all."
30. "That couple resembles each other a lot."
31. "I bought a decoration that looks like sweets."
32. "It looks similar to that."
33. "The box looks light."

Answer Keys

34. "I guess your younger sibling is still too young."
35. "I guess the speed is faster than the other cars."
36. "I guess the temperature (of the weather) is higher than our country."

Chapter 14

1. 철수를 만난 지 1 일이 됐어요.
2. 다이어트를 시작한 지 벌써 10 일 됐어요.
3. 등산을 좋아하기 시작한 지 얼마나 됐어요?
4. 한국에 온 지 몇 년이 됐어요.
5. 설거지를 하고 나서 집을 청소할 거예요.
6. 운동을 하고 나서 잠을 잘 거예요.
7. 친구와 만나자마자 밥을 먹었어요.
8. 영희는 남자 친구랑 헤어지자마자 새로운 사람을 만났어요.
9. 그렇게 생각할 수밖에 없어요.
10. 케이크를 좋아할 수밖에 없어요.
11. 내일 일찍 일어나기 위해서 지금 자러 갈 수밖에 없어요.
12. "It's been two hours since I met the reporter and started doing the interview."
13. "It's been 3 days since I started singing practice with dad."
14. "It's been only a little (while) since I started learning swimming."
15. "I weighed myself after going to the sauna (and coming back)."
16. "The teacher cried after reading the words that Chul-soo wrote."
17. "I'll look for a place to work after I graduate."
18. "I did running right away after eating."
19. "The movie started as soon as I sat in the seat."
20. "The baby stopped crying as soon as dad hugged her."
21. "That person acts well so they can't be anything but internationally famous."
22. "In order to succeed you can't help but sleep a little."

Chapter 15

1. 약속(이) 되다
2. 배달(이) 되다
3. 마음(이) 바뀌다
4. 책(이) 쓰이다
5. 겁(이) 나다
6. 케이크(가) 만들어지다
7. 소리(가) 들리다
8. 사람(이) 보이다
9. 주문(을) 하다
10. 찍다
11. 놓다

Answer Keys

12. 팔다
13. 살(을) 빼다
14. 차다
15. 허락(을) 하다
16. 화(를) 내다
17. 싫어하는 음식을 먹게 됐어요.
18. 한국어를 많이 배우게 될 거예요.
19. 옷이 작아졌어요.
20. 아기가 더 귀여워졌어요.
21. 1 시간 전에 시작됐어요.
22. 사과는 어제 다 팔렸어요.
23. 한국어를 배우는 데에 시간이 오래 걸려요.
24. 빨리 만들어질 수 있길 바라요.
25. 사탕이 어린이들에게 주어졌어요.
26. "I ended up singing in front of people I don't know."
27. "If you fix the computer it'll get much faster."
28. "I thought it was already completed."
29. "The book was written in English too."
30. "I can't hear it because it's far (away)."
31. "I can't see well because it's dark."
32. "The teacher got angry at the student who was late to class."
33. "There was a loud sound from far away."
34. "The mirror broke by a ball that someone threw."

Chapter 16

1. 추가(가) 되어 있다
2. 티비가 켜져 있다
3. 티비가 꺼져 있다
4. 사랑에 빠져 있다
5. 규칙이 바뀌어 있다
6. 한글로 쓰여 있다
7. 도둑이 잡혀 있다
8. 건물이 지어져 있다
9. 책이 펴져 있다
10. 눈이 떠져 있다
11. 팔이 부러져 있다
12. 정해져 있다
13. 6 월 말까지 못 만나요.
14. 에어컨이 꺼져 있어요.
15. 문이 잠겨 있어요?
16. 쓰레기가 이미 분리(가) 돼 있어요.
17. 그 남자는 가수로서 최고예요.

Answer Keys

18. 100원짜리 사탕을 샀어요.
19. 공주는 10층짜리 탑에서 살고 있어요.
20. 춥지 않은 척했어요. Or, 안 추운 척했어요.
21. 집으로 가는 길이에요.
22. 학교로 가는 길에 제레미를 만났어요.
23. "The flowers have all blossomed in the garden."
24. "I came home and the window was broken."
25. "I opened the door that was closed."
26. "I'll tell you as a representative."
27. "I pretended that I didn't do it."
28. "I'll go on a trip as soon as the money is earned."
29. "Please throw away the trash on your way out."
30. "He's addicted to that snack."
31. "I'm not adjusted to the time difference yet."

Chapter 17

1. 이 파자마를 입곤 했어요 (or 입었었어요).
2. 땅콩을 싫어하곤 했어요 (or 싫어했었어요).
3. 여기서 살곤 했어요 (or 살았었어요).
4. 밤 10시에 자곤 했어요 (or 잤었어요).
5. 주말마다 친구들을 만나곤 했어요 (or 만났었어요).
6. 엄마와 함께 영화를 보러 가는 걸 좋아하곤 했어요 (or 좋아했었어요).
7. 생각보다 쉬웠어요.
8. 이건 제가 자주 읽었던 (or 읽던) 책이에요.
9. 그건 제가 좋아했던 (or 좋아하던) 영화가 아니에요.
10. 제가 살았던 (or 살던) 집을 팔았어요.
11. 잘생겼던 선생님이 할아버지가 되셨어요.
12. "I used to take (daytime) naps when I was young."
13. "I used to ski when it's winter."
14. "The quality is good (I recall) so it'll be okay to buy only one."
15. "He was continually next to me but he couldn't recognize me."
16. "It was a lot different from what I had heard."
17. "Where did the baby go that was crying next to me?"
18. "The website I used to go to every day disappeared."
19. "The machine that sprinkled water in the garden each morning broke down yesterday."
20. "I don't remember it at all."
21. "Do you know the title of the song we'd listened to a short time ago?"
22. "I met my older sister who used to be short, and now she's much taller than me."

Answer Keys

Chapter 18

1. 공부하느라고 공원으로 가지 못했어요.
2. 기침을 하느라고 말을 못했어요.
3. 돈을 줄 테니까 지금 해 주세요.
4. 내일 해도 될 테니까 집에 가세요.
5. 아무도 예상할 수 없을 텐데요.
6. 그걸 컴퓨터로 하면 좋을 텐데요.
7. 재미있을 걸요.
8. 서울에 눈이 오고 있을 걸요.
9. 운동을 (하면) 할수록 더 건강해져요.
10. 철수를 (만나면) 만날수록 더 좋아하게 될 거예요.
11. "I'm exercising because I'm losing weight."
12. "I stayed up all night because I was watching a drama."
13. "I took off my glasses because I was washing my face and hands."
14. "It took a long time due to putting on makeup."
15. "If you sleep more, you'll regret it."
16. "Because the two players' levels are similar, don't worry."
17. "If we work while helping each other, then it can become an advantage."
18. "Buy it today, because I'll make it as cheap as possible (for you)."
19. "If you donate gradually, we can help many people."
20. "Your Korean skill will improve so study hard."
21. "I'll (probably) be able to finish it quickly."
22. "My older brother (probably) ate dinner too."
23. "She'll (probably) remember me."
24. "If you drive like that, there'll (probably) be an accident."
25. "I cried because I saw the baby hurting."
26. "The more you try to do it precisely, the more time it will take."
27. "The more you study, the easier it gets."
28. "I get angry the more I think about it."
29. "It will hurt the more you endure it."
30. "The more the doctor kept explaining, the more serious mom's face became."

Chapter 19

1. 그렇게 간단하지 않던데요.
2. 비싸던데요.
3. 줄이 너무 길던데요.
4. 아빠도 그 가수를 좋아하시던데요.
5. 선생님은 지금 시간이 없다고 하시던데요.
6. 알다시피 저는 학생이에요.
7. 저는 피자를 좋아하지 않거든요.

Answer Keys

8. 제가 아직 집에 없거든요.
9. 제가 요리를 잘할 수 있거든요.
10. 하든지 안 하든지 상관없어요.
11. 사든지 만들든지 맛은 똑같을 거예요.
12. 한국어를 어디서 배우든지 상관없어요.
13. 오히려 혼자 공부하는 게 더 쉬웠어요.
14. 차라리 어린이 영화를 보고 싶어요.
15. "As you see, they were all sold."
16. "(For your information...) I'm the boss here."
17. "(For your information...) I didn't even get one present."
18. "They're selling it cheap because it's a sale."
19. "It's harder than I had heard."
20. "It's okay if you only breathe, whether you breathe through your nose or breathe through your mouth."
21. "Give me anything quickly, whether it's a pencil or a pen."
22. "Anything matches well."
23. "Even my mom came to the birthday party."
24. "Anyway you won't listen to me."

Chapter 20

1. 생일 파티에 갈까 (생각)해요.
2. 자동차를 새로 살까 (생각)했어요.
3. 그렇게 하면 좋지 않을까 (생각)해요.
4. 왜 케이크를 만들까 싶었어요.
5. 이 집은 너무 작지 않을까 싶어요.
6. 제 친구가 책을 한 권 더 쓸까 싶어요.
7. 피자를 좋아하나 싶어요.
8. 너무 많나 싶었어요.
9. 그 생각이 괜찮지 않나 싶어요.
10. 잘 만들 수 있지 싶어요.
11. 한국의 7월 날씨는 덥지 싶어요.
12. 시계를 이미 두 개를 가지고 있지 싶어요.
13. 영희가 저를 안 좋아할까 봐요.
14. 시험에 늦을까 봐 뛰었어요.
15. 배가 고플까 봐 가져왔어요.
16. 비싸더라도 사고 싶어요.
17. 늦더라도 오세요.
18. 가격에 비해서 크기가 너무 작아요.
19. 위치에 비해서 꽤 저렴해요.
20. "I'm thinking of starting from tomorrow."
21. "It's so much later than I thought, so I thought of leaving first."
22. "I'm wondering if I had to have bought an expensive present."

Answer Keys

23. "I called because I wondered if I had to cook tonight."
24. "I wonder if I arrived too early."
25. "I wonder if my friend will come because it's too far."
26. "I worried if I would smell, so I changed my clothes."
27. "I wonder if it's (not) okay to do this."
28. "Even if I don't have time next year, I'll go on a trip no matter what."

Answer Keys

Appendix A. Introduction to Onomatopoeia

"What is onomatopoeia?"

Onomatopoeia are words that describe the *sound* of something. For example, let's take a look at this sentence: 나는 수영장에 뛰어들었다 ("I jumped into the pool."). This sentence is perfectly correct, but we could add onomatopoeia here to give the sentence a little extra style. One example of onomatopoeia that we could add to describe the *sound* of something falling into the water would be "splash." In Korean, this sound of "splashing" into the water is 풍덩, so we could instead write this: 나는 수영장에 **풍덩** 뛰어들었다 ("I splashed into the pool."). Or more literally, "I jumped with a *splash* into the pool."

You will also find onomatopoeia used regularly in comics and children's books. For example, you might read "KA-POW!" when the hero punches a bad guy, or "SKREECH!" when a car makes a sudden turn at high speeds. However, there are still many uses for onomatopoeia in regular conversation as well.

Adv | The word for onomatopoeia is 의성어.

Another common example of onomatopoeia is animal sounds. In English, cats say "meow," cows say "moo," and geckos say... well, most animals have a written sound of what they say. For example, let's look at the sentence 고양이가 울었다 ("The cat cried."). This sentence is grammatically fine, but it would probably sound more natural to say "The cat meowed." We can do this with the onomatopoeia 야옹 ("meow") like this: 고양이가 **야옹** 울었다 ("The cat meowed."). Or more literally, "The cat cried '*meow*'."

Since Korean culture is different from other cultures, there are many onomatopoeia that one language has but the other does not. For example, 텅(텅) is the sound of something hollow (empty), but there is no equivalent onomatopoeia in English. You could say 머리가 텅 비어 있다 ("His head is completely empty.") and 텅 could translate naturally as "completely," but not as an onomatopoeia in English. You will find examples like these often, so do not worry if you are unable to translate them exactly.

Appendix A. Introduction to Onomatopoeia

This section will introduce several of the most common and useful onomatopoeia that you might come across or want to use when speaking and writing in Korean. This section is not intended to be a complete list of onomatopoeia, but it should help to get you started.

Memorizing and using onomatopoeia is not a requirement to speaking Korean at a conversational level, but will be necessary for higher stages. You will usually be able to understand a sentence, even if you have not yet learned onomatopoeia, simply by removing that word from the sentence as you hear it or by looking it up in a dictionary as you read it.

거리다, 하다, 대다, 이다

Onomatopoeia will only be used together with certain verbs. For example, you can make a "splash" *jumping* into the water (using 뛰어들다), but you can not make a "splash" when you *close* the door (using 닫다).

Each onomatopoeia will have its own verbs that it works with, but some can also work on their own as well. For example, 빤짝(빤짝) is the sound of something sparkling, twinkling, or glittering, and it can also be used by itself when attached to the verb 거리다, which means "to go (onomatopoeia)" – such as "to go twinkle." You can then make the sentence 별이 빤짝거렸다 ("The stars twinkled.").

Other onomatopoeia can be used by themselves with the verb 하다, such as 말랑말랑 (feeling of something soft and weak); you can enjoy a nice piece of 말랑말랑한 떡 ("soft rice cake"). Other onomatopoeia can be used with 대다 and 이다, or a combination of these four verbs, depending on the sentence.

It can be helpful if you are able to recognize onomatopoeia through noticing these four verbs, and through finding words that seem to repeat themselves (such as 빤짝빤짝 or 말랑말랑), but it is not necessary. Instead, it would be faster, and therefore more effective in the beginning to simply memorize onomatopoeia one at a time using examples.

Example Sentences

The best way to learn onomatopoeia is through seeing examples of them (in this book, and in your own extra studies), taking notes which verbs were used with each, and practicing them yourself. Also practice translating them on your own, as there can be multiple ways to correctly translate sentences using onomatopoeia. Here are several examples, with the onomatopoeia highlighted in bold.

Appendix A. Introduction to Onomatopoeia

쾅: "slam," "thud" (sound of door slamming, loud falling, hitting against something)

머리를 벽에 **쾅** 부딪쳤어요.
"I bumped my head against the wall with a thud."
"I slammed my head against the wall."

따르릉: "ring" (sound of telephone, bicycle bell, alarm clock)

잠을 자다가 **따르릉**하는 소리에 깼어요.
"While sleeping I awoke to a ringing sound."

주룩(주룩): (sound of rain)

밖에 비가 **주룩주룩** 오고 있어요.
"It's pouring rain outside."

끽: (sound of creaking, screeching)

차가 내 앞에서 **끽**하고 멈춰 섰어요.
"The car screeched to a stop in front of me."

똑(똑): "knock knock" (sound of knocking)

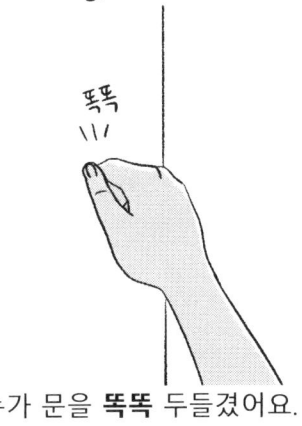

누가 문을 **똑똑** 두들겼어요.
"I knocked on the door."

Appendix A. Introduction to Onomatopoeia

쿵: "thud" (sound of falling)

책이 **쿵** 소리를 내면서 떨어졌어요.
"The book fell with a thud."

빵(빵): "beep (beep)" (sound of car honking, gun)

차가 뒤에서 **빵빵**거렸어요.
"The car honked from behind."

펑: "boom" (sound of explosion, loud pop)

티비가 **펑** 소리를 내면서 터졌어요.
"The television made a boom sound and popped."

지글(지글): (sound of something sizzling)

고기가 **지글지글** 익고 있어요.
"The meat is cooking with a sizzle."
"The meat is sizzling."

쪽: (sound of kissing)

쪽 소리가 나도록 키스했어요.
"They kissed loudly."

드르렁: (sound of snoring)

아빠가 **드르렁 드르렁** 코를 골아요.
"Dad snores loudly."

Appendix A. Introduction to Onomatopoeia

짝(짝): "clap" (sound of clapping)

우리가 박수를 **짝짝** 쳤어요.
"We applauded loudly."

콜록(콜록): (sound of coughing)

옆에서 계속 **콜록**거려요.
"He keeps coughing next to me."

꼬르륵: (sound of stomach growling)

배에서 **꼬르륵** 소리가 나고 있어요.
"A growling sound is coming from my stomach."
"My stomach is growling."

쿨(쿨): (sound of sleeping)

강아지가 **쿨쿨** 자고 있어요.
"The dog is sleeping soundly."

엉(엉): "boo hoo" (sound of crying)

너무 슬퍼서 **엉엉** 울었어요.
"I was so sad I cried, 'Boo hoo!'"
"I was so sad I cried a lot."

두근(두근): (sound of heartbeat)

그 남자만 보면 심장이 **두근두근**해요.
"If I only look at that guy, my heart beats fast."

Appendix A. Introduction to Onomatopoeia

깜빡(깜빡): (sound of something blinking)

신호등이 **깜빡깜빡**하고 있어요.
"The traffic light is blinking."

> **Adv**
> 깜빡(깜빡) is also commonly used to mean "forgetting" such as in the verb 깜빡(을) 하다, which means to mean "to forget" or "to slip (one's) mind" and is a *casual* expression. It can also be used together with 잊다 ("to forget"), which has the same meaning and usage. Here is an example.
>
> 자꾸 깜빡 잊어 버려요.
> "I keep forgetting."

멍(멍): "woof" (sound of dog)

강아지가 밖을 보면서 **멍멍** 짖고 있어요.
"The puppy is barking 'woof woof' while looking outside."
"The puppy is barking while looking outside."

개굴(개굴): "ribbit" (sound of frog)

여름에는 개구리가 **개굴개굴** 울어요.
"Frogs cry 'ribbit ribbit' in the summer."
"Frogs ribbit in the summer."

꽥(꽥): "quack" (sound of duck)

오리가 **꽥꽥** 소리를 내면서 수영을 하고 있어요.
"The ducks are swimming while making a 'quack quack' sound."
"The ducks are swimming while quacking."

꼬끼오: "cluck," "cock-a-doodle-doo" (sound of chicken or rooster)

새벽에 닭이 **꼬끼오**하고 울었어요.
"The rooster cried 'cock-a-doodle-doo' in the early morning."

> **Adv**
> 닭 ("chicken") is also commonly used to refer to *roosters*.

New Onomatopoeia

풍덩	"splash" (sound of falling in water)
텅(텅)	(sound of something hollow)

Appendix A. Introduction to Onomatopoeia

빤짝(빤짝)	"twinkle" (sound of something sparkling, glittering, twinkling)
말랑말랑	(feeling of something soft and weak)
우르릉	(sound of thunder)
따르릉	"ring" (sound of telephone, bicycle bell, alarm clock)
주룩(주룩)	(sound of rain)
끽	(sound of creaking, screeching)
쾅	"slam," "thud" (sound of door slamming, loud falling, hitting against something)
딩동	"ding dong" (sound of door bell)
똑(똑)	"knock knock" (sound of knocking)
쿵	"thud" (sound of falling)
빵(빵)	"beep (beep)" (sound of car honking, gun)
펑	"boom" (sound of explosion, loud pop)
땡	"clang" (sound of hitting metal bell)
보글(보글)	(sound of boiling)
지글(지글)	(sound of something sizzling)
톡(톡)	(sound of tapping)
쪽	(sound of kissing)
드르렁	(sound of snoring)
짝(짝)	(sound of clapping)
콜록(콜록)	(sound of coughing)
꼬르륵	(sound of stomach growling)
쿨(쿨)	(sound of sleeping)
엉(엉)	"boo hoo" (sound of crying)
흑(흑)	(sound of crying)
에취	"achoo" (sound of sneezing)
끄덕(끄덕)	(sound of nodding in agreement)
두근(두근)	(sound of heartbeat)
후루룩	"slurp" (sound of slurping)
킁킁	"sniff" (sound of smelling)
깜빡(깜빡)	(sound of something blinking)

Appendix A. Introduction to Onomatopoeia

야옹	"meow" (sound of cat)
멍(멍)	"woof" (sound of dog)
찍(찍)	"squeak" (sound of mouse)
어흥	"roar" (sound of tiger)
꿀꿀	"oink" (sound of pig)
개굴(개굴)	"ribbit" (sound of frog)
매애	"bah" (sound of sheep)
음매	"moo" (sound of cow)
꽥꽥	"quack" (sound of duck)
꼬꼬(댁)	"cluck" (sound of chicken)
꼬끼오	"cluck," "cock-a-doodle-doo" (sound of chicken or rooster)
삐악(삐악)	"cheep" (sound of chick)
짹(짹)	"tweet" (bird sound)

Appendix B. Introduction to Dialects

Disclaimer

This appendix will cover only a small selection of traits that you might come across when listening to different Korean dialects. It is not meant to be a complete guide to dialects, nor will it go into much detail. Learning everything about every dialect in Korea (including North Korean dialects) would require a much larger book. If your goal is to become fluent in Korean, you will eventually learn more about the dialect in the location(s) that you are most interested in through your normal daily studies and interactions with native Koreans.

This section is also not intended to be a "rulebook" on dialects. In dialects, there unfortunately are not many rules. Vocabulary, grammar, spelling, and pronunciation can vary from person to person, and over time. The best way to learn the dialect of an area is to speak with people who are from there, to copy what you hear, or to live there yourself.

What is Dialect?

If you have ever traveled around the United States or in any country that speaks English, you will probably have found that the farther away you travel from where you are the more different the language can sound. This is known as a person's 말투 ("way of speaking"). For example, listen to someone speaking English in California, and compare that to someone speaking English in England, Africa, Australia, New Zealand, the Philippines, and many other countries. Even within the same country, and the same state or region, different people can speak the same language slightly differently from each other.

The same applies to the Korean peninsula. Although Korea is a relatively small country compared to others, people living in different regions and cities of Korea will speak the same language differently from others. Although each person can speak Korean uniquely due to their background, location, and upbringing, typically people within each region of South Korea will have similar language traits with each other. These similarities that appear within each region are what is known as "dialects" (사투리, or 방언).

Fortunately, although a person born in California will speak differently from a person born in England, the same two people can still communicate without any major issues (except arguing over whether "football" or "soccer" is correct). The same applies in Korea, and people all over Korea will have no problem understanding 표준어 ("standard Korean"). All of the Korean that we have learned so far has been 표준어. Using 표준어 means that anyone in Korea will be able to understand you. 표준어 is also what Koreans themselves learn in grammar classes, and is what is used when writing school essays, newspaper articles, and books. The majority of dialects in Korean will only be used when *spoken*, not when written.

Appendix B. Introduction to Dialects

Note that most younger people these days will not use any strong dialect when speaking, regardless of where they are originally from. Instead of using different vocabulary and grammar, younger people born and raised in each region of Korea might have slightly different intonation, or prefer different styles of speech. Since language constantly changes, you will notice the most difference in speaking between younger and older generations.

Since not everyone in Korea – especially older generations – will avoid speaking using a dialect, it can be helpful if you have been introduced to the basics of Korean dialects in order to enjoy traveling around Korea more freely, or even living there.

There are six major dialects – one for each major area of South Korea. These areas are 경기도, 강원도, 충청도, 경상도, 전라도, and 제주도.

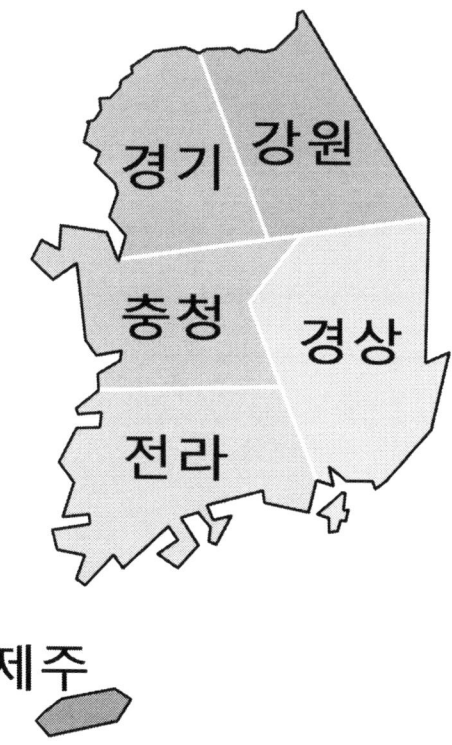

The Basics: Intonation

The most common thing that will differ between each dialect is the *intonation* of the sentence (the way that words and syllables rise and fall when spoken in a sentence). Even the phrase 안녕하세요 will sound different depending on where you are in Korea and who you talk to. For example, older generations in 강원도 might say 안녕하시구레, people in 충청도 might say 안녕하세유, people in 경상도 might say 안녕하이소, people in 전라도 might say 안녕하쇼, and people in 제주도 might say 안녕하수다.

Appendix B. Introduction to Dialects

These examples are included simply as an introduction to how different each dialect *can* sound. Note that most people in all areas of Korea will simply say 안녕하세요.

Not only can words and phrases change, the intonations of sentences can change as well. A good way to understand this is to listen to them spoken by native Koreans. Because intonation can be different from person to person, focus more on the *style* of intonation (in general, how sentences sounds to you), than the actual specific intonation used on each word and syllable.

To hear the specific differences of each dialect's intonation, ask a pen pal or an acquaintance to read the story 흥부와 놀부 (written below) out loud. You will notice that although he or she is merely reading a story as it is written, some things will be spoken a bit differently.

흥부와 놀부

흥부와 놀부 is a traditional Korean fairy tale about greed. Here is the story written using 표준어 (followed with a translation).

옛날 한마을에 착한 동생 흥부와 욕심 많은 형 놀부가 살고 있었습니다.
아들과 딸이 많은 흥부는 배고픈 아이들을 위해서 형의 집에 먹을 것을 빌리러 갔다가 밥주걱으로 뺨을 맞고 돌아왔습니다.
어느 날 흥부는 다리가 다친 제비를 발견해서 다리를 고쳐 주었습니다.
다리가 나은 제비는 흥부에게 박 씨를 가져다주었습니다.
제비에게 받은 씨앗에서 박이 나왔고 흥부는 그것을 잘랐습니다.
그런데 박에서 여러 가지 보석이 나왔습니다.
그 얘기를 들은 놀부는 제비를 잡아서 다리를 부러뜨린 후에 다리를 고쳐 주었습니다.
다리가 나은 제비는 놀부에게 박 씨를 가져다주었습니다.
놀부가 박을 잘랐더니 보석이 없었습니다.
그 박에서는 도깨비가 나와서 집을 무너뜨리고 놀부 가족을 쫓아냈습니다.
가난해진 놀부는 동생 흥부에게 도움을 청했고, 착한 흥부는 놀부 형의 가족과 함께 살았습니다.

Appendix B. Introduction to Dialects

Heung-boo and Nol-boo

A long time ago Heung-boo, the nice younger brother, and Nol-boo, the greedy older brother, lived in the same town. Heung-boo, who had many sons and daughters, went to ask to borrow food from his older brother Nol-boo's house for his hungry children, but then was hit in the face with a rice scoop and went back home. One day Heung-boo discovered a swallow with a broken leg, and fixed its leg. The swallow with the mended leg brought a gourd seed to Heung-boo. A gourd came out from the seed that Heung-boo received from the swallow, and he cut it open. He cut the gourd, and many jewels came out. Nol-boo, who heard what happened, caught a swallow and after breaking its leg, fixed it. The swallow with the mended leg brought a gourd seed to Nol-boo. Nol-boo cut open the gourd, but there were no jewels. From the gourd came a goblin, which destroyed his house and kicked his family out. Nol-boo, who became poor, asked for help from his younger brother Heung-boo, and the nice Heung-boo lived together with his older brother Nol-boo's family.

New Vocabulary

한마을	"the same village," "the same town"
밥주걱	"rice scoop"
뺨(을) 맞다	"to be hit/slapped in the face"
어느 날	"one day" (literally, "a certain day")
제비	"swallow (bird)"
박	"gourd"
가져다주다	"to bring (from somewhere) and give (to someone)"
보석	"jewel," "gem"
부러뜨리다	"to break (bone)," "to fracture," "to snap"
도깨비	"goblin"
무너뜨리다	"to destroy," "to demolish," "to tear down"
쫓아내다	"to kick someone out," "to throw someone out"
청하다	"to ask for," "to request (something)"

Appendix B. Introduction to Dialects

The Basics: Vocabulary

Another common thing that will change is the vocabulary that is used. For example 김치 can be said as 짐치 in 강원도, or as 짠지 in 경상도. Remember that nearly all Koreans are familiar with 표준어, so it is not necessary to memorize specific dialect vocabulary in order for people to be able to understand you (but it can be fun).

In addition, many dialect words and grammar features are shared between different areas. This means that you might hear parts of the dialect from one area used in a different area. This is normal. Instead of focusing on learning "this word comes from this place," it is better to think "I might hear this dialect word no matter where I go in the countryside."

The Basics: Grammar

Pay close attention to *verb endings* used in each dialect, as this will be one of the easiest ways to distinguish what dialect a person is speaking.

Some dialects can use their own completely unique verb endings. For example, you might hear the 노 ending in 경상도 (for example, 뭐하노?), or the 잖소 ending used in parts of 강원도 (for example, 했잖소.).

Other dialects will simply use certain verb endings more commonly. For example, you might hear the 나 ending and the 데 form used more frequently in 경상도 than in other areas.

경기도

The majority of Korean that you will come into contact with through media (television, music, movies, etc.) will use this "dialect" of Korean.

The region of 경기도 surrounds the cities of 서울 (the largest city in Korea) and 인천, but does not actually include these two cities.

And while many people typically think of the Korean spoken in 서울 as being 표준어, this is not completely true. 서울 has its own dialect too (called 서울말) which is slightly different from "official" 표준어 taught in textbooks, but it is the closest example. To keep things simple, it is fine to think of the Korean used in 서울 (or in 경기도) as 표준어.

Appendix B. Introduction to Dialects

경기도: Intonation

고맙습니다.

The intonation used in 경기도 (표준어) sounds the smoothest of the dialects of Korea. If you were to draw the intonation it would usually look like smooth hills going up and down through the sentence, ending just a bit below the top. You can hear this intonation used throughout all of the audio files for the conversations of the three books in this series (which you can download for free on my web site).

경기도: The Vowel Sound ㅏ

While not specific to only 경기도 – Koreans all throughout Korea might use the same pronunciation "quirks" used in 경기도 – the ㅏ sound can be pronounced as ㅓ when part of the 요 form conjugation. This pronunciation is more common when the 요 is not added.

표준어	경기도
아파(요)	아퍼(요)
받아(요)	받어(요)
앉아(요)	앉어(요)
알아(요)	알어(요)
많아(요)	많어(요)

강원도

Most of 강원도 is surrounded by trees and mountains, and the area is famous for its agriculture. The majority of people living in 강원도 are not far from 서울, which is just to the west, so they will speak similarly to people in 경기도. However, people who live farther east, such as in the city of 강릉, will have a slightly more distinct dialect.

강원도: Grammar

A feature of 강원도 dialect that is well known to other Koreans is using (이)래(요) instead of 이에요 and 예요. This also applies to the past tense, as (이)랬어(요).

Appendix B. Introduction to Dialects

표준어	강원도
한국이에요.	한국이래요.
학교예요.	학교래요.
이었어요. Or, 였어요.	(이)랬어요.

You might hear the 세요 ending replaced with 시라요 or 시구레.

표준어	강원도
하세요.	하시라요. Or, 하시구레.

Another ending is (잖)소, which is a combination of the 잖다 ending we learned (지 않다) and the 소 ending, an old fashioned, honorific verb ending equivalent to 세요. 잖소 can take the place of the 죠 ending, or the 니다 ending.

표준어	강원도
집에 갔습니다. Or, 집에 갔죠.	집에 갔(잖)소.

You might hear the verb ending 드래요 (or 뜨래요) used by some Koreans who are not 강원도 residents. This is an *incorrect* grammar form that became popular as a stereotype of the 강원도 dialect.

강원도: Vocabulary

Here are some examples of different words that are sometimes used in 강원도.

표준어	강원도
김치	짐치
음식	음석
아버지	아부지
어머니	어머이
지금	시방
학생	학상
나쁘다	매했다
토요일	반공일
화장실	정낭
먹다	묵다

Appendix B. Introduction to Dialects

충청도

Since the northern parts of 충청도 are close to 서울, most people will speak similarly to people in 경기도. You will notice more unique traits in southern parts of the region, such as in the city of 대전, and especially in the countryside.

People in 충청도 might speak a bit more slowly than people in other areas. Because of this, it might sound a bit more *friendly* than other dialects.

충청도: Grammar

The 요 ending can be pronounced as 유 instead.

표준어	충청도
감사해요.	감사해유.
집에 가요.	집에 가유.
한국어를 공부하나요?	한국어를 공부하나유?

시유 (or 슈) is a shortening of the sound 세요 or the past tense 쓰어요 form. It can be used in place of either.

표준어	충청도
하세요.	하시유. Or, 하슈.
했어요.	했시유. Or, 했슈.
밥 드셨어요?	밥 드셨슈?

Instead of 입니다, (이)여 can be used. In addition, (이)여 can also replace the 반말 ending (이)야.

표준어	충청도
아닙니다. Or, 아니야.	아니여.
한국인입니다. Or, 한국인이야.	한국인이여.
할 것입니다. Or, 할 거야.	할 거여.*

*거여 can be shortened to 겨.

Appendix B. Introduction to Dialects

경상도

경상도 includes the major cities of 부산, 울산, and 대구. A main feature of 경상도 speakers is using shorter sentences in general when compared to speakers of other dialects. This means that you can say more by saying less. A stereotypical father from 경상도, upon returning from work, is said to speak only these three words to his wife: 1) 밥도. (밥을 줘.) 2) 아는? (아이는 잘 있어요?) 3) 자자.

Among the different dialects spoken within 경상도, 부산 사투리 is the most well known and the most popular. We will mostly focus on 부산 사투리 in this section.

경상도: Intonation

경상도 dialects have the most varied intonation – especially 부산 사투리. If you were to draw the intonation it would usually look more bumpy, like small hills going up and down through the sentence.

Among native Koreans, men who speak 부산 사투리 are typically seen as masculine, and women who speak it are seen as cute. It is the harshest sounding dialect among all Korean dialects. When hearing this dialect for the first time, it can sound almost as if people are arguing with each other *angrily* even when they are just speaking in a friendly way.

경상도: Vowels and Consonants

부산 사투리 speakers prefer simpler ways of speaking. For example, the vowels ㅡ and ㅓ are sometimes pronounced similarly. In addition, diphthongs can also be pronounced more simply by only pronouncing the final vertical vowel. For example, ㅝ can be said as ㅓ, ㅢ as ㅣ, and ㅘ as ㅏ.

표준어	경상도
음식	엄식
추워.	추어.
어디	으디
의사	이사
사과	사가

Appendix B. Introduction to Dialects

| 되다 | 대다 |
| 뭐 | 머 or 모 |

The consonant ㅆ can simply be pronounced as ㅅ.

표준어	경상도
쌀	살
씨앗	시앗

경상도: Grammar

The 요 form can be replaced with 예. This includes 이에요 and 예요, which can become (이)예.

표준어	경상도
안녕하세요.	안녕하세예.
했어요.	했어예.
그렇죠?	그렇제.

A common polite ending is (으)이소 or (으)시이소 which can replace the 세요 ending.

표준어	경상도
수고하세요.	수고하이소. Or, 수고하시이소.
받으세요.	받으이소. Or, 받으시이소.

The 니다 form can be replaced by 니데이, or 소이다.

표준어	경상도
합니다.	합니데이. Or, 하소이다.
반갑습니다.	반갑습니데이. Or, 반갑소이다.

Another common 반말 ending is 아이가, which is used in a similar way to the 잖아 ending (지 않아). However, 아이가 is used after the Plain Form (instead of after a verb stem). 아이가 can also be used directly after a noun to mean (이)잖아. You can think of 아이가 as meaning 맞지? ("That's right, huh?") at the end of a sentence.

표준어	경상도
하잖아.	한다 아이가.
우리 친구잖아.	우리 친구 아이가.

Appendix B. Introduction to Dialects

When asking questions, two commonly used endings are 노 and 나 (from Chapter 9 of the second book). While using the 나 ending in 부산 사투리 means that you would like a "yes" or "no" answer, using the 노 ending means that you would prefer an *explanation*, instead of just a "yes" or "no." These endings are only appropriate when speaking in 반말.

표준어	경상도
뭐해?	뭐하노? Or, 뭐하나?
집에 있어?	집에 있나?
가고 싶어?	가고 싶나?

The 데 form can be used for asking questions when used with question words. Although 표준어 can use the 데 form in this way as well, note that the form will have a *falling intonation* (not rising as in 표준어) when used in this dialect. This ending is only appropriate when speaking in 반말.

표준어	경상도
뭐해?	뭐하는데?
어디 가?	어디 가는데?
어떻게 했어?	어떻게 했는데?

When asking questions, the (이)고 ending or the (이)가 ending can be used instead of (이)야. These two endings are only appropriate when speaking in 반말.

표준어	경상도
몇 살이야?	몇 살이고? Or, 몇 살이가?
학교야?	학교고? Or, 학교가?

The 반말 words for 너 ("you") and 네 ("your") are pronounced as 니. In addition, 나 ("I," "me") can be pronounced as 내.

표준어	경상도
네 집	니 집
네가	니가
너는	니는
나는	내는
나도	내도

도 can replace the conjugation 줘 (from 주다), such as when asking for items or asking favors using verbs. This usage is only appropriate when speaking in 반말.

Appendix B. Introduction to Dialects

표준어	경상도
숙제를 해 줘.	숙제를 해 도.

A common grammar form is 가지고 (pronounced as 가꼬), which can be used in place of the 서 ending or 고 ending attached to a verb to show one action happening after another.

표준어	경상도
식당에 가서 밥을 먹었어요.	식당에 가가꼬 밥을 묵었어예.

경상도: The Consonants ㄱ and ㅎ

You will often hear (그)카 used in 경상도 사투리, which is a shortened form of the ㄱ consonant followed by the ㅎ consonant. For example, 그렇게 하다 can be shortened to 그카다 because 그렇게 uses a ㄱ (in 게) followed by a ㅎ (in 하). When 그카다 is used after a question word, it will shorten further to 카다 – this verb can then be conjugated normally.

Long Version (경상도)	Shortened Version (경상도)
그렇게 할래?	그칼래?
왜 그렇게 하는데?	와 카는데?
왜 그렇게 하노?	와 카노?
뭐라고 (말)하노?	뭐라카노?
뭐라고 (말)했노?	뭐라켔노?*

*케 can be used instead of 카 when the following sound is not ㅏ. For example, in (말)했노, the sound is ㅐ (from 했). 카 and 케 are both shortened forms of the sounds made when the ㄱ consonant is followed by the ㅎ consonant.

경상도: Vocabulary

Here are some examples of different words that are sometimes used in 경상도.

표준어	경상도
김치	짠지
매우 or 너무	억수로
많이	마이
아이	아
왜	와
제대로	단디

Appendix B. Introduction to Dialects

얘 (이 아이)	야 (이 아)
걔 (그 아이)	가 (그 아)*
쟤 (저 아이)	쟈 (저 아)
죽이다	직이다*
먹다	뭇다 or 묵다

*This can lead to interesting sounding sentences when combined with the (이)가 ending, such as 가가 가가? (meaning 그 아이가 그 아이인가?).

*A common *slang* word in 표준어 is 죽이다 (literally "to kill"), which means "to be wonderful" or "to be fantastic." For example, the sentence 와, 죽인다! means "Wow, that's fantastic!" In 경상도 dialect, this can also be pronounced as 직이다 (와, 직인다!).

경상도: Phrases

Here are a few more common expressions in 경상도 dialect. Note that these expressions (except 욕봤습니데이) should only be used when speaking in 반말.

표준어	경상도
어떻게 알아?	우째 아나?
수고했습니다.	욕봤습니데이.
와라!	온나!
그래? Or, 정말?	맞나?
아주 좋다. Or, 괜찮다.	살아 있네!*

*This is a slang expression, and literally means "is alive" (from 살아 있다).

전라도

The 전라도 area includes the city of 광주. This area is also referred to as 호남, a word that comes from Chinese characters and means "south of the lake."

전라도: Grammar

Instead of the 세요 ending, you might find 시요, which can be shortened to 쇼.

표준어	전라도
안녕하세요.	안녕하시오. Or, 안녕하쇼.

Appendix B. Introduction to Dialects

Instead of the 니다 ending, you might find 당께요. This is used at the end of the Plain Form, in place of the final 다. For example, 합니다 would become 한당께(요) because the Plain Form of 하다 is 한다. This form is originally from the 다니까(요) ending. 이다 ("to be") will become (이)랑께(요) when used with this form.

표준어	전라도
합니다.	한당께(요).
있습니다.	있당께(요).
아닙니다.	아니랑께(요).
반갑습니다.	반갑당께(요).

Another common ending is 부러, which can be used to add *emphasis* to a sentence. It is added after conjugating a verb to the 요 form, but without adding the 요. 부러 originally comes from 버려 (from the verb 버리다). However, it can only be used with action verbs if the sentence is a *command*. It should only be used when speaking in 반말.

표준어	전라도
좋아요!	좋아 부러!
집에 가!	집에 가 부러!

전라도: Vocabulary

Here are some examples of different words that are sometimes used in 전라도.

표준어	전라도
고양이	괭이
강아지	갱아지
얼굴	상판
아주 or 매우	겁나게
어떻게	어쩨서
이것, 그것, or 저것	거시기*
아직	당아

*거시기 can be used to refer to something when you are not certain what to call it. In this way it can take the place of 이것, 그것, or 저것. It can also be used for a person, when you are not certain of their name. While 거시기 itself is not a dialect word, it is used most frequently in 전라도.

Appendix B. Introduction to Dialects

제주도

제주도 is to Korea what Hawaii is to the United States, with its own unique culture and history, warmer weather, clean beaches, local meats and seafood, fresh fruits and vegetables, and plenty of spots for taking photos. Due to it being an island, 제주도 has been isolated from the rest of Korea throughout much of its history. That allowed it to develop and maintain such a different style of speaking.

Many parts of the 제주도 dialect have been borrowed from the languages of other countries, such as Japanese (due to Japan being so close), and even Mongolian (it was once ruled by Mongolia).

Although this appendix is about dialects, it might be more appropriate to call the dialect of this area a "language" instead. This is because the dialect spoken by older generations living in 제주도 is different enough from 표준어 that people from other areas of Korea are *unable* to understand someone speaking in strong 제주도 dialect. This is because over 75% of the 제주도 dialect uses words that are not found in 표준어 or in other areas of Korea. However, this does not mean that people in 제주도 are unable to communicate together with people from the mainland. In fact, only a small number of people who live in 제주도 are still fluent in 제주도 dialect, and these days the language is only promoted and maintained in order to preserve the culture of the island and the historical importance of the language. The majority of people living in 제주도 are still able to speak and understand standard Korean as well due to most media coming from the mainland.

제주도: The Lost Vowel

When 한글 was first created, there were originally more consonants and vowels than there are remaining today. Over time 한글 was standardized and simplified, and this left us with what we have now. At the time of its creation, the Korean language had an additional vowel sound that is no longer used today in 표준어. This vowel is called 아래아 ("arae-a"), and it survives today in the 제주도 dialect. It is written as a dot, and has a sound similar to saying 아으 quickly. Words that were originally written with the 아래아 in older Korean are now written in 표준어 using ㅏ (when at the start of a word) or ㅡ (when not at the start of a word). We will not be writing words using this vowel in this appendix in order to keep things simple, but be able to recognize what it is when you see it on your next trip to 제주도.

Appendix B. Introduction to Dialects

제주도: Grammar

In 제주도 dialect, there is much less of a need to speak *honorifically* to older people. It is perfectly fine to use 있다 instead of 계시다, and 엇다 (없다) instead of 안 계시다. While 제주도 people still show respect to older people through their actions, this respect is not shown through formal or honorific speech as it is in 표준어. The standard ending 수다 that we will learn soon will be appropriate for both informal and formal situations.

The 니다 (or 요) ending can be replaced with 암수다 (or 엄수다) when used with *action verbs*, or 수다 when used with *descriptive verbs*. This attaches directly to the verb stem. For questions, change the 다 at the end to 과 (or 꽈). You might also find the endings 우다 (for statements) and 우과 (for questions) used in the same way.

표준어	제주도
압니다.	알암수다.
했습니다.	했수다.
했습니까?	했수과?
있습니다.	있수다.
안녕하세요.	안녕하수다.
반갑습니다.	반갑수다.*
좋습니다.	좋수다.
좋습니까?	좋수과?
한국입니다.	한국이우다.
아니요.	아니우다.
얼마입니까?	얼마우과?

*Note that 반갑수다 can also commonly used in place of 안녕하수다 (안녕하세요) when seeing someone, even if you have already met them before. Or you can ask 펜안하우과? (from 편안하다, meaning "to be peaceful"), which can be used in the same way as asking 안녕하십니까? to someone.

Alternatively, you might see 마씀 (or 마씸) used in place of the 니다 or 니까 forms. This can also be used in place of 입니다 and 입니까. When used with a verb, it will be used after the 요 form (without the 요).

표준어	제주도
한국입니다.	한국 마씀.
학교입니까?	학교 마씀?
모릅니다.	몰라 마씀.

Appendix B. Introduction to Dialects

| 갑니다. | 가 마씀. |

When making a *command*, the 세요 form can be replaced with ㅂ서 after a *vowel*, or 읍서 after a *consonant*.

표준어	제주도
오세요.	옵서.
주세요.	줍서.
받으세요.	받읍서.

제주도: Vocabulary

Here are some examples of different words that are sometimes used in 제주도.

표준어	제주도
아버지	아방
어머니	어멍
할아버지	하르방
할머니	할망
남자	소나리
여자	지집아이
따뜻하다	맨도롱하다
비싸다	빗나다
감자	지실
고구마	감저
많이	하영
무엇	무싱거
왜	무사
삼촌	삼춘*

*The word 삼춘 (originally from 삼촌, meaning "uncle"), has a different meaning in 제주도 dialect. It can be used to *call out* to anyone – a friend or a stranger, regardless of age.

제주도: Phrases

Here are a few more common expressions in 제주도 dialect.

Appendix B. Introduction to Dialects

표준어	제주도
어서 오세요!	혼저 옵서예!
잘 먹었습니다!	잘 먹쿠다!
안녕히 가세요!	혼저 갑서!
안녕히 계세요!	잘 이십서!
매우 고맙습니다.	잘도 고맙수다.
수고했습니다.	폭싹 속았수다.
뭐예요?	무싱거 마씀?

Special Thanks

I could not have made this book without the support of the following individuals. You helped this book to transform into something special, and it's thanks to you that it even exists. I'd like to give a special thank you to each person here who has contributed to this book's creation.

trevarr
Joel Tersigni
Leeza Perez
Kat Morrill
Thea Brune
George Trombley
Tyler D. Smith
Richard Hamilton
Jennifer Weglarz
Mark Canlas
Chris Morlang (chris3spice)
Papp1s
Wade Mayfield
James D. Garza
Bennett Seacrist
AVFN
Jan Kuffer
Evan
Perry Hwang Willems
B.J. Williamson
Brittney Raphael
Charles Vought
Anthony Biddle
dr_root
Edward Voss
Joseph Davis
Rachel "토끼" Bibb
Eike
Ben S.
Natalie Tae Matheson
Nektarios Machner
James Valleroy
Nelson Morris
Nathan Clingan
Victoria Lynn Yoak
Merrill Grady
손소현

Glossary

ㄱ

가난하다 "to be poor"	Ch. 2
가만히 있다 "to stay still," "to keep still"	Ch. 11
가입(을) 하다 "to become a member," "to join (a group)"	Ch. 7
가져다주다 "to bring (from somewhere) and give (to someone)"	App. B
가지 "a type," "a kind"	Ch. 8
각도 "angle"	Ch. 13
간 "liver"	Ch. 11
갈아입다 "to change (clothes)"	Ch. 20
감각 "a sense," "a sensation"	Ch. 20
감각(이) 있다 "to have sense," "to have taste" (idiom)	Ch. 20
감동(을) 받다 "to be moved (emotionally)," "to be touched (emotionally)"	Ch. 15
감동(을) 시키다 "to move (emotionally)," "to touch (emotionally)"	Ch. 15
값 "value," "worth"	Ch. 2
갚다 "to repay"	Ch. 2
개구쟁이 "troublemaker"	Ch. 4
개굴(개굴) "ribbit" (sound of frog)	App. A
개인 "personal" (adjective)	Ch. 1
개인적 "personal"	Ch. 12
걔 "that guy/girl"	Ch. 3
거부 "rejection (of suggestion, demand)"	Ch. 20
거부(를) 하다 "to reject (suggestion, demand)"	Ch. 20
거북이 "turtle"	Ch. 7
거스름돈 "change (from a transaction)"	Ch. 8
거절 "rejection (of item, request, suggestion, demand)"	Ch. 20
거절(을) 하다 "to reject (item, request, suggestion, demand)"	Ch. 20
거품 "bubble"	Ch. 4
걱정(이) 되다 "to become a worry," "to become worried"	Ch. 20
건강하세요! "Be healthy!"	Ch. 5
건너가다 "to cross (to somewhere)"	Ch. 9
건너오다 "to cross (to here)"	Ch. 9
건너편 "the other side (of something)"	Ch. 9
걸어 다니다 "to walk around," "to move about"	Ch. 12
겁 "cowardice," "fear"	Ch. 15
겁(을) 내다 "to show (one's) cowardice"	Ch. 15
겁(이) 나다 "to be afraid," "to be cowardly"	Ch. 15
겁쟁이 "a coward"	Ch. 15
게으르다 "to be lazy"	Ch. 4
게으름쟁이 "lazy person"	Ch. 4
겪다 "to go through," "to experience"	Ch. 9
결심(을) 하다 "to be determined to do," "to resolve to do"	Ch. 12
결정(이) 되다 "to be decided"	Ch. 15
경우 "a case," "a circumstance"	Ch. 9
경제적 "economical"	Ch. 12
경찰차 "police car"	Ch. 10
경치 "view," "scenery"	Ch. 6
경험 "an experience"	Ch. 9
경험(을) 하다 "to experience"	Ch. 9
계란 "(chicken) egg" (slightly casual)	Ch. 1
계절 "season"	Ch. 1
고객님 "customer," "client"	Ch. 9
고급 "advanced (level)," "high-grade"	Ch. 9
고등학생 "high school student"	Ch. 8
고생(을) 하다 "to go through a difficult working experience," "to go through a hardship"	Ch. 2
고생하셨어요. "You've suffered to help me," "Thank you for your hard work (to a worker)"	Ch. 2
고소하다 "to be savory," "to be nutty"	Ch. 1
공장 "factory"	Ch. 11
과외 "tutoring"	Ch. 1
과외 선생님 "tutor"	Ch. 1
과학적 "scientific"	Ch. 12

Glossary

Korean	English	Chapter
관광	"sightseeing," "tourism"	Ch. 16
관광(을) 하다	"to sightsee," "to tour"	Ch. 16
관광객	"sightseer," "tourist"	Ch. 16
관리	"maintenance," "administration"	Ch. 8
관리(를) 하다	"to maintain," "to administer"	Ch. 8
관리자	"supervisor," "administrator"	Ch. 8
괴로워하다	"to suffer"	Ch. 5
괴롭다	"to be distressed," "to be in pain"	Ch. 5
굉장히	"extremely," "awfully"	Ch. 1
교재	"teaching materials," "textbook(s)"	Ch. 1
구경	"sightseeing," "looking around"	Ch. 8
구경(을) 하다	"to sightsee," "to look around"	Ch. 8
구급차	"ambulance"	Ch. 10
구멍	"a hole"	Ch. 8
구체적	"concrete," "specific"	Ch. 12
국내	"national," "domestic" (adjective)	Ch. 14
국내 전화	"domestic phone call"	Ch. 14
국물	"(soup) broth"	Ch. 1
국자	"ladle"	Ch. 1
국제	"international" (adjective)	Ch. 14
국제 전화	"international phone call"	Ch. 14
국제적	"international"	Ch. 14
굳이	"really," "absolutely," "obstinately" (adverb)	Ch. 18
귀여워하다	"to adore"	Ch. 5
귀찮다	"to be tiresome," "to be troublesome"	Ch. 1
규칙적	"regular," "orderly"	Ch. 12
그 때에	"at that time"	Ch. 17
그러게(요).	"Yes (in answer to your question)."	Ch. 19
그러다	"to say so"	Ch. 2
그런 것 같아요.	"I think so."	Ch. 3
그렇게 생각해요.	"I think so."	Ch. 3
그립다	"to miss," "to long for"	Ch. 5
그만	"stop" (adverb)	Ch. 12
근	"geun" (600 grams)	Ch. 6
글	"(written) words," "letters"	Ch. 14
기간	"a period (of time)," "a term (of time)"	Ch. 7
기계적	"mechanical"	Ch. 12
기념	"commemoration"	Ch. 16
기념일	"anniversary"	Ch. 16
기념품	"souvenir"	Ch. 16
기능	"function (of something)"	Ch. 10
기대(가) 되다	"to be expected," "to look forward"	Ch. 16
기말고사	"final exam," "final test"	Ch. 1
기말시험	"final exam," "final test"	Ch. 1
기부	"donation"	Ch. 18
기부(를) 하다	"to donate"	Ch. 18
기분	"(one's) mood"	Ch. 5
기분(이) 안 좋다	"to not feel good"	Ch. 5
기분(이) 좋다	"to feel good"	Ch. 5
기분이 어떻습니까?	"How do you feel?"	Ch. 5
기사	"news article"	Ch. 13
기숙사	"dormitory," "dorms"	Ch. 6
기억(이) 나다	"to remember," "to come to mind"	Ch. 7
기억력(이) 좋다	"to have a good memory (ability)"	Ch. 9
기온	"temperature (of weather)"	Ch. 13
기자	"reporter"	Ch. 14
기초	"(the) basics," "base," "foundation"	Ch. 1
길 건너편	"the other side of the street"	Ch. 9
길 맞은편	"the other side of the street"	Ch. 9
길(을) 물어보다	"to ask the way," "to ask (for) directions"	Ch. 6
길(이) 막히다	"road is blocked," "road is obstructed"	Ch. 15
길거리	"street," "road"	Ch. 2
길이	"length"	Ch. 20
김	"flat, dry seaweed"	Ch. 5
깊다	"to be deep"	Ch. 13
깎다	"to trim," "to mow"	Ch. 11

Glossary

깜빡(깜빡) (sound of something blinking)	App. A
깜짝 "surprise," "with a startle" (adverb)	Ch. 10
깜짝 생일 파티 "surprise birthday party"	Ch. 10
깨 "sesame seeds"	Ch. 1
깨(어)지다 "to be broken," "to be smashed"	Ch. 15
깨다 "to awake"	Ch. 10
깨다 "to break (something)," "to smash (something)"	Ch. 15
깨닫다 "to realize"	Ch. 8
깨우다 "to make (someone) wake up," "to awaken"	Ch. 10
꺼지다 "to be turned off"	Ch. 15
껍질 "peel," "wrapper"	Ch. 10
껍질(을) 벗기다 "to take off the peel," "to take off the wrapper"	Ch. 10
꼬꼬(댁) "cluck" (sound of chicken)	App. A
꼬끼오 "cluck," "cock-a-doodle-doo" (sound of chicken or rooster)	App. A
꼬르륵 (sound of stomach growling)	App. A
꽤 "quite," "comparatively," "fairly" (adverb)	Ch. 20
꽥꽥 "quack" (sound of duck)	App. A
꿀꿀 "oink" (sound of pig)	App. A
끄덕(끄덕) (sound of nodding in agreement)	App. A
끌다 "to drag (someone)"	Ch. 9
끌어가다 "to drag (someone somewhere)"	Ch. 9
끌어오다 "to drag (someone here)"	Ch. 9
끽 (sound of creaking, screeching)	App. A

ㄴ

나긋나긋하다 "to be gentle and soft"	Ch. 4
나비 "butterfly"	Ch. 7
나이(가) 들다 "to get older"	Ch. 9
낙서 "scribbling," "scribbles," "doodling"	Ch. 20
낙서(를) 하다 "to scribble," "to doodle"	Ch. 20
낙엽 "leaf (on the ground)"	Ch. 10
낙원 "a paradise"	Ch. 19
남기다 "to make left over," "to leave (over)"	Ch. 10
남성 "male"	Ch. 18
남성스럽다 "to be masculine"	Ch. 18
남자 친구(가) 생기다 "to get a boyfriend"	Ch. 11
남자 친구(를) 사귀다 "to date a boyfriend"	Ch. 9
남친 남자 친구 (casual)	Ch. 9
남학생 "male student"	Ch. 19
납작하다 "to be flat"	Ch. 5
낭비 "a waste" (noun)	Ch. 20
낭비(를) 하다 "to waste"	Ch. 20
낮추다 "to make low," "to lower"	Ch. 10
내게 나에게 (casual)	Ch. 1
내려가다 "to go down," "to descend (to somewhere)"	Ch. 9
내용 "content(s)"	Ch. 8
냄비 "a pot"	Ch. 7
냄새(를) 맡다 "to smell (something)"	Ch. 20
넓이 "width," "area"	Ch. 20
네게 너에게 (casual)	Ch. 1
네모나다 "to be square (shaped)"	Ch. 4
녹음(을) 하다 "to record (audio)"	Ch. 3
논쟁 "argument"	Ch. 9
논쟁(을) 하다 "to argue"	Ch. 9
놀리다 "to make fun of," "to mock," "to tease"	Ch. 10
높이 "height"	Ch. 20
높이다 "to make high," "to raise"	Ch. 10
놓이다 "to be put down," "to be let go"	Ch. 15
누구든지 "whoever," "anyone"	Ch. 19
누르다 "to push (a button)," "to press"	Ch. 4
눈(을) 감다 "to close (one's) eyes"	Ch. 16
눈(을) 깜빡이다 "to blink (eyes)"	Ch. 16
눈(을) 뜨다 "to open (one's) eyes"	Ch. 16
눈(이) 감기다 "(one's) eyes close"	Ch. 16
눈(이) 그치다 "to stop snowing"	Ch. 14
눈(이) 내리다 "to snow (down)"	Ch. 14

Glossary

Korean	Meaning	Chapter
눈(이) 떠지다	"(one's) eyes open"	Ch. 16
눈물(을) 흘리다	"to shed tears," "to cry"	Ch. 14
눈썹	"eyebrow"	Ch. 16
눌리다	"to be pressed down," "to be held down"	Ch. 10
느끼다	"to feel," "to sense"	Ch. 5
느낌	"a feeling," "a sensation"	Ch. 5
늘다	"to be increased," "to be improved"	Ch. 8
늘리다	"to make increase/improve," "to increase/improve (something)"	Ch. 10
늦잠(을) 자다	"to sleep late"	Ch. 11

ㄷ

Korean	Meaning	Chapter
다리(가) 부러지다	"to break a leg" (literally, "a leg breaks")	Ch. 7
다리미	"(clothes) iron"	Ch. 3
다리미질(을) 하다	"to iron (clothes)"	Ch. 3
다양하다	"to be various"	Ch. 1
다운(을) 받다	"to download"	Ch. 8
다치다	"to get (physically) hurt"	Ch. 7
다행이다	"to be fortunate," "to be a good thing"	Ch. 8
다행이에요.	"That's fortunate.," "I'm glad."	Ch. 8
다행히	"fortunately" (adverb)	Ch. 8
단점	"a weakness," "a con"	Ch. 18
단체	"group," "organization"	Ch. 5
단추	"(clothes) button"	Ch. 4
닫히다	"to be closed"	Ch. 15
달걀	"(chicken) egg"	Ch. 10
달라지다	"to get/become different"	Ch. 17
달리기	"running"	Ch. 8
달리기(를) 하다	"to do running," "to run"	Ch. 8
닮다	"to resemble," "to look like"	Ch. 13
당겨지다	"to be pulled"	Ch. 15
당분간	"for the time being," "for awhile," "for now"	Ch. 18
당황하다	"to be confused and flustered"	Ch. 5
대	generation counter, "a person who's in their #s," "(one's) #0s"	Ch. 3
대단히	"greatly," "incredibly"	Ch. 6
대단히 감사합니다.	"Thank you very much." (formal)	Ch. 6
대충	"roughly," "approximately" (adverb)	Ch. 4
대학생	"college student," "university student"	Ch. 8
대학원	"graduate school"	Ch. 12
대화	"conversation," "dialogue"	Ch. 2
대화(를) 하다	"to converse," "to hold a conversation"	Ch. 2
더 이상	"anymore," "any longer" (negative)	Ch. 17
덩어리	"a pile," "a lump"	Ch. 15
데	"place," "location"	Ch. 4
데우다	"to heat/warm up (something)"	Ch. 7
도깨비	"goblin"	App. B
(도)대체	"in the world" (adverb)	Ch. 6
도시락	"a box lunch," "a packed lunch"	Ch. 1
도움(이) 되다	"to be helpful"	Ch. 3
돈(을) 쓰다	"to use money"	Ch. 2
돈(이) 많다	"to have a lot of money," "to be rich"	Ch. 2
(돈[이]) 모아지다	"to be saved up (money)"	Ch. 16
동감(을) 하다	"to agree (with someone's feelings)"	Ch. 5
동감입니다.	"I feel the same way (about it)."	Ch. 5
동갑	"same age" (casual)	Ch. 9
동네	"neighborhood"	Ch. 6
동시에	"at the same time" (adverb)	Ch. 17
동의(를) 하다	"to agree (with someone's idea)"	Ch. 3
되게	"terribly," "exceedingly," "very (much)" (casual)	Ch. 17
두근(두근)	(sound of heartbeat)	App. A
두다	"to put down"	Ch. 11

Glossary

두들기다	"to knock (door)," "to beat (drum)"	Ch. 15
두부	"tofu"	Ch. 10
둘	"the two of them/us"	Ch. 3
드르렁	(sound of snoring)	App. A
듣다시피...	"as you hear..."	Ch. 19
들다	"to enter," "to go in"	Ch. 16
들리다	"to be heard"	Ch. 15
디자인	"design"	Ch. 20
딩동	"ding dong" (sound of door bell)	App. A
따다	"to pick (a plant)"	Ch. 16
따르릉	"ring" (sound of telephone, bicycle bell, alarm clock)	App. A
딱딱하다	"to be hard," "to be firm"	Ch. 5
땀	"sweat"	Ch. 15
땀(이) 나다	"to sweat"	Ch. 15
땅콩	"peanut"	Ch. 17
땡	"clang" (sound of hitting metal bell)	App. A
또	"again" (adverb)	Ch. 4
똑(똑)	"knock knock" (sound of knocking)	App. A
뛰어들다	"to jump in(to)"	Ch. 9

ㄹ

라면	"ramen (soup and noodles)"	Ch. 5

ㅁ

마다	"each" (particle)	Ch. 9
마무리(를) 하다	"to finish (up)," "to complete (something)"	Ch. 12
마을	"village," "town"	Ch. 4
마음	"(one's) mind," "(one's) heart," "(one's) feelings"	Ch. 5
마음(을) 바꾸다	"to change (one's) mind"	Ch. 15
마음(이) 바뀌다	"(one's) mind changes"	Ch. 15
마음(이) 아프다	"to be hurting (emotionally)," "to feel sad"	Ch. 5
마음(이) 편하다	"to feel at ease (emotionally)"	Ch. 5
마카롱	"macaron"	Ch. 8
막다	"to block," "to obstruct"	Ch. 15
막히다	"to be blocked," "to be obstructed"	Ch. 15
만족	"satisfaction"	Ch. 18
만족스럽다	"to be satisfying"	Ch. 18
만족하다	"to be satisfied"	Ch. 18
만지다	"to touch"	Ch. 4
말	"end"	Ch. 16
말랑말랑	(feeling of something soft and weak)	App. A
말하다시피...	"as you say..."	Ch. 19
망치	"hammer"	Ch. 7
망하다	"to be destroyed," "to be messed up," "to completely fail," "to go bankrupt" (casual)	Ch. 1
맞은편	"the opposite side," "the other side (of something)"	Ch. 9
맞혀 보다	"to try to guess"	Ch. 7
맞히다	"to guess (correctly)"	Ch. 7
매다	"to wear (seatbelt, backpack)"	Ch. 2
매번	"every time"	Ch. 9
매애	"bah" (sound of sheep)	App. A
매우	"very," "greatly"	Ch. 17
맨	"the most," "the very"	Ch. 7
맨발	"barefoot"	Ch. 7
맨손	"bare hands"	Ch. 7
머리(를) 감다	"to wash (one's) hair"	Ch. 12
먹이	"(animal) food," "feed"	Ch. 15
먹이다	"to make (someone) eat," "to feed"	Ch. 10
먹히다	"to be eaten"	Ch. 15
멀쩡하다	"to have no problems," "to be/feel fine"	Ch. 8
멈춰 서다	"to come to a halt"	Ch. 12
멍(멍)	"woof" (sound of dog)	App. A
면접	"interview"	Ch. 9
멸망(을) 하다	"to collapse," "to be destroyed," "to end (the world, etc.)"	Ch. 1
명령	"a command"	Ch. 2
명령(을) 하다	"to command"	Ch. 2
명함	"business card"	Ch. 9

Glossary

모두 "everyone"		Ch. 7
모습 "figure," "image"		Ch. 18
모임 "meeting"		Ch. 2
목도리 "scarf"		Ch. 2
목욕탕 "bath house"		Ch. 10
몸 조리 잘하세요. "Take care of yourself.," "Get well soon."		Ch. 15
몸무게 "body weight," "weight (of someone)"		Ch. 14
몹시 "terribly," "exceedingly," "very (much)"		Ch. 17
무게 "weight (of something)"		Ch. 14
무너뜨리다 "to destroy," "to demolish," "to tear down"		App. B
무늬 "pattern (on something)," "design (on something)"		Ch. 20
무서워하다 "to feel scared"		Ch. 5
무시(를) 하다 "to ignore," "to look down on (someone)"		Ch. 3
묶이다 "to be tied"		Ch. 15
문화 차이 "culture difference"		Ch. 4
문화 충격 "culture shock"		Ch. 4
문화 충격(을) 받다 "to experience culture shock"		Ch. 4
문화적 "cultural"		Ch. 12
물건 "an item," "stuff"		Ch. 6
뭐든지 "whatever," "anything" (or 무엇이든지)		Ch. 19
미신 "superstition"		Ch. 3
미안. "Sorry.," "Oops." (casual)		Ch. 1
미역 "(edible) seaweed"		Ch. 5
미치다 "to be crazy/insane," "to go crazy/insane"		Ch. 5
민감하다 "to be touchy," "to be sensitive (emotionally)"		Ch. 5
민속촌 "folk village"		Ch. 8
밀리다 "to be pushed"		Ch. 15
밉다 "to be detestable," "to be hated"		Ch. 5

ㅂ

바꾸다 "to change (something)"		Ch. 15
바뀌다 "to be changed"		Ch. 15
바라다 "to hope"		Ch. 11
바로 "right away" (adverb)		Ch. 14
박 "gourd"		App. B
박수 "applause"		Ch. 9
박수(를) 하다 "to applaud"		Ch. 9
반드시 "certainly," "surely," "no matter what" (adverb)		Ch. 20
발견 "discovery"		Ch. 13
발견(을) 하다 "to discover"		Ch. 13
발톱 "toenail"		Ch. 13
발표 "a presentation"		Ch. 3
발표(를) 하다 "to present"		Ch. 3
밤 늦게 "late at night"		Ch. 4
밤(을) 새다 "to stay up all night"		Ch. 18
밥주걱 "rice scoop"		App. B
배 fold counter		Ch. 7
배달 "delivery"		Ch. 15
배달(을) 하다 "to deliver"		Ch. 15
배달(이) 되다 "to be delivered"		Ch. 15
백화점 "department store"		Ch. 6
버튼 "(mechanical) button"		Ch. 4
번 item number counter		Ch. 6
번개 "lightning"		Ch. 2
변하다 "to change," "to transform"		Ch. 17
변화 "change," "transformation" (noun)		Ch. 17
보글(보글) (sound of boiling)		App. A
보너스 "bonus"		Ch. 12
보다시피... "as you see..."		Ch. 19
보석 "jewel," "gem"		App. B
보이다 "to be seen," "to appear"		Ch. 13
본토 "(the) mainland"		Ch. 16
봉사 "service (to others)"		Ch. 8
봉사(를) 하다 "to do service (to others)"		Ch. 8
봉지 bag (of something) counter		Ch. 9
부끄러워하다 "to feel embarrassed"		Ch. 5
부담 "burden"		Ch. 15
부담(이) 되다 "to be a burden"		Ch. 15
부드럽다 "to be soft," "to be smooth"		Ch. 5
부딪(치)다 "to bump into/against"		Ch. 15

Glossary

Korean	Meaning	Ch.
부딪치이다	"to be bumped into/against"	Ch. 15
부러뜨리다	"to break (bone)," "to fracture," "to snap"	App. B
부러워하다	"to feel jealous"	Ch. 5
부모	"parents"	Ch. 9
부부	"married couple," "husband and wife"	Ch. 13
부인	"(another person's) wife" (hon.)	Ch. 9
부자	"a wealthy person"	Ch. 2
부지런하다	"to be diligent," "to be hard working"	Ch. 4
부츠	"boots"	Ch. 20
부탁	"request," "favor"	Ch. 2
부탁(을) 드리다	"to request" (hon.)	Ch. 2
부탁(을) 하다	"to request"	Ch. 2
분리(가) 되다	"to be separated"	Ch. 16
분리(를) 하다	"to separate"	Ch. 16
분위기	"atmosphere," "an image"	Ch. 13
불(이) 나다	"to have a fire"	Ch. 15
불평	"complaint"	Ch. 2
불평(을) 하다	"to complain"	Ch. 2
불행하게도	"unfortunately" (adverb)	Ch. 8
비(가) 그치다	"to stop raining"	Ch. 14
비(가) 내리다	"to rain (down)"	Ch. 14
비교	"a comparison"	Ch. 20
비교(를) 하다	"to compare," "to make a comparison"	Ch. 20
비우다	"to make empty," "to make blank," "to empty"	Ch. 10
비율	"proportion," "ratio"	Ch. 19
비키다	"to move out of the way"	Ch. 10
비타민	"vitamin"	Ch. 8
비타민(을) 먹다	"to take vitamins"	Ch. 8
빈대떡	"mung bean pancake"	Ch. 4
빗기다	"to make (someone) brush," "to make (someone) comb"	Ch. 10
빗다	"to brush," "to comb"	Ch. 10
빚	"debt"	Ch. 2
빤짝(빤짝)	"twinkle" (sound of something sparkling, glittering, twinkling)	App. A
빵(빵)	"beep (beep)" (sound of car honking, gun)	App. A
뺨(을) 맞다	"to be hit/slapped in the face"	App. B
뽀뽀(를) 하다	"to kiss" (children's word)	Ch. 14
뽑다	"to pick out (something)," "to choose (someone)"	Ch. 4
뿌리다	"to sprinkle," "to spray"	Ch. 17
삐약(삐약)	"cheep" (sound of chick)	App. A

ㅅ

사고(가) 나다	"to have an accident"	Ch. 15
사귀다	"to date," "to go out with," "to associate with"	Ch. 9
사기	"scam"	Ch. 13
사기꾼	"a scammer"	Ch. 13
사랑(을) 받다	"to be loved"	Ch. 15
사이	"space," "gap," "relationship"	Ch. 20
사이(가) 좋다	"to have a good relationship," "to be on good terms"	Ch. 20
사이에	"between (things)"	Ch. 20
사이에서	"among (people)"	Ch. 20
사장	"a boss"	Ch. 5
사춘기(가) 되다	"to enter puberty"	Ch. 9
사회적	"social"	Ch. 12
살(을) 빼다	"to lose weight"	Ch. 8
살(이) 빠지다	"weight is lost"	Ch. 15
살(이) 찌다	"weight is gained"	Ch. 15
30 대	"a person who's in their 30s," "(one's) 30s"	Ch. 3
상	"prize," "reward"	Ch. 4
상관없이	"regardless" (adverb)	Ch. 20
상상(을) 하다	"to imagine"	Ch. 3
상상력(이) 좋다	"to have a good imagination (ability)"	Ch. 9
상처	"wound," "injury"	Ch. 5
상처(를) 주다	"to hurt someone's feelings"	Ch. 5
상큼하다	"to be refreshing"	Ch. 1
상태	"state," "condition," "situation"	Ch. 16
상품	"a product," "merchandise"	Ch. 6
상황	"a situation"	Ch. 9

Glossary

새 "new" (adjective)	Ch. 3
새 집 "new house"	Ch. 3
새 차 "new car"	Ch. 3
새로 "new(ly)," "anew" (adverb)	Ch. 7
새집 "bird house"	Ch. 3
새해 "new year"	Ch. 3
새해 복 많이 받으세요. "Happy New Year."	Ch. 3
생각(이) 나다 "to come to mind," "to think (of something from the past)"	Ch. 3
생각보다... "... than (one) thought/thinks"	Ch. 17
생강 "ginger"	Ch. 2
생기다 "to come up," "to arise," "to happen"	Ch. 9
생신 "birthday" (hon.)	Ch. 10
서랍 "drawer"	Ch. 7
서로 "each other" (adverb)	Ch. 3
서류 "document," "paper(s)"	Ch. 15
서명 "signature"	Ch. 9
서투르다 "to be unskilled," "to be poor at"	Ch. 16
선 "a line (in geometry)," "a wire"	Ch. 6
선배 "(one's) senior"	Ch. 9
설명 "instruction"	Ch. 2
설명(을) 하다 "to explain"	Ch. 2
설명서 "(instruction) manual"	Ch. 2
섭씨 "Celsius"	Ch. 1
성 "last name"	Ch. 7
성형 수술 "plastic surgery"	Ch. 15
세금 "tax"	Ch. 8
세일 "sale"	Ch. 7
세탁 "dry cleaning"	Ch. 3
세탁(을) 하다 "to dry clean"	Ch. 3
세탁소 "the (dry) cleaner's"	Ch. 3
세트 "a set (of things)"	Ch. 20
셀카 "selfie" (slang)	Ch. 7
셋 "the three of them/us"	Ch. 3
소개(를) 시키다 "to introduce (someone else)"	Ch. 9
소리(가) 나다 "a sound is made," "a noise is made"	Ch. 15
소리(를) 내다 "to make a sound," "to make a noise"	Ch. 15
소리(를) 지르다 "to scream," "to cry out"	Ch. 2
소방관 "firefighter"	Ch. 12
소방서 "fire station"	Ch. 12
소식 "news"	Ch. 8
소원 "a desire," "a wish"	Ch. 11
속눈썹 "eyelash"	Ch. 16
속다 "to be tricked," "to be deceived"	Ch. 15
속도 "speed"	Ch. 13
속삭이다 "to whisper"	Ch. 2
속상하다 "to be upset"	Ch. 5
속이다 "to trick (someone)," "to deceive (someone)"	Ch. 15
손목 "wrist"	Ch. 13
손잡이 "handle"	Ch. 7
손톱 "fingernail"	Ch. 13
솔직하다 "to be honest," "to be frank"	Ch. 3
솔직히 "honestly," "frankly"	Ch. 3
솔직히 말하면... "To be honest...," "To be frank..."	Ch. 3
쇠 "metal"	Ch. 15
수고(를) 하다 "to work hard," "to put effort into a job"	Ch. 2
수고하세요! "Keep up the good work!," "Goodbye (to a worker)"	Ch. 2
수고하셨어요! "You did good work!"	Ch. 2
수능(시험) "college entrance exam"	Ch. 1
수상하다 "to be suspicious" (descriptive verb)	Ch. 13
수선 "mending," "repair"	Ch. 20
수선(을) 하다 "to mend," "to repair"	Ch. 20
수술 "surgery," "operation"	Ch. 15
수염 "beard," "mustache"	Ch. 11
수준 "level," "standard"	Ch. 18
숙소 "residence," "lodging"	Ch. 6
순서 "order," "sequence"	Ch. 16
순종(을) 하다 "to obey," "to be obedient"	Ch. 2
숨 "a breath"	Ch. 8
숨(을) 쉬다 "to breathe"	Ch. 8

Glossary

Korean	Meaning	Ch.
숨기다	"to make (something) hidden," "to hide (something)"	Ch. 10
숨다	"to be hidden"	Ch. 10
스님	"monk"	Ch. 9
스키	"ski(s)," "skiing"	Ch. 17
스키(를) 타다	"to ski"	Ch. 17
스트레스(를) 받다	"to get stress"	Ch. 1
스포츠카	"sports car"	Ch. 4
시내	"downtown"	Ch. 17
시민	"citizen"	Ch. 8
시작(이) 되다	"to be started"	Ch. 15
시차	"time difference"	Ch. 16
시키다	"to order (food)"	Ch. 10
식탁	"(kitchen) table"	Ch. 7
신선하다	"to be fresh"	Ch. 1
신청	"application," "petition"	Ch. 2
신청(을) 하다	"to apply for," "to petition for"	Ch. 2
신호등	"traffic light"	Ch. 12
신혼여행	"honeymoon"	Ch. 16
신혼여행(을) 가다	"to go on a honeymoon"	Ch. 16
실력	"skill," "ability"	Ch. 8
실력(이) 늘다	"to get better (at something)," "a skill/ability improves"	Ch. 8
실망	"disappointment"	Ch. 18
실망스럽다	"to be disappointing"	Ch. 18
실망하다	"to be disappointed"	Ch. 18
실수(를) 하다	"to make a mistake"	Ch. 1
심각하다	"to be serious"	Ch. 18
심지어	"even (still)" (adverb)	Ch. 19
10 대	"teenager," "the teenage years"	Ch. 3
쌓다	"to stack," "to pile (up)"	Ch. 15
쌓이다	"to be stacked," "to be piled (up)"	Ch. 15
쑥스럽다	"to be bashful"	Ch. 5
쓰레기통	"trashcan"	Ch. 10
쓰이다	"to be used," "to be written"	Ch. 15
씨(앗)	"seed(s)"	Ch. 1
씻어가다	"to wash and take (somewhere)"	Ch. 9
씻어오다	"to wash and bring (here)"	Ch. 9

ㅇ

Korean	Meaning	Ch.
아, 참!	"Ah!"	Ch. 16
아기(를) 낳다	"to have a baby"	Ch. 9
아껴 먹다	"to eat without wasting," "to not waste (food)"	Ch. 20
아껴 쓰다	"to spend (money) wisely," "to use wisely"	Ch. 20
아끼다	"to cherish," "to save (by not using)"	Ch. 20
아무래도...	"Anyway...," "Either way..."	Ch. 19
아예	"at all," "absolutely," "completely" (negative)	Ch. 20
아침 일찍	"early in the morning"	Ch. 4
악수	"handshake"	Ch. 9
악수(를) 하다	"to shake hands"	Ch. 9
안	"within/in (time)"	Ch. 5
안마	"massage"	Ch. 18
안마(를) 받다	"to get a massage"	Ch. 18
안마(를) 하다	"to massage," "to give a massage"	Ch. 18
안부(를) 전하다	"to give (one's) regards"	Ch. 2
안아주다	"to hug"	Ch. 14
안전벨트	"seatbelt"	Ch. 2
앉히다	"to make (someone) sit," "to seat"	Ch. 10
알게 되다	"to find (out)"	Ch. 15
알다시피...	"as you know..."	Ch. 19
알려지다	"to be (made) known," "to be understood"	Ch. 15
알리다	"to make known," "to inform"	Ch. 10
알아듣다	"to understand (by hearing)"	Ch. 3
알아채다	"to recognize," "to notice"	Ch. 17
앞으로	"from now on," "in the future"	Ch. 17
앵무새	"parrot"	Ch. 7
야근	"(overtime) night work"	Ch. 12
야시장	"(outdoor) night market"	Ch. 16
야식	"late-night snack"	Ch. 7
야옹	"meow" (sound of cat)	App. A
양	"quantity"	Ch. 20
(양)초	"candle"	Ch. 16

Glossary

얕다	"to be shallow"	Ch. 13
얘	"this guy/girl"	Ch. 3
어?	"Huh?," "Oh?"	Ch. 4
어느 날	"one day" (literally, "a certain day")	App. B
어디든지	"wherever," "anywhere"	Ch. 19
어떡하다	"to do what/how"	Ch. 10
어쩐지	"for some reason," "somehow"	Ch. 20
어쩔 수 없어요.	"It can't be helped."	Ch. 11
어쩔 수(가) 없다	"to be inevitable," "to be nothing one can do about something"	Ch. 11
어차피	"anyway," "in any case," "one way or the other" (adverb)	Ch. 19
어흥	"roar" (sound of tiger)	App. A
억지로	"by force," "forcefully" (adverb)	Ch. 10
언제든지	"whenever," "anytime"	Ch. 19
없애다	"to make not exist," "to get rid of"	Ch. 10
없어지다	"to disappear"	Ch. 15
엉(엉)	"boo hoo" (sound of crying)	App. A
에스컬레이터	"escalator"	Ch. 7
에이….	"Come on…."	Ch. 4
에취	"achoo" (sound of sneezing)	App. A
엘리베이터	"elevator"	Ch. 7
여러	"a number of," "many" (adjective)	Ch. 8
여러 가지	"a number of types," "many types," "various types"	Ch. 8
여러 번	"a number of times," "many times," "repeatedly"	Ch. 8
여러 사람	"a number of people," "many people"	Ch. 8
여분(의)	"extra," "surplus" (adjective)	Ch. 7
여성	"female"	Ch. 18
여성스럽다	"to be feminine"	Ch. 18
여자 친구(가) 생기다	"to get a girlfriend"	Ch. 11
여자 친구(를) 사귀다	"to date a girlfriend"	Ch. 9
여친	여자 친구 (casual)	Ch. 9
여학생	"female student"	Ch. 19
여행객	"traveler," "tourist"	Ch. 16
역사적	"historic"	Ch. 12
연결	"connection"	Ch. 16
연결(이) 되다	"to be connected"	Ch. 16
연구	"research"	Ch. 15
연구(가) 되다	"to be researched"	Ch. 15
연구(를) 하다	"to research"	Ch. 15
연기	"act," "acting"	Ch. 14
연기(를) 하다	"to act"	Ch. 14
연락처	"contact information"	Ch. 17
연봉	"(yearly) salary," "(yearly) pay"	Ch. 9
열리다	"to be opened"	Ch. 15
염소	"goat"	Ch. 11
염소 수염	"goatee" (literally, "goat beard")	Ch. 11
예민하다	"to be sensitive (physically/emotionally)"	Ch. 5
예방	"prevention"	Ch. 8
예방(을) 하다	"to prevent"	Ch. 8
예뻐하다	"to favor and like"	Ch. 5
예상	"expectation," "prediction"	Ch. 18
예상(을) 하다	"to expect," "to predict"	Ch. 18
예약	"reservation"	Ch. 8
예약(을) 하다	"to reserve," "to make a reservation"	Ch. 8
예정	"schedule"	Ch. 12
오디션	"audition"	Ch. 8
오래되다	"to be old (an object)"	Ch. 1
오븐	"oven"	Ch. 8
오이	"cucumber"	Ch. 17
오토바이	"motorcycle"	Ch. 12
오픈	"open(ing)"	Ch. 16
오히려	"on the contrary" (adverb)	Ch. 19
온도	"temperature (of a thing)"	Ch. 13
온돌	"heated floor"	Ch. 8
올리다	"to put up," "to upload"	Ch. 8
옷걸이	"(clothes) hanger"	Ch. 7
(옷[을]) 빨다	"to wash (clothes)"	Ch. 12
옷장	"closet"	Ch. 7

Glossary

와.	"Wow.," "Nice."	Ch. 12
완료(가) 되다	"to be completed"	Ch. 15
완료(를) 하다	"to complete"	Ch. 15
완전하다	"to be complete," "to be perfect"	Ch. 6
완전히	"completely"	Ch. 6
왕복	"round trip"	Ch. 14
왜냐(하)면...	"If you ask why...," "Because..."	Ch. 19
왠지	"for some reason," "somehow"	Ch. 1
외국 사람	"foreigner"	Ch. 8
외로워하다	"to feel lonely"	Ch. 5
외롭다	"to be lonely"	Ch. 5
외치다	"to shout," "to yell"	Ch. 2
요금	"a fee," "a charge"	Ch. 8
욕심	"greed"	Ch. 4
욕심(이) 많다	"to be greedy"	Ch. 4
욕심쟁이	"greedy person"	Ch. 4
욕조	"bathtub"	Ch. 10
용기	"courage"	Ch. 15
용기(를) 내다	"to be courageous," "to show (one's) courage"	Ch. 15
용돈	"allowance," "pocket change"	Ch. 4
용서	"forgiveness"	Ch. 9
용서(를) 하다	"to forgive"	Ch. 9
우르릉	(sound of thunder)	App. A
우선	"First of all..."	Ch. 12
우연	"coincidence"	Ch. 17
우연히	"by coincidence," "by chance" (adverb)	Ch. 17
우와.	"Wow."	Ch. 19
우회전(을) 하다	"to turn to the right (when driving)"	Ch. 12
운	"luck"	Ch. 3
운(이) 안 좋다	"to be unlucky"	Ch. 3
운(이) 좋다	"to be lucky"	Ch. 3
울려지다	"to be made to cry"	Ch. 15
울리다	"to make (someone) cry"	Ch. 10
웃기다	"to make (someone) laugh"	Ch. 10
월급	"(monthly) salary," "(monthly) pay"	Ch. 9
위치	"location"	Ch. 20
유감입니다.	"I'm sorry (to hear that)."	Ch. 9
유일하게	"only" (adverb)	Ch. 1
유일하다	"to be the only one"	Ch. 1
유일한	"only" (adjective)	Ch. 1
유치원	"preschool," "kindergarten"	Ch. 19
은퇴(를) 하다	"to retire (from working)"	Ch. 12
음매	"moo" (sound of cow)	App. A
음식점	"restaurant"	Ch. 17
응급실	"emergency room"	Ch. 10
의사 선생님	"doctor" (formal)	Ch. 9
의외로	"unexpectedly" (adverb)	Ch. 4
이럴 때	"(at) times like these"	Ch. 19
이사	"a move (to another residence)"	Ch. 12
이상	"more than"	Ch. 19
이쑤시개	"toothpick"	Ch. 7
20 대	"a person who's in their 20s," "(one's) 20s"	Ch. 3
이용하다	"to use (someone)," "to exploit"	Ch. 10
이하	"less than"	Ch. 19
이해(가) 되다	"to be understood"	Ch. 15
익숙하다	"to be used to" (descriptive verb)	Ch. 15
익숙해지다	"to become/get used to" (action verb)	Ch. 15
인내심	"patience"	Ch. 15
인내심(이) 많다	"to be (very) patient"	Ch. 15
인류	"human race"	Ch. 19
인식(을) 하다	"to realize," "to recognize"	Ch. 8
인증(을) 하다	"to authorize," "to confirm"	Ch. 1
인터넷	"internet"	Ch. 8
인터뷰	"interview"	Ch. 16
일(을) 다니다	"to go to work," "to commute to work"	Ch. 9
읽히다	"to be read"	Ch. 15
잃다	"to lose (something)"	Ch. 5
임신(을) 하다	"to get pregnant"	Ch. 9
입구	"entrance"	Ch. 9

Glossary

입히다	"to make (someone) wear," "to put (clothes) on (someone)," "to dress"	Ch. 10
잎	"leaf (on a tree)"	Ch. 10

ㅈ

자....	"Well... (shall we?)," "Here/there (you go)...."	Ch. 4
자기	"yourself," "oneself"	Ch. 4
자꾸	"repeatedly" (adverb)	Ch. 10
자동적	"automatic"	Ch. 12
자랑	"pride," "bragging," "boasting"	Ch. 18
자랑스럽다	"to be proud," "to be boastful"	Ch. 18
자발적	"voluntary"	Ch. 12
자세하다	"to be detailed"	Ch. 18
자판기	"vending machine"	Ch. 7
잘 자(요).	"Good night." (casual)	Ch. 2
잘리다	"to be cut (off)," "to be severed"	Ch. 15
잘못	"an error," "a mistake"	Ch. 13
잘못	"incorrectly," "wrong(ly)" (adverb)	Ch. 13
잘못(을) 하다	"to do something wrong," "to make a misake"	Ch. 13
잠(이) 오다	"to feel tired," "to feel like (one) wants to sleep" (literally, "sleep comes")	Ch. 2
잠그다	"to lock"	Ch. 15
잠기다	"to be locked"	Ch. 15
잠옷	"sleep wear," "night clothes" (literally, "sleep clothes")	Ch. 17
잠자리	"dragonfly"	Ch. 7
잡지	"magazine"	Ch. 13
잡히다	"to be grabbed," "to be caught"	Ch. 15
장님	"a blind person"	Ch. 9
장마	"rainy season"	Ch. 13
장면	"(movie) scene"	Ch. 6
장식	"decoration," "ornament"	Ch. 13
장점	"an advantage," "a pro"	Ch. 18
재다	"to weigh"	Ch. 14
재우다	"to make (someone) sleep," "to put to sleep"	Ch. 10
쟤	"that guy/girl"	Ch. 3
저렇다	"to be so"	Ch. 5
적다	"to write down," "to note," "to jot down"	Ch. 2
적다	"to be few (in number)"	Ch. 19
적당하다	"to be adequate (for something)," "to be suitable"	Ch. 20
적응(을) 하다	"to adapt to," "to adjust to"	Ch. 16
적응(이) 되다	"to be adapted to," "to be adjusted to"	Ch. 16
전 남자 친구	"ex-boyfriend"	Ch. 9
전 여자 친구	"ex-girlfriend"	Ch. 9
전기	"electricity"	Ch. 7
전문가	"expert"	Ch. 1
전부	"whole (thing)," "entire (thing)," "all"	Ch. 15
전자레인지	"microwave"	Ch. 7
전자레인지에 데우다	"to microwave (something)"	Ch. 7
전쟁	"war"	Ch. 15
전쟁(이) 나다	"to have a war"	Ch. 15
전통	"tradition"	Ch. 12
전통적	"traditional"	Ch. 12
전하다	"to tell," "to let (someone) know"	Ch. 2
접수(가) 되다	"to be received (and accepted)"	Ch. 15
접수(를) 하다	"to receive (and accept)"	Ch. 15
정거장	"(train/bus) stop," "(train/bus) station"	Ch. 6
정류장	"(bus) stop," "(bus) station"	Ch. 6
정신(이) 없다	"to be out of it," "to be extremely busy"	Ch. 5
정하다	"to set (something)"	Ch. 15
정해지다	"to be set"	Ch. 15
정확하다	"to be precise"	Ch. 18
젖다	"to be wet"	Ch. 10
젖히다	"to make wet," "to wet"	Ch. 10

411

Glossary

Korean	Meaning	Ch.
제가 실수하면 고쳐 주세요.	"If I make a mistake, please correct me."	Ch. 9
제게	저에게	Ch. 1
제대로	"properly," "correctly," "right" (adverb)	Ch. 4
제목	"title (of something)," "name (of something)"	Ch. 17
제비	"swallow (bird)"	App. B
제안	"offer," "proposal," "suggestion"	Ch. 20
제출(을) 하다	"to submit," "to turn in"	Ch. 15
제출(이) 되다	"to be submitted," "to be turned in"	Ch. 15
제품	"(manufactured) good," "(manufactured) product"	Ch. 15
조건	"qualification," "a condition (for something)"	Ch. 11
조금 전에	"a short time ago," "a little while ago"	Ch. 17
조금씩	"little by little," "gradually" (adverb)	Ch. 18
조심스럽다	"to be cautious" (adjective)	Ch. 18
조심하다	"to be careful" (descriptive verb)	Ch. 10
조심히	"carefully"	Ch. 10
조심히 하다	"to be cautious," "to be careful" (action verb)	Ch. 18
조언	"advice," "counsel"	Ch. 12
존경(을) 받다	"to be respected," "to be looked up to"	Ch. 15
종교	"religion"	Ch. 19
좌회전(을) 하다	"to turn to the left (while driving)"	Ch. 12
죄책감	"(feeling of) guilt"	Ch. 15
죄책감(을) 느끼다	"to feel guilt(y)"	Ch. 15
주룩(주룩)	(sound of rain)	App. A
주름(이) 생기다	"to get wrinkles"	Ch. 9
주문(이) 되다	"to be ordered"	Ch. 15
주어지다	"to be given"	Ch. 15
죽이다	"to make (someone) die," "to kill"	Ch. 10
준비	"preparations"	Ch. 10
준비(가) 되다	"to be prepared"	Ch. 11
줄	"a line (for waiting)"	Ch. 6
줄(을) 서다	"to make a (standing) line," "to stand in line"	Ch. 6
줄거리	"plot," "story"	Ch. 20
줄이다	"to make decrease/get worse," "to decreasen/worsen (something)"	Ch. 10
중급	"intermediate (level)"	Ch. 9
중독	"addiction"	Ch. 16
중독(이) 되다	"to be addicted"	Ch. 16
중독성(이) 있다	"to be addicting"	Ch. 16
중순	"middle (of a month)"	Ch. 16
중학생	"middle school student"	Ch. 8
즐거워하다	"to feel cheerful," "to feel merry"	Ch. 5
즐겁다	"to be cheerful," "to be merry"	Ch. 5
증거	"proof," "evidence"	Ch. 1
증명(을) 하다	"to prove"	Ch. 1
지글(지글)	(sound of something sizzling)	App. A
지내다	"to live," "to associate with"	Ch. 3
지도서	"guide book"	Ch. 2
지리적	"geographical"	Ch. 12
지어지다	"to be built"	Ch. 15
지옥	"hell"	Ch. 19
지우다	"to erase"	Ch. 15
지워지다	"to be erased"	Ch. 15
지진	"earthquake"	Ch. 2
직장	"(one's) place of work"	Ch. 14
직진(을) 하다	"to drive straight (forward)"	Ch. 12
진심	"sincerity"	Ch. 5
진작	"before(hand)" (adverb)	Ch. 14
질(이) 안 좋다	"to be bad quality"	Ch. 17
질(이) 좋다	"to be good quality"	Ch. 17
질리다	"to get sick (of something)," "to be tired (of something)"	Ch. 5
집다	"to pick up"	Ch. 2

Glossary

Korean	Definition	Chapter
집어가다	"to pick up and take (somewhere)"	Ch. 9
집어오다	"to pick up and bring (here)"	Ch. 9
집중(을) 하다	"to focus"	Ch. 3
짓다	"to build"	Ch. 15
짖다	"to bark"	Ch. 2
짜리	"worth (of)," "amount (of)"	Ch. 16
짜증(을) 내다	"to get annoyed (at someone/something)"	Ch. 15
짜증(이) 나다	"to be annoyed (by someone/something)"	Ch. 15
짝(짝)	(sound of clapping)	App. A
짹(짹)	"tweet" (bird sound)	App. A
쪽	(sound of kissing)	App. A
쫓아내다	"to kick someone out," "to throw someone out"	App. B
쭉 가다	"to go straight"	Ch. 12
찍(찍)	"squeak" (sound of mouse)	App. A
찍히다	"to be chopped," "to be hacked (up)," "to be taken (a photo)"	Ch. 15
찜질방	"sauna"	Ch. 10
찢기다	"to be torn," "to be ripped (up)"	Ch. 15
찢다	"to tear," "to rip (up)"	Ch. 15

ㅊ

Korean	Definition	Chapter
차라리	"rather" (adverb)	Ch. 19
차례	"a turn"	Ch. 4
차이다	"to be kicked"	Ch. 15
참석(을) 하다	"to attend"	Ch. 8
찾아가다	"to go visit"	Ch. 9
찾아오다	"to come visit"	Ch. 9
척(을) 하다	"to pretend (to/like)," "to act (like)"	Ch. 16
천국	"heaven"	Ch. 19
천둥	"thunder"	Ch. 2
청첩장	"wedding invitation"	Ch. 9
청하다	"to ask for," "to request (something)"	App. B
쳐다보이다	"to be stared at"	Ch. 15
초	"beginning"	Ch. 16
초급	"beginner (level)"	Ch. 9
초대	"an invitation"	Ch. 9
초대장	"(written) invitation"	Ch. 9
초등학생	"elementary student"	Ch. 8
초보자	"beginner"	Ch. 1
초콜릿	"chocolate"	Ch. 1
최대한	"as (much as) possible," "maximum" (adverb)	Ch. 18
최소한	"as (little as) possible," "minimum" (adverb)	Ch. 18
추가(가) 되다	"to be added (to something)"	Ch. 15
추억	"a memory (of something)"	Ch. 9
출구	"exit"	Ch. 9
출근	"leaving to work"	Ch. 5
출근(을) 하다	"to leave to work"	Ch. 5
출입구	"entrance and exit"	Ch. 9
출장	"company trip"	Ch. 12
충격	"a shock," "an impact"	Ch. 4
충격(을) 받다	"to experience shock"	Ch. 4
충격적이다	"to be shocking"	Ch. 12
충전(을) 하다	"to charge (electronics)"	Ch. 7
취소(가) 되다	"to be cancelled"	Ch. 15
취소(를) 하다	"to cancel"	Ch. 15
취업	"getting/finding a job"	Ch. 11
취직(을) 하다	"to get a job"	Ch. 11
치실	"floss"	Ch. 7
치실질(을) 하다	"to floss"	Ch. 7
치우다	"to clean up," "to tidy up," "to clear (away)"	Ch. 10
치이다	"to be hit"	Ch. 15
치킨집	"chicken restaurant"	Ch. 18
친구(를) 사귀다	"to make friends"	Ch. 9
친척	"a relative," "relatives"	Ch. 9
친하게 지내다	"to have a close relationship (with someone)"	Ch. 3
친하다	"to be close (as friends)"	Ch. 3
침낭	"sleeping bag"	Ch. 12

ㅋ

Korean	Definition	Chapter
카드	"card"	Ch. 1
커플티	"couple t-shirt"	Ch. 14
커지다	"to be turned on"	Ch. 15

Glossary

코(를) 골다	"to snore"	Ch. 16
코끼리	"elephant"	Ch. 7
콜록(콜록)	(sound of coughing)	App. A
콩	"bean"	Ch. 17
쾅	"slam," "thud" (sound of door slamming, loud falling, hitting against something)	App. A
쿠폰	"coupon"	Ch. 16
쿨(쿨)	"sniff" (sound of sleeping)	App. A
쿵	"thud" (sound of falling)	App. A
크기	"size"	Ch. 20
큰 일(이) 나다	"to be a big problem"	Ch. 15
킁킁	"sniff" (sound of smelling)	App. A
키스(를) 하다	"to kiss"	Ch. 14

ㅌ

타다	"(something) burns"	Ch. 8
탑	"tower"	Ch. 16
탓	"(one's) fault"	Ch. 4
탓(을) 하다	"to blame"	Ch. 4
태우다	"to burn (something)"	Ch. 8
태풍	"typhoon"	Ch. 2
터지다	"to burst," "to pop"	Ch. 1
텅(텅)	(sound of something hollow)	App. A
텐트	"tent"	Ch. 12
토론	"discussion"	Ch. 9
토론(을) 하다	"to discuss"	Ch. 9
토(를) 하다	"to vomit," "to throw up"	Ch. 14
톡(톡)	(sound of tapping)	App. A
퇴근	"leaving from work"	Ch. 5
퇴근(을) 하다	"to leave from work"	Ch. 5
퇴직(을) 하다	"to resign (from a job)," "to retire (from work, from a task)"	Ch. 12
트럭	"truck"	Ch. 12

ㅍ

파일	"(computer) file"	Ch. 8
파자마	"pajamas"	Ch. 17
팔리다	"to be sold"	Ch. 15
패키지	"package"	Ch. 16
펑	"boom" (sound of explosion, loud pop)	App. A
펴다	"to open up (something)," "to unfold"	Ch. 11
펴지다	"to be opened up," "to be unfolded"	Ch. 15
편	"a side"	Ch. 9
편도	"one-way trip"	Ch. 14
편리하다	"to be convenient"	Ch. 5
평가	"review"	Ch. 20
평가(를) 받다	"to be reviewed," "to get a review"	Ch. 20
평가(를) 하다	"to review"	Ch. 20
평균	"average," "mean"	Ch. 19
평범하다	"to be plain," "to be ordinary"	Ch. 4
평소(에)	"normally," "usual(ly)"	Ch. 13
평화	"peace"	Ch. 9
포기(를) 하다	"to give up"	Ch. 12
폭발	"explosion"	Ch. 1
폭발(을) 하다	"to explode"	Ch. 1
표정	"(facial) expression"	Ch. 18
표현	"a (spoken) expression"	Ch. 2
표현(을) 하다	"to express"	Ch. 2
풀리다	"to be untied," "to be solved"	Ch. 15
품질	"quality (of an item)"	Ch. 20
풍덩	"splash" (sound of falling in water)	App. A
풍선	"balloon"	Ch. 7
프라이팬	"(frying) pan"	Ch. 7
피다	"to blossom (flowers)"	Ch. 8
필요	"a necessity," "a need"	Ch. 11
핑계	"an excuse"	Ch. 2
핑계(를) 대다	"to make an excuse"	Ch. 2

ㅎ

하나도	"not one bit," "not at all" (negative)	Ch. 17
학교에 다니다	"to go to school," "to attend school"	Ch. 9
학기	"(school) term," "semester/trimester/quarter"	Ch. 9
학년	"school year"	Ch. 3
한가하다	"to be free," "to have (spare) time," "to be at leisure"	Ch. 15

Glossary

한마을 "the same village," "the same town"		App. B
할인 "a discount"		Ch. 8
해결(을) 하다 "to resolve," "to settle," "to take care of (a problem)"		Ch. 15
해결(이) 되다 "to be resolved," "to be settled," "to be taken care of (a problem)"		Ch. 15
해초 "seaweed"		Ch. 5
행복하세요! "Be happy!"		Ch. 5
행사 "an event"		Ch. 3
허락 "permission"		Ch. 12
허락(을) 받다 "to get permission"		Ch. 12
허락(을) 하다 "to permit," "to allow"		Ch. 15
헤어지다 "to break up (with someone)"		Ch. 9
헷갈리다 "to be confused (about something)"		Ch. 5
혜택 "benefit"		Ch. 15
혜택(이) 되다 "to (be a) benefit"		Ch. 15
호기심 "curiosity"		Ch. 15
호기심(이) 많다 "to be curious"		Ch. 15
혼(을) 내다 "to scold," "to tell off"		Ch. 15
혼(이) 나다 "to be scolded," "to be told off"		Ch. 15
홍수 "flood"		Ch. 2
홍콩 "Hong Kong"		Ch. 16
화(가) 나다 "to be angry (due to someone/something)"		Ch. 10
화(를) 내다 "to get angry (at someone/something)"		Ch. 15
화씨 "Fahrenheit"		Ch. 1
화재 "fire (disaster)"		Ch. 2
환불 "refund"		Ch. 20
환불(을) 하다 "to refund"		Ch. 20
회식 "a company meal"		Ch. 9
회장 "a president (of a company)"		Ch. 9
회화 "conversation (in person)"		Ch. 2
회화(를) 하다 "to converse (in person)," "to hold a conversation (in person)"		Ch. 2
효과 "effect"		Ch. 12
효과적 "effective"		Ch. 12
후루룩 "slurp" (sound of slurping)		App. A
후배 "(one's) junior"		Ch. 9
후진(을) 하다 "to reverse (when driving)"		Ch. 12
훨씬 "much (more)" (adverb)		Ch. 1
휴대폰 "mobile phone"		Ch. 7
흐르다 "to flow (liquid)"		Ch. 14
흑(흑) (sound of crying)		App. A
힘(이) 들다 "to be hard," "to be difficult"		Ch. 3
힘들어하다 "to have a hard time," "to have trouble"		Ch. 5

Printed in Great Britain
by Amazon